Lecture Notes in Computer Science 14131

The series Lecture Notes in Computer Science (LNCS), including its subseries Lecture Notes in Artificial Intelligence (LNAI) and Lecture Notes in Bioinformatics (LNBI), has established itself as a medium for the publication of new developments in computer science and information technology research, teaching, and education.

LNCS enjoys close cooperation with the computer science R & D community, the series counts many renowned academics among its volume editors and paper authors, and collaborates with prestigious societies. Its mission is to serve this international community by providing an invaluable service, mainly focused on the publication of conference and workshop proceedings and postproceedings. LNCS commenced publication in 1973.

Silvia Bonfanti · Angelo Gargantini ·
Paolo Salvaneschi
Editors

Testing Software and Systems

35th IFIP WG 6.1 International Conference, ICTSS 2023
Bergamo, Italy, September 18–20, 2023
Proceedings

Springer

Editors
Silvia Bonfanti 🆔
University of Bergamo
Bergamo, Italy

Angelo Gargantini 🆔
University of Bergamo
Bergamo, Italy

Paolo Salvaneschi
Salvaneschi & Partners
Bergamo, Italy

ISSN 0302-9743   ISSN 1611-3349 (electronic)
Lecture Notes in Computer Science
ISBN 978-3-031-43239-2   ISBN 978-3-031-43240-8 (eBook)
https://doi.org/10.1007/978-3-031-43240-8

This Springer imprint is published by the registered company Springer Nature Switzerland AG
The registered company address is: Gewerbestrasse 11, 6330 Cham, Switzerland

Paper in this product is recyclable.

Preface

It is our great pleasure to welcome you to the proceedings of the 35th IFIP WG 6.1 International Conference on Testing Software and Systems, ICTSS 2023, held in Bergamo, Italy, from September 18th to September 20th, 2023.

ICTSS is a series of international conferences addressing conceptual, theoretical, and practical problems of testing software systems, including communication protocols, services, distributed platforms, middleware, embedded and cyber-physical systems, and security infrastructures. The conference is dedicated to researchers, developers, testers, and users from industry to present and discuss the most recent innovations, experiences, and open challenges related to testing software and systems and measuring software quality. In this edition, we received 63 papers, of which 7 were desk rejected. In the review phase, each submission was single-blind reviewed by at least 3 reviewers of the program committee, which was followed by a discussion phase. At the end of the discussion, we accepted 20 papers divided into the following categories: 13 regular papers, 6 short papers, and 1 journal-first paper. We would like to thank all program committee members for their efforts in both reviewing and discussing the submissions. The process of reviewing and selecting the papers was significantly simplified using EquinOCS. In these conference proceedings, the papers are divided into the following topical subheadings: Test generation, Test automation and design, Model-based testing, and AI and smart contracts.

We were very glad to have Leonardo Mariani as keynote of ICTSS 2023. He presented a talk on Failure Analysis in CPS Simulink Models. We thank him for agreeing to give an invited presentation at IFIP-ICTSS 2023.

Moreover, in this edition, we actively involved participants from industry, who presented in a dedicated session their experience in software testing.

We want to acknowledge IFIP (International Federation for Information Processing) for its sponsorship of ICTSS 2023 as well as Springer for having published this volume.

Finally, we are very grateful to the University of Bergamo for contributing to the event by making available the conference room and funds to cover some expenses.

On behalf of the IFIP-ICTSS organizers, we hope that you find the proceedings useful, interesting, and challenging.

September 2023

Silvia Bonfanti
Angelo Gargantini
Paolo Salvaneschi

Organization

Program Committee Chairs

Bonfanti, Silvia	University of Bergamo, Italy
Gargantini, Angelo	University of Bergamo, Italy
Salvaneschi, Paolo	Salvaneschi & Partners, Italy

Steering Committee

Casola, Valentina	Università di Napoli Federico II, Italy
Cavalli, Ana	Télécom SudParis, France
Clark, David	University College London, UK
De Benedictis, Alessandra	Università di Napoli Federico II, Italy
Gaston, Christophe	CEA-LIST, France
Hierons, Robert	University of Sheffield, UK
Kosmatov, Nikolai	CEA-LIST, France
Le Gall, Pascale	CentraleSupélec, France
Menéndez, Héctor	Middlesex University London, UK
Merayo, Mercedes	Universidad Complutense de Madrid, Spain
Rak, Massimiliano	Università degli studi della Campania, Italy

Program Committee

Aichernig, Bernhard K.	Graz University of Technology, Austria
Amrani, Moussa	University of Namur, Belgium
Arcaini, Paolo	National Institute of Informatics, Japan
Barkaoui, Kamel	Conservatoire National des Arts et Métiers, Paris
Bertolino, Antonia	Italian National Research Council, Italy
Camilli, Matteo	Politecnico di Milano, Italy
Campos, José	University of Porto, Portugal
Cavalli, Ana	Télécom SudParis, France
El-Fakih, Khaled	American University of Sharjah, UAE
Gaston, Christophe	CEA-LIST, France
Gomes, Francisco	University of Gothenburg, Sweden
Hierons, Robert	University of Sheffield, UK
Higashino, Teruo	Osaka University, Japan
Khendek, Ferhat	Concordia University, Canada
Kushik, Natalia	SAMOVAR, Télécom SudParis, Institut Polytechnique de Paris, France

Le Gall, Pascale	CentraleSupélec, France
Lefticaru, Raluca	University of Bradford, UK
Lei, Yu	University of Texas at Arlington, USA
Lopez, Jorge	Airbus, France
Mallouli, Wissam	Montimage, France
Medina-Bulo, Inmaculada	University of Cádiz, Spain
Menéndez, Héctor	Middlesex University London, UK
Merayo, Mercedes	Universidad Complutense de Madrid, Spain
Montes de Oca, Edgardo	Montimage, France
Mousavi, Mohammad Reza	King's College London, UK
Núñez, Manuel	Universidad Complutense de Madrid, Spain
Pecchia, Antonio	University of Sannio, Italy
Peleska, Jan	University of Bremen, Germany
Petke, Justyna	University College London, UK
Pietrantuono, Roberto	Università di Napoli Federico II, Italy
Polo, Macario	University of Castilla-La Mancha, Spain
Rak, Massimiliano	Università degli studi della Campania, Italy
Tramontana, Porfirio	Università di Napoli Federico II, Italy
Trubiani, Catia	Gran Sasso Science Institute, Italy
Türker, Uraz Cengiz	University of Leicester, UK
Villano, Umberto	University of Sannio, Italy
Wotawa, Franz	Graz University of Technology, Austria
Yenigün, Hüsnü	Sabancı University, Türkiye
Yevtushenko, Nina	Ivannikov Institute for System Programming of the RAS, Russia
Zaidi, Fatiha	Université Paris Saclay, France

Additional Reviewers

Nguyen, Huu Nghia	Montimage, France
Barboni, Morena	University of Camerino, Italy
Khadka, Krishna	University of Texas at Arlington, USA
Lallali, Mounir	Universite de Bretagne Occidentale, France
Mahe, Erwan	CentraleSupélec, France
Ouffoué, Georges	APL Data Center, France
Petersen, Erick	Télécom SudParis, France
Sachtleben, Robert	University of Bremen, Germany
Shree, Sunny	University of Texas at Arlington, USA
Sikder, Fadul	University of Texas at Arlington, USA
Vinarskii, Evgenii	Lomonosov Moscow State University, Russia

Failure Analysis in CPS Simulink Models (Keynotes)

Leonardo Mariani ⓘ

University of Milano Bicocca, 20126 Milan, Italy
leonardo.mariani@unimib.it

Abstract. Failures observed in Simulink models are particularly hard to debug and explain, since any computation normally involves every, or most of, the elements in a model, and localization strategies based on the detection of the elements (only) activated by failed tests cannot work in this context.

To address this challenge, approaches that explore the behavioural space of Simulink models to discover the internal behaviors that may characterize failing tests have been proposed. In particular, we recently worked on the generation and comparison of close passing and failing executions, to isolate the internal behaviors likely responsible for the failures. We investigated this approach both using models inferred from passing executions, which are then compared to failing executions [1–3], and by the straight comparison of pairs of passing and failing executions [4].

Experimenting these approaches require a large number of faults, which are seldom available in practice. In these cases, mutation testing is particularly helpful to run large experiments with synthetic faults. Unfortunately, the regular notion of mutant killing (i.e., the condition to reveal a fault) that requires generating a test that produces different outputs for the original and mutated version of a model, is not particularly useful in the context of CPS Simulink models. In fact, faults are normally trivial to activate and propagate to the output, thus being trivial to kill. Yet, a mutant-killing test might not be particularly useful, especially when a model must be validated against specific properties. In fact, the output difference generated by a mutant-killing test might not be enough to violate the available property, resulting in a test that would not expose the problem in a target model, even when it exercises the fault. To address this problem, we investigated the notion of *property-based mutation testing*, which requires the generation of tests that exercise faults, while magnifying their impact on the model up to causing the violation of the available properties [5, 6].

The talk will discuss recent advances obtained in failure analysis and fault injection in CPS Simulink models.

References

1. Bartocci, E., Manjunath, N., Mariani, L., Mateis, C., Ničković, D.: Automatic failure explanation in CPS models. In: Ölveczky, P., Salaün, G. (eds.) SEFM 2019. LNCS, vol. 11724, pp. 69–86. Springer, Cham (2019). https://doi.org/10.1007/978-3-030-30446-1_4
2. Bartocci, E., et al.: CPSDebug: automatic failure explanation in CPS models. Int. J. Softw. Tools Technol. Transfer **23**, 783–796 (2021). https://doi.org/10.1007/s10009-020-00599-4
3. Bartocci, E., et al.: CPSDebug: a tool for explanation of failures in cyber-physical systems. In: Proceedings of the 29th ACM SIGSOFT International Symposium on Software Testing and Analysis, Tool Demo (2020)
4. Bartocci, E., Mariani, L., Nickovic, D., Yadav, D.: Search-based testing for accurate fault localization in CPS. In: 33rd International Symposium on Software Reliability Engineering (ISSRE) (2022)
5. Bartocci, E., Mariani, L., Nickovic, D., Yadav, D.: Property-based mutation testing. In: IEEE Conference on Software Testing, Verification and Validation (ICST) (2023)
6. Bartocci, E., Mariani, L., Ničković, D., Yadav, D.: FIM: fault injection and mutation for simulink. In: Proceedings of the 30th ACM Joint European Software Engineering Conference and Symposium on the Foundations of Software Engineering, Tool Demo Paper (2022)

Contents

Model Based Testing

AI and Smart Contracts Testing

Test Case Generation

A Rapid Review on Fuzz Security Testing for Software Protocol Implementations

Alessandro Marchetto(✉) (iD)

University of Trento, Trento, Italy
alessandro.marchetto@unitn.it

Abstract. Nowadays, devices and systems are always connected for providing everyday services. Hence, there is a growing interest concerning the adoption of secure software implementations of communication protocols that allow heterogeneous systems to exchange information and data. In the last decade, several approaches and techniques for applying fuzz security testing to such implementations have been proposed. Fuzz security testing is a promising approach to discover software vulnerabilities. It aims at exercising the implementation under test by means of unexpected and potentially invalid inputs and data, aiming at triggering misbehaviors, exceptions, and system crashes.

This paper presents a Rapid Review (RR) conducted to study fuzz security testing for software implementations of communication protocols. The following evidences emerged from our RR: (i) Industrial Control System and Internet of Thing protocols are among the most studied ones; (ii) black-box fuzz security testing is frequently investigated and, often, the proposed approaches require protocol or data specifications as input; (iii) most of the detected vulnerabilities are related to memory management and, less frequently, to input and data management and validation, and (iv) only few tools are publicly available.

Keywords: Fuzzing Testing · Software Vulnerability · Rapid Review

1 Introduction

Modern devices and systems are widely and continuously connected for providing everyday services. For instance, in the last years, embedded systems and Internet of Things (IoT) are more and more connected and used in several domains, e.g., automotive, aerospace, telecommunications, and healthcare. The global market of such systems is expected to still grow [6], thanks to technologies such as virtualization, artificial intelligence, automation, high-performance hardware, and 5G low-latency communication.

Cyber-attacks that exploit weaknesses and vulnerabilities of such connected systems are also growing [7] and can cause dramatic cyber-physical damages. Several approaches and techniques for *fuzz security testing* (also referred as *fuzz testing* or *fuzzing*) have been proposed in the literature for discovering such system and software vulnerabilities. Fuzz testing exercises the target system

© IFIP International Federation for Information Processing 2023
Published by Springer Nature Switzerland AG 2023
S. Bonfanti et al. (Eds.): ICTSS 2023, LNCS 14131, pp. 3–20, 2023.
https://doi.org/10.1007/978-3-031-43240-8_1

under test by means of a large set of unexpected and potentially invalid inputs and data, aiming at triggering system's failures (e.g., misbehaviors, exceptions, and crashes). A system failure could reasonably be due to the presence of an exploitable vulnerability in the target system [9]. Different types of fuzz testing exist depending on the type of the target system, e.g., application fuzzing, file format fuzzing and protocol fuzzing.

This paper presents a Rapid Review (RR) conducted to study the literature of the last decade concerning fuzz security testing for software implementations of communication protocols (software implementing communication protocols). A protocol enables the communication between entities by defining rules, syntax, semantics, synchronization, and possible errors of the communication. In this paper, we aim at investigating: (i) the type of protocols tested with fuzz testing; (ii) the type of fuzz testing approaches and techniques investigated in the literature; (iii) the existing tools that can support protocol fuzz testing; and (iv) the types of software vulnerabilities typically discovered by fuzz testing.

Rapid Reviews (RRs) [4] are a recent type of review approach proposed for conducting evidence-based studies [10]. These studies aim at identifying the current best evidence from the literature in a specific domain, thus improving the decision making process in that domain. Differently from a conventional Systematic Literature Review (SLR), a RR takes into account constraints related to practical situations and cases, such as the need of delivering evidence promptly, with low costs, the need of reporting evidence in a clear and simple way without formal synthesis. RRs omit and simplify some steps of conventional SLRs, thus in a sense, lowering the generalizability of results, while preserving a systematic and rigorous approach. RRs are not intended to replace SLRs: SLRs provide in-depth insights, while RRs are lightweight review studies to easily and quickly transfer knowledge to practitioners, through *evidences*. Indeed, differently from SLRs, RRs

i start from a practical need and problem of practitioners [1], e.g., the beginning of a new engineering project, the need of increasing the practitioners confidence on decisions or to let them quickly acquire new information, concepts and pointers concerning a specific problem or technology.

ii focus on a single source of data and involve a single researcher [4], thus reducing costs, time (e.g., weeks rather than months required by conventional SLRs) and resources at the expenses of the number of paper analyzed. RRs are not expected to be exhaustive on the analysis of the literature studies, this is not their goal;

iii apply a rigorous, even if simplified process, with respect to SLRs. For instance, RRs do not conduct a rigorous quality appraisal of the literature studies. However, it is worthy highlight that RRs are not informal reviews.

iv aim at collecting evidences and, even they can represent a preliminary step towards the identification of research challenges and open issues, however, this is not their goal;

v report the results in a narrative and descriptive form by focusing on the evidence emerged, according to the goal of communicating to practitioners [4]. RRs do not analyze data and present results by using a formal synthesis.

RRs are conducted through a 4-step process [4]: (1) analysis of the literature studies identified to familiarize with concepts related to problem and domain of interest; (2) creation of an initial set of themes/criteria, by classifying the literature studies according to their concepts; (3) searching for data that support or refute the criteria in the studies; and (4) production of the final report by focusing on emerged evidences.

We opted for a RR because it better fits our needs with respect to a SLR. As often happens for RRs, our RR has been triggered by the beginning of a new project demanding for a fast screening of the literature to deliver evidences and guidelines to the involved practitioners. To the best of our knowledge, only few SLRs have investigated, from a research-oriented perspective, fuzz testing for communication protocols and mainly by focusing on specific technologies (e.g., IoT) and application domains (e.g., Industrial Control Systems).

2   Related Works

Fuzz Security Testing. Fuzz testing exercises the target system under test by a large set of inputs with the aim of triggering system's failures. The typical fuzz testing process [16] includes: (1) definition of input tests (named "seeds") to exercise the target system; (2) generation of fuzzing test data for the seeds; (3) execution of the tests; (4) monitor of the target system and analysis of exceptions and crashes to detect exploits. There are two main traditional approaches to fuzzing: mutation-based and generation-based fuzzing. Tools such as American Fuzzing Loop (AFL[1]) and LibFuzzer[2] implement two gray-box fuzzing approaches based on mutation. They start from some initial seeds (typically, real data recorded during user sessions or a preliminary test session) then mutated for producing inputs' variants by flipping, replacing, and adding bits or bytes. They also instrument the code of the target system and use heuristics to guide both generation and mutation of test inputs. Several extensions of such tools exist, e.g., AFLFast [2] uses Markov Chain Models to increase the code coverage while producing tests. Tools such as Peach[3], Boofuzz[4] and Sulley [16] support generation-based fuzzing approaches. They require user-provided data models to generate inputs and, often, can use also templates and data/protocol specifications (e.g., data model, format, grammar). For instance, both Peach and Boofuzz support black-box fuzzing and require a state machine of the protocol software (protocol states and transitions) and data specifications as inputs. Other fuzzing tools exist for specific purposes, domains and technologies. For instance, syzkaller[5] is an unsupervised code-coverage guided tool developed for Linux-kernel fuzzing. ZDHCP[6] is a black-box fuzzing tool for DHCP servers.

---

[1] https://github.com/google/AFL.
[2] https://github.com/enovella/libfuzzer-workshop.
[3] https://www.peach.tech.
[4] https://github.com/jtpereyda/boofuzz.
[5] https://github.com/google/syzkaller.
[6] https://github.com/zdnscloud/zdhcp.

kittyfuzzer[7] and Mutiny[8] are fuzz testing frameworks for non-TCP and TCP channels. Snipuzz [5] is a black-box fuzzing tool for IoT firmwares. The effectiveness of fuzz testing is strongly dependent on the target system under test. This paper focuses on software implementations of communication protocols, one of the area in which fuzz testing is widely adopted.

Secondary Studies. A few systematic literature reviews (SLRs) exist about fuzz security testing for software implementations of communication protocols. [8] presents the basic principles and the typical process applied to network protocol fuzzing, as well as the fundamental structure of a fuzzing system. The paper also focuses on the adoption of machine learning algorithms for fuzz testing. [11] surveys on protocol fuzz testing adopted for Industrial Control Systems. [12] surveys on network protocol fuzz testing for information systems and applications. [12] conducts an in-depth analysis on a few selected studies that mainly apply fuzz testing to network TCP/IP protocols. [15] reviews the techniques, e.g., symbolic execution, taint analysis, artificial intelligence, that can be combined with conventional fuzz testing approaches applied, in particular, to IoT protocols and firmwares. [13] contextualizes the adoption of fuzz testing with respect to others vulnerability discovery strategies (e.g., static analysis), without focusing to software implementations of communication protocols. Despite these SLRs are related to our RR, they did not fit our research goal, i.e., not address our RQs. We do not focus on a specific domain (e.g., Industrial Control Systems) or technology (e.g., IoT), as well as done by these SLRs. Furthermore, these SLRs adopt a more research-oriented point of view with respect to our RR, they discuss about general principles and processes to conduct fuzz testing. Differently form these SLRs, we mainly focus on how the investigated approaches and tools work, targeting practitioners. To the best of our knowledge, this paper is the first one that presents a RR on the field of fuzz security testing for software protocol implementations and that reports the result by using an evidence briefing method.

3   Rapid Review

To plan and design the RR, according to Cartaxo et al. [3], we defined: (i) our research questions (RQs); (ii) both data source and search strategy; (iii) the criteria to analyze the literature papers; and (iv) the threats to validity limiting our study.

3.1   Research Questions

The following research questions have been defined according to our **goal** of *identifying and analyzing existing approaches and tools, presented in the last*

---

[7] https://pypi.org/project/kittyfuzzer.
[8] https://github.com/Cisco-Talos/mutiny-fuzzer.

decade, to apply fuzz security testing to software implementations of communication protocols.

- **RQ1** *What are the types of protocols tested?*
  RQ1 aims at identifying the type of protocols (e.g., telecommunication, proprietary, web, IoT) tested in the literature by fuzz security testing. By starting from the protocol's type, we aim at identifying both the architecture (e.g., server-client, web/mobile, desktop, embedded software, publisher and subscriber) and the application domain (e.g., telecommunications, aerospace, space, automotive, industrial system, network service) of the target system under test.
- **RQ2** *What are the types of fuzzing testing approaches investigated?*
  RQ2 aims at characterizing the type of approaches (e.g., black-box, white-box, gray-box) applied to conduct fuzz security testing for software implementations of communication protocols. To answer to RQ2, we have to go deeper in the fuzz testing approach for identifying: (i) the required artifact (e.g., application requirements, application/protocol specifications, data specification – model, grammar, format, data samples, execution samples, application code); (ii) the adopted input and data generation strategy (e.g., generative, grammar-based, mutation-based, smart - with knowledge on data, dumb - without knowledge on data, evolutionary); and (iii) the adopted test oracles and results verification procedure (e.g., exceptions, error-handling, software crashes, assertion-based, comparison responses, memory checks).
- **RQ3** *What are the existing tools that support protocol fuzz testing?*
  RQ3 aims at identifying the available tools that support the investigated fuzz testing approaches for software implementations of communication protocols.
- **RQ4** *What are the types of the software vulnerabilities discovered?*
  RQ4 aims at identifying the software vulnerabilities (e.g., memory leaks and assertion failure, missing access control or authentication, improper or insufficient input check, wrong error handling routines) that are typically discovered by fuzz security testing when dealing with software implementations of communication protocols. It is also of interest, to identify the typical attacks (e.g., denial of services, man-in-the-middle, remote code execution) that can exploit such vulnerabilities.

We believe that these RQs are of interest for both practitioners and researchers. For instance, RQ1 and RQ3 can be useful for practitioners to know if some work exists in the literature about the communication protocols they are adopting in their business and to identify the fuzz testing tool that can better fits their needs. RQ2 can help practitioners in identifying potential strategies that they can adopt to improve the security of the software protocol implementations they are adopting and developing. Finally, RQ4 can help practitioners in getting a quick inside into the vulnerabilities that can be exploited by cyber-attackers. Nevertheless, the answers to the RQs can help researchers in identifying the non-adequately studied areas that can be require further investigation.

3.2   Data Source and Search Strategy

As suggested by Cartaxo et al. [3] for conducting a RR, we adopted Scopus as a single database since it is a quite large source of peer-reviewed literature [14] provided by several editors, e.g., ACM, IEEE, Springer, Elsevier, and Wiley.

We defined our search string by deriving terms and phrases of interest from our RQs, such as: "Protocol", "Fuzzing", and "Vulnerability", we then combined them by using both *AND* and *OR* operators, thus obtaining the following search query string in the Scopus syntax:

TITLE-ABS-KEY ("PROTOCOL") **AND** (TITLE-ABS-KEY ("VULNERABILITY") **OR** TITLE-ABS-KEY ("SECURITY")) **AND** (TITLE-ABS-KEY ("FUZZING") **OR** TITLE-ABS-KEY ("FUZZ"))

"TITLE-ABS-KEY" is the Scopus command to search on titles, abstracts, or keywords of each paper. The used query included also: (i) plurals and variants of the listed terms and phrases (e.g., "vulnerabilities", "fuzz"); and (ii) automatic filtering criteria, i.e., we filter out papers published before the year 2012, aiming at addressing contributions related to recent technologies and tools (as stated by our goal), and we limit our search to papers published in conference proceedings and journals (i.e., book were not considered) and written in English. From the obtained list of 48 papers published, we removed the not accessible and the abstract-only ones, thus obtaining a final list of 45 papers.

3.3   Analysis Criteria

According to the analysis strategy delineated by Cartaxo et al. [3] for a RR, we conducted a thematic analysis [1] on each selected literature paper, by searching on it notions and concepts according to some criteria identified for investigating our RQs. Table 1 summarizes such criteria in terms of aspects and examples of values. Four groups of aspects are considered:

- **Work**: goal and description of the paper under analysis, e.g., presentation of a new fuzzing approach or a new technique, experimentation, reviewing fuzzing techniques;
- **Target system**: aspects related to the target system under test, i.e., type of the protocol, architecture and application domain of the protocol implementation;
- **Investigated solution**: in-depth aspects related to the investigated fuzz testing approach;
- **Available solution**: aspects related to the presented or used tool that support the investigated solution;
- **Vulnerability and attack**: aspects related to the type of vulnerabilities that can be discovered and the attacks that can exploit such vulnerabilities.

A three-step procedure has been applied to define such criteria: (1) an initial set has been defined; (2) the initial set has been applied to some papers, aiming at collecting feedback to refine and finalize the criteria. Finally, (3) all papers have been analyzed and evidences collected. The objective is to use these criteria for extracting evidences from the literature, thus investigating our RQs. In detail, **Target system** is used for **RQ1**, both **Investigated solution** and **Work** are used for **RQ2**, **Available solution** is used for **RQ3**, and, finally, **Vulnerability and attack** is used for **RQ4**.

Table 1. Analysis criteria for the detailed analysis

Work
Goal: Presentation of a new technique/approach, experiment/assessment, tool presentation, review
Goal description: One-sentence text description of the paper's goal

Target system
Type of protocol: E.g., telecommunication, 5G/6G, proprietary, web, mobile, Internet of Things
Type of architecture: E.g., server/client, web/mobile, embedded software, publisher/subscriber
Application domain: E.g., telecommunications, aerospace, automotive, industrial system, networks

Vulnerability and attack
Type of Vulnerability: E.g., memory leaks and assertion failure, missing access control or authentication, improper or insufficient input check, wrong error handling routines
Type of the attack: E.g., denial of services, man-in-the-middle, remote code execution, malware

Investigated solution
Types of solution: E.g., black-box, white-box, gray-box
Analysis source: E.g., application requirements, application/protocol specifications, random values, data grammar, data samples, execution samples, app. source code
Generation strategy: E.g., generative, grammar-based, mutation-based, mutation with template, smart -knowledge on data structure, dumb -no knowledge on data structure, evolutionary
Strategy description: One-sentence text description of the paper's input data generation strategy
Types of oracles: E.g., exceptions, error-handling, software craches, assertion-based, comparison of the responses, checks of the memory

Available solution
Tool name: Free text description about the analysis method
Tool availability: E.g., yes - the tool is available, no - the tool is not available
Tool link: http/s link to the tool web site
Extended tool: Tool/techniques extended of of inspiration, if any

3.4 Limitations of the Study

The main limitation of the study affects the generalization of the RR's findings and it concerns the analysis of the literature (i) conducted by only one author, which might have introduced a bias, and (ii) the adoption of only one data source for searching the literature to be analyzed, that can have left some papers out of the review. Another threat to the validity of our RR concerns (iii) the set of criteria adopted in the in-depth analysis of each papers. We are conscious that different criteria could be adopted and could lead to different results and findings. These threats can limit the validity of our work but they are expected for a RR [3].

4 Results

In order to present the results of our RR according to Cartaxo et al. [3], we high-light relevant concepts and notions that emerged from our study, thus focusing on the evidence. The complete list of the analyzed literature papers, details (e.g., authors, publication venues, year of publication), and results of the reported in-depth analysis are available online[9].

RQ1. Table 2 summarizes the relevant concepts emerged for the criterion **Target system**, used to derive the evidences concerning *RQ1*.

- *Evidence 1.1*. A large number of papers investigate industrial control systems and Internet of Things (IoT) protocols (respectively 10 and 6 out of 45 papers), such as Modbus, MQTT, HTTP, Zigbee, just to cite a few of them.
- *Evidence 1.2*. Among the specified ones, such protocols are used in particular within embedded systems (8 out 24 papers) and client/server (7 out 24 papers) architectures.

Table 2. RR results: Target system

Type of protocol

Industrial control systems (10), Network (8), Internet of Things (6), Stateful network (4), Internet Key Exchange (2), In-vehicle networks (2), Non-IP based wireless (2), Telecommunication (2), Center to field and center to center communications (1), Ethereum network (1), HMI-device communication (1), Hypervisor peripherals (1), Multimedia network (1), Routing network (1), Smart metering (1), Universal Serial Bus (1), and Wireless sensor networks (1)

Examples of protocols: Industrial control systems (DNP3, EtherCAT, Ethernet/IP, HTTP, ICMP, IEC104, IEC61850, MMS, Modbus, MQTT, Profinet, proprietary protocol, Siemens S7), Network (DHCP, DNS, DNS, HTTP, NTP, POP, QQ, SNMP), Internet of Things (HTTP, Modbus, MQTT, Zigbee, Z-Wave), Stateful network (DBMS, FTP, LightFTP, RTSP,SMTP, SSL, tinyDTLS), Internet Key Exchange (IKE, IKEv2), In-vehicle networks (SOME/IP, ZeroMQ), Non-IP based wireless (Bluetooth LE, ZigBee), telecommunication (5G, 5G RRC), Center to field and center to center communications (IETF HTTP, IETP FTP, NTCIP, SOAP), Ethereum network (RPLx), HMI-device communication (ICMP, IEC61850, Modbus-TCP), Multimedia network (DVB/MPEG2-TS, VoIP), Routing network (ICMP), Smart metering (DLMS/COSEM), and Wireless sensor networks (ZigBee)

Type of architecture

Embedded systems (8), client/server (5), web/mobile (3), client/server with stateful application (2), decentralized client/ server or publisher/ subscriber (2), publisher/subscriptor (2), cooperative centralized systems (1), hypervisors (1)

Application domain

Network services (12), industrial control systems (6), IoT devices (6), industrial systems (3), automotive (2), industrial remote control systems (2), telecommunication systems (2), blockchain (1), home network (1), hypervisor containers (1), intelligent transportation systems (1), medical (1), multimedia services (1), smart meter devices (1), and storage devices (1)

---

[9] https://tinyurl.com/k2s9d5pz.

– *Evidence 1.3*. In terms of application domain, industrial systems, including industrial control systems, IoT-based and remote control systems (17 out of 41) and network services (12 out of 41) attract most of the attention and effort of the community.

RQ2. In terms of **Work**, we can see that (*Evidence 2.1.*) the goal of almost all the analyzed papers is to introduce a new fuzzing approach and technique (respectively 28 and 6 out of 45 papers considered). Some of the papers (5 out of 45) present a framework that supports fuzzing testing and only one paper reports an empirical assessment of existing fuzzing techniques. Finally, some papers (5 out of 45) are devoted to review the state-of-the-art for specific domains or technologies. More interesting for our purpose, Tables 3, 4, 5 and Fig. 1 present the relevant concepts emerged for the criterion **Investigated solution**, used to derive the evidences concerning *RQ2*.

Table 3. RR results: Investigated solution - Types of solution and Analysis Source

Artifact	Papers per Types of solution					
	Black-box		Gray-box		White-box	
	Required	Inferred	Required	Inferred	Required	Inferred
Attack model, execution samples	1					
Attack model, data samples	1					
Code			2			
Code (source code) + execution samples					1	
Code + data model			3			
Code + data model + execution samples			1			
Code + execution samples			2		1	
Code + protocol specification + data model			1			
Code + state model			1			
Code + state model, data model			1			
Data model	2	8		2		
Data model + state model		1		1		
Data samples + data model	2					
Data-flow model (CFG)						1
Execution samples	10		1			
Execution samples + protocol specification	3					
Protocol specification	4	1				
State model	1	2		2		
Structural model + data model				1		
Not-detailed	2	14		6		1

Table 3 reports the number of papers, per type of the investigated solution (e.g., black, gray, and white -box approach), that require a specific data artifact as input or that recover such an artifact (respectively column "Required" and "Inferred"). For instance, the table shows that one black-box approach (row

4, column 2) requires both an attack model and a set of execution samples as input, while 8 of such approaches (row 14, column 3) recover a data model (e.g., type, format or grammar of protocol data), typically, by analyzing the execution samples provided by the user or automatically collected by a crawler.

Table 4. RR results: Investigated solution - Generation strategy

Generation strategy	Papers per Types of solution		
	black-box	gray-box	white-box
Mutation	2		
Mutation (Dump)	5	2	
Mutation (Smart)		6	2
Generative	4		
Generative (Dump)	1		
Generative (Smart)	2	2	
Generative + Mutation (Dump)	1		
Generative + Mutation (Smart)		1	
Evolution	1	1	

We applied a two-step approach to analyze the one-sentence descriptions, manually written in the analysis phase by the author for each considered paper, and that briefly summarizes the data generation strategy of fuzzing approaches and techniques (**Strategy description**). (1) Group the one-sentence descriptions, based on the their textual commonality, and (2) analyze the inter-cluster descriptions, by looking for relevant terms and their connection. We excluded the papers reviewing the literature from this analysis. To this aim, we first used Lexos[10]. Lexos analyzes each sentence (i.e., document) by: (i) tokenizing it, (ii) removing stop-words, (iii) computing Term Frequency-Inverse Document Frequency (TF-ID), with the aim of reflecting the relevance of each term with respect to the whole term's corpus (terms of all sentences), and finally, (iv) applying the K-Means clustering algorithm to group sentences according to their terms. Figure 1(a) shows the clusters of the one-sentence strategy descriptions. Figure 1(a) clearly shows that three groups of strategy descriptions emerged from the investigated papers. We then used Voyant[11] to extract the Collocated Graphs built by considering all the one-sentence strategy descriptions within each group/cluster. A collocated graph represents terms of a text that occur in close proximity as a force-directed network graph; dark boxes in the graph are the most frequent terms, while edges are relations between contextual terms. In our case, such a graph highlights the relationship among relevant and common terms used to describe the input/data generation strategy of each approach presented in each paper. Figure 1(b) (c) (d) present the three Collocated Graphs built by considering all the one-sentence strategy descriptions within

---

[10] http://lexos.wheatoncollege.edu.
[11] https://voyant-tools.org.

Table 5. RR results: Investigated solution - Types of oracles

Types of oracles	Papers per Types of solution		
	black-box	gray-box	white-box
State-based monitoring and analysis Monitoring of the network and device status	4	2	
(e.g., "Ping", abnormal content)	3		
Capture responses, identify exceptions and crashes	7	4	1
Detect crashes and use differential testing (i.e., compare normal/fuzzy responses)		1	
Analysis of responses and state-based monitoring	1		
Identification of crashes from a log-based post-analysis	2	2	
Post-verification of assertions in log-based analysis	3		
Memory error detection	1	2	1
Verification of response time and response content analysis	4		
Response content analysis and memory error detection	1	1	

each group/cluster in Fig. 1(a). For instance, the cluster in Fig. 1 groups: (b) network fuzzing based on protocol specifications; (c) generation approaches that capture data packet structure; and (d) approaches that use state machines and message mutation. Overlaps can be observed, e.g., packets and generation are common terms between (c) and (d).

- **Evidence 2.2.** The large majority of the papers (26 out 39) proposed a new black-box fuzzing approach/technique and most of them (9 out 26) require at least the protocol specifications as input while other ones recover protocol or data specifications during the approach execution (respectively 5 and 4 papers out of 26).
- **Evidence 2.3.** Only very few papers (2 out of 39) proposed new white-box fuzzing approaches. This is quite expected since in most of the cases, the source code of the software implementing communication protocols is not available.
- **Evidence 2.4.** In terms of artifacts used as source of information, execution or data samples are required by almost half of the black-box approaches (14 out 26) and of the gray-box approaches (6 our of 12).
- **Evidence 2.5.** Binary and bytecode -level code coverage is widely used (14 out of 39 papers) by all types of approaches to collect feedback during the fuzz testing, e.g., decide when stop testing.

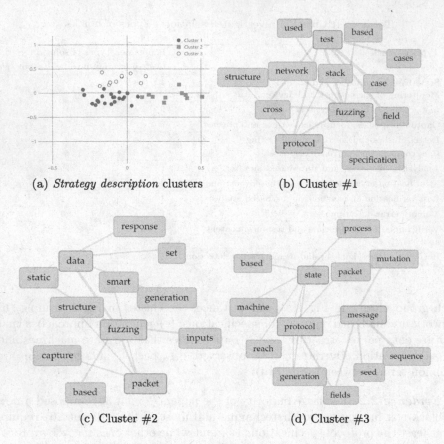

(a) *Strategy description* clusters

(b) Cluster #1

(c) Cluster #2

(d) Cluster #3

Fig. 1. Clusters of *Strategy description* and related collocates graphs

- **_Evidence 2.6_**. Mutation is widely used to produce new fuzzing test cases or data (19 out of 39) and, in almost half of the cases, the applied mutation is driven by some degree of "smartness" related to predefined or inferred knowledge.
- **_Evidence 2.7_**. In terms of test oracles, most of the approaches use: detection of system's exceptions and crashes, memory verification (e.g., wrong allocation, out-of-bound), analysis of the responses to the fuzzy requests (in terms of time needed to the target system to respond and response content).

RQ3. Table 6 summarizes the relevant concepts emerged for the criterion **Available solution**, used to derive the evidences concerning *RQ3*.

Table 6. RR results: Available solution

Tool availability	Tool name
Available	ContractFuzzer, CyberExploit, libFuzzer, Polar-Fuzz, SIoTFuzzer, Snout, StateFuzzer, V-Shuttle, Z-Fuzzer
Non-available	APREFuzz, Charon, ENIPFuzz, EUFuzzer, FIoTFuzzer, FUZZUSB, GANFuzzer, IKEProFuzzer, NDFuzz, NPSFUZZER, Ori, PAVFuzz, PCFuzzer, Peach*, SATFuzz, SGPFuzzer, Vfuzz, other ad-hoc prototypes

Tool	Programming Language	Link
ContractFuzzer	Go 80%, JS 8%, C 6.6%	https://github.com/gongbell/ContractFuzzer
CyberExploit	Phython 87%, Shell 11%	https://github.com/CyberExploitProject/CyberExploit
libFuzzer	C/C++	https://llvm.org/docs/LibFuzzer.html
Polar-Fuzz	C 85%, Shell 7%, C++ 4%	https://github.com/fouzhe/Polar-Fuzz
SIoTFuzzer	Phython 74%, Shell 24%	https://github.com/yinfeidi/Firmware-fuzz-tool
Snout	Phython 99%	https://github.com/nislab/snout
StateFuzzer	Java	https://gitee.com/z11panyan/state-fuzzer
V-Shuttle	C 90%, Shell 6%	https://github.com/hustdebug/v-shuttle
Z-Fuzzer	Phython 92%, C 3%	https://github.com/zigbeeprotocol/Z-Fuzzer

Parent tool	List of tools that use/extend the parent one
AFL	NDFuzz, NPSFUZZER, Polar-Fuzz, Ori, V-Shuttle, ad-hoc prototypes
AFLFast	Polar-Fuzz
Boofuzz	SIoTFuzzer
KittyFuzzer	PCFuzzer
Mutiny	NDFuzz
Peach	Charon, NPSFUZZER, Peach*, PAVFuzz, ad-hoc prototypes
Snipuzz	FIoTFuzzer
Sulley	ad-hoc prototypes
syzkaller	FUZZUSB
ZDHCP	NDFuzz

To obtain an overall view, we built a Sankey diagram that relates relevant aspects from RQ1 and notions on tools. A Sankey diagram is a flow diagram that shows the flow between source and destination nodes, in which the width of the connection of each flow is proportional to the flow rate of the relevance of the depicted flow property. Figure 2 shows the built diagram that represents the flow among: artifacts required (first layer in the diagram), artifacts inferred (second layer), available tools (third layer), and extended or used tools (last layer).

- **Evidence 3.1.** Most of the analyzed papers (31 out of 45) introduce a tool, the adopted technology (e.g., tool architecture, libraries and programming language) and, often, provide a name to their tool. Python and C/C++ are the most popular programming languages.
- **Evidence 3.2.** Only a small portion of these tools (9 out of 27), however, is available online for testing purposes and almost all of them are provided by Github[12].

---

[12] https://github.com.

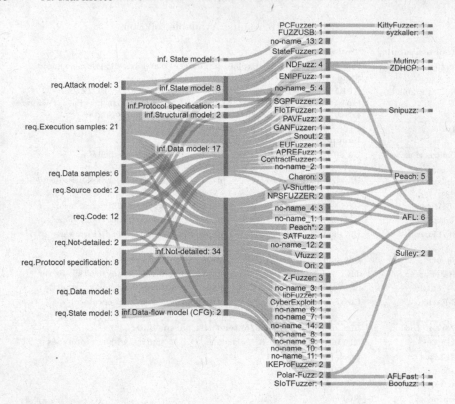

Fig. 2. Sankey diagram: required artifacts, inferred artifacts, tools and used tools

- **Evidence 3.3**. A large number of tools (11 our of 18) that extend or use an existing tools, use Peach or AFL.
- **Evidence 3.4**. It seems that most of the tools do not recover a structured artifact source (e.g., model or specification) or, at least, the related papers do not explicitly describe it. In cases in which it happens, data models (e.g., data types, structure and grammar) are most frequently recovered.

RQ4. Table 7 summarizes the relevant concepts emerged for the criterion **Vulnerability and attack**, used to derive the evidences concerning *RQ4*.

- **Evidence 4.1**. Most of the detected and documented vulnerabilities are related to memory management (e.g., buffer overflow, heap/stack buffer overflow, null pointers, use-after-free) and, less frequently, to input and data management and validation (e.g., improper input validation, response timeout, integer overflow, malformed packets, cross-site scripting).
- **Evidence 4.2**. Among the specified ones, Denial of Service (DoS) and Remote code execution (RCE) are the most frequent cyber-attacks that can exploit such vulnerabilities.

Table 7. RR results: Vulnerability and attack

Type of Vulnerability
Buffer overflow (7), Heap buffer overflow (5), Null-pointer-de/referenced (5), Stack buffer overflow (5), Memory errors (4), Use-after-free (4), Improper Input Validation (3), Improper Memory Allocation (3), Response timeout - DoS (3), Divide by Zero (2), Integer overflow (2), Invalid sequence (2), Malformed packets (2), Out-of-bound read (2), Segmentation Fault (2), Assertion violation (1), Authentication vulnerabilities (1), Command injection (1), Cross-site scripting - XSS (1), Display error happens (1), Ethereum specific vulnerabilities (e.g., message and function calls, timestamps/block number dependencies, exceptions) (1), Global buffer overflow (1), Improper data-access in messages (1), Improper variable assignment (1), Infinite Loop (1), Memory leakage (1), Overheating (1), Power loss (1), String vulnerabilities (1), switch set (1), Uncontrolled resources (1), Unexpected device behavior (1), Vulnerability due to communication latency (1), Web-type vulnerabilities (1)

Type of the attack
Denial of Service - DoS (15), Remote code execution - RCE (4), Information leakage (2), Advanced Persistent Threats (1), Command injection (1), Control-flow attacks (1), Data tampering (1), Eavesdropping (1), Elevation of privilege (1), Impersonation (1), Integrity attack (1), Man-in-the-middle -MITM (1), Memory corruption (1), Ping of Death (1), Security bypass (1), Web-based attacks (1)

5 Final Remarks

This section collects observations and evidences we derived from our RR, that is essential questions that can guide us when we have to start fuzzing, limitations of the literature, and paper's conclusions.

Start Fuzzing. We observe that when we have to start working with fuzz testing, we have to clearly identify the target protocol and the target protocol implementation that we have to test. We need to acquire some essential knowledge about the protocol (e.g., Do we know type and format of the protocol data and the protocol specifications?) and also about the specific protocol implementation (e.g., What is the technology adopted? Which type of system architecture is implemented?). By analyzing such an information, relevant aspects of the protocol have to be clearly identified (e.g., Is it a state or stateless protocol? Do the protocol adopt protection mechanisms such as authentication and message encryption?). Then, we have to identify the artifacts that we can use as input source for fuzzing (e.g., Do we have the protocol specifications? Is the data model available? Do we have some data samples? Do we have the implementation source code or a binary image of the protocol implementation? Can we capture some real traffic data? Do we have functional test cases to be used as seeds?). Another aspect to consider is the type of vulnerability we are mainly interested to discover (e.g., Which type of vulnerability and attack we are interested in limiting?). This is also related to the capability of monitoring the target system and to analyze its response during fuzzing (e.g., What can be monitored in the target system?). Finally, a key aspect concerns the selection of the tool (e.g., Can I use an existing tool to fuzzing my target system?). We can select an existing tool or, in most of the cases, plan to dedicate effort to extend an existing tool to customize it for our target system.

Limitations of Fuzz Approaches and Tools. We observe the following limitations of the existing approaches that need to be considered by practitioners that have to work with fuzz testing.

- It is often unclear and under-investigated how initial seeds are composed and generated. Even if it is a crucial enabler for fuzzing, in most of the cases, the seeds' composition is not considered.
- Only few tools are available and most of them are based on only two "parents" tools. Furthermore, since fuzzing depends on the technology of the target system, some development effort to customize such tools is expected before adopting them.
- Often, the smartness/intelligence degree of existing tools appears limited and they require manually-defined data/protocol models and specifications. This implies human effort and domain knowledge, thus limiting the adoption of fuzzing.
- Modern tools recover data/protocol models and specifications from traffic samples, aiming at reducing the required human involvement. However, the adoption of these tools is limited by several factors, e.g., ad-hoc recovery capabilities are needed for dealing with specific protocols, which require specific knowledge and a non-trivial amount of traffic samples. Furthermore, the use of data encryption and protection mechanisms can make these tools inefficient.
- Tools have a limited capability of monitoring and analyzing both the target system and the responses received from such a system, when the system is exercised during fuzzing. In particular, often, in embedded and IoT systems, the monitoring is limited to system crashes and memory management. This strongly restricts the discovery of sets of vulnerabilities.
- The complexity of fuzz testing increases when state-based protocols or protocols that use authentication and protection mechanisms have to be tested. Most of existing tools are based on single-data sessions, or pairs of fuzz test requests and response checks; however, this is not enough for such kind of situations.

Conclusions. This paper reports the findings of our RR on fuzz security testing for software implementations of communication protocols. We can summarize the main evidences as follows: (i) Industrial Control System and IoT protocols are the most studied ones; (ii) black-box fuzz testing is often investigated and the proposed approaches require protocol or data specifications as input; (iii) the investigated gray-box fuzzing approaches, often, drive the test generation with code coverage information; (iv) most of the detected vulnerabilities are related to memory management and, less frequently, to input and data management and validation; and (v) only a limited number of the investigated approaches is supported by publicly available tools.

The results of this RR represent the starting point to create the knowledge base needed to identify the requirements of a new fuzz testing tool we are developing in a new project. Furthermore, we believe that the emerged evidences can be of interest for practitioners and researchers since they can be used to characterize existing approaches and tools, thus being able to: (i) select the most appropriate tool for fuzz testing the software implementation of communication protocols in use, and (ii) identify new areas that need to be further investigated.

References

1. Braun, V., Clarke, V.: Using thematic analysis in psychology. Qual. Res. Psychol. **3**(2), 77–101 (2006)
2. Böhme, M., Pham, V.T., Roychoudhury, A.: Coverage-based greybox fuzzing as Markov chain. IEEE Trans. Softw. Eng. **45**(5), 489–506 (2019). https://doi.org/10.1109/TSE.2017.2785841
3. Cartaxo, B., Pinto, G., Soares, S.: Rapid reviews in software engineering. In: Felderer, M., Travassos, G. (eds.) Contemporary Empirical Methods in Software Engineering, pp. 357–384. Springer, Cham (2020). https://doi.org/10.1007/978-3-030-32489-6_13
4. Cartaxo, B., Pinto, G., Vieira, E., Soares, S.: Evidence briefings: towards a medium to transfer knowledge from systematic reviews to practitioners. In: ACM/IEEE International Symposium on Empirical Software Engineering and Measurement. ESEM, ACM (2016). https://doi.org/10.1145/2961111.2962603
5. Feng, X., et al.: Snipuzz: black-box fuzzing of IoT firmware via message snippet inference. In: ACM SIGSAC Conference on Computer and Communications Security, pp. 337–350. ACM, New York (2021)
6. Globe Newswire: Embedded system market predicted to garner (2023)
7. Grand View Research: Next generation technology - cyber security market size, share & trends report, 2023–2030 (2022)
8. Hu, Z., Pan, Z.: A systematic review of network protocol fuzzing techniques. In: IEEE 4th Advanced Information Management, Communicates, Electronic and Automation Control Conference (IMCEC), vol. 4, pp. 1000–1005 (2021). https://doi.org/10.1109/IMCEC51613.2021.9482063
9. Juuso, A., Takanen, A., Kittilä, K.: Proactive cyber defense: understanding and testing for advanced persistent threats (APTs). In: European Conference on Information Warfare and Security (2013)
10. Kitchenham, B., Dyba, T., Jorgensen, M.: Evidence-based software engineering. In: Proceedings of 26th International Conference on Software Engineering, pp. 273–281. ACM/IEEE (2004). https://doi.org/10.1109/ICSE.2004.1317449
11. Lan, H., Sun, Y.: Review on fuzz testing for protocols in industrial control systems. In: IEEE Sixth International Conference on Data Science in Cyberspace (DSC), pp. 433–438 (2021). https://doi.org/10.1109/DSC53577.2021.00068
12. Munea, T.L., Lim, H., Shon, T.: Network protocol fuzz testing for information systems and applications: a survey and taxonomy. Multimedia Tools Appl. **75**(22), 14745–14757 (2015). https://doi.org/10.1007/s11042-015-2763-6

13. Pan, Z., Liu, C., Liu, S., Guo, S.: Vulnerability discovery technology and its applications. JSW **8**(8), 2000–2007 (2013)
14. Schotten, M., M'hamed., E., Meester, W., Steiginga, S., Ross, C.: A Brief History of Scopus: The World's Largest Abstract and Citation Database of Scientific Literature, pp. 31–58. CRC Press (2017). https://doi.org/10.1201/9781315155890
15. Shen, Q., Wen, M., Zhang, L., Wang, L., Shen, L., Cheng, J.: A systematic review of fuzzy testing for information systems and applications. In: 2nd International Conference on Electronics, Communications and Information Technology (CECIT), pp. 156–162 (2021). https://doi.org/10.1109/CECIT53797.2021.00035
16. Sutton, M., Greene, A., Amini, P.: Fuzzing: Brute Force Vulnerability Discovery. Pearson Education, London (2007)

Enhancing Synthetic Test Data Generation with Language Models Using a More Expressive Domain-Specific Language

Chao Tan[1,2]($\boxtimes$) (iD), Razieh Behjati[2], and Erik Arisholm[2]

[1] University of Oslo, Oslo, Norway
[2] Testify AS, Oslo, Norway
chao.tan@testify.no

Abstract. Generating production-like test data that complies with privacy regulations, such as the General Data Protection Regulation (GDPR), is a significant challenge in testing data-intensive software systems. In our previous research, we posed this challenge as a language modeling problem. We trained a language model to capture the statistical properties of production data, and showed that it can effectively generate production-like test data. However, the richness of the generated data in our earlier work was limited by the information capacity of the domain-specific language that we used for representing the data and the training corpus. In this paper, we present an enhanced approach, by using a more expressive domain-specific language with a higher information capacity. We show that using the new domain specific language allowes better leveraging the deep-learning technology and generate even richer, production-like test data. Our experiment results show that with higher information capacity and constraints complexity, the new language performs better regarding generated data quality, with an affordable increase on computational cost.

Keywords: synthetic data generation · domain specific language · deep learning · language modelling

1 Introduction

Production-like test data are essential at higher levels of the testing pyramid, where the goal is to gain confidence in the correct behavior of a fully integrated and deployed system. As the privacy protection regulations like GDPR prohibit the use of production data containing personal and private information, the demand for synthetic and production-like test data arises. Specifically, synthetic test data need to be statistically representative of the production data and conform with the business constraints of the domain and application.

The authors acknowledge the collaboration and support from the Norwegian Population Registry, and the financial support from the Research Council of Norway.

© IFIP International Federation for Information Processing 2023
Published by Springer Nature Switzerland AG 2023
S. Bonfanti et al. (Eds.): ICTSS 2023, LNCS 14131, pp. 21–39, 2023.
https://doi.org/10.1007/978-3-031-43240-8_2

To address the need for synthetic production-like test data, we previously proposed a language modelling approach [24]. This approach involves building a language model that captures the statistical characteristics of production data, and using it to generate synthetic test data. We also proposed an evaluation framework to measure the quality of the generated data in terms of statistical representativeness and business constraint conformance. We applied our solution to our case study, the Norwegian Population Registry (NPR), for integration testing with other public and private organizations that exchange a large amount of population data. We experimented with Char-RNN [23] algorithm and built a language model that generates highly representative data that conforms to the NPR domain's business constraints. Our research demonstrates the effectiveness of language modelling in generating synthetic production-like test data.

Our previous research highlights the potential of deep learning for generating high-quality test data suitable for high-level testing of complex systems. However, a crucial step is constructing a training corpus from production data.

Modern software systems often use structured document formats like XML or JSON to store and exchange data. However, raw production data is not suitable for model training for several reasons. In application domain where raw production data contain sensitive information, such data cannot be exposed outside of production due to privacy protection regulations. Moreover, not all data in raw form is important for testing, with some text or non-essential information having little impact on system behavior. Thus, a training corpus should only include the most important and non-sensitive information from production data.

To represent the selected information extracted from raw data, we use a domain-specific language (DSL). In our previous experiments, we designed the *Steve132* DSL for the NPR domain, but it has limitations. *Steve132* uses a fixed-length format, where information fields are marked by their ordinal positions, and there are no field delimiters. This format is efficient for representing records with similar semantics, where all fields are relevant and present. But when it comes to encoding many varying types of records, the fixed-length format results in sparse sequences, and can easily become inefficient and impractical. Moreover, the fixed-length format hampers the expression of complex domain constraints, which is essential for generating realistic and valid test data.

This paper proposes a novel approach for designing DSLs with wider applicability. Instead of relying on the position of information fields within the text string, it uses structural tokens and a grammar to indicate information fields. We apply this new design approach to the NPR domain and design a new DSL, *Steveflex*. We experiment with this language by training a Char-RNN language model with a *Steveflex* corpus and compare the generated data quality with the *Steve132*. The results show that with higher information capacity and constraints complexity, *Steveflex* performs better than *Steve132* regarding generated data quality, with affordable increase on computational cost.

Our contributions of this paper are as follows:

- we propose of an effective approach for designing DSLs with high information capacity and expressiveness, to enhance the utility of deep-learning techniques for test data generation,

– we measure and quantify the impact of the choice of the DSL on the model-training performance and quality of the generated data, by applying our approach to a real-world case study.

The remainder of the paper is organized as follows. We introduce our case study in Sect. 2 before we present the two DSLs and discuss their expressiveness and information capacity in Sect. 3. Section 4 presents our language model evaluation framework, and Sect. 5 presents our experiments, results and comparison between the two languages. We discuss related work in Sect. 6 and conclude the paper in Sect. 7.

2   Case Study

The Norwegian National Population Registry (NPR) collects, stores and manages the personal data of all the residents of Norway and distributes electronic personal information to more than 2000 organisations (which are referred to as data consumers) so that they can provide service to society. The software system in NPR is undergoing a modernisation process, and so are the software systems of many of its data consumers. An effective setup for cross-organisational integration testing, which is critical for a successful transition, requires a large amount of production-like data that can stimulate realistic test scenarios.

Under the restriction of GDPR, production data are strictly prohibited in such testing. Therefore, our collaboration with the NPR aims to provide synthetic, dynamic and production-like data to support the cross-organisational integration testing between NPR and its data consumers. Dynamic in this context refers to the test data not being static, but rather evolve and adapt, similar to how the production data changes in a real production environment. To apply our proposed solution and train a language model to generate a synthetic population representative of the Norwegian population synthetically, the first and essential step is designing a domain-specific language to form a training corpus from the NPR data.

2.1   Abstract Data Model

The software systems of the NPR and its data consumer organisations are event-based systems. In these systems, each record of personal data, and any event that happens to a person (birth, marriage or relocation) that gets registered into NPR, are stored as XML documents.

We model the NPR data as an abstract event-based model in Fig. 1. An event-based system can be seen as a collection of *StatefulEntities*, whose states can be altered by events. Each stateful entity (or entity for short) consists of a collection of *StateDescriptors*. The *StateDecriptors* are typed, and each type of *StateDescriptor* describes one group of information about the entity. At any time, an entity contains only one currently applicable instance of one type of *StateDescriptor*. An event consists of one or more *StateDescriptors*. An event happening to an entity adds its *StateDescriptor* into the entity and the added ones become currently applicable; if the entity has that type of *StateDescriptor* from before, the existing instances are set to historical.

In the NPR domain, each personal data record is an *StatefuEntity*; each aspect of the personal data, for example, birth information, civil status, residence address and many others, is a type of *StateDescriptor*. The collection of all the personal data forms the population.

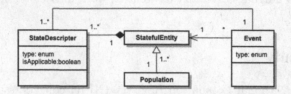

Fig. 1. Abstract data model for event-based systems. Note that the *StateDescriper* has a boolean attribute *isApplicable*, which allows the data model to accommodate historical information about an entity: *isApplicable: True* means that this *StateDescriptor* instance is currently applicable, and *isApplicable: False* indicates historical.

2.2   Conceptual Model of Event Generator and Event Specification

Based on the abstract data model of the event-based system, we propose a conceptual model of an event generator, as shown in Fig. 2. At the heart of the event generator is a *StatisticalModel*, which captures the statistical characteristics of the events and of the states of the involved entities. The *StatisticalModel* samples for *EventSpecifications*. An *EventSpecification* is an abstraction over an event in an event-based containing important information fields.

Here is an example of a simplified event specification in the population registry domain:

Example 1 (Example EventSpecification). A single woman born in 1991 gets married to a divorced man born in 1981.

Note that the real event would normally refer to the people involved in the event by their personal identification numbers: e.g., "Person with Id M gets married to Person with Id N". However, since a personal identification number is generally a random sequence of digits, it does not carry any interesting statistical information. Therefore, in the formation of event specifications we replace the identities with basic information that carries statistical meaning for the model to learn.

Algorithm 1 shows the event generation process. The algorithm takes four inputs: (1) $P^{(t)}$, the state of the system at time t, which is essentially composed of the states of all the stateful entities in the system at time t; (2) the statistical model, M; (3) a collection of constraints, C; and (4) the number of events to

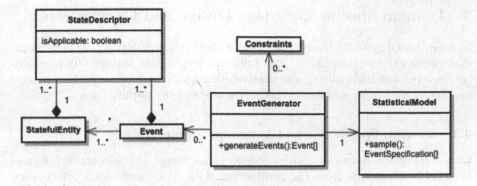

Fig. 2. Conceptual Model of the Event Generator

Algorithm 1. Event Generator

1: **function** GENERATEEVENTS($P^{(t)}, M, C, N$)
2:     $E \leftarrow \emptyset;\ P \leftarrow P^{(t)}$
3:     **for** $i \leftarrow 1, N$ **do**
4:         $e_{spec} \leftarrow M.sample(N)$
5:         $e \leftarrow createEvent(e_{spec}, P, C)$
6:         $E \leftarrow E \cup \{e\}$
7:     **end for**
8:     $P^{(t+1)} \leftarrow updatePopulation(P, E)$
9:     **return** $P^{(t+1)}, E$
10: **end function**

---

generate N. The algorithm returns a collection of events E and the updated state of the system $P^{(t+1)}$.

In Algorithm 1, each iteration in the *for* loop in lines 3–7 generates an event e and adds it to E. Event generation in each iteration involves two steps. In the first step, an event specification e_{spec} is sampled from M, in Line 4. To construct a fully specified event, other details that are not captured by the *StatisticalModel* must be added to this event specification. This is the second step of event generation and is done by calling *createEvent* in Line 5. Based on the information provided by the e_{spec}, the *createEvent* function fills out the missing information by random sampling from a valid data range, while making sure that the resulting event conforms to the business constraints C.

From the previous example of event specification, a simplified concrete synthetic event can be generated, with the added details in angle brackets:

Example 2 (Example generated event). A single woman <named Beautiful Flower>, born on <01-02-> 1991 <with ID xxxxxxxxxxx>, gets married to a divorced man <named Green Tree> born on <02-01-> 1981 <with ID xxxxxxxxxxx>

In particular, the *createEvent* function requires a domain-specific implementation and will not be discussed in depth in this paper.

3   Domain Specific Language Design and Comparison

In event-based systems, in order to build a synthetic population that is dynamic and statistically representative, it is sufficient to generate statistically representative events. Statistically representative events propagate through the systems and maintain a statistically representative state of the population.

3.1   Domain Specific Formal Language - *Steve132*

Construction of *Steve132* strings follow these steps: (1) select the information fields to include from the production data, (2) encode each information field's possible values using fixed-length character-level tokens, (3) concatenate the encoded information fields in a predetermined order to form a fixed-length sequence of characters, and (4) if any included information field is absent in a specific record of the production data, use filler characters of the same length to denote the absence and take up the corresponding position in the text string.

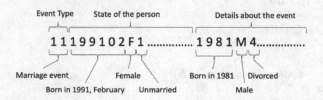

Fig. 3. *Steve132* example sentence, which describes a marriage event of a unmarried female born in Febrary 1991. The spouse is a divorced male born in 1981.

Figure 3 illustrates the structure of a *Steve132* sentence with an example, which consists of three parts: the event type, the current state of the person, and the event details. The string contains 132 characters, representing 48 information fields, with 1 for event type, 18 for the state of the person, and 29 for details of the event. The first two characters denote the event type (in this case, a marriage event of type *11*), followed by the state of the person and the details of the event, respectively. The state of the person contains information such as birth year, birth month, gender, and civil status, while the details of the event include information about the spouse and the location and date of the marriage event.

3.2   Domain Specifical Language - *Steveflex*

The *Steveflex* language design is also based on the abstract data model. We design a set of structural tokens to denote the elements in the abstract data model, as listed in Table 1. The event type, the current state of the entity and the event details are denoted with token **T**, **S** and **E**. A state descriptor consists of the state type and the state description. Angle brackets $<>$ encloses the type

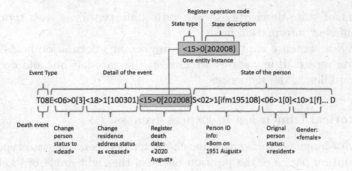

Fig. 4. *Steveflex* example sentence

Table 1. Structural tokens

Token	Description
T	Start of event type
E	Start of event detail
S	Start of statefull entity status
D	End of sequence
<>	Encloses type of state
[]	Encloses description of state

of the state and square brackets [] encloses the description of the state. Token **D** denotes the end of a sequence.

Besides the structural tokens, we utilize number characters to denote types, specifically, event type and state type. And for construction of state description, we utilize a similar approach as for the *Steve132* language, i.e., (1) identify information fields in this state description to include, (2) for each information field, identify all its possible values and encode with fixed length character-level tokens and (3) concatenate these information fields together to form a character sequence. Further more, *Steveflex* uses lowercase characters and numbers for state description tokens for better readability for humans and to avoid confusion with the capital structural tokens.

Figure 4 shows an example of a *Steveflex* sequence. This sentence describes a death event of event type *08*. The event detail part shows that this event modifies three states of a person: alters *status* to *dead*, changes the *residence address* status to *ceased*, and registers a *date of death*, August 2020. The state of the person part contains the person's state before this event happens. This person is a female born in August 1951. In "date of death" state in the event detail part, we see that a pair of angle brackets enclose the state, which is of type *15*. The state description part is a sequence of six digits, denoting the year and the month, and is enclosed in rectangular brackets. Note that the length and content of state descriptions vary with state types, as each type of state contains different information fields.

A *Steveflex* sentence captures all the important information fields in a production data record. If any states are absent, they are left out and do not need any position filler in the sequence.

3.3   Historical Dimension in Expressiveness

The *Steveflex* language designates one character between the state type and the state description part, i.e. the position between the right angle bracket '>' and the left rectangular bracket '[', for extra information for each state descriptor, i.e. meta data. The grammar for meta data in the NPR domain, as shown in Table 2: The meta data field in a state in the event detail represents the register operation code in the NPR, as shown in Fig. 4. It takes value from $0, 1, 2$ and 3, representing four types of register operations: register a new state, alter the current state, cancel the current state or alter the historical state. The meta data field in the person state part takes value from 0 and 1, representing whether the state is historical or currently applicable. Furthermore, if one state type has multiple instances present in the person state, only one can have meta data 1, meaning currently applicable, and all the others must have meta data 0, i.e. historical.

Introducing the meta data highly increases the expressiveness of the *Steveflex* language. Comparing to the *Steve132* language, which cannot describe a person's historical state or different type of action of an event, the *Steveflex* language provides a new dimension for expressing information in the NPR domain.

Table 2. Meta data grammar in *Steveflex*

meta data in state in the event detail		meta data in state of the person state description	
0	Register new state	0	historical
1	Alter current state	1	currently applicable
2	Cancel state		If there are multiple instances of one type state, only one of them can have meta data 1, and all the others must have meta data 0
3	Alter historical state		

3.4   Higher Information Capacity

Due to its limited length, the *Steve132* language excludes many important information fields from the production data, such as contact information for death residence, identification document from another country, shared residence for children with divorced parents, parental responsibility and use of the Sami language, and more. Excluding these important information fields leads to the inability to simulate test scenarios that rely on these inputs. In contrast, the *Steveflex* language captures all types of states and includes as many information fields as needed. *Steveflex* defines 30 types of states; if all the defined states and information fields present, a *Steveflex* sequence contains 141 information fields, which is almost 3 times as many as that of the *Steve132*.

Not requiring filler characters makes the *Steveflex* language more efficient in conveying information. To illustrate, in our *Steve132* training corpus, the sequences have an average of 68.03 filler characters for each, indicating that only about 48.5% of the sequence length conveys information. In contrast, 100% of the *Steveflex* sequence length conveys information.

4   Evaluation Framework

Language models are evaluated based on their performance in downstream tasks. In the context of deep learning language models applied to generate production-like data, we conduct experiments to address the following research questions:

- Syntactic validity: to what extent is the generated data valid?
- Statistical representativeness: to what extent is the generated data representative?
- Semantic validity: to what extent does the generated data conform to the con- straints?

While only syntactically valid data holds value for testing purposes, it is the combination of representative and semantically valid data that creates realistic testing scenarios. It is important to note that the evaluation of statistical representativeness and semantic validity is carried out exclusively on the subset of data that meets the criteria for syntactic validity.

Syntactic Validity. The syntactic validity rate represents the percentage of generated data that comply with the syntax and grammar of the DSL.

Representativeness. Representativeness is evaluated by measuring the similarity between the distributions (and joint distributions) of information fields in the generated and training data, but only on syntactically valid data. A person's data record in the NPR has many fields, including name, gender, birth date, address, marital status, family relation, and many others. The events in NPR also have many fields, and event type is one of them, and many event specific information fields, such as spouse information for marriage event, and original country for immigration event. Similarity of distributions and joint distributions of these information fields indicates how well the generated person and events represents the real data in the NPR

We measure distribution similarity with the symmetric and bounded Jensen-Shannon divergence (JSD) metric [5], which is zero when two probability distributions are identical and grows to a maximum value of 1.0 as the distributions diverge.

Semantic Validity. The semantic validity rate represents the percentage of generated data that conforms to the application domain's constraints. These constraints can be specified in any logic language, and we use Python in Example 3 to illustrate the format of the constraints: given a logical expression as the condition, the semantic validity equals the evaluation result of a logical expression. A constraint with such a definition specifies a relationship between two or more data fields.

Example 3 (Constraint definition).

```
if condition:
  semantic_validity = expression
```

The following is an example of a constraint in the NPR domain:

```
if EventType == "Marriage":
  semantic_validity = (person.age >= 18)
    and (person.civilStatus not in ["pertnership", "married"
    ])
    and (person.currentSpouseOrPartnerInfo = null)
    and (event.spouseAge >= 18)
```

This constraint specifies that if an event is of type marriage, the person it happens to should be at least 18 years, has a civil status that is neither married nor partnership and has no registered spouse or partner in the national registry. Additionally, the event must state that the new spouse is also at least 18 years old.

The validity rate for each constraint is the ratio of the number of generated strings that are valid for this constraint, to the total number of generated strings. Given a set of constraints, the aggregated or total validity rate is the ratio of the number of total data records for which all of the constraints are valid to the total number of data records.

Due to the complexity of real-world domains and applications, exhaustively checking every constraint in a domain is impossible. High conformance to a representative subset of the constraints can indicate that the model has learned the business rules of the domain well. Therefore, a high semantic validity rate for a subset of the constraints implies that the majority of the other constraints will also hold for the majority of the generated data.

5   Experiment, Result and Comparison

We experiment with the Char-RNN algorithm to train the language model for the *Steveflex* language. We obtain more than 108k of data records from the NPR domain and transform the records into *Steveflex* sequences to form our training corpus. For privacy protection reasons, we opt anonymized data instead of raw production data. The anonymization process in NPR is standard, automated and managed by a dedicated data processing team. The algorithm used for anonymization, to a great extent, preserves the statistical properties of the production data. The amount of anonymized data available equals the amount of real population data. However, for our experiments, we collected event documents recorded for 100 days to keep the data size and computational cost manageable. Note that although the anonymized data is available for internal testing in NPR, the anonymization algorithm is not sufficiently privacy-preserving to make the data eligible for cross-organizational integration testing. However, the synthetic data from the language model does not suffer from this restriction. This is because no one-to-one correspondence exists between the generated event or person documents and the event and person documents in production.

5.1   Result and Comparison

Syntactic Validity. We evaluated 850k generated sequences from our trained Char-RNN language model. The syntactic validity rate of the generated data is 99.55%, demonstrating that the model learns the *Steveflex* syntax exceptionally well.

The definition of syntactic validity for *Steve132* is the same, and the generated data has a syntactic validity rate of 96.06%. The model learns the *Steve132* language well, but the *Steveflex* language model outperforms it for this criteria.

Table 3. *JSD* and joint *JSD*

distributions	Steveflex	Steve132
seqLength	0.0093	0
eventType	0.0073	0.0032
person_birth_year	0.0061	0.0102
person_birth_month	0.0036	0.0072
person_civil_status	0.0011	0.0028
person_residence_municipality	0.0127	0.0267
person_death_yearn	0.0015	0.0001
person_death_month	0.0109	0.0002
person_immigrant_from_country	0.0088	0.0066
person_emigrate_to_country	0.0013	0.0018
partner_birth_year	0.0000	0.0021
joint_eventType_municipality	0.0267	0.0404
joint_eventType_birthYear_civilStatus	0.0310	0.0383
joint_birthYear_gender_fromCountry	0.0266	0.0285
joint_eventType_stateChange	0.0083	-
joint_personStatus_state	0.0173	-

Representativeness. Table 3 summarizes the results for both *Steveflex* and *Steve132*, including single information field JSDs in the first part of the table and joint JSDs of multiple information fields in the second part.

The first item in the table, *seqLength*, indicates the similarity of the sequence length distributions for training and generated data. Although sequence length is not an information field in the *Steveflex* or *Steve132* sequence, it is an important indication of the similarity between generated data and training data.

For *Steve132*, the JSD for sequence length is 0, indicating that the distribution of sequence length is identical between the generated data and training data. In fact, all the generated data from the *Steve132* model have a fixed length of 132 characters, matching the training data. In contrast, the length of the *Steveflex* sequences varies significantly. The sequence length in the training corpus ranges from 82 to 1049 with an average of 179.8. For *Steveflex*, the JSD for sequence length is 0.0073, indicating that the sequence length distributions of the generated data and training data are highly similar. The JSD values for the other single information fields for both *Steveflex* and *Steve132* are relatively small, indicating that the distributions of the generated data are similar to those of the training data.

Note that in the second part of the table, two joint distributions are missing for *Steve132*: *joint_ eventType_ stateChange* and *joint_ personStatus_ state*. The *joint_ eventType_ stateChange* represents the joint distribution of event types and the type of states they alter, i.e., what type of events alters what type of information. And the *joint_ personStatus_ state* is the joint distribution of the person status, and the presence of type of state descriptors for the person. These distributions involve typed states, which do not exist in the *Steve132* language.

It is not practical to examine all the distributions and joint distributions of the synthetic data and training data. Overall, however, we can confidently conclude that both the *Steveflex* and *Steve132* models learn the statistical properties of the training data of its language, and can generate highly-representative data. Despite the higher complexity of *Steveflex*, the JSDs and joint JSDs are comparable to or even better than those of *Steve132*.

Table 4. Constraint conformity - Steve132

Event type	Cyclomatic complexity	Valid rate
Marriage	4	98.25%
Birth	3	99.94%
Death	2	100%
Relocation within municipality	3	99.95%
Relocation between municipality	3	99.89%
Immigration	2	99.43%
Emigration	3	99.64%
Change name	2	100%
Over all	2.73(average)	**97.12%**

Semantic Validity. Table 4 provides a summary of the constraint checks for 8 event types in the generated *Steve132* sequences, including marriage, birth, and death events, etc. The constraints are expressed as Python functions (see Appendix A). To evaluate of the complexity of these constraints, we check the cyclomatic complexity, i.e., the number of decisions in the validation function for each event type, as listed in the table. On average, each event type has a cyclomatic complexity of 2.73. In the generated data, two types of events have 100% valid rate, five types have more than 99% valid rate, and one has 98.25%. In total, the generated data have a 97.12% valid rate.

Steveflex has more complex constraints than *Steve132*. These constraints apply to either a single state, between multiple states or to the whole event. Table 5 shows the constraint-checking results for two types of states and two types of events, which are shown in Appendix B.

Steveflex defines 10 types of civil status, and in the NPR domain, there is one rule for each civil status type; besides, the state must have valid meta data indicating it is currently applicable. Hence, the constraint for state "civil status" has 11 checks. The constraints for events are more complex than those for the states because they usually involve checking multiple states in both the event details and person state descriptions. For example, the constraint for event type "death" involves the checks for state *Death, Residence Address, and Status*, and their operation codes and metadata. This constraint has 20 checks. The constraint for "change of civil status" event has 27 checks. On average, these four constraints have a cyclomatic complexity of 15, which shows that *Steveflex* constraints are much more complex than *Steve132* constraints. The valid rates for all these constraints are more than 99%, and the overall valid rate is 99.74%. Despite the higher complexity of the constraints, the *Steveflex* generated data overperforms that of the *Steve132* regarding semantic validity.

The above three subsections demonstrate that, despite its higher information capacity and greater complexity in terms of language syntax and domain constraints, the data generated using *Steveflex* is of comparable or superior quality to that of *Steve132*. These results showcase the impressive learning ability of the Char-RNN algorithm for complex DSLs and suggest its potential application for data generation with language modeling in other domains.

Table 5. Constraint conformity - Steveflex

State or event type	Cyclomatic complexity	Valid rate
State ID number	2	99.99%
State civil status	11	99.99%
Event death	20	99.97%
Event Change in civil status	27	99.76%
Overall	15(average)	**99.74%**

5.2   Experimental Setup

Our training utilized a Tesla T4-4C virtual GPU with 4GB of available GPU memory for both *Steve132* and *Steveflex* experiments. We employed a PyTorch Char-RNN implementation [1] and fine-tuned various hyperparameters to identify the best model based on model loss and generated data quality.

Table 6. Experiment setup comparison

	Steveflex	Steve132
Network size	Two layers network, each with 400 GRU units	Two layers network, each with 100 GRU units
Training data size	113M	23M
Training epochs	13	28
Training time	26 h	4 h
Generation time for 100k sequences	100 min	less than 5 min

Our training setup is summarized in Table 6. The best performing *Steveflex* model has two layers, with 400 GRU units in each layer, and employs the Adam optimizer [10]. The network has over 2 million parameters and was trained for 27 epochs. The lowest validation loss is achieved after 26 hours of training, at the end of the 13th epoch, and we use the model at the end of this epoch for data generation. Using this model, it takes approximately 100 minutes to generate $100k$ sequences.

Comparing to the *Steve132* setup, the network size for the *Steveflex* model is four times larger, and the training time is more than six times longer. This is expected due to the larger model size and training corpus size. As a consequence, the data generation time is also longer for the same number of sequences.

The NPR domain expects population data statistics to change slowly, so retraining the model frequently is not necessary. The training corpus is composed of 100 days of production data, making quarterly retraining a reasonable option. A 26-hour training time for quarterly retraining is feasible for this application. On average, there are about 1,000 events per day in the NPR domain, so generating 100,000 sequences is enough to simulate a production-like data flow for a quarter. A 100-minute data generation time every quarter is manageable s well. Overall, the increase on computational cost for adopting *Steveflex* is entirely affordable.

6   Related Work

Generating test data is a well-researched topic, with various techniques proposed, such as combinatorial [13,18,19], metaheuristic search [6,8,14], model-based [2, 22,26], fuzzing [12,15], and machine learning algorithms [4,7,9,27]. While many of these approaches focus on increasing test coverage at lower testing levels, high-level testing, such as integration and end-to-end testing, is essential for quality assurance of large-scale complex software systems. However, simulating realistic test scenarios at this level is challenging without access to production-like test data. This is where our research comes in, as it addresses this challenge.

Along with the flourishing of deep learning techniques, language models, especially large language models (LLMs), have progressed rapidly in recent years [3,11,17,20,25]. It is also reported that LLMs are used for bug fixing [16,21]. However, the computational cost of training such models is huge. Hoffman et al. [25] proposed a relation between scaling up model size and increasing the number of training tokens, However, this relation cannot be applied to our approach of training language models for DSL for data generation purpose. Our language models, *Steve132* and *Steveflex-NPR*, differ from LLMs in multiple ways, including the learning objective, complexity, and evaluation methods. Additionally, our models are trained on epochs, and we do not have an unlimited corpus like many of the LLM training, making it challenging to scale up the number of training tokens as language size scales up. Nonetheless, the proposed relation offers a potential direction for optimizing model training.

7 Conclusion

In this paper, we present a novel approach for designing domain-specific languages for synthetic data generation using language models. We apply this design approach to the Norwegian Population Registry domain and design a more expressive DSL with higher information capacity and constraint complexity, the *Steveflex*. Through the training of a language model for *Steveflex* and an evaluation of the generated data, we show that the new language outperforms the previous DSL, *Steve132* in terms of data quality. Moreover, we demonstrate that the increase in computational cost associated with using *Steveflex* is affordable, making it a feasible choice for synthetic data generation in the NPR domain. Our approach can also be applied to other domains to design DSLs for synthetic data generation, which can result in high-quality synthetic data with a lower cost and effort compared to manual data synthesis. Overall, our work contributes to the advancement of synthetic data generation in various domains, with potential applications in privacy-preserving data collection, data analysis and machine learning.

A Steve132 constraints

```
""" check state validity """
""" State ID number """
def isStateValid_IDnumber(state):
  semantic_validity = (state.
      hasOneApplicable == True)
    and (state.year in range(1900,2023))
  return semantic_validity

""" State Civil Status """
def isStateValid_CivilStatus(state):
  semantic_validity = True
    if state.hasOneApplicable == False
      semantic_validity = False
      return semantic_validity
  match state.civilStatus:
    case "single":
      semantic_validity = not state.
      hasSpouseInfo
```

```
    case "married":
      semantic_validity = state.
      hasSpouseInfo
    case "widowed":
      semantic_validity = not state.
      hasSpouseInfo
    case "divorced":
      semantic_validity = not state.
      hasSpouseInfo
    case "separated":
      semantic_validity = not state.
      hasSpouseInfo
    case "registeredPartnership":
      semantic_validity = state.
      hasSpouseInfo
    case "separatedPartner":
      semantic_validity = not state.
      hasSpouseInfo
    case "divorcedPartner":
      semantic_validity = not state.
      hasSpouseInfo
```

```
        case "survivingPartner":
            semantic_validity = not state.
        hasSpouseInfo
        case "unknown":
            semantic_validity = not state.
        hasSpouseInfo
    return semantic_validity


""" check event validity """
""" Event Death """
def isEventValid_death(event, personState
    ):
    if event.hasEntityDeath == False:
        return False
    match event.entityDeath.operationCode:
        case "RegisterNew":
            if personState.hasEntityDeath ==
        True:
                if personState.entityDeath.
        hasOneApplicable == True:
                    return False
        case ["AlterCurrentState" | "
        CancelState" ]:
            if personState.hasEntityDeath ==
        False:
                return False
            if personState.entityDeath.
        hasOneApplicable == False:
                return False
        case "AlterHistoricalState":
            if personState.hasEntityDeath ==
        False:
                return False
            if personState.entityDeath.
        hasOneNonApplicable == False:
                return False
    if personState.
        hasEntityResidencyAddress == True:
        if event.hasEntityResidencyAddress ==
        False
            return False
        if event.entityResidencyAddress.
        hasOneApplicable == False
            return False
    if personState.hasEntityStatus == False
        return True
    if person.entityStatus.hasOneApplicable
        == False
        return True
    if event.hasEntityStatus == True:
        if event.entityStatus.operationCode
        == "CancelState" and
            event.entityStatus.stateus == "
        Dead":
            return True
    if personState.hasEntityStatus == False
        :
        return False
    if not (personState.entityStatus.
        hasOneApplicable and
        personState.entityStatus.status == "
        Dead"):
        return False
    if (event.entityDeath.hasOneApplicable
        and
        event.entityDeath.hasDate):
        return True
    return False


""" Event Change Civil Status """
def isEventValid_ChangeCivilStatus(event,
    personState):
    semantic_validity = True
    if event.hasEntityCivilStatus == False
        return False
    match event.entityCivilStatus.
        civilStatus:
        case ["married" | "
        registeredPartnership"]:
            if event.entityCivilStatus.
        hasSpouseInfo == False:
                return False
        case ["unknown"]:
            pass
        case _:
            if event.entityCivilStatus.
        hasSpouseInfo == True
                return False
```

```
    match event.entityCivilStatus.
        operationCode:
        case "RegisterNew":
            if personState.hasEntityCivilStatus
        == False:
                return True
            if personState.entityCivilStatus.
        hasOneApplicable == False:
                return True
            match event.entityCivilStatus.
        civilStatus:
                case "unknown":
                    if personState.
        hasEntityCivilStatus == True
                        return False
                case ["married" | "
        registeredPartnership"]:
                    if personState.
        entityCivilStatus.civilStatus in ["
        married", "registeredPartnership"]:
                        return False
                case _:
                    if personState.
        entityCivilStatus.civilStatus in ["
        married", "registeredPartnership"]
                        return True
            return False
        case "AlterCurrentState":
            if personState.hasEntityCivilStatus
        == False:
                return False
            if personState.entityCivilStatus.
        hasOneApplicable == False:
                return False
            if event.entityCivilStatus.
        civilStatus == personState.
        entityCivilStatus.civilStatus
                return False
            return True
        case "CancelState":
            if personState.hasEntityCivilStatus
        == False:
                return False
            if personState.entityCivilStatus.
        hasOneApplicable == False:
                return False
            if event.entityCivilStatus.
        civilStatus == personState.
        entityCivilStatus.civilStatus
                return True
            return False
        case "AlterHistoricalState":
            if personState.hasEntityCivilStatus
        == False:
                return False
            if personState.entityCivilStatus.
        hasNonApplicable == False:
                return False
            if event.entityCivilStatus.
        civilStatus == personState.
        entityCivilStatus.history.
        civilStatus
                return False
    return semantic_validity
```

B Steveflex constraints

```
""" check state validity """
""" State ID number """
def isStateValid_IDnumber(state):
    semantic_validity = (state.
        hasOneApplicable == True)
    and (state.year in range(1900,2023))
    return semantic_validity

""" State Civil Status """
def isStateValid_CivilStatus(state):
    semantic_validity = True
    if state.hasOneApplicable == False
        semantic_validity = False
        return semantic_validity
    match state.civilStatus:
        case "single":
            semantic_validity = not state.
        hasSpouseInfo
        case "married":
            semantic_validity = state.
        hasSpouseInfo
```

```
      case "widowed":
        sementic_validity = not state.
        hasSpouseInfo
      case "divorced":
        sementic_validity = not state.
        hasSpouseInfo
      case "separated":
        sementic_validity = not state.
        hasSpouseInfo
      case "registeredPartnership":
        sementic_validity = state.
        hasSpouseInfo
      case "separatedPartner":
        sementic_validity = not state.
        hasSpouseInfo
      case "divorcedPartner":
        sementic_validity = not state.
        hasSpouseInfo
      case "survivingPartner":
        sementic_validity = not state.
        hasSpouseInfo
      case "unknown":
        sementic_validity = not state.
        hasSpouseInfo
    return sementic_validity


""" check event validity """
""" Event Death """
def isEventValid_death(event, personState
    ):
    if event.hasEntityDeath == False:
        return False
    match event.entityDeath.operationCode:
      case "RegisterNew":
        if personState.hasEntityDeath ==
        True:
            if personState.entityDeath.
        hasOneApplicable == True:
              return False
      case ["AlterCurrentState" | "
      CancelState" ]:
        if personState.hasEntityDeath ==
        False:
            return False
        if personState.entityDeath.
        hasOneApplicable == False:
            return False
      case "AlterHistoricalState":
        if personState.hasEntityDeath ==
        False:
            return False
        if personState.entityDeath.
        hasOneNonApplicable == False:
            return False
    if personState.
    hasEntityResidencyAddress == True:
        if event.hasEntityResidencyAddress ==
        False
            return False
        if event.entityResidencyAddress.
        hasOneApplicable == False
            return False
    if personState.hasEntityStatus == False
        return True
    if person.entityStatus.hasOneApplicable
        == False
        return True
    if event.hasEntityStatus == True:
        if event.entityStatus.operationCode
        == "CancelState" and
        event.entityStatus.stateus == "
        Dead":
            return True
    if personState.hasEntityStatus == False
        :
        return False
    if not (personState.entityStatus.
    hasOneApplicable and
    personState.entityStatus.status == "
    Dead"):
        return False
    if (event.entityDeath.hasOneApplicable
    and
    event.entityDeath.hasDate):
        return True
    return False
```

```
""" Event Change Civil Status """
def isEventValid_ChangeCivilStatus(event,
    personState):
    sementic_validity = True
    if event.hasEntityCivilStatus == False
        return False
    match event.entityCivilStatus.
    civilStatus:
      case ["married" | "
      registeredPartnership"]:
        if event.entityCivilStatus.
        hasSpouseInfo == False:
            return False
      case ["unknown"]:
        pass
      case _:
        if event.entityCivilStatus.
        hasSpouseInfo == True
            return False
    match event.entityCivilStatus.
    operationCode:
      case "RegisterNew":
        if personState.hasEntityCivilStatus
        == False:
            return True
        if personState.entityCivilStatus.
        hasOneApplicable == False:
            return True
        match event.entityCivilStatus.
        civilStatus:
          case "unknown":
            if personState.
        hasEntityCivilStatus == True
                return False
          case ["married" | "
        registeredPartnership"]:
            if personState.
        entityCivilStatus.civilStatus in ["
        married", "registeredPartnership"]:
                return False
          case _:
            if personState.
        entityCivilStatus.civilStatus in ["
        married", "registeredPartnership"]
                return True
        return False
      case "AlterCurrentState":
        if personState.hasEntityCivilStatus
        == False:
            return False
        if personState.entityCivilStatus.
        hasOneApplicable == False:
            return False
        if event.entityCivilStatus.
        civilStatus == personState.
        entityCivilStatus.civilStatus
            return True
        return True
      case "CancelState":
        if personState.hasEntityCivilStatus
        == False:
            return False
        if personState.entityCivilStatus.
        hasOneApplicable == False:
            return False
        if event.entityCivilStatus.
        civilStatus == personState.
        entityCivilStatus.civilStatus
            return True
        return False
      case "AlterHistoricalState":
        if personState.hasEntityCivilStatus
        == False:
            return False
        if personState.entityCivilStatus.
        hasNonApplicable == False:
            return False
        if event.entityCivilStatus.
        civilStatus == personState.
        entityCivilStatus.history.
        civilStatus
            return False
    return sementic_validity
```

References

1. char-rnn.pytorch. https://github.com/spro/char-rnn.pytorch. Accessed Aug 2019
2. Ali, S., Iqbal, M.Z., Arcuri, A., Briand, L.C.: Generating test data from OCL constraints with search techniques. IEEE Trans. Software Eng. **39**(10), 1376–1402 (2013)
3. Brown, T., et al.: Language models are few-shot learners. Adv. Neural. Inf. Process. Syst. **33**, 1877–1901 (2020)
4. Čegiň, J., Rástočný, K.: Test data generation for MC/DC criterion using reinforcement learning. In: 2020 IEEE International Conference on Software Testing, Verification and Validation Workshops (ICSTW), pp. 354–357. IEEE (2020)
5. Fuglede, B., Topsoe, F.: Jensen-Shannon divergence and Hilbert space embedding. In: Proceedings of International Symposium on Information Theory, ISIT 2004, p. 31. IEEE (2004). https://doi.org/10.1109/ISIT.2004.1365067
6. Gois, N., Porfírio, P., Coelho, A.: A multi-objective metaheuristic approach to search-based stress testing. In: 2017 IEEE International Conference on Computer and Information Technology (CIT), pp. 55–62. IEEE (2017)
7. Ji, S., Chen, Q., Zhang, P.: Neural network based test case generation for data-flow oriented testing. In: 2019 IEEE International Conference on Artificial Intelligence Testing (AITest), pp. 35–36. IEEE (2019)
8. Khari, M., Kumar, M., et al.: Analysis of software security testing using metaheuristic search technique. In: 2016 3rd International Conference on Computing for Sustainable Global Development (INDIACom), pp. 2147–2152. IEEE (2016)
9. Kim, J., Kwon, M., Yoo, S.: Generating test input with deep reinforcement learning. In: 2018 IEEE/ACM 11th International Workshop on Search-Based Software Testing (SBST), pp. 51–58. IEEE (2018)
10. Kingma, D.P., Ba, J.: Adam: a method for stochastic optimization. arXiv preprint arXiv:1412.6980arXiv:1412.6980 (2014)
11. Lewis, P., et al.: Retrieval-augmented generation for knowledge-intensive NLP tasks. Adv. Neural. Inf. Process. Syst. **33**, 9459–9474 (2020)
12. Li, J., Zhao, B., Zhang, C.: Fuzzing: a survey. Cybersecurity **1**(1), 1–13 (2018)
13. Li, N., Lei, Y., Khan, H.R., Liu, J., Guo, Y.: Applying combinatorial test data generation to big data applications. In: 2016 31st IEEE/ACM International Conference on Automated Software Engineering (ASE), pp. 637–647. IEEE (2016)
14. McMinn, P.: Search-based software testing: past, present and future. In: 2011 IEEE Fourth International Conference on Software Testing, Verification and Validation Workshops, pp. 153–163. IEEE (2011)
15. Padhye, R., Lemieux, C., Sen, K., Papadakis, M., Le Traon, Y.: Semantic fuzzing with zest. In: Proceedings of the 28th ACM SIGSOFT International Symposium on Software Testing and Analysis, pp. 329–340 (2019)
16. Prenner, J.A., Babii, H., Robbes, R.: Can OpenAI's codex fix bugs? An evaluation on QuixBugs. In: Proceedings of the Third International Workshop on Automated Program Repair, pp. 69–75 (2022)
17. Rae, J.W., et al.: Scaling language models: methods, analysis & insights from training gopher. arXiv preprint arXiv:2112.11446 (2021)
18. Salecker, E., Glesner, S.: Combinatorial interaction testing for test selection in grammar-based testing. In: 2012 IEEE Fifth International Conference on Software Testing, Verification and Validation, pp. 610–619. IEEE (2012)
19. Simos, D.E., Kuhn, R., Voyiatzis, A.G., Kacker, R.: Combinatorial methods in security testing. IEEE Comput. **49**(10), 80–83 (2016)

20. Smith, S., et al.: Using DeepSpeed and megatron to train megatron-turing NLG 530B, a large-scale generative language model. arXiv preprint arXiv:2201.11990 (2022)
21. Sobania, D., Briesch, M., Hanna, C., Petke, J.: An analysis of the automatic bug fixing performance of ChatGPT. arXiv preprint arXiv:2301.08653 (2023)
22. Soltana, G., Sabetzadeh, M., Briand, L.C.: Synthetic data generation for statistical testing. In: 2017 32nd IEEE/ACM International Conference on Automated Software Engineering (ASE), pp. 872–882. IEEE (2017)
23. Sutskever, I., Martens, J., Hinton, G.E.: Generating text with recurrent neural networks. In: Proceedings of the 28th International Conference on Machine Learning (ICML 2011), pp. 1017–1024 (2011)
24. Tan, C., Behjati, R., Arisholm, E.: Application of deep learning models to generate representative and scalable synthetic test data for the Norwegian population registry. J. Syst. Softw. (2020, submitted)
25. Thoppilan, R., et al.: LaMDA: language models for dialog applications. arXiv preprint arXiv:2201.08239 (2022)
26. Yano, T., Martins, E., de Sousa, F.L.: A model-based approach for robustness test generation. In: 2011 Fifth Latin-American Symposium on Dependable Computing Workshops, pp. 33–34. IEEE (2011)
27. Zhou, X., Zhao, R., You, F.: EFSM-based test data generation with multi-population genetic algorithm. In: 2014 IEEE 5th International Conference on Software Engineering and Service Science, pp. 925–928. IEEE (2014)

On the Evaluation of Photometric Stereo Applications Testing Using Image Modifications

Franz Wotawa[1]($\boxtimes$) iD, Ledio Jehaj[1], and Nicole Brosch[2]

[1] Graz University of Technology, Institute for Software Technology, Inffeldgasse 16b/2, 8010 Graz, Austria
{wotawa,ljehaj}@ist.tugraz.at
[2] AIT Austrian Institute of Technology, Giefinggasse 4, 1210 Vienna, Austria

Abstract. Computer vision is vital for various applications like object tracking for autonomous driving or quality assurance. Hence, assuring that computer vision fulfills given quality criteria is essential and requires sufficient testing. In previous work, authors introduced a testing method relying on image modifications for a photometric stereo application. Image modifications include pixel errors or the rotation of images to be analyzed, revealing a substantial impact on the computed outcome of the photometric stereo application, depending on the applied modification. This paper focuses on whether we can reproduce the impact of image modifications in a real-world setup. In particular, we compare the impact of the rotation of the analyzed sample with the rotation modification applied to the image of the sample. The comparison indicates a similar effect when using rotation, showing that testing based on image modifications is valuable for verifying computer vision applications.

Keywords: Testing computer vision applications · Test automation · Test case generation

1 Introduction

Testing, i.e., finding interactions between a system and its environment that lead to unexpected or unwanted behavior, is essential to the development and accounts for up to 50% of the total development costs [1]. To reduce these costs, we require test automation, which appears in two flavors, i.e., the automation of test execution and the automated test suite (or test case) generation. When testing pure software, automated test execution only requires appropriate frameworks. However, when testing systems comprising hardware and software that interact with the natural world, the automation of test execution requires additional hardware that emulates the outside world, which is costly and often only valid for a particular system under test. The alternative, i.e., testing the system itself, requires building it, which is costly and prevents testing the system as early as possible during development.

© IFIP International Federation for Information Processing 2023
Published by Springer Nature Switzerland AG 2023
S. Bonfanti et al. (Eds.): ICTSS 2023, LNCS 14131, pp. 40–51, 2023.
https://doi.org/10.1007/978-3-031-43240-8_3

Therefore, industries like automotive introduce methods for testing systems at all stages of development utilizing physical and 3D simulation. Especially in the case of autonomous driving, such virtual verification becomes inevitable because of the vast number of potential interactions between the autonomous car and its environment that we need to consider for quality assurance [7,14,17]. However, when relying on simulation, someone might be interested in answering whether testing based on simulation is sufficient for fault detection. Unfortunately, there is only little scientific work tackling this question. Sotiropoulos and colleagues [11] carried out experiments in the area of mobile robotics, where they used simulation to detect faults already discovered in reality. The paper indicates that a substantial part of all faults can be identified in simulation too. However, utilizing the simulation for testing also comes with challenges. El Mostadi and colleagues [9] discussed several technical challenges influencing simulation outcomes to virtual testing.

In this paper, we contribute to the question regarding the difference between virtual and real verification and validation. In particular, we consider the area of computer vision and focus on testing photometric stereo applications. Such applications use pictures from different angles or lightning conditions to extract 3D models. In our case, we consider an implementation for quality assurance of riblet surfaces. Riblets, which mimic natural surfaces like shark skin, are microstructures aiming at reducing drag. Application areas are wind turbines, airplanes, and other devices where drag negatively influences performance. Therefore, any damages in riblets decrease drag reduction (see e.g. [8]) and may lead to replacing the surface. For more information regarding the system under test and its testing, we refer to previous publications [15,16], where we utilized an image modification framework for generating tests. We used modification operators that mimic faults potentially occurring in practice, like changing light conditions, missing pixels, or rotations.

In particular, we focus on the rotation operator. We compare the outcome of the riblet inspection tool [2] on surfaces where we apply manual rotation and rotations of images utilizing the corresponding operator from an image modification framework. This comparison partially answers whether testing based on an image modification framework captures reality and is the main contribution of this paper.

It is worth noting that besides the already introduced papers, there is little research on testing riblet inspection tools and photometric stereo systems. Research in riblet inspection focuses mainly on improving photometric stereo and other algorithms rather than on testing implementations and systems. For example, [5] presents a CNN-based photometric stereo method that learns the relationship between the input and surface normals of the scene. It improves conventional BRDF-based photometric stereo algorithms by taking the global light into account and not only the artificial light sources. Alternatively, [6] introduces a photometric stereo method that makes the photometric stereo more robust from image noise, and [10] develops a method for testing drag-reduction riblet-surfaces based on the Spaldig formula.

Most of the papers dealing with testing computer vision focus on the underlying methods, e.g., neural networks. Applications of testing include checking the robustness of neural networks. [3] creates perturbations (modifications) of images that a neural network fails to detect or classify correctly. The main focus is road signs since they are the most vulnerable objects allowing easy manipulation with potentially catastrophic effects. [4] suggest types of attacks on data that a machine learning algorithm uses to train and test itself. It also points out machine learning algorithms that cannot defend against these attacks. [12] shows that different realistic image transformations, like contrast or the presence of fog, can be used to generate tests that increase neuron coverage. Their experiments show that we can use these images for retraining neural networks. Their paper uses the testing results as new input for the system to learn and improve. [13] is another paper considering image misclassification of neural networks due to adversarial manipulation. In contrast to these papers, we do not focus on a particular computer vision method like neural networks for image classification. Instead, we are interested in the impact of real versus simulated modifications on the outcome of computer vision algorithms like photometric stereo.

We organize this paper as follows: We start introducing the underlying overall framework and setup of photometric stereo. Afterward, we discuss the carried-out experiments. The experimental part of this paper is central. We discuss the setup, the obtained results, and threats to validity. Finally, we summarize the paper.

2   The System Under Test

The system under test is a computer vision application developed to inspect the quality of riblet surfaces [2]. Riblet surfaces have tiny symmetric structures about $50\,\mu m$ high and are used to reduce drag, based on the shark skin effect. These structures are commonly used, e.g., in aviation, to lower fuel consumption, but over time they deteriorate and need to be replaced. Therefore, there is a need for tools that can assess the quality of riblet surfaces. The riblet surface inspection tool relies on the photometric stereo, which involves using one camera and multiple light sources to capture images of the same object under different lighting conditions (see Fig. 1). Photometric stereo applications use these images to generate a 2.5D model of the object, which computer vision methods can use to extract object information. The inspection tool we use for our experiments returns the percentages of defect pixels, scratch pixels, and abrasion pixels of provided riblets. Defect pixels refer to any destroyed parts of the riblet surface. The tool categorizes defect pixels as follows: Scratch pixels refer to a group of pixels that indicate a scratch on the riblet surface, whereas abrasion pixels refer to any shape of pixel errors that are not scratch-shaped. Hence, the number of defect pixels is the sum of scratch and abrasion pixels.

We can divide the riblet inspection tool into two main parts: 1) the photometry and 2) the inspection part. The photometry part comprises hardware and software. As shown in Fig. 1, the tool uses a camera setup with four lights from four different angles to capture the four image samples of the riblet. Python software implements the hardware control to capture the four images, one for

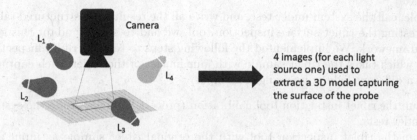

Camera

4 images (for each light source one) used to extract a 3D model capturing the surface of the probe

Fig. 1. Principle of the photometric stereo application.

each lighting angle. In addition, the software implements the photometric stereo algorithms. For this, it requires a calibration procedure, which uses a sample of four images of the riblet and an image of five spheres. The calibration procedure shall be performed before each new experiment. Afterward, the implemented algorithm takes the image sample and constructs a 2.5D model. The output of this process using the four images is information about the surface normals in x, y, and z directions. These normals are vectors that show the surface orientation. In addition, the tool provides the Albedo map that gives information about the reflectivity or brightness of the surface. It is a 2D image that shows the variations in the surface's reflectance properties across different regions.

The photometry output information is input for the inspection part, which is implemented in Matlab. The inspection output is a defect map showing the defect, scratch, and abrasion pixels detected. Apart from the defect map, the inspection tool also outputs a general info text file, which shows all the inspection results in a textual format. We use the provided textual information for evaluation.

In our previous work [15], we tested the described riblet inspection tool using different image modification methods. These methods include: increasing and decreasing image brightness, changing the pixel color in random areas of the image, image rotation, color inversion, and simulating camera lens distortion. We used three different samples of riblet surfaces to apply the modifications. The carried-out tests revealed a significant impact on the system's output under the test of the modification method used. Therefore, we developed an automation framework for computer vision applications to generate and carry out the tests.

We implemented this general framework for testing computer vision applications in Python, utilizing native and third-party libraries for data management, image modification, and user interface. We presented the first version of the framework in a previous paper (see [16]), and the latest version in [15]. The framework handles three main components (see Fig. 2). The first is the system under test. It is used without any changes and connected to the rest of the framework via a user interface. The second component is the modification component. The modification component implements several modification methods and is independent of the image format. The last component is the evaluation component. In this component, we call the modification methods on the image sample, call the system under test, and write all the results in a structured table. For testing the riblet surface inspection tool, we had to slightly adapt this general framework. We implemented the following steps to test the riblet inspection tool, which takes the riblet sample with four images of the riblet, each captured with a different light source angle, as input.

1. Run the riblet inspection tool calibration (process happens inside the system under test).
2. Run the riblet inspection tool with the original riblet sample as input and save the inspection results.
3. Perform image modification on the original sample.
4. Run the riblet inspection tool with the modified riblet images as input and save the inspection results.
5. Output a table with all obtained results for the original and modified images.

In the next section, we discuss the evaluation of the rotation operator considering manual rotation as the baseline.

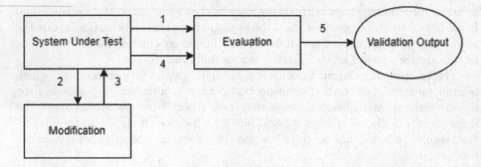

Fig. 2. Framework general architecture with numbered steps of its workflow.

3   Experiments

All the experiments are based on an existing framework comprising an image modification part and the photometric stereo application, i.e., the riblet inspection tool, we want to test (see [16]). In our experiments, we focussed on evaluating the precision of the rotation modifier in comparison with manual rotation. Figure 3 depicts the used **test setup**. Rotations are performed arround the center of the riblet under analysis. The experimental setup has two paths. The first path starts from the images taken from the riblet without rotations (A). The image snapshot is rotated (B) and passed to the image analysis framework (PSA) in step (B). This path is referred to the rotation path utilizing the image modification framework. The second path applies manual rotation in step (1). Afterward, in step (2) we take the image snapshot and pass this to the analysis

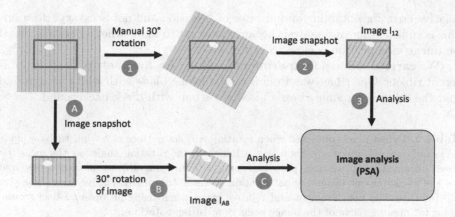

Fig. 3. Image modification versus manual application. The basic experimental setup.

in step (3). Again we use the same image analysis framework (PS) for computing the quality of the riblet.

It is worth mentioning that there is a difference in both paths. In the case of manual rotation, we always obtain a snapshot covering the riblet. This is not the case when applying the image modification framework where rotation leads to small areas (which are in white in Fig. 3). Hence, we cover not the whole riblet surface anymore. Note that in our first experiments, the areas which are not covered, are replaced with black color. In a further experiment, we used the following method, which we implemented in python. This method utilizes the *floodfill* method from *cv2* library[1]. The method connects every pixel to it's neighbor pixels. The connection happens when the difference of two pixels is within some threshold. If the neighbor pixel is more than 50% different in color, we make the neighbors pixel color the same as our current pixel. In this way we fill the black areas with the mostly used color of the entire image.

There are a lot of different **quality measures** used for comparing results of different methods. In our case we have the results obtained from manual inspection, which serve as the baseline. In the experiments, we want to know how far away results from automated rotation utilizing the image modification framework are. For measuring the difference between the values obtained from rotation using the image modification framework and the one from manual rotation, we rely on the relative error defined as follows:

$$\delta = \left| \frac{v_A - v_E}{v_E} \right| \cdot 100\% \qquad (1)$$

In this formula, v_A indicates the actual value, i.e., the value obtained using the image modification framework, and v_E the expected value, i.e., the one we get when applying manual rotation. Note that we do not know the real value of the quality of the riblet part from which we take the snapshot. Hence, we use the

---

[1] See https://opencv.org.

relative error for obtaining an indicator of precision and not accuracy. However, this is sufficient for our analysis because we want to know whether testing based on image modification is close to expectations.

We **carried out the experiments using the first setup** using two different riblets. One riblet was from a wind turbine blade with white background and the other was mounted on a piece of carbon with black background.

Table 1. Defect pixels obtained when rotating a riblet surface of a wind turbine blade (A), and one on a piece of carbon (B). α indicates the rotation angle. v_A the measurement obtained when rotating the riblet using the image modification framework, and v_E the measurement using manual rotation. δ is the computed relative error. The star "*" indicates the measurement and relative error when using an optimal background color for missing parts of the image occurring during rotation.

		Black backgr.		Opt. backgr.				Black backgr.		Opt. backgr.	
α	v_E	v_A	δ	v_A^*	δ^*	α	v_E	v_A	δ	v_A^*	δ^*
0	5.08	5.08	0.00%	5.08	0.00%	0	2.99	2.99	0.00%	2.99	0.00%
1	5.04	5.84	15.87%	6.04	19.84%	1	2.93	3.82	30.33%	3.88	32.38%
5	4.84	6.44	33.20%	7.16	48.09%	5	3.08	3.93	27.64%	4.05	31.54%
10	4.81	7.09	47.40%	9.07	88.57%	10	3.05	4.34	42.53%	4.42	45.16%
20	4.85	7.25	49.61%	8.68	79.12%	20	3.39	5.00	4.95%	4.95	45.89%
30	6.19	7.24	16.91	11.37	83.59%	30	3.16	4.83	52.75	5.20	64.45%
40	33.25	7.49	77.48%	7.11	78.62%						
45	49.82	7.55	84.84%	5.75	88.46%						
90	88.39	-	-	-	-						
Avg.			40.66%		60.79%	Avg.			33.44%		36.57%

(A) Wind turbine riblet   (B) Carbon riblet

Table 1 summarizes the obtained experimental results utilizing the available riblet inspection tool. The rotation angle (α) varies from 0 to 90° in case of the wind turbine blade and from 0 to 30 for the carbon riblet. In column v_E, we see the expected values, i.e., the defect pixels obtained using manual rotation. Column v_A shows the results when using the image modification framework and black color for filling unknown areas occurring during rotation. Column v_A^* states the defect pixels when using the optimized coloring instead of black. δ and δ^* show the computed relative error for both cases of coloring. When using black, we have one case of rotation (90°) for the wind turbine blade riblet where the riblet inspection tool reveals an error message and does not give back any information about the defect pixel rate.

Regarding the results, we see the following. In both coloring cases, the relative error is rather large varying between 4.95% in the best case for the carbon riblet to 84.84% for the wind turbine blade riblet. We see also no substantial changes for the different background colors for missing riblet parts occurring during automated image rotation. However, we see also that the obtained defect pixel values are always larger for rotations using the image modification framework in the range from 0 to 30°. Hence, it seems that the results obtained using the image modification framework overestimate the real impact of rotation. We see also that there is an impact of rotation, which automatically modified images using rotation also are able to reveal.

However, two questions remain after carrying out the first experimental setup. First, the impact of filling empty areas occurring during rotation is unclear. Second, there are substantial differences in case of rotations larger than 30°. To answer the first one, we are going to carry out a second experimental setup. For the second question, we manually analysed the rotated images. In Fig. 4, we see a difference between manual and automated rotation, which should not occur. We also had a look at the images of manual rotation of the wind turbine blade riblet showing that the manual rotation was not carried out very precisely. This explains at least partially, the larger differences between manual and automated rotation.

Fig. 4. Wind turbine blade riblets used for comparing the defect rate when applying manual and automated rotation of 45°. On the left, we see the manually rotated image, and on the right, the image that we rotated using the image modification framework.

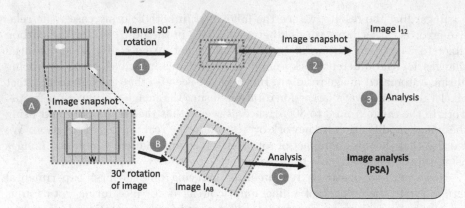

Fig. 5. The second experimental setup where we take a subarea of the original snap-shots for rotation to minimize empty parts with no riblet information.

To obtain more information regarding the influence of empty areas occur-ring during rotation when using the image modification framework, we slightly adapted the original experimental setup and conducted the experiments again using a **second experimental setup**. Figure 5 shows the extended setup where we take a sub-image from the original snapshot (A) having the same height-to-width ratio but a width w allowing us to perform rotation without empty areas. For the second experimental setup we focus on rotations between 0 and 30° only.

Table 2. Defect pixels obtained for the second experiment using the wind turbine riblet (A) and the carbon riblet, where we only consider sub-images for minimizing empty areas during image rotation. v_A is the measurement obtained when rotating the riblet using the image modification framework, and v_E is the measurement using manual rotation. δ is the computed relative error.

α	v_E	v_A	δ	α	v_E	v_A	δ
0	1.78	1.78	0.00%	0	4.74	4.74	0.00%
1	2.52	1.71	32.12%	1	4.79	4.96	3.48%
5	4.57	1.44	68.52%	5	4.76	5.13	7.80%
10	10.40	0.92	91.15%	10	4.47	5.21	16.45%
20	10.91	0.76	93.03%	20	4.41	4.35	1.29%
30	11.95	0.81	93.22%	30	3.36	3.84	14.35%
Avg.			67.77%	Avg.			7.23%
(A) Wind turbine riblet				(B) Carbon riblet			

Table 2 comprises the results of the second experiment. For rotations up to 30°, we see no improvements in case of the wind turbine riblet but substantial improvements for the carbon riblet. We further analysed the manual rotation for the wind turbine riblet for smaller rotations. We found that even for smaller manual rotations there are visible differences that cannot be explained using rotational effects. Hence, it seems that the whole manual rotation for the wind turbine blade was not carried out with sufficient precision.

Hence, in the following analysis, we only focus on the carbon riblet case. There we see a substantially smaller relative error compared to the first experiments. On average, we obtain 7.23% relative error, which is an excellent precision. This value is also substantially smaller compared to the results from the first experimental setup. Hence, we can conclude that when relying on rotations not introducing areas to be filled, the overall results of defect pixels obtained from the image modification framework are within the range of manual rotation. Hence, image modification can be used for carrying out testing providing reasonable precision, where reasonable means that the automated modifications are close to the manual modifications.

In summary, we can conclude the following from the two experiments:

- A high precision of manual rotation is required to allow comparing its outcome with the one of automated rotation.
- The precision of automated rotation for testing is sufficient when eliminating influencing factors like missing area information.
- Using image modification frameworks is able to indicate influences like rotation on the computed number of defects even in cases where precision is not that appropriate.
- Testing using image modification may overestimate the influence of faults like rotation on the overall result.

Threats to validity mainly comprise internal threats. We only used two particular riblets for carrying out the experiments. We did not select the riblet accordingly to specific influencing parameters if there are even any. Hence, we do not expect substantial differences when using more riblets. We may used the riblet inspection tool wrongly when carrying out the experiments leading to different results. This threat is very unlikely because of several reasons. First, we used the same setup in previous work, gaining sufficient experience for using the image analysis framework. Second, we checked our toolchain for shortcomings several times. Finally, we used the same setup for carrying out all the experiments. Because we carried out all experiments automatically using a program, there cannot be any direct human influence on the results of image modification. However, of course, we have an indirect influence caused by manual rotations, where the center of rotation or the degrees of rotation might not be 100% precise. We evaluated images of manual rotation as part of analysis.

For external threats, we may have an interaction effect of selection biases and the experimental variable, i.e., the number of pixel defects measured using the image analysis framework. However, we do not see it very likely that manual rotation and automated rotation are substantially different for other riblet surfaces.

4   Conclusions

This paper tackled investigations on the differences between image modification based on programs and manual modifications. The motivation behind this is to contribute to the clarification of whether simulations used in testing are accurate enough to reveal faults or any other conclusions. In particular, we focused on testing computer vision applications (and, in this case, a riblet inspection tool) where testing relies on automated image modification frameworks. We compared the results obtained using manual rotations of riblets with the ones computed using image rotation. The experiments reveal that there are several influencing parameters on the outcome. First, the precision of manual rotation cannot always be guaranteed, obviously influencing the outcome of the analysis. Second, we must pay attention to the effects of automatic rotation, like empty areas.

We do not see any substantial difference in the computed outcome when considering mentioned pitfalls. Moreover, even the first experiments show that using image modification operators reveal potential relationships between faults and their impact. For example, image modification already showed the impact of image rotation on the outcome of the riblet inspection tool but overestimated this. Hence, testing computer vision using image modification can provide good results, which are sufficient for practice. In future research, we want to extend this evaluation to other types of image modifications.

Acknowledgements. This work is funded by the Austrian Research Promotion Agency (FFG) within the project RiSPECT (874163).

References

1. Beizer, B.: Software Testing Techniques. Van Nostrand Reinhold (1990)
2. Brosch, N., Ginner, L., Schneider, S., Antensteiner, D., Traxler, L.: Quality inspection of translucent and micro-structured functional surfaces. In: Jalali, B., ichi Kitayama, K. (eds.) AI and Optical Data Sciences III, vol. 12019, pp. 173–184. International Society for Optics and Photonics, SPIE (2022). https://doi.org/10.1117/12.2605273
3. Eykholt, K., et al.: Robust physical-world attacks on deep learning visual classification. CVPR J. (2018)
4. Goodfellow, I., McDaniel, P., Papernot, N.: Making machine learning robust against adversarial inputs. Commun. ACM **61**(7), 56–66 (2018). https://doi.org/10.1145/3134599
5. Ikehata, S.: CNN-PS: CNN-based photometric stereo for general non-convex surfaces. In: Proceedings of the European Conference on Computer Vision (ECCV) (2018)
6. Ikehata, S., Wipf, D., Matsushita, Y., Aizawa, K.: Robust photometric stereo using sparse regression. In: 2012 IEEE Conference on Computer Vision and Pattern Recognition, pp. 318–325 (2012). https://doi.org/10.1109/CVPR.2012.6247691
7. Klück, F., Wotawa, F., Neubauer, G., Tao, J., Nica, M.: Analysing experimental results obtained when applying search-based testing to verify automated driving functions. In: DSA, pp. 213–219. IEEE (2021)

8. Leitl, P.A., Wotawa, F., Naughton, J.W., Feichtinger, C., Husen, N.M., Flanschger, A.: Measurements of macroscopic and microscopic riblet defects and their impact on performance. In: Proceedings of the AIAA SCITECH 2022 Forum, vol. 37, San Diego, CA & Virtual (2022). https://doi.org/10.2514/6.2022-0916

9. Mostadi, M.E., Waeselynck, H., Gabriel, J.M.: Seven technical issues that may ruin your virtual tests for ADAS. In: 2021 IEEE Intelligent Vehicles Symposium (IV), pp. 16–21 (2021). https://doi.org/10.1109/IV48863.2021.9575953

10. Song, B.W., Liu, Z.Y., Xu, T., Hu, H.B., Huang, M.M.: A method for testing drag-reduction on riblet surfaces based on the Spalding formula. J. Mar. Sci. Appl. **8**(4), 333–337 (2009). https://doi.org/10.1007/s11804-009-8073-5

11. Sotiropoulos, T., Waeselynck, H., Guiochet, J., Ingrand, F.: Can robot navigation bugs be found in simulation? An exploratory study. In: 2017 IEEE International Conference on Software Quality, Reliability and Security (QRS), pp. 150–159 (2017). https://doi.org/10.1109/QRS.2017.25

12. Tian, Y., Pei, K., Jana, S., Ray, B.: Deeptest: automated testing of deep-neural-network-driven autonomous cars. In: Proceedings of the 40th International Conference on Software Engineering, ICSE 2018, pp. 303–314. Association for Computing Machinery, New York (2018). https://doi.org/10.1145/3180155.3180220

13. Wicker, M., Huang, X., Kwiatkowska, M.: Feature-guided black-box safety testing of deep neural networks. In: International Conference on Tools and Algorithms for Construction and Analysis of Systems (2017)

14. Wotawa, F.: On the importance of system testing for assuring safety of AI systems. In: AISafety@IJCAI. CEUR Workshop Proceedings, vol. 2419. CEUR-WS.org (2019)

15. Wotawa, F., Jahaj, L.: Testing photometric stereo applications. In: 2022 9th International Conference on Dependable Systems and Their Applications (DSA) (2022). https://doi.org/10.1109/DSA56465.2022.00029

16. Wotawa, F., Klampfl, L., Jahaj, L.: A framework for the automation of testing computer vision systems. In: 2021 IEEE/ACM International Conference on Automation of Software Test (AST), pp. 121–124 (2021). https://doi.org/10.1109/AST52587.2021.00023

17. Wotawa, F., Peischl, B., Klück, F., Nica, M.: Quality assurance methodologies for automated driving. Elektrotech. Informationstechnik **135**(4–5), 322–327 (2018)

Seeding Contradiction: A Fast Method for Generating Full-Coverage Test Suites

Li Huang[1], Bertrand Meyer[1,2]($\boxtimes$) (ID), and Manuel Oriol[1]

[1] Constructor Institute, Schaffhausen, Switzerland
{li.huang,bm,mo}@sit.org
[2] Eiffel Software, Santa Barbara, CA, USA
https://constructor.org, https://eiffel.com

Abstract. The regression test suite, a key resource for managing program evolution, needs to achieve 100% coverage, or very close, to be useful. Devising a test suite manually is unacceptably tedious, but existing automated methods are often inefficient. The method described in this article, "Seeding Contradiction", inserts incorrect instructions into every basic block of the program, enabling an SMT-based Hoare-style prover to generate a counterexample for every branch of the program and, from the collection of all such counterexamples, a test suite. The method is static, works fast, and achieves excellent coverage.

Keywords: Testing · Coverage · Software verification · Eiffel

1 Overview

In the modern theory and practice of software engineering, tests have gained a place of choice among the artifacts of software production, on an equal footing with code. One particularly important rule is that every deployed program should come accompanied with a *regression test suite* achieving high branch coverage and making it possible to check, after any change to the software, that previous functionality still works: no "regression" has occurred.

Producing a high-coverage regression test suite is a delicate and labor-intensive task. Tools exist (such as RANDOOP [23], Pex [25], AutoTest [4] and Korat [7]) but they are typically *dynamic*, meaning that they require numerous executions of the code. The Seeding Contradiction (SC) method and the supporting tools presented in this article typically achieve 100% coverage (excluding unreachable code, which they may help detect) and involve no execution of the code, ensuring very fast results.

The principal insight of Seeding Contradiction is to exploit the power of modern program provers, which attempt to generate a counterexample of program correctness. In normal program proving, we hope that the prover will *not* find such a counterexample: a proof follows from the demonstrated *inability* to *disprove* the program's correctness. Switching the focus from proofs to tests, we may look at counterexamples in a different way: as test cases. We may call this

S. Bonfanti et al. (Eds.): ICTSS 2023, LNCS 14131, pp. 52–70, 2023.
https://doi.org/10.1007/978-3-031-43240-8_4

approach *Failed Proofs to Failing Tests* or FP-FT. Previous research (including by some of the present authors) has exploited FP-FT in various ways [13,14,20]. Seeding Contradiction extends FP-FT to a new goal: generating a full-coverage test suite, by applying FP-FT to *seeded* versions of the program in which a branch has on purpose been made incorrect. For every such variant, the prover generates a counterexample exercising the corresponding branch. Combining the result for all branches yields a high-coverage test suite. In fact coverage is normally 100%, with the following provisions:

- Some branches may be unreachable. Then by definition no test could cover them; the tool may help identify such cases. (Terminology: we will use the term **exhaustive coverage** to mean 100% coverage of reachable branches.)
- Limitations of the prover may prevent reaching 100%. In our examples so far such cases do not arise.

The method involves no execution of the code and on examples tried so far produces a test suite much faster than dynamic techniques (Sect. 5).

The current setup involves the AutoProof [3,26] verification framework for contract-equipped Eiffel [19] code, relying internally on the Boogie proof system [5,18] and the Z3 SMT solver [11]. It is generalizable to other approaches.

The discussion is organized as follows. Section 2 presents the approach by considering a small example. Section 3 examines the theoretical correctness of that approach. Section 4 describes the extent to which we have applied it so far, and Sect. 5 assesses the results. Section 6 discusses limitations of the current state of the work and threats to validity of the evaluation results. Section 7 reviews related work and Sect. 8 presents conclusions and future work.

2 The Method

A simple code example will illustrate the essential idea behind Seeded Composition.

2.1 Falsifying a Code Block

Consider a small routine consisting of a single conditional instruction:

```
simple (a: INTEGER)
    do
        if a > 0 then x := 1 else x := 2 end
    end
```

where x is an integer attribute of the enclosing class. In a Design-by-Contract approach intended to achieve correctness by construction, the routine might include the following postcondition part (with $\implies$ denoting implication):

```
ensure
    a > 0 ⟹ x = 1
    a ≤ 0 ⟹ x = 2
```

With or without the postcondition, how can we obtain a regression test suite that will exercise both branches?

Various techniques exist, discussed in Sect. 7 and generally requiring execution of the code. The Seeding Contradiction technique is, as noted, static (it does not involve executing the code); it assumes that we have a toolset for proving program correctness. Specifically, we rely on the AutoProof environment [3, 26], with a tool stack presented in Fig. 1, in which the Boogie prover is itself based on an SMT solver, currently Z3. A characteristic of this style of proof is that it relies on a *disproof* of the *opposite* property: the SMT solver tries to construct at least one counterexample, violating the desired result. If it cannot find one, the proof is successful.

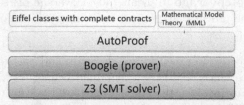

Fig. 1. AutoProof tool stack

In this work, as in previous articles using the general FP-FT approach [13, 14], we are interested in a proof that actually fails: then the counterexample can be useful on its own, yielding a directly usable test.

In contrast with the earlier FP-FT work, the proof that will fail is not a proof of the actual program but of a modified version, into which we have inserted ("seeded") incorrect instructions. In the example, we change the first branch, so that the routine now reads

```
simple (a: INTEGER)
    do
        if a > 0 then
            check False end -- This is the added instruction
            x := 1 -- The rest is unchanged.
        else
            x := 2
        end
    end
```

A "check C end" instruction (assert C in some other notations [17]) states that the programmer expects condition C to hold at the corresponding program point. Specifically, its semantics is the following, from both a dynamic perspective (what happens if it gets executed) and a static, proof-oriented perspective:

- From a dynamic viewpoint, executing the instruction means: if condition C has value True at that point, the check instruction has no effect other than evaluating C; if C evaluates to False and the programmer has enabled run-time assertion monitoring, as possible in EiffelStudio, execution produces a violated-assertion exception, usually implying that it terminates abnormally.

- In the present discussion's static approach, the goal is to prove the program correct. The semantics of the `check` instruction is that it is correct if and only if the condition C alway has value `True` at the given program point. If the prover cannot establish that property, the proof fails.

In a general FP-FT approach, the key property is that in the static view, if the proof fails, an SMT-based prover will generate a **counterexample**. In the Seeding Contradiction approach, C is `False`: the proof *always* fails and we get a counterexample exercising the corresponding branch—exactly what we need if, as part of a regression test suite, we want a test exercising the given branch.

For the `simple` code seeded with a `check False end`, such a counterexample will, by construction, lead to execution of the first branch (a > 0) of the conditional. If we have an efficient mechanism to turn counterexamples into tests, as described in earlier work [13,14], we can get, out of this counterexample, a test of the original program which exercises the first branch of the conditional.

Such a generated test enjoys several interesting properties:

- It can be produced even in the absence of a formal specification (contract elements such as the postcondition above).
- Unless the enclosing code (here the routine `simple`) is unreachable, the test can be produced whether the program is correct or incorrect.
- If the program is correct, the test will pass and is useful as a regression test (which may fail in a later revision of the program that introduces a bug).
- Generating it does not require any execution.
- That generation process is fast in practice (Sect. 5).

The next sections will show how to generalize the just outlined idea to produce such tests not only for one branch as here but for *all* branches of the program, as needed to obtain an exhaustive-coverage regression test suite.

2.2 Block Variables

To generalize the approach, the following terminology is useful. So far it has been convenient to talk informally of "branches", but the more precise concept is **basic block**, defined in the testing and compilation literature as a sequence of instructions not containing conditionals or loops. (This definition is for a structured program with no branching instructions. In a more general approach, a basic block is any process node—as opposed to decision nodes—in the program's flowchart.) "Block" as used below is an abbreviation for "basic block".

The method illustrated on the `simple` example generates a test guaranteed to exercise a specific block of a correct program: seed the program by adding to the chosen block one `check False end` instruction. Then, as seen in the example, we run the prover and apply the FP-FT scheme: since the program is now incorrect, the proof fails and the prover generates a counterexample, which we turn into a runnable test guaranteed to exercise the given block in the original program.

To generalize this approach so that it will generate a test suite exercising all blocks, a straightforward idea is "*Multiple Seeded Programs*" (MSP): generate such a seeded program for each of its blocks in turn; then run the prover on every such program, in each case producing a counterexample and generating a test from it. Subject to conditions in Sect. 3 below, the MSP approach is correct, in the sense that together the generated tests exercise all reachable blocks. It is, however, impractical: for a single original program, we would need to generate a possibly very large number of seeded programs, and run every one of them through the prover.

To obtain a realistic process, we can instead generate a single seeded program, designed to produce the same counterexamples as would all the MSP-generated programs taken together. A helpful property of a good counterexample-based prover is that it can deal with a program containing several faults and generate a set of counterexamples, each addressing one of the faults. In the example above, we can submit to the prover a single seeded program of the form

```
simple (a: INTEGER)
    do
        if a > 0 then
            check False end
            x := 1 -- Instruction 1
        else
            check False end
            x := 2 -- Instruction 2
        end
    end
```

which will produce two counterexamples, one for each branch. We call this approach "RSSP" (Repeatedly Seeded Single Program). With AutoProof, the FP-FT tools generate tests with $a = 1$ and $a = 0$. (More precisely, the prover initially generates larger and less intuitive values, but a minimization technique described in earlier work [14] produces 1 and 0.)

This approach does not suffice for more complex examples. Assume that after the conditional instruction the routine simple includes another conditional:

```
-- This code comes after the above conditional (Instructions 1-2)
if a^2 > a then
    x := 3 -- Instruction 3
else
    x := 4 -- Instruction 4
end
```

With the program seeded as above, even if we insert a check False end into each of the two new blocks (before Instructions 3 and 4), we will get tests covering only two cases (1-4, 2-4), not four (1-3, 1-4, 2-3, 2-4) as needed. These two tests, $a = 1$ and $a = 0$, fail to cover Instruction 3. The reason is that the prover does not generate specific tests for the branches of the second conditional (3–4) since it correctly determines that they are unreachable as both branches of the first conditional (1–2) now include a check False end. They were, however, both reachable in the original! The test suite fails to achieve exhaustive coverage.

The solution to this "*Seeded Unreachability*" issue is to make the `check` them-selves conditional. In the seeded program, for every routine under processing, such as `simple`, we may number every basic block, from 1 to some N, and add to the routine an argument bn (for "block number") with an associated precondition

```
require
    bn ≥ 0 -- See below why 0 and not 1.
    bn ≤ N
```

To avoid changing the routine's interface (as the addition of an argument implies), we will instead make bn a local variable and add an initial instruction that assigns to bn, non-deterministically, a value between 0 and N. Either way, we now use, as seeded instructions, no longer just `check False end` but

```
if bn = i then check False end end
```

where i is the number assigned to the block. In the example, the fully seeded rou-tine body for the extended version of `simple` with two conditionals, is (choosing the option of making `bn` a local variable rather than an argument):

```
bn := "Value chosen non−deterministically between 0 and N"
if a > 0 then
        if bn = 1 then check False end end
        x := 1 -- Instruction 1
else
        if bn = 2 then check False end end
        x := 2 -- Instruction 2
end

if a² > a then
        if bn = 3 then check False end end
        x := 3 -- Instruction 3
else
        if bn = 4 then check False end end
        x := 4 -- Instruction 4
end
```

As in the previous attempt, there are four incorrect `check False` instruc-tions, but all are now reachable for bn values ranging from 1 to 4. The prover generates counterexamples exercising all the paths of the original program (with appropriately generated values for its original variables). In this case there is only one relevant variable, a; AutoProof's prover generates, for the pair $[bn, a]$, the test values $[1, 1]$, $[2, 0]$, $[3, -1]$, $[4, 0]$. These four tests provide 100% branch coverage for the program and can serve as a regression test suite. We call this technique **Conditional Seeding**; it addresses the Seeded Unreachability issue.

As noted above, we accept for bn not only values between 1 and N (the num-ber of basic blocks) but also 0. This convention has no bearing on test generation and coverage but ensures that the behavior of the original program remains pos-sible in the seeded version: for $bn = 0$, none of the seeded `check False` will execute, so the program behaves exactly as the original. If the original was cor-rect, the prover will not generate any counterexample for that value.

3   Correctness

The goal of a test-suite-generation strategy is to produce high-coverage test suites. The Seeding Contradiction strategy is more ambitious: we consider it correct if it achieves **exhaustive coverage** (as defined in Sect. 1: full coverage of reachable branches). More precisely, we will now prove that SC is "coverage-complete" if the prover is "reachability-sound", "correctness-sound" and "counterexample-complete". Section 3.1 defines these concepts and Sect. 3.2 has the proof.

3.1   Definitions and Assumptions

Establishing the correctness of SC requires precise conventions and terminology.

A general assumption is the availability of an "FP-FT" mechanism which, as described in previous articles [13], can produce directly executable tests (expressed in the target programming language, in our case Eiffel) from counterexamples produced by the SMT-based prover. As a consequence, the rest of this discussion does not distinguish between the notions of counterexample and test.[1]

The definition of basic block, or just **block** for short, appeared earlier (Sect. 2.2).

For simplicity, we assume that the programs are **structured**, meaning that they use sequences, loops and conditionals as their only control structures. Also, we consider that a conditional always includes exactly one "else" part (possibly empty), and that a loop has two blocks, the loop body and an empty block (corresponding to the case of zero iterations). Further, expressions, particularly conditional expressions used in conditional instructions, are side-effect-free. Thanks to these conventions, instruction coverage (also known as statement coverage) and branch coverage are the same concept, called just "coverage" from now on.

A (possibly empty) block of a program is **reachable** if at least one set of input values will cause it to be executed, and otherwise (if, regardless of the input, it cannot be executed) *unreachable*. Reachability is an undecidable property for any realistic programming language, but that need not bother us since this work relies on a prover of which we will only require that it be **reachability-sound**: if a block is reachable, the prover will indeed characterize it as reachable. (The prover might, the other way, wrongly characterize a block as reachable when in fact it is not: with `if cos`^{2} `(x) + sin`^{2} `(x) = 100 then y := 0 else y := 1 end`, the prover might consider $y = 0$ as a possible outcome if it does not have enough built-in knowledge about trigonometric functions. That too-conservative determination does not endanger the SC strategy.)

A program may contain instructions of the form `check C end`, with no effect on execution (as previewed in Sect. 2). Such an instruction is **correct** if and only if the condition C will hold on every execution of the instruction. This property is again undecidable, and again we only need the prover to be **correctness-sound**: if it tells us that an instruction is correct, it is. (We hope the other way

---

[1] Counterexamples that the prover generates at first can use arbitrary values, sometimes too large to be meaningful to programmers; as noted in Sect. 2.2, a minimization strategy is available to produce more intuitive values. The SC technique and its analysis are independent of such choices of counterexamples.

around too, but do not require it.) For the SC strategy we are interested in the trivial case for which C is `False`.

Also for simplicity, we assume that all correctness properties are expressed in the form of `check` instructions; in particular, we replace any contract elements (preconditions, postconditions, loop invariants and variants, class invariants) by such instructions added at the appropriate places in the program text.

With this convention, a **block** is correct if all its `check` instructions are, and a **program** is correct if all its blocks are. For a normally written program, this definition means that the program is correct in the usual sense; in particular, if it has any contracts, it satisfies them, for example by having every routine ensure its postcondition. The SC strategy, by adding `check False end` to individual blocks, makes these blocks—and hence the program as a whole—incorrect.

A **test suite** is a collection of test cases for a program.

A test suite achieves **exhaustive coverage** if for every reachable block in the program at least one of its test cases causes that block to be executed. (Note the importance of having a reachability-sound prover: if it could wrongly mark some reachable blocks as unreachable, it could wrongly report exhaustive coverage, which is not acceptable. On the other hand, if it is reachability-sound, it may pessimistically report less-than-exhaustive coverage for a test suite whose coverage is in fact exhaustive, a disappointing but not lethal result. This case does not occur in our examples thanks to the high quality of the prover.)

A test-suite-generation method (such as Seeding Contradiction) is **coverage-complete** if the generated test suite achieves exhaustive coverage for any correct program. In other words, for each reachable basic block of a correct program, at least one test in the suite will execute the block.

Finally, consider a prover that can generate counterexamples for programs it cannot prove correct. The prover is **counterexample-complete** if it generates a counterexample for every block that it determines to be reachable and incorrect.

With these conventions, the correctness of the Seeding Contradiction method is the property (proven next) that

> *If the prover is reachability-sound, correctness-sound and counterexample-complete, SC is coverage-complete.*

3.2 Proof of Correctness

To establish that correctness holds, on the basis of the preceding definitions, we first establish the following two lemmas:

1 Any test case of a seeded program (the program modified by addition of `check` instructions as described above) yields, by omitting the `bn` variable, a test case of the original program, exercising the same basic block.
2 Any reachable block of the original program is reachable in the seeded one.

The proof of both lemmas follows from the observation that the seeded program has the same variables as the original except for the addition of the `bn` variable, which only appears in the conditional `check` instructions and hence does not affect the behavior of the program other than by possibly causing execution of one of these instructions in the corresponding block. If bn has value i in such an execution, the execution of all blocks other than the block numbered i (if any—remember that we accept the value 0 for bn), in particular the execution of any block in an execution path *preceding* the possible execution of block i, proceeds exactly as in the original unseeded program. As a result:

- Any test executing block number i in the seeded program for any i has, for all other variables (those of the original program), values that cause execution of block i in the original program too, yielding Lemma 1.
- Consider a reachable block, numbered i, of the original program. Since it is reachable, there exists a variable assignment, for the variables of the original program, that causes its execution. That variable assignment complemented by bn = i causes execution of block i in the seeded program, which is therefore reachable, yielding Lemma 2.

To prove that SC satisfies the definition of correctness (given at the end of Sect. 3.1):

- Assume that the original program is correct; then the only incorrect instructions in the seeded program are the added conditional check instructions (the if C then check False end at the beginning of every block).
- Consider an arbitrary reachable basic block B, of the original program. Because of Lemma 2, it is also reachable in the seeded program.
- If the prover is reachability-sound, it indeed determines that block B is (in the seeded program) reachable.
- If the prover is also correctness-sound, it determines that B's seeded check instruction is incorrect, and hence (by definition) that B itself is incorrect.
- Then if it is counter-example-complete it will generate a counterexample that executes B in the seeded program.
- By Lemma 1, that counterexample yields a test that executes block B in the original program.
- As a consequence, by the definition of correctness above, the Seeding Contradiction strategy is correct.

3.3   Correctness in Practice

To determine that SC as implemented is correct, we depend on properties of the prover: the definition assumes that the prover is reachability-sound, correctness-sound and counterexample-complete.

To our knowledge, no formal specification exists for the relevant tools in our actual tool stack (Fig. 1), particularly Z3 and Boogie. In their actual behavior as observed pragmatically, however, the tools satisfy the required properties.

4   Implementation

We have implemented Seeding Contradiction strategy in the form of a new option of the AutoProof program-proving framework, called "Full-coverage Test Generation" (FTG)[2]. The implementation relies on the FP-FT [13,14] feature of Auto-Proof, which enables automatic generation of failed tests from failed proofs. The objective is to add the incorrect **check** instructions at the appropriate program locations so that the verification of the seeded program results in proof failures, yielding an exhaustive-coverage test suite as described above.

Like the rest of AutoProof, seeding is modular: routine by routine. It is applied at the Boogie level, so that the Eiffel program remains untouched. The Boogie equivalent of the **check** instruction is written **assert**. Depending on the structure of the code for a routine **r**, five cases arise, reviewed now.

A - Plain Block. If the body of **r** includes no conditional and hence has only one path, the SC strategy inserts a single **assert false** at the beginning of the body. Verification of **r** results in failure of the assertion; by applying FP-FT, we obtain a valid test case of **r** (whose test input satisfies the precondition).

B - Implicit Else Branch. If **r** contains a conditional whose **else** branch is implicit, SC makes it explicit and produces a test case covering the branch. Figure 2 shows an example: SC inserts two **assert** clauses, one in the **then** branch and the other in the **else** branch that it creates. Running the proof produces two counterexamples for the two injected **assert** clauses, hence two tests.

```
r                          implementation r () {
   do                          𝒯(B0)
      B0                       if (c){
      if c then                   assert false;  𝒯(B1) }
         B1                    else{
      end                         assert false; }
      B2                       𝒯(B2)
   end                                                  }
```

Fig. 2. Instrumentation for **r** with implicit **else** branch. Left: original Eiffel code of **r**. Right, seeded Boogie code. B_i ($i \in \{0, 1, 2\}$) is a basic block in Eiffel, **c** a branch predicate evaluating to **true** or **false**, $\mathcal{T}(B_i)$ the Boogie translation of B_i.

C - Cascading Branches. If **r** has a series of branches placed sequentially, as in Fig. 3, the SC algorithm inserts an·**assert false** clause in each branch. The resulting tests cover all branches.

D - Nested Branches. When conditionals are nested, SC only generates tests targeting the *leaf* branches—those with no embedded conditionals. This approach is sound since any program execution that exercises a leaf branch must also go through all the branches leading to it. Figure 4 has three leaf branches

---

[2] AutoProof including the FTG option is available for download at github.com/huangl223/ES-AP-Installation.

```
r                    implementation r (){
  do                    T(B0)
    B0                  if (c1){
    if c1 then             assert false;  T(B1) }
      B1                else{
    elseif c2 then        if (c2){ assert false;  T(B2) }
      B2                  else{ assert false;  T(B3) } }
    else  B3  end        T(B4)
    B4                                              }
  end
```

Fig. 3. Instrumentation for cascading branches: three `assert false` clauses are inserted for the three branches in `r`; note that the `elseif` instruction in Eiffel, together with the last `else` instruction, is mapped to a nested `if−else` instruction in Boogie.

for blocks B2, B3 and B5. Any execution going through B2 and B3 will exercise B1; SC only inserts `assert` instructions for leaves (none for B1).

```
r                    implementation r (){
  do                    T(B0)
    B0                  if (c1){
    if c1 then             T(B1)
      B1                   if (c2){
      if c2 then             assert false;  T(B2) }
        B2                 else{ assert false;  T(B3) }
      else  B3  end        T(B4) }
      B4                else{ assert false;  T(B5) }
    else  B5  end       T(B6)                        }
    B6
  end
```

Fig. 4. Instrumentation for nested branches

E - Sequential Decisions. If `r` has multiple successive decision instructions, as in Fig. 5, SC inserts the conditional `assert false` instructions as explained in Sect. 2.2. It declares a variable `bn` for the block number and adds "`if (bn == i)` `assert false;`". Since the value of `bn` is between 0 and N (number of target blocks), it adds a clause "`requires bn≥0 && bn≤N`" to the precondition of `r`.

5   Evaluation and Comparison with Dynamic Techniques

We performed a performance evaluation of Seeding Contradiction as implemented in AutoProof per the preceding section, comparing it to two existing test generation tools: IntelliTest [25] (previously known as Pex, a symbolic execution test-generation tool for .NET) and AutoTest [4], a test generation tool for Eiffel using Adaptive Random Testing, specifically ARTOO [10]).

```
r                              implementation r (){
  do                             int bn;
    B0                           T(B0)
    if c1 then                   if (c1){
      B1                           if (bn == 1) assert false;  T(B1) }
    else  B2   end               else{ if (bn == 2) assert false;  T(B2) }
    B3                           T(B3)
    if c2 then                   if (c2){
      B4                           if (bn == 3) assert false; T(B4) }
    else  B5   end               else{ if (bn == 4) assert false; T(B5) }
    B6                           T(B6)
  end                          }
```

Fig. 5. Instrumentation for sequential conditionals

5.1   Comparison Criteria and Overview of the Results

The experiment applies all three tools to generate tests for 20 programs adapted from examples in the AutoProof tutorial[3] and benchmarks of previous software verification competitions [6,15,27]. Table 1 lists their characteristics, including implementation size (number of Lines Of Code) and number of branches.

Table 1. Examples

	Account	Clock	Heater	Lamp	Max	Linear Search	Insertion Sort	Gnome Sort	Square root	Sum and max	Arithmetic
LOC	214	153	102	95	49	64	122	62	56	56	204
Branches	14	10	8	8	3	5	5	5	5	4	14

	Binary search	Recursive binary search	Dutch flag	Two way max	Two way sort	Quick sort	Selection Sort	Bubble Sort	Optimized gnome sort	Total
	74	89	188	49	85	232	167	165	183	**2409**
	5	7	11	4	6	9	5	5	8	**141**

The comparison addresses three metrics: coverage; time needed to generate the tests; size of the test suite. All code and results are available at https://github.com/huangl223/ICTSS2023.

The examples are originally in Eiffel; we translated them manually into C# for IntelliTest. The experiment includes a test generation session for every example in every tool. For AutoTest, whose algorithms keeps generating tests until a preset time limit, it uses 10 min (600 s) as that limit; there is no time limit for the other two approaches.

All sessions took place on a machine with a 2.1 GHz Intel 12-Core processor and 32 GB of memory, running Windows 11 and Microsoft .NET 7.0.203. Versions used are: EiffelStudio 22.05 (used through AutoProof and AutoTest); Boogie 2.11.10; Z3 solver 4.8.14; Visual Studio 2022 (integrated with IntelliTest).

Table 2 shows an overview of the results. SC and IntelliTest handle the examples well, with coverage close to 100%; SC reaches exhaustive coverage (100% coverage of reachable branches) for all 20 examples and IntelliTest for 19 examples. AutoTest, due to its random core, achieves the lowest coverage, reaching exhaustive coverage for only 7 examples.

---

[3] http://autoproof.sit.org/autoproof/tutorial.

Table 2. Overall result

Metrics	SC	IntelliTest	AutoTest
Avg. branch coverage	99.37%	97.15%	81.2%
Number of examples reaching exhaustive coverage	20	19	7
Avg. time for reaching exhaustive coverage (s)	0.487	27	259
Avg. number of generated tests for reaching exhaustive coverage	6.26	10.47	623.28

To reach exhaustive coverage, SC performs significantly faster than the other two: it needs less than 0.5 s on average—about 50 times less than IntelliTest and 500 times than AutoTest. SC also generates the smallest test suite; the average size of the exhaustive-coverage test suite from IntelliTest is slightly larger than SC, and both are much smaller than AutoTest. The importance of minimizing the size of test suites has become a crucial concern [22].

5.2   Detailed Results

Table 3 shows coverage results. For each example, we executed the generated test suite and calculated coverage as the ratio of *number of exercised branches* over *number of branches*. SC always reaches exhaustive coverage (the maximum possible for Lamp is 87.5% as it contains an unreachable branch). IntelliTest reaches exhaustive coverage for most examples but misses it for Account and Lamp. AutoTest's coverage varies from 50% to 100%. Occasionally, it performs better than IntelliTest, reaching the maximum 87.5% for Lamp against IntelliTest's 50%.

Table 3. Result: branch coverage

	Account	Clock	Heater	Lamp	Max	Linear Search	Insertion Sort	Gnome Sort	Square root	Sum and max
SC	100%	100%	100%	87.5%	100%	100%	100%	100%	100%	100%
IntelliTest	92.85%	100 %	100%	50%	100%	100%	100%	100%	100%	100%
AutoTest	78.6%	70%	62.5%	87.5%	66.7%	100%	80%	60%	100%	100%

Arithmetic	Binary search	Recursive binary search	Dutch flag	Two way max	Two way sort	Quick sort	Selection Sort	Bubble Sort	Optimized gnome sort
100%	100%	100%	100%	100%	100%	100%	100%	100%	100%
100%	100%	100%	100%	100%	100%	100%	100%	100%	100%
100%	100%	85.7 %	72.7 %	75%	83.3%	100%	80%	80%	50%

Table 4 gives the time needed to produce the test suite in the various approaches, using the following conventions:

- For SC, time for test generation includes two parts: proof time (for Auto-Proof) and time for extracting tests from failed proofs (time for FP-FT).
- For AutoTest, the time is always the 10-minute timeout, chosen from experience: within that time, test generation of examples usually reaches a plateau.

- IntelliTest does not directly provide time information. We measure duration manually by recording the timestamps of session start and termination.

In Table 4 results, SC is the fastest of the three, with all its test generation runs taking less than 1 s. For IntelliTest, test generation takes less than 40 s for most examples, but three of them out of 20 require more than one minute. For AutoTest, test generation time varies from 1.71 s for `Square root` to more than 20 min for `Sum and max`.

Table 4. Result: time (in seconds) to reach maximum coverage

	Account	Clock	Heater	Lamp	Max	Linear Search	Insertion Sort	Gnome Sort	Square root	Sum and max
SC	0.56	0.44	0.85	0.39	0.37	0.36	0.42	0.52	0.26	0.37
IntelliTest	9.58	7.44	8.06	–	8.19	9.63	11.77	10.89	12.86	10.99
AutoTest	–	–	–	233.03	–	21.95	–	–	1.71	1322.61

Arithmetic	Binary search	Recursive binary search	Dutch flag	Two way max	Two way sort	Quick sort	Selection Sort	Bubble Sort	Optimized gnome sort
0.415	0.44	0.48	0.43	0.52	0.39	0.90	0.50	0.59	0.54
32.98	99.29	13.07	31.36	9.59	80.91	111.57	17.81	14.74	12.32
14.49	150.86	–	330.89	–	–	78.37	–	–	–

Another important criterion, when a tool covers all the branches of a program, is how many redundant tests it produces. Table 5 presents the sizes of the generated test suites of the three tools when reaching exhaustive coverage. From a software engineering viewpoint, particularly for the long-term health of a project, a smaller size achieving the same coverage is better, since it results in a more manageable test suite giving the project the same benefits as a larger one.

Among the three tools, SC generates the fewest tests. In most cases, the number of tests is the same as the number of blocks: as each generated test results from a proof failure of an incorrect instruction, seeded at one program location, each test covers just the corresponding block and introduces no redundancy. If nested branches are present, the size of the test suite can actually be less than the number of branches: SC only generates tests targeting the innermost branches (the leaf nodes of the control structure), as explained in Sect. 4; each test going through these branches automatically covers all its enclosing branches. Intellitest also generates small test suites, but is slower. The reason is Intellitest's use of concolic testing [24], which tests all feasible execution paths: since a branch can occur in several paths, a test will often identify a branch that was already covered by a different path. AutoTest, for its part, produces much larger test suites: as an Adaptive Random Testing tool, it often generates multiple test cases covering the same branches.

Tables 2, 3, 4 and 5 provide evidence of the benefits of the approach (subject to the limitations examined in the next section): SC is fast and efficient; it uses less than 1 s to produce an exhaustive-coverage test suite with the fewest number of test cases. Other observations:

Table 5. Result: number of generated tests to reach exhaustive coverage

	Account	Clock	Heater	Lamp	Max	Linear Search	Insertion Sort	Gnome Sort	Square root	Sum and max
SC	13	10	8	7	3	3	3	3	4	3
IntelliTest	13	13	8	–	4	7	5	7	5	5
AutoTest	–	–	–	656	–	127	–	–	18	1784
Arithmetic	Binary search	Recursive binary search	Dutch flag	Two way max	Two way sort	Quick sort	Selection Sort	Bubble Sort	Optimized gnome sort
14	4	7	9	2	5	9	5	4	7
25	6	15	27	4	9	18	12	8	8
531	905	–	–	–	–	342	–	–	–

- AutoTest does not guarantee that the test inputs satisfy the routine's precondition, while SC and IntelliTest always generate precondition-satisfying test inputs. The reason is that SC and IntelliTest rely on the results of constraint solving, where the routine's precondition is encoded as an assumption and will always be satisfied.
- The SC approach is has a prerequisite: the program under test has to be proved correct (the proof of the original program has no failure), while AutoTest and IntelliTest have no such constraint.
- As to the values of the generated test inputs, IntelliTest and AutoTest always apply small values that are easy to understand. SC initially produces test inputs that may contain large values; its "minimization" mechanism [14] corrects the problem.

6   Limitations and Threats to Validity

The setup of the SC approach assumes a Hoare-style verification framework (of which Boogie is but one example), and the availability of a test generation mechanism that supports generating test cases from proof failures. We have not studied the possible application of the ideas to different verification frameworks, based for example on abstract interpretation or model checking.

The current version of SC is subject to the following limitations:

- SC is not able to handle programs with non-linear computations (such as derivation and exponentiation); this restriction comes from the underlying SMT solver.
- SC does not support the more advanced parts of the Eiffel system, in particular generic classes. Data structures are limited to arrays and sequences.

These limitations will need to be removed for SC to be applicable to industrial-grade programs.

The following considerations may influence the generalization of the results achieved so far:

- The number of repeated experiments increased the potential threats to internal validity. We hope that further experiments with large number of iterations will provide more conclusive evidence.
- Although a few of the examples classes that we processed so far are complex and sophisticated, most are of a small size and not necessarily representative of industrial-grade object-oriented programs. In the future, we intend to use the EiffelBase library[4], which has yielded extensive, representative results in the evaluation of AutoProof and AutoTest, and exhibits considerable variety and complexity in terms of size (according to various metrics), richness of program semantics, and sophistication of algorithms and software architecture.

7 Related Work

Previous work has taken advantage of counterexamples generated by failing proofs, but for other purposes, in particular automatic program repair [21] and generation of failing tests [13,20]. These techniques work on the original program and not, as here, on a transformed program in which *incorrect* instructions have been inserted with the express purpose of making the proof fail.

The earliest work we know to have applied this idea [1,2] generates tests for low-level C programs using Bounded Model Checking (BMC) [16], producing test suites with exhaustive branch coverage. A more recent variant, for Java bytecode, is JBMC [8]. In contrast with SC, each verification run only activates one assertion at a time, producing one counterexample. This approach is conceptually similar, in the terminology of the present work (Sect. 2.2), to the "MSP" (Multiple Seeded Programs) technique, although the C version [1] uses compile-time macros, one for each block, to avoid the actual generation of multiple programs. In contrast, the present work uses RSSP (Repeatedly Seeded Single Program), relying on a single *run-time* variable representing the block number. BMC-based approaches rely on the correctness of the *bound* of the execution trace: if the bound is not set correctly, some branches might not be covered, requiring more verification runs to obtain a better bound.

Other techniques that apply constraint solving for generating inputs includes test generations based on symbolic execution, such as Pex/IntelliTest [25], KLEE [9], PathCrawler [28]. None of the strategies proposed guarantees exhaustive branch coverage; they can achieve it when a systematic test generation strategy, rather than one based on heuristics or randomization, is applied.

A very recent development (published just as the present work was being submitted) is DTest, a toolkit [12] for generating unit tests for Dafny programs, applying ideas similar to those of SC. As the generated Dafny tests are not directly executable, test generation requires transformation of Dafny programs and tests into a mainstream language. In contrast, the present approach works directly on Eiffel programs. The DTest coverage results cited in the referenced

---

[4] EiffelBase Data Structures: https://www.eiffel.org/doc/solutions/EiffelBase_Data_Structures_Overview.

article are 100% on only 2 of its examples, and go down to as low as 58% on the others. One should not draw definite conclusions from these figures, since the examples are different, their program sizes too (more precisely, most of the examples are of comparable sizes, but the cited work has three between 1100 and 1900 LOCs, which we have not handled yet), and the article does not mention any presence of unreachable code (which makes it impossible to distinguish between full coverage and exhaustive coverage). It should be noted, however, that the article also makes no mention of the "Seeded Unreachability" issue discussed in Sect. 2.2; in fact, it states that "*DTest enters a loop where it systematically injects trivially failing trap assertions (meaning assert false)*", a technique which generally leads, for any program with a non-trivial control structure, to Seeded Unreachability and hence to decreased coverage. That omission may be the reason for the relatively low coverage results reported in the article. The Conditional Seeding technique of SC, introduced by the present work, addresses Seeded Unreachability and has made it possible to reach exhaustive coverage in all examples so far. In addition, to obtain small test suites, DTest seems to require a separate minimization strategy, which takes from 8 to 1860 s on the cited examples, far beyond the times of running SC. In discussing minimization, the authors appear to come close to recognizing the Seeded Unreachability issue, without using the Conditional Seeding technique, when they write that "*we determine the feasibility of a path via a query to the SMT solver, in which a trap assertion is added that fails only if all the blocks along the path are visited*", a technique that is "*exponential in the number of SMT queries (running on all benchmarks* [cited in the article] *would take weeks)*". SC does not appear to need any such technique.

8   Conclusions and Future Work

The approach presented here, Seeding Contradiction (SC), automatically generates test suites that achieve exhaustive branch coverage very fast. The presentation of the approach comes with a proof of correctness, defined as the guarantee that the generated test suite achieves exhaustive coverage (full coverage of reachable branches). While technical limitations remain, the evaluation so far demonstrates the effectiveness and efficiency of the SC approach through the comparison with two existing test generators IntelliTest and AutoTest, in terms of achieved coverage, generation time, and size of the test suite.

Ongoing work includes handling larger examples, processing entire classes instead of single routines, providing a mechanism to generate tests covering branches that a given test suite fails to cover, and taking advantage of the SC strategy to identify dead code.

Acknowledgement. We are particularly grateful, for their extensive and patient help, to Yi Wei (AutoTest) and Jocelyn Fiat (EiffelStudio and AutoProof). The paper benefitted from perceptive comments by the anonymous referees on the original version.

References

1. Angeletti, D., Giunchiglia, E., Narizzano, M., Palma, G., Puddu, A., Sabina, S.: Improving the automatic test generation process for coverage analysis using CBMC. In: International RCRA Workshop (2009)
2. Angeletti, D., Giunchiglia, E., Narizzano, M., Puddu, A., Sabina, S.: Automatic test generation for coverage analysis using CBMC. In: Moreno-Díaz, R., Pichler, F., Quesada-Arencibia, A. (eds.) EUROCAST 2009. LNCS, vol. 5717, pp. 287–294. Springer, Heidelberg (2009). https://doi.org/10.1007/978-3-642-04772-5_38
3. AutoProof. https://autoproof.sit.org/
4. AutoTest. https://www.eiffel.org/doc/eiffelstudio/Using_AutoTest
5. Barnett, M., Chang, B.-Y.E., DeLine, R., Jacobs, B., Leino, K.R.M.: Boogie: a modular reusable verifier for object-oriented programs. In: de Boer, F.S., Bonsangue, M.M., Graf, S., de Roever, W.-P. (eds.) FMCO 2005. LNCS, vol. 4111, pp. 364–387. Springer, Heidelberg (2006). https://doi.org/10.1007/11804192_17
6. Bormer, T., et al.: The COST IC0701 verification competition 2011. In: Beckert, B., Damiani, F., Gurov, D. (eds.) FoVeOOS 2011. LNCS, vol. 7421, pp. 3–21. Springer, Heidelberg (2012). https://doi.org/10.1007/978-3-642-31762-0_2
7. Boyapati, C., Khurshid, S., Marinov, D.: Korat: automated testing based on java predicates. ACM SIGSOFT Softw. Eng. Notes **27**(4), 123–133 (2002)
8. Brenguier, R., Cordeiro, L., Kroening, D., Schrammel, P.: JBMC: A Bounded Model Checking Tool for Java Bytecode. arXiv:2302.02381 (2023)
9. Cadar, C., Dunbar, D., Engler, D.R., et al.: KLEE: unassisted and automatic generation of high-coverage tests for complex systems programs. In: USENIX Symposium on Operating Systems Design and Implementation (OSDI), vol. 8, pp. 209–224 (2008)
10. Ciupa, I., Leitner, A., Oriol, M., Meyer, B.: ARTOO: adaptive random testing for object-oriented software. In: International Conference on Software Engineering (ICSE), pp. 71–80 (2008)
11. de Moura, L., Bjørner, N.: Z3: an efficient SMT solver. In: Ramakrishnan, C.R., Rehof, J. (eds.) TACAS 2008. LNCS, vol. 4963, pp. 337–340. Springer, Heidelberg (2008). https://doi.org/10.1007/978-3-540-78800-3_24
12. Fedchin, A., et al.: A Toolkit for Automated Testing of Dafny (2023)
13. Huang, L., Meyer, B.: A Failed Proof Can Yield a Useful Test. arXiv:2208.09873 (2022)
14. Huang, L., Meyer, B., Oriol, M.: Improving counterexample quality from failed program verification. In: International Symposium on Software Reliability Engineering Workshops (ISSREW), pp. 268–273. IEEE (2022)
15. Klebanov, V., et al.: The 1st verified software competition: experience report. In: Butler, M., Schulte, W. (eds.) FM 2011. LNCS, vol. 6664, pp. 154–168. Springer, Heidelberg (2011). https://doi.org/10.1007/978-3-642-21437-0_14
16. Kroening, D., Tautschnig, M.: CBMC – C bounded model checker. In: Ábrahám, E., Havelund, K. (eds.) TACAS 2014. LNCS, vol. 8413, pp. 389–391. Springer, Heidelberg (2014). https://doi.org/10.1007/978-3-642-54862-8_26
17. Leino, K.R.M.: Program Proofs. MIT Press, Cambridge (2023)
18. Leino, K.R.M., Rümmer, P.: The Boogie 2 Type System: Design and Verification Condition Generation. https://citeseerx.ist.psu.edu/viewdoc/summary?doi=10.1.1.146.4277
19. Meyer, B.: Object-Oriented Software Construction, 2nd edn. Prentice Hall, Hoboken (1997)

20. Nilizadeh, A., Calvo, M., Leavens, G.T., Cok, D.R.: Generating counterexamples in the form of unit tests from hoare-style verification attempts. In: International Conference on Formal Methods in Software Engineering (FormaliSE), pp. 124–128. IEEE (2022)
21. Nilizadeh, A., Calvo, M., Leavens, G.T., Le, X.B.D.: More reliable test suites for dynamic APR by using counterexamples. In: International Symposium on Software Reliability Engineering (ISSRE), pp. 208–219. IEEE (2021)
22. Orso, A., Hsu, H.Y.: MINTS: a general framework and tool for supporting test-suite minimization. In: International Conference on Software Engineering (ICSE), pp. 419–429 (2009)
23. Pacheco, C., Ernst, M.D.: Randoop: feedback-directed random testing for java. In: Companion to the 22nd ACM SIGPLAN Conference on Object-Oriented Programming Systems and Applications Companion, pp. 815–816 (2007)
24. Sen, K., Marinov, D., Agha, G.: CUTE: a concolic unit testing engine for C. In: The ACM Joint European Software Engineering Conference and Symposium on the Foundations of Software Engineering (ESEC-FSE), pp. 213–223 (2005)
25. Tillmann, N., de Halleux, J.: Pex–white box test generation for .NET. In: Beckert, B., Hähnle, R. (eds.) TAP 2008. LNCS, vol. 4966, pp. 134–153. Springer, Heidelberg (2008). https://doi.org/10.1007/978-3-540-79124-9_10
26. Tschannen, J., Furia, C.A., Nordio, M., Polikarpova, N.: AutoProof: auto-active functional verification of object-oriented programs. In: Baier, C., Tinelli, C. (eds.) TACAS 2015. LNCS, vol. 9035, pp. 566–580. Springer, Heidelberg (2015). https://doi.org/10.1007/978-3-662-46681-0_53
27. Weide, B.W., et al.: Incremental benchmarks for software verification tools and techniques. In: Shankar, N., Woodcock, J. (eds.) VSTTE 2008. LNCS, vol. 5295, pp. 84–98. Springer, Heidelberg (2008). https://doi.org/10.1007/978-3-540-87873-5_10
28. Williams, N.: Towards exhaustive branch coverage with PathCrawler. In: International Conference on Automation of Software Tests (AST), pp. 117–120. IEEE (2021)

Test Automation and Design

Automated Testing of Systems of Systems

Özge Akat[1,2] and Hasan Sözer[2(✉)]

[1] Vestel Electronics, Manisa, Turkey
ozge.akat@ozu.edu.tr
[2] Ozyegin University, İstanbul, Turkey
hasan.sozer@ozyegin.edu.tr

Abstract. There are various kinds of software applications like mobile and Web applications. These applications have different types of user interfaces and user interaction methods. Hence, test automation tools are either dedicated or configured for a particular kind of application. Test scenarios can be implemented in the form of scripts and test execution can be automated separately for each type of application. However, there are systems of systems that embody multiple types of applications deployed on various platforms. Test scenarios might cross-cut these applications to be controlled collectively in the test script. In this paper, we propose an approach for testing cross-platform systems of systems. We present an application of it on a real system that involves a mobile and a Web application that are supposed to work in coordination. Our approach integrates a set of existing tools to facilitate test automation. It provides testers with a unified interface for developing test scripts that involve both mobile and Web applications. We conduct an industrial case study and show that our tool can reduce the testing effort significantly.

Keywords: Test automation · Systems of systems · Mobile applications · Web applications · Behaviour driven development

1 Introduction

The cost of testing activities may account for at least half of the development costs [2,16]. The cost can further increase depending on the required reliability level and the size of the system under test. Test automation is adopted to reduce this cost [3,17] in almost every domain including Web applications [4,15,18] and mobile applications [12]. These applications possess distinct user interfaces and user interaction methods. Consequently, test automation tools are either specifically designed or configured to cater to a particular type of application and platform. Test scenarios can be implemented in the form of scripts, and test execution can be automated separately for each type of application. However, certain complex systems, known as systems of systems, incorporate multiple types of applications. Usage scenarios that should be tested for these systems may cut across various platforms, and it might be necessary to control them

Published by Springer Nature Switzerland AG 2023
S. Bonfanti et al. (Eds.): ICTSS 2023, LNCS 14131, pp. 73–79, 2023.
https://doi.org/10.1007/978-3-031-43240-8_5

collectively in a single test script (See Fig. 1). For instance, a user of a Web application might need to observe the result of an action that is performed by another user on a mobile application. However, there is no direct automation support for the execution of such test scripts.

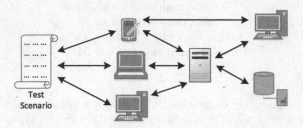

Fig. 1. A test scenario that interacts with multiple cross-platform applications.

There have been studies [6–8,10] to explore test automation strategies when dealing with multiple platforms. However, these studies focus on testing a single system that is deployed on various platforms. Their aim is to identify inconsistencies across platforms, such as cross-platform inconsistencies for mobile applications [10] and cross-browser inconsistencies for Web applications [8]. Additionally, in cases where different user interfaces are adopted for a wide range of platforms, the research goal is to reduce duplicated testing efforts for these platforms [6]. We tackle a different problem in this paper. Our goal is to facilitate the automated testing of multiple, cross-platform systems that are supposed to work in coordination. We integrate a set of existing tools to provide testers with a unified interface for developing test scripts involving both mobile and Web applications. We facilitate test automation by following the Behavior-Driven Development (BDD) approach [13]. Test scripts can be developed as a composition of natural-language constructs that access multiple platforms concurrently. We present an application of our approach on a real system that involves a mobile and a Web application working in coordination. We conduct an industrial case study and show that our approach can reduce the testing effort significantly.

The remainder of this paper is organized as follows. We summarize the related studies in Sect. 2. We explain the implementation of our approach in Sect. 3. We present a motivating example and a case study from the industry in Sect. 4. Finally, in Sect. 5, we conclude the paper.

2   Related Work

The behavior and the Graphical User Interface (GUI) of a software application might change depending on the deployed platform. Research efforts so far focus on the identification of these platform inconsistencies, especially for Web applications [8] and mobile applications [10] that can be deployed on a variety of platforms. In this work, we focus on the testing of systems of systems, where each involved system is deployed on a different platform.

The increasing number and variety of platforms increase test automation efforts as well [6]. Frameworks like Apache Cordova, Xamarin, and React Native enable the development of a single application that can be deployed on multiple platforms. However, a separate test script has to be developed for testing the application on each platform. x-PATeSCO [14] automatically generates test scripts for multiple platforms. However, it focuses on testing a single application at a time, unlike our approach.

Test scripts can be fragile due to changes in the GUI layout or code, as well as differences among the deployed platforms. Visual GUI Testing (VGT) [1] gained popularity due to its adaptability and resilience to these changes and differences. However, VGT approaches proposed so far focus on testing a single application rather than multiple types of applications on various platforms at the same time.

Appium [9] supports test automation across many platforms covering mobile (iOS, Android, Tizen), browser (Chrome, Firefox, Safari), desktop (macOS, Windows), and TV (Roku, tvOS, Android TV, Samsung) applications. It also supports several programming languages (e.g., Java, Pyhton, Ruby) for developing test scripts. However, to use Appium, one needs to set up a set of drivers and plugins depending on the target platform, and programming experience is necessary to develop test scripts. Our goal is to provide support test automation for multiple platforms at the same time and at a hig level of abstraction by following BDD principles [13]. With our approach, test scripts can be written using natural-language constructs that access multiple platforms concurrently, without worrying about the underlying setup. In the following section, we discuss our approach and its implementation in detail.

3 The Approach and Implementation

An overview of our approach is depicted in Fig. 2, where a set of tools are integrated. In particular, our approach employs Cucumber [13], Selenium [5] and Appium [9] for enabling test automation. A Selenium driver is used for steering a Web application on a Chrome browser. An Appium driver is used for controlling a mobile application that works on an Android phone. Cucumber is used for developing test scenarios. The test steps listed in these scenarios are mapped to executable test scripts by test fixtures that we developed in Java.

Test scenarios are developed in Gherkin format, where test steps are specified in structured natural language. Each of these test steps are mapped to a test fixture by Cucumber. Test steps are annotated to differentiate among a number of target applications and platforms. Text fixtures use these annotations to execute the intended user actions by employing the corresponding driver and interface. The implementation of the test fixtures is available online at a public repository[1]. While our current implementation utilizes Selenium and Appium, it

---

[1] https://github.com/ozgeakat4/toss.

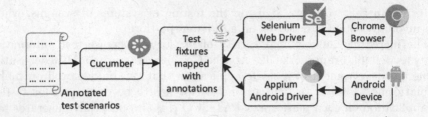

Fig. 2. Implementation of the approach with an integrated set of tools.

can be enhanced with alternative tools to accommodate diverse platforms. We used the Bridge Pattern [11] for abstracting away platform details from the set of possible generic test steps. In the following section, we present an application of our approach on a real system from the industry.

4   Motivating Example from the Industry

Our approach is motivated by the testing processes of a system called Charge Point Management System (CPMS). It is developed by a multi-industry manufacturer, Vestel, for managing Electric Vehicle Chargers (EVCs)[2]. CPMS is composed of 3 systems. There is a backend system that resides on the Azure cloud platform to keep track of EVC resources and the relevant IoT protocols. There is a Web application used by Charging Point Operators (CPOs) to control the charging process, EVCs and users. There is also a mobile application used by electrical vehicle owners for interacting with an EVC.

A user can start the charging process via the mobile application with or without registration. After the charging process is completed, the payment is made via Internet banking and checked through the CPO Web portal. The charging process can be initiated by using QR codes via the mobile application. Registered users can make reservations through the mobile application, depending on the availability of the connectors of EVCs. Reservations can be canceled via the mobile application or the CPO Web portal. New charging points can be added by CPOs, and users can locate these charging points on the map. When a faulty charging point is to be removed from use, it can be deleted by CPOs, so that users cannot access this device via the mobile application anymore.

CPMS has been subject to testing at various levels, including unit tests, integration tests, and system tests. These tests could be automated for a single system. For example, executable test scripts could be developed with Selenium for the CPO Web portal. However, programming expertise is required and it was not possible to automate end-to-end tests that involve multiple systems at the same time. For instance, when a user reserves a particular EVC from the mobile application, a status update should be visible at the CPO Web portal. Likewise, when a new EVC is introduced by a CPO, it should be visible on the

---

[2] http://vestelinternational.com/en/ev-charging-stations.

map presented by the mobile application. Our approach facilitated the specification and automated execution of such scenarios, without requiring programming expertise. A sample test scenario is specified in Gherkin format in the following.

```
Scenario: Reserved charger
Given open webpage "<webpage>"
When login web with username "<username>" and password "<password>"
When search charger on web
Then charger is unreserved
When login app  with username "<username>" and password "<password>"
And search charger on app
And reserve charger on app
Then search charger on web
Then charger is reserved
```

In the above scenario, the operator is logged on the portal first and the charging point is added. Then, the charging point is searched on the portal and verified by searching the charging point on the map presented by the mobile application. This confirms that the charging point has been successfully added. In one of the other scenarios, the user becomes a member via the mobile application and the user is activated via the operator portal, enabling the user to start charging thereafter. Listing 1.1 shows a sample snippet from the test fixture code. Lines 1–4 correspond to the test setup, where drivers are initialized. Lines 5–9 correspond to the second line in the scenario listed above. Lines 10–19 correspond to the 4, 5 and 6th lines, where a charger is searched.

```
1   public StepDefinition()throws IOException, ParseException {
2     AppTest = new AppiumTest();
3     WebTest = new SeleniumTest();
4   }
5   @Given("open webpage {string}")
6   public void open_webpage(String string) {
7     this.WebTest.driver.get(string);
8     this.WebTest.driver.manage().window().maximize();
9   }
10  @Then("search charger on {word}")
11  public void search_charger_on(String system ) ... {
12  try {
13  if(system.equals("web")) {
14    this.WebTest.driver.get("https://vesteuwebapptest.net/CP");
15    this.WebTest.driver.findElement(By.id("Filter")).click();
16    this.WebTest.driver.findElement(By.id("Filter")).
17      sendKeys("DV-6");
18    this.WebTest.driver.findElement(By.id("dropdown")).click();
19  }
20  else if(system.equals("app")){
21    this.AppTest.driver.findElement(By.id("button")).click();
22    this.AppTest.driver.findElementByXPath(("buton")).click();
23    this.AppTest.driver.findElementByXPath(("EditText")).
24      sendKeys("DV-6");
25  }
26  }
```

Listing 1.1. A sliced sample snippet from the test fixture code.

Table 1 lists the properties of the implemented test scenarios, the time it takes to execute them manually and their execution time with our approach. The scenario listed above is S2. We observe an order of magnitude reduction in testing time. Every execution of the listed test scenarios saves more than half an hour time and it does not require any manual effort. The test fixture code has to be developed for new types of user actions and platforms. The last column of Table 1 lists the time it took to develop these fixtures. However, this is a one-time investment only and it can be amortized after a dozen test executions.

Table 1. Test scenarios and their execution time before and after automation.

Test scenario	# of test steps	Manual testing time (min)	Test execution time (min)	Test development time (hrs)
S1	6	7	0.63	0.12
S2	9	6	0.56	1.5
S3	7	5	0.42	0.5
S4	5	5	0.37	0.33
S5	6	4	0.35	1.5
S6	3	2	0.18	0.33
S7	3	3	0.20	1
S8	3	2	0.15	0.5
S9	4	4	0.29	0.33
Total	46	38	3.06	6.11

5   Conclusion and Future Work

We introduced an approach for testing systems of systems. We integrated a set of existing tools for implementing a generic approach. Our approach provides testers with a unified interface for developing test scripts that involve multiple applications deployed on various platforms at the same time. Currently it supports Web and Android applications that are supposed to work in coordination. We also illustrated an application of our approach for the test automation of a real system. We observed significant effort reduction for tests that were previously performed manually.

As future work, we plan to increase the variety of platforms supported. We also plan to conduct additional case studies and experiments for measuring the effectiveness of our approach in test automation and effort reduction.

Acknowledgment. We would like to thank software developers and test engineers at Vestel for supporting our case study.

References

1. Alegroth, E., Feldt, R., Ryrholm, L.: Visual GUI testing in practice: challenges, problems and limitations. Empir. Softw. Eng. **20**, 694–744 (2015)
2. Beizer, B.: Software Testing Techniques, 2nd edn. Van Nostrand Reinhold Co., New York (1990)
3. Berner, S., Weber, R., Keller, R.K.: Observations and lessons learned from automated testing. In: Proceedings of the 27th International Conference on Software Engineering, pp. 571–579 (2005)
4. Biagiola, M., Stocco, A., Ricca, F., Tonella, P.: Dependency-aware web test generation. In: Proceedings of the IEEE 13th International Conference on Software Testing, Validation and Verification, pp. 175–185 (2020)
5. Bruns, A., Kornstadt, A., Wichmann, D.: Web application tests with selenium. IEEE Softw. **26**(5), 88–91 (2009)
6. Choudhary, S.: Cross-platform testing and maintenance of web and mobile applications. In: Proceedings of the 36th International Conference on Software Engineering, pp. 642–645 (2014)
7. Choudhary, S., Prasad, M., Orso, A.: Cross-platform feature matching for web applications. In: Proceedings of the International Symposium on Software Testing and Analysis, pp. 82–92 (2014)
8. Choudhary, S., Prasad, M., Orso, A.: X-PERT: a web application testing tool for cross-browser inconsistency detection. In: Proceedings of the International Symposium on Software Testing and Analysis, pp. 417–420 (2014)
9. Das, K.: Creating Android, iOS, and Web Drivers on Demand, pp. 45–60. Apress, Berkeley (2022)
10. Fazzini, M., Orso, A.: Automated cross-platform inconsistency detection for mobile apps. In: Proceedings of the 32nd IEEE/ACM International Conference on Automated Software Engineering, pp. 308–318 (2017)
11. Gamma, E., Helm, R., Johnson, R., Vlissides, J.M.: Design Patterns: Elements of Reusable Object-Oriented Software. Addison-Wesley Professional, Boston (1994)
12. Kong, P., Li, L., Gao, J., Liu, K., Bissyandé, T., Klein, J.: Automated testing of android apps: a systematic literature review. IEEE Trans. Reliab. **68**(1), 45–66 (2019)
13. Lawrence, R., Rayner, P.: Behavior-Driven Development with Cucumber. Addison-Wesley Professional, Boston (2019)
14. Menegassi, A., Endo, A.: Automated tests for cross-platform mobile apps in multiple configurations. IET Softw. **14**(1), 27–38 (2020)
15. Mesbah, A., van Deursen, A., Roest, D.: Invariant-based automatic testing of modern Web applications. IEEE Trans. Softw. Eng. **38**(1), 35–53 (2012)
16. Myers, G., Badgett, T., Sandler, C.: The Art of Software Testing, 3rd edn. John Wiley and Sons Inc., Hoboken (2012)
17. Rafi, D., Moses, K., Petersen, K., Mäntylä, M.: Benefits and limitations of automated software testing: systematic literature review and practitioner survey. In: Proceedings of the 7th International Workshop on Automation of Software Test, pp. 36–42 (2012)
18. Sunman, N., Soydan, Y., Sözer, H.: Automated web application testing driven by pre-recorded test cases. J. Syst. Softw. **193**, 111441 (2022)

Empirical Verification of TQED - A New Test Design Heuristic Technique

Adam Roman[✉][iD], Michał Mnich[iD], and Jarosław Hryszko[iD]

Faculty of Mathematics and Computer Science, Division of Software Engineering,
Jagiellonian University, Łojasiewicza 6, 30 -348 Krakow, Poland
{adam.roman,michal.mnich,jaroslaw.hryszko}@uj.edu.pl

Abstract. TQED is a universal test heuristic that assists testers in creatively designing effective test cases. It involves defining the test problem
in terms of component elements, each of which is classified into one of
the four so-called dimensions, which are: time (T), quantity (Q), event
(E) and data (D). Then, test ideas are created by considering specific
combinations of the components, aided by the interpretation of combinations of dimensions.

In this article, we compare the TQED model with other well-known
test heuristics and risk analysis techniques, and then present an empirical verification of the effectiveness of the TQED model. We compare
the effectiveness of tests written by 24 developers who were asked to
implement code for the same problem, together with the unit tests. The
developers were divided into two groups, one of which used TQED when
designing unit tests and the other did not. Effectiveness was measured
in terms of code coverage, mutation coverage and failure rate of test
cases. To increase the objectivity of the study, a cross-experiment was
conducted in which each developer's tests were run on the source code of
all other developers. Our research showed that TQED can significantly
support testers in creating strong tests that are more likely to detect
defects in code.

Keywords: test heuristics · test case design · test technique · TQED ·
creativity

1 Introduction

The IT systems being developed today are very complex products. Effective
control of their quality often requires sophisticated testing methods. This makes
testing itself a both technologically and intellectually challenging undertaking.
One of the key steps in the testing process is the analysis and design of test
cases. For test cases to be effective, that is, to detect existing defects in the
work product with the highest possible probability, they must be properly and
carefully designed. The variety and complexity of the problems a tester faces
in their daily work means that despite the existence of a number of specific

S. Bonfanti et al. (Eds.): ICTSS 2023, LNCS 14131, pp. 80–96, 2023.
https://doi.org/10.1007/978-3-031-43240-8_6

test design approaches and techniques, they are never sufficient to achieve the aforementioned goal. An essential ingredient of an effective design process is the tester's creativity, which is difficult to put into a precise, technical framework.

In Winograd's book creativity is defined as "the process that results in novel and useful products" [31]. In software testing, creativity can be viewed as the ability to generate original and valuable test ideas or solutions to testing problems. It involves divergent thinking (i.e., the ability to explore multiple possibilities and perspectives), as well as convergent thinking (i.e., the ability to analyze and synthesize information to obtain a set of effective and efficient test cases that can reveal defects in the software system and help to improve the overall software quality). Creative test cases can often help uncover issues that might not have been identified by more conventional approaches, like formal test design techniques.

There are surprisingly few studies on creativity and its impact on software engineering [15], not mentioning the software testing. It is quite striking, especially when we realize that the main task of a tester is to provide good and effective tests that detect software failures with high probability. Achieving this goal definitely relies on the tester's creativity. In [9] a method for assessing the creativity of software products is introduced. The authors say that it should be measured in terms of the novelty and usefulness. This aligns with Winograd's definition. We adapt this definition for the tester's creativity and assume that from the tester's point of view: *novelty* should be understood as the non-redundancy of test cases, while *usefulness* should be understood as the ability to detect with high probability a failure in the system under test.

It is well-known that creativity is one of the most important characteristics of the software engineer [14] apart from factors like: team quality, fun, professionalism, having an ideology, non-financial benefits, penalty policies and good relationship with users/customer. But how can testers increase their creativity? To the best of our knowledge, there is no research on this topic. Some papers mention the creativity only as a general method used in a given technique. The example may be [1], where exploratory testing is described as a technique which utilizes well the tester's creativity. The same technique is mentioned in [11], where it is said that the improvement of the DevOps process results in the fact that manual (exploratory) tests basically complement automated tests (focus on tests that require creativity).

Study conducted by Deak et al., concentrated on the motivations behind selecting software testing as a career. They formulated a concise questionnaire, guided by the research questions: How do computer science students perceive software testing? What factors encourage or discourage students to pursue a career in software testing? The research involved a sample of bachelor's and master's students from the Norwegian University of Science and Technology, as well as computer engineering students from University College. The survey received a total of 161 responses. Among the negative aspects related to a career in software testing, respondents characterized software testing as boring (48 participants) and not creative (15 participants) [12].

Similar observations may be found in [15]. The authors performed an experiment involving 68 students split into 12 teams. The aim was to check the creativity involvement in different software development phases. In one survey the students had to decide if a given phase should be considered discipline-based or creative. The creativeness for the phases: documenting with demanded format, architecture design, architecture assessment, and programming was chosen by resp. 33, 97, 44 and 81 percent. The testing phase was considered creative only by... 19 percent of the students (sic!). This means that software testing is perceived rather as a discipline-based phase, with well-defined techniques, processes and activities that do not require any creativity at all.

The authors conclude: "If we classify (...) [the above mentioned] activities into two categories: producing activities, including architecture design and programming, and improving activities (quality assuring activities), including completing document with demanded format, architecture assessment and testing, the results tell us that students perceive there is more creative work in producing activities than in improving activities".

However, it is obvious to any tester that improvement activities require at least the same amount of creativity as the design phases. Formal test design techniques can be used as such tools, but despite their concreteness, they are not universal – each technique is very prescriptive and focuses only on some particular aspect of the system under test. This can hinder the creative process, because when applying a particular, formal test design technique, the tester is always limited to a certain way of thinking (e.g., in case of Equivalence Partitioning technique – to domain analysis).

Unlike scripted testing, where the tester follows a pre-defined set of steps to verify that the software behaves as expected, *exploratory testing* is a more flexible, unscripted approach. Thus, exploratory testing is often considered a *creative* process by researchers and practitioners. For example, Mårtensson et al. [23] shared interview findings from 20 participants, who had experience ranging from 4 to 46 years (averaging over 13 years). These participants were associated with four different companies, each involved in the development of large-scale software systems. According to these experienced professionals, exploratory testing provides a more inventive, creative approach to their work. Therefore, they believe it optimizes the skills and potential of the testers. Similar findings regarding creativity during testing can be found in Pfahl et al. [26] survey results from an online survey among Estonian and Finnish software developers and testers. The authors find that among three most frequently indicated by respondents advantages of exploratory testing, apart from efficiency and effectiveness is, indeed, creativity. Some authors have even likened exploratory testing to scientific exploration or detective work, both of which require a high degree of creativity and problem-solving skills. Like a detective trying to solve a mystery, an exploratory tester must use their observational skills, intuition, and creativity to find and investigate potential issues with the software [2,20].

The previously mentioned works allow us to state that creativity is an important factor in the attractiveness of the work of a software tester. Other research seem to support this statement. For example, the primary reason why de Jesus et al. [18] began investigating the gamification usage in software testing was the claim that, testing is considered unpleasant, dull and tedious". In their work, they recognize the *development of creativity* as one of the important goals to be pursued through gamification in software testing. Moreover, De Souza et al. [28] constructed a survey-based tool to explore the motivational factors among software testers, which was rooted in a pre-existing theory of motivation within the realm of software engineering. From a group of 80 software testers, they gathered views on the nature of work in software testing and the elements of this work that impact the testers' motivation. As a result, they observed that among other factors, like acquisition of knowledge and work variety, what profoundly influences software testers motivation to work is creativity.

There are papers in the literature devoted to comparing the effectiveness of testing techniques (e.g., directly comparing the effectiveness of the techniques themselves [16], comparing the effectiveness of tests generated by different tools [8], or comparing the effectiveness of test prioritization strategies [22]). However, they mainly concern formal test design techniques, such as black-box or white-box techniques. To the best of our knowledge, there is no such work, involving empirical approach, devoted to less formal approaches (e.g., defect-based or experience-based test techniques), let alone techniques or models that support testers' creativity.

In this study, we set out to fill this gap by empirically investigating the effectiveness of one such technique for helping testers' creativity. This is the TQED model, proposed in [27]. In the experiment we conducted, we compared the code and tests of programmers divided into two groups. Programmers in one group were required to use the TQED model when writing tests. Programmers in the other group did not use this technique. Then, in a crossover experiment, by executing each programmer's tests on the other programmers' source codes, we tested the effectiveness of tests written using TQED against tests written without TQED. Our ultimate goal is to answer the following research question:

(RQ) Does the TQED technique help testers increase their creativity and allow them to design stronger and more effective test cases?

The article is structured as follows. In Sect. 2 we briefly discuss the requirements for test creativity techniques. We introduce and classify, according to these requirements, different test approaches and techniques. We compare these methods with the TQED approach, against these requirements, justifying why the TQED approach is interesting from a practical, tester's point of view. In Sect. 3 we present the TQED model in detail, together with an example of using it in practice. Section 4 describes the results of the controlled experiment performed to assess the effectiveness of the TQED method. Section 5 follows with conclusions.

2   TQED and Effectiveness of Test Design Techniques

There are many test design techniques, but their impact on tester's creativity varies. In order to compare these techniques and see where the TQED model can be located against them, we introduce two factors to evaluate test design techniques: versatility (universality) and concreteness (prescriptiveness). By versatility, we mean the variety of projects and contexts in which a technique can be successfully applied. By concreteness, we mean the degree to which a method provides us with detailed information about test cases, coverage items, test data or test ideas. Note that from a practical point of view, these are the two most important features of test design techniques, because they allow the tester to achieve the goal of creating effective test cases, regardless of the context.

In general, these two factors can be at odds with each other: a method that can be applied to any situation is usually unable to provide a specific test idea or meaningful test data. A very specific method, on the other hand, is usually limited to some particular, narrow context of use. The ideal test technique should be versatile (we should be able to apply it to every possible situation), and at the same time its application should give us specific test cases and test data. Of course, ideal techniques do not exist, but using these two characteristics we can compare different techniques with each other. Figure 1 shows several types of test techniques, in terms of their versatility and concreteness.

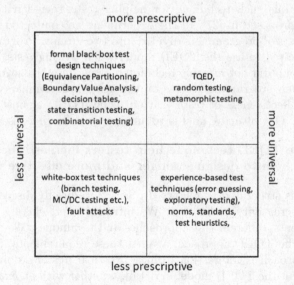

Fig. 1. Comparison of different test design approaches and techniques, regarding their universality and concreteness.

Formal black-box test design techniques (cf. [4,7,19,21]) tend to be very specific, as they allow us to, among other things, provide specific test cases by covering the relevant elements of the models they use. For example, Boundary Value Analysis gives us the *exact* test data values that test cases should cover. However, each of these techniques is a model of only one specific aspect of the system under test. Hence, their universality is limited.

White-box techniques can be considered not very prescriptive and not very versatile. This is because each white-box technique can only be applied to a specific work product (e.g., source code). In addition, these techniques do not provide specific test data, but only define criteria for covering structural elements of the test object. Fault attacks are based on specific defects and failures and do not provide the specific test data needed to cause those failures or reveal those defects.

Experience-based test techniques [4,30], standards, standards and norms (e.g., the quality model [17]) are universal, but do not allow the derivation of any specific test data – this task fully rests with the tester, who is assumed to be experienced and can best design the most appropriate test data. Testing heuristics, such as those proposed by Bach [3] or Edgren [13], are also quite general. However, compared to formal test design techniques, they are less specific. For example, the "test each function, one at a time" heuristics proposed by Bach can be applied to any type of functional testing, but provides no guidance on *how* to do so.

The TQED approach, like random testing [5,24] or metamorphic testing [6,29] techniques, can be considered a universal yet specific approach. All of these techniques offer some general test case generation mechanisms that can be applied to virtually any context of use. On the other hand, these procedures are specific enough to derive specific test data (e.g., a random number generator in the case of random testing) or give specific instructions on how to obtain such data (e.g., metamorphic relations in the case of metamorphic testing). In the case of the TQED approach, the generality of the test case generation mechanism is due to the generality of the concept of the so-called problem dimensions, while the ability to derive specific test data is related to the interpretation of the combination of elements belonging to each problem dimension.

The above analysis shows that the TQED method may be an interesting and useful approach with a very nice trade-off between versatility and concreteness. In Sect. 3 we give a detailed description of the method, and in Sect. 4 we verify empirically the effectiveness of the TQED.

3   TQED Model

The TQED model can be seen as a very simple (but universal) fault model based on a few basic software features, although its purpose is to support test design and enhance testers' creativity. The theoretical basis of the model is inspired by physics. Physics describes our world in terms of a few basic concepts, such as mass, distance, time, or force. All other more complex characteristics can be expressed as a combination of basic concepts, for example, speed is a function of distance and time.

Similarly, software can be described by four basic "dimensions": data (D), events (E), quantity (Q), and time (T). These act as building blocks for each type of software and its behavior. Using these four concepts, we can build a model to describe the operation of any software system at any level of abstraction, since any software system involves processing (E) different amounts of data (D, Q) over time (T). But this also means that we are able to derive many different fault models from this model. Error models based on relationships between software dimensions describe how software can fail, so they can be a very helpful tool for generating ideas for effective and creative test cases.

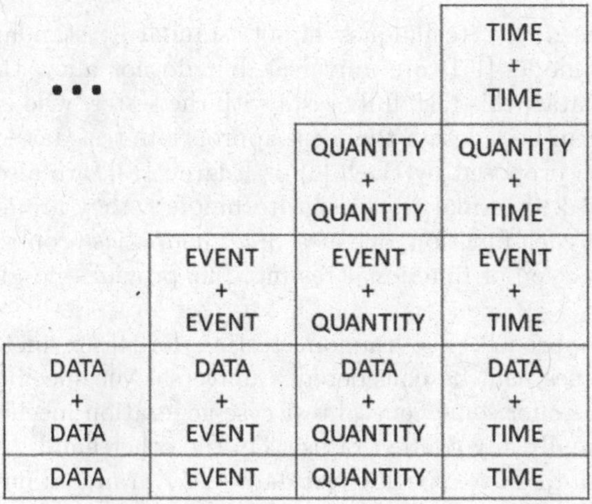

•••			TIME + TIME	
			QUANTITY + QUANTITY	QUANTITY + TIME
		EVENT + EVENT	EVENT + QUANTITY	EVENT + TIME
	DATA + DATA	DATA + EVENT	DATA + QUANTITY	DATA + TIME
	DATA	EVENT	QUANTITY	TIME

Fig. 2. TQED model

The TQED model is shown in Fig. 2. It depicts all four primary dimensions and their compositions. The three dots in the upper left corner suggest that there may be more combinations, covering three, four, etc. of the basic dimensions. Each dimension and each combination of dimensions can be interpreted by the tester in terms of actual software characteristics, which should help the tester come up with creative test ideas. The primary dimensions can stand for various concepts related to the actual software – an example interpretation is shown in table 1.

The procedure for using the TQED model is as follows. First, identify the basic features of the software that can be classified into one of the basic dimensions (D, E, Q, T). Then, various sensible combinations of these features are considered. Each corresponds to a combination of their dimensions (for example, D+D, E+T, D+D+E+Q, etc.), which is subject to interpretation in terms of test conditions or test ideas. These form the basis for the test cases. Example heuristics for interpreting certain combinations of dimensions are as follows:

Table 1. The possible meaning of the TQED model components.

Dimension	Represents	Intuition	Examples
Data	immutable, premanent entity (variable, object, element, part of a system or environment)	something fixed in time, persistent object	number, string, file, file name, document, object, GUI element, database record
Event	phenomenon that, when it occurs, can change the state of a system, environment or user	something that has short, almost zero duration in time	use of a variable, filling in a form, pressing a button, performing an operation
Time	a continuous progression of existence	an irreversible succession from the past, through the present, to the future	ordering, succession, parallel, duration, forward, backward
Quantity	amount or number of some part of a system or environment	number, volume, size of something	length, minimum, maximum, boundary value, part of, superset

- D+D: data merging, high-dimensional representation, element comparison, relationships between data elements;
- D+E: data-driven event, event parameters, object operations;
- D+T: data persistence over a given period of time;
- D+Q: amount or volume of data, minimum or maximum value of data, number of objects;
- E+E: combination of events, business logic rules (if-then), sub-event within an event;
- E+T: sequence of events, long-term event, short-term event, event duration;
- T+T: concurrency, time comparison, sum of time periods, race condition.

Note that the interpretation of the dimensions and their combinations is always up to the tester. The method itself does not dictate anything here – it is only a framework to be filled with the tester's interpretation of the elements suggested by the model (dimension combinations).

Comparison of TQED with Other Models. The TQED approach may seem similar to the Category-Partition method, a formal test design technique proposed by Ostrand and Blacer [25], but the latter is limited to functional tests only. Category-Partition, moreover, is a hierarchical, combinatorial approach that divides certain predefined categories into partitions and then combines different partitions from different categories. Hence, its versatility is less than that of TQED.

The TQED approach is also similar to test heuristics in terms of universality – it can be applied to any type of system, be it software or hardware, regardless of the type of test, software lifecycle, etc. However, compared to test heuristics, TQED is more specific. We showed earlier that the use of TQED involves some normative rules for combining software dimensions, but it is always left to the tester to interpret them.

Finally, TQED shares some similarities with the Hazard and Operability (HAZOP) approach [10] – a form of risk management to identify, evaluate, and control hazards and risks in complex processes. The HAZOP approach first identifies operational processes. From these, parameters or safe operating limits of the process elements are defined so that deviations can be identified and so-called "guide words" selected. Examples of common HAZOP guiding words are: No or Not, More, Less, High, Low. With the use of guide words, workplace hazards can be clearly defined as deviations that fall outside acceptable parameters or safe operating limits. However, HAZOP was designed for use in the chemical, pharmaceutical, oil and gas, and nuclear industries, not in software engineering. In addition, the set of guide words is closed, limited and directed at describing the parameters of industrial processes. TQED is flexible and open in this regard.

An Example of Using the TQED Approach. In this chapter, we show a simple application of the TQED that results in a failure triggering. We will test the most important feature of the well-known web-based time management application, Google Calendar - adding an event to the calendar. When we want to add an event to the calendar, we see a window like the one in Fig. 3a.

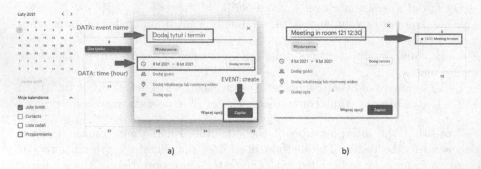

a)   b)

Fig. 3. Adding an event to Google Calendar (in Polish)

The creative process assisted by the TQED is figuratively shown in Fig. 4. From the interface itself, we know that before clicking the 'Save' button, the application wants us to add both the event name and its time in the field. From here we can derive the following dimensions: D1 (event name), D2 (time), E (click the 'Save' button). The tester can interpret the combination D1+D2 as "the name contains the time." Using the "part of something" heuristic for the Q dimension, we can go one level down this structure and derive the idea that the hour contains numbers.

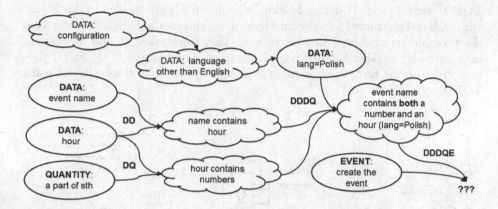

Fig. 4. Creative process supported with the TQED method.

At this point, we have the following idea for a test: see if we can add an appointment with a name that contains *both* a number and an hour. For example, we could try adding an event called "Meeting in room 121 12:30". This works fine if the application language is set to English. Since configuration items are a typical example of a data dimension (D), we can think about changing this setting, for example, we can change the language to Polish. Now things get interesting. When we combine our test idea (add an event containing a number and time, with the language set to Polish) with the obvious "click Save" dimension E, we get our final idea of the test case that triggers the failure (Fig. 3b). Google Calendar misinterprets the title of the event, assuming that the room number is the time of the meeting.

4   Experiment

Experimental Setup. In order to empirically test the effectiveness of the TQED approach and answer the research question posed at the beginning of the article, we conducted an experiment. 24 programmers were asked to implement the same application in Java language – a simple payment card management program. The program consisted of three classes (Account, Atm, CreditCard) containing 4, 7 and 8 methods, respectively. The programmers also had to implement unit tests for the code they wrote. When implementing the code, participants were not allowed to create public fields, only to use methods from defined interfaces. In addition, participants were not allowed to add their own methods, modify interfaces, or change the established version of the Java language and the JUnit library. It was also not possible to create new (custom) constructors, but only to use existing ones – parameter-free. Thanks to these rules, it was possible to cross-execute tests written by one developer on the code of any other developer.

The developers were divided into two groups of 12: TQED (T) and non-TQED, control group (0). The developers in group T were trained in the TQED approach and instructed to write unit tests using this methodology. To verify that the programmers followed this instruction, they were asked to add a comment next to each test about which combinations of dimensions (T, Q, E, D) they used to write the test. Programmers in group 0 wrote unit tests without using TQED.

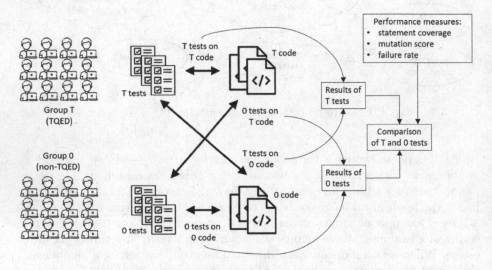

Fig. 5. Experimental design.

The experimental design is shown in Fig. 5. After all programmers wrote the code and tests, each code was tested with each test set, so a total of $24 \times 24 = 576$ test runs were performed. By using the cross-validation approach, greater objectivity was achieved in evaluating the tests. This is because the tests were evaluated on code for which they were not intended, since the respective test author did not know the code implementations of the other participants in the experiment. In this way, the effectiveness of the tests of the two groups, T and 0, could be compared more objectively. Three measures were adopted to evaluate the effectiveness of the tests: statement coverage, mutation coverage (also known as mutation score) and failure rate.

Statement coverage is defined as $SCov = (X/Y) \cdot 100\%$, where X is the number of statements executed during testing and Y is the total number of executable statements in the code. $SCov$ measures what portion of the code was covered by tests and can be considered a basic (albeit very simple) measure of test thoroughness.

Mutation coverage measures the ability of tests to detect defects. In the mutation testing process, a number of so-called mutants are created from the source code. A mutant is the original code with an artificially introduced change (defect) that simulates the programmer's mistake. Tests are run on both the original code and the mutant. If for each test the result on the original code and on the mutant is the same, it means that the mutant was not detected by either test, so either the tests are weak or the mutant happens to be equivalent to the original code. If for at least one test the result on the original code and on the mutant is different, it means that the test detected the mutant (the mutant is said to be killed by the test). The more killed mutants, the stronger the tests are. Mutation coverage is defined as $MCov = (X/Y) \cdot 100\%$, where X is the number of mutants killed by the tests and Y is the total number of mutants generated. For mutant generation, in our experiment we used the PIT Mutation Testing tool (https://pitest.org/).

Failure rate is defined as $FR = (X/Y) \cdot 100\%$, where X is the number of test cases that failed and Y is the total number of test cases run. FR is the percentage of test cases that failed, so it is a similar measure to $MCov$ in that it describes the ability of tests to detect defects. The difference between $MCov$ and FR is that FR is measured on actual code, while $MCov$ rather takes into account the potential power of tests also if the tests are run on code that is changed in the future.

Results and Discussion. Table 2 shows the basic statistics of the code, test cases and mutants, by group (T and 0) and implemented classes. The programs written by the two groups are similar both in terms of their size, the number of tests written, and the number of mutants generated for each class.

Table 2. Statistics on code, tests and mutants for both groups.

Category	Class	Group 0 $\mu \pm \sigma$	Group T $\mu \pm \sigma$	Total $\mu \pm \sigma$
Lines of Code	Account.java	10.75 ± 3.64	11.17 ± 3.34	10.96 ± 3.50
	Atm.java	17.92 ± 5.48	22.33 ± 7.50	20.13 ± 6.92
	CreditCard.java	33.75 ± 6.52	35.58 ± 8.17	34.67 ± 7.44
	Total	62.4 ± 10.47	69.08 ± 10.21	65.75 ± 11.63
Number of tests	Account.java	6.42 ± 3.90	7.00 ± 3.57	6.71 ± 3.67
	Atm.java	15.75 ± 10.93	14.67 ± 7.34	15.21 ± 9.12
	CreditCard.java	15.08 ± 8.73	19.33 ± 8.90	17.21 ± 8.89
Number of mutants	Account.java	9.00 ± 1.22	8.23 ± 2.26	8.60 ± 1.88
	Atm.java	15.58 ± 4.54	18.31 ± 7.40	17.00 ± 6.34
	CreditCard.java	25.25 ± 7.51	22.62 ± 8.60	23.88 ± 8.20

μ = mean value, σ = standard deviation.

Each of the 24 test sets was executed on each of the 24 programs written, as well as on the mutants generated for these programs. For each of the $24 \times 24 = 576$ test/code combinations, statement coverage, mutation coverage and failure rate were measured for the test cases run. The results were averaged across groups 0 and T. In the tables below, the results are reported separately for the four test/code combinations: 0/T (group 0 tests run on group T programs), T/0, 0/0 and T/T. The measures are also reported for group 0 tests and group T tests performed on all programs (from both groups).

The results of code coverage compared to mutation coverage are interesting. Table 3 shows the average statement coverage achieved by the tests of one group on the code of the other group. It is noticeable that the tests of group 0 achieve higher coverage compared to those of group T. The difference is about 7% (83% vs. 76.2%). This difference is statistically significant (two-sample t-test, N=288, p-value=5.07×10^{-5} for homoscedastic groups (F-test, p-value=0.125)). However, as can be seen in Table 4, Group T tests achieve 3% higher mutation coverage than Group 0 tests (68.8% vs. 65.7%). This difference is also statistically significant (two-sample t-test, N=288, p-value = 0.003 for heteroscedastic groups (F-test, p-value=5.5×10^{-5})). These results can be interpreted as follows. Using the TQED approach makes it possible to create tests that cover a smaller but more quality-relevant portion of the code. Although these tests cover less code than Group 0 tests, they are more effective, as shown by the mutation coverage.

Table 3. Statistics on statement coverage.

Tests from ↓ on code from →	Group 0	Group T	All
Group 0	85.3%	80.8%	83.0%
Group T	77.6%	74.8%	76.2%
All	81.5%	77.8%	79.6%

Table 4. Statistics on mutation coverage.

Tests from ↓ on code from →	Group 0	Group T	All
Group 0	63.7%	67.6%	65.7%
Group T	66.8%	70.8%	68.8%
All	65.3%	69.2%	67.2%

Finally, Table 5 shows the failure rate results. As in the case of mutation coverage, the failure rate turned out to be significantly higher (by more than 8%) for the tests from group T (37.6% vs. 29.3%). This difference is statistically significant (two-sample t-test, $n_1 = 900$, $n_2 = 975$, p-value = 4.5×10^{-9}). Thus, despite achieving lower statement coverage, tests written using the TQED approach were failing 28% more often $((37.6-29.3)/29.3)$ than tests written without using this approach.

Table 5. Statistics on failure rate.

Tests from ↓ on code from →	Group 0	Group T	All
Group 0	23.6%	34.5%	29.3%
Group T	39.2%	35.8%	37.6%
All	30.0%	37.0%	33.6%

The observed both higher mutation coverage and higher failure ratio for Group T tests allows us to positively answer the research question posed at the beginning of the article: the TQED approach supports testers in creatively developing better, more efficient tests capable of detecting defects more frequently. Thus, the TQED approach can be considered a valuable tool in a tester's work during test analysis and design.

Threats to Validity. Although the results of the experiment showed the positive impact of the TQED approach on the effectiveness of the test cases, the following threats to validity should be taken into account:

- (internal validity) The experiment included a small group of developers ($N = 24$). However, the number of code/test combinations of $24 \times 24 = 576$ was sufficient to draw statistically significant conclusions within the experiment. In addition, participants were randomly assigned to groups 0 and T to avoid systematic bias between the study groups.
- (external validity) The participants in the experiment were first- and second-year graduate students in computer science. Although most of them were working professionally as programmers at the time of the experiment, their professional experience in both programming and testing was not very extensive. The effectiveness of the TQED method may prove to be different when applied, for example, by experienced testers.
- (external validity) The tests involved a single, small program written in Java (in most cases, the number of lines of code written was 54–76), with only 3 classes and a total of 19 methods. The effectiveness of the method may prove to be different in production applications, where the software has thousands of classes and millions of lines of code, and is written in languages other than Java.
- (external validity) The test cases involved only functional tests and were written only at the level of unit tests and very simple component integration tests. The effectiveness of the method was not tested at higher levels of testing (e.g., system integration tests, system tests or acceptance tests) or for non-functional testing.

5   Conclusions

In this paper, we described the TQED technique for supporting testers' creativity during the test analysis and design phase. We compared it with other similar approaches, justifying its relatively high generality while being highly prescriptive when it comes to providing ideas for test data or test ideas. We conducted an experiment that showed that the use of TQED increases the strength of test cases, expressed in terms of mutation coverage and failure rate. The results of the study allow us to conclude that TQED can be successfully applied in practice as an effective heuristics for test case design.

Links to Data Files. The code containing the definitions of the interfaces the participants were to implement, as well as the solutions provided by the participants, can be found at github.com/Software-Engineering-Jagiellonian/TQED-experiment

References

1. Afzal, W., Ghazi, A.N., Itkonen, J., Torkar, R., Andrews, A., Bhatti, K.: An experiment on the effectiveness and efficiency of exploratory testing. Empirical Softw. Eng. **20**(3), 844–878 (2014). https://doi.org/10.1007/s10664-014-9301-4
2. Bach, J.: Exploratory testing explained. https://wwwsatisfice.com/articles/et-article.pdf (2003)
3. Bach, J.: Heuristic test strategy model (2019). https://www.satisfice.com/download/heuristic-test-strategy-model
4. Beizer, B.: Black-Box Testing. Techniques for Functional Testing of Software and Systems, Wiley (1995)
5. Chen, J., Chen, H., Wu, Y., Mao, C., Cai, S.: Adaptive random testing based on the modified metric-memory tree and information entropy. In: 2022 9th International Conference on Dependable Systems and Their Applications (DSA), pp. 615–623 (2022). https://doi.org/10.1109/DSA56465.2022.00088
6. Chen, T., Cheung, S., Yiu, S.: Metamorphic testing: a new approach for generating next test cases. Technical Report HKUST-CS98-01, University of Science and Technology, Hong Kong (1998)
7. Copeland, L.: A Practitioner's Guide to Software Test Design. Artech House Publishers, Norwood (2003)
8. Corradini, D., Zampieri, A., Pasqua, M., Ceccato, M.: Empirical comparison of black-box test case generation tools for restful APIS. In: 2021 IEEE 21st International Working Conference on Source Code Analysis and Manipulation (SCAM), pp. 226–236 (2021). https://doi.org/10.1109/SCAM52516.2021.00035
9. Crawford, B., Crawford, K., Soto, R., de la Barra, C.L.: Creativity in agile software development methods. Commun. Comput. Inf. Sci. **529**, 131–135 (2015)
10. Crawley, F., Tyler, B.: HAZOP: Guide to Best Practice, 3rd edn. Elsevier (2015). https://doi.org/10.1016/C2014-0-04859-9
11. Cruzes, D.S., Melsnes, K., Marczak, S.: Testing in a DevOps Era: perceptions of testers in norwegian organisations. In: Misra, S., et al. (eds.) ICCSA 2019. LNCS, vol. 11622, pp. 442–455. Springer, Cham (2019). https://doi.org/10.1007/978-3-030-24305-0_33

12. Deak, A., Stålhane, T., Cruzes, D.: Factors influencing the choice of a career in software testing among norwegian students. Softw. Eng. **796** (2013)
13. Edgren, R.: The little black book on test design (2012). https://www.thetesteye. com/papers/TheLittleBlackBookOnTestDesign.pdf
14. Franca, C., Gouveia, T., Santos, P., Santana, C., Silva, F.: Motivation in software engineering: a systematic review update. In: IET Seminar Digest, pp. 154–163. EASE 2011 (2011). https://doi.org/10.1049/ic.2011.0019
15. Gu, M., Tong, X.: Towards hypotheses on creativity in software development. In: Bomarius, F., Iida, H. (eds.) PROFES 2004. LNCS, vol. 3009, pp. 47–61. Springer, Heidelberg (2004). https://doi.org/10.1007/978-3-540-24659-6_4
16. Henard, C., Papadakis, M., Harman, M., Jia, Y., Le Traon, Y.: Comparing white-box and black-box test prioritization. In: 2016 IEEE/ACM 38th International Conference on Software Engineering (ICSE), pp. 523–534 (2016). https://doi.org/10. 1145/2884781.2884791
17. ISO/IEC: ISO/IEC 25010. Systems and software engineering - Product quality. ISO/IEC (2011)
18. de Jesus, G.M., Ferrari, F.C., de Paula Porto, D., Fabbri, S.C.P.F.: Gamification in software testing: a characterization study. In: Proceedings of the III Brazilian Symposium on Systematic and Automated Software Testing, pp. 39–48 (2018)
19. Jorgensen, P.C.: Software Testing. A Craftsman's Approach, CRC Press, Boca Raton (2014)
20. Kaner, C.: Exploratory testing. In: Quality Assurance Institute Worldwide Annual Software Testing Conference, pp. 1–14 (2006). https://kaner.com/pdfs/ETatQAI. pdf
21. Kaner, C., Padmanabhan, S., Hoffman, D.: The Domain Testing Workbook. Context Driven Press (2013)
22. Luo, Q., Moran, K., Poshyvanyk, D.: A large-scale empirical comparison of static and dynamic test case prioritization techniques. In: Proceedings of the 2016 24th ACM SIGSOFT International Symposium on Foundations of Software Engineering, pp. 559–570. FSE 2016, Association for Computing Machinery, New York, NY, USA (2016). https://doi.org/10.1145/2950290.2950344
23. Mårtensson, T., Martini, A., Ståhl, D., Bosch, J.: Excellence in exploratory testing: success factors in large-scale industry projects. In: Franch, X., Männistö, T., Martínez-Fernández, S. (eds.) PROFES 2019. LNCS, vol. 11915, pp. 299–314. Springer, Cham (2019). https://doi.org/10.1007/978-3-030-35333-9_21
24. Mayer, J., Schneckenburger, C.: An empirical analysis and comparison of random testing techniques. In: Proceedings of the 2006 ACM/IEEE International Symposium on Empirical Software Engineering, ISESE 2006, pp. 105–114. Association for Computing Machinery, New York, NY, USA (2006). https://doi.org/10.1145/ 1159733.1159751
25. Ostrand, T., Blacer, M.: The category-partition method for specifying and generating functional tests. Commun. ACM **31**(6), 676–686 (1988)
26. Pfahl, D., Yin, H., Mäntylä, M.V., Münch, J.: How is exploratory testing used? a state-of-the-practice survey. In: Proceedings of the 8th ACM/IEEE International Symposium on Empirical Software Engineering and Measurement, pp. 1–10 (2014)
27. Roman, A.: Thinking-Driven Testing. The Most Reasonable Approach to Quality Control. Springer Nature (2018). https://doi.org/10.1007/978-3-319-73195-7
28. de Souza Santos, R.E., De Magalhaes, C.V.C., da Silva Correia-Neto, J., Da Silva, F.Q.B., Capretz, L.F., Souza, R.: Would you like to motivate software testers? ask them how. In: 2017 ACM/IEEE International Symposium on Empirical Software Engineering and Measurement (ESEM), pp. 95–104. IEEE (2017)

29. Weyuker, E.J.: On testing non-testable programs. Comput. J. **25**(4), 465–470 (1982). https://doi.org/10.1093/comjnl/25.4.465

30. Whittaker, A.: Exploratory Software Testing. Addison-Wesley, Boston (2009)

31. Winograd, T.: Bring Design to Software. Addison Wesley, Boston (1996)

How Do Different Types of Testing Goals Affect Test Case Design?

Dia Istanbuly, Max Zimmer, and Gregory Gay(✉) ⓘ

Chalmers, University of Gothenburg, Gothenburg, Sweden
{gusistdi,gusmaxzi}@student.gu.se, greg@greggay.com

Abstract. Test cases are designed in service of goals, e.g., functional correctness or performance. Unfortunately, we lack a clear understanding of how specific goal types influence test design. In this study, we explore this relationship through interviews and a survey with software developers, with a focus on identification and importance of goal types, quantitative relations between goals and tests, and personal, organizational, methodological, and technological factors.

We identify nine goal types and their importance, and perform further analysis of three—correctness, reliability, and quality. We observe that test design for correctness forms a "default" design process that is modified when pursuing other goals. For the examined goal types, test cases tend to be simple, with many tests targeting a single goal and each test focusing on 1–2 goals at a time. We observe differences in testing practices, tools, and targeted system types between goal types. In addition, we observe that test design can be influenced by organization, process, and team makeup. This study provides a foundation for future research on test design and testing goals.

Keywords: Software Testing · Test Design · Testing Goals · Functional Testing · Non-Functional Testing

1 Introduction

Software testing is a process where input is applied to a system-under-test (SUT) and observations of the reaction to the input are used to verify that the SUT operates correctly [19]. It is the most common verification technique, and can be conducted in many forms and at different levels of granularity within the code of the SUT [4]. Testers may write test cases before or after writing the code-under-test [20], and according to different personal problem-solving models [9,12].

Unifying all testing approaches, practices, and technologies is that tests are designed in service of *goals*. These goals can vary in nature and type—for example, a test might be written to verify functional requirements, to show that known security risks are mitigated, or to ensure that performance thresholds are met [17]. The nature of problem-solving implies that developers must have goals

Support provided by Software Center Project 30: "Aspects of Automated Testing".

S. Bonfanti et al. (Eds.): ICTSS 2023, LNCS 14131, pp. 97–114, 2023.
https://doi.org/10.1007/978-3-031-43240-8_7

that they wish to achieve through the act of designing tests, even if those goals are not explicitly enumerated in requirements or other documentation [9,18].

Despite the prominence of testing as a development practice, we lack a clear understanding of how specific types of testing goals influence the practice of test design. For example, Enoiu et al. proposed a model of test case design as a problem solving process [9]. This model makes it clear that tests are designed to show the attainment of specific goals, but does not discuss what common types of goals are, or how different goal types could influence this process.

The purpose of this research is to explore the types of goals that testers pursue and the influence of these goal types on the process that developers follow to design tests that assess attainment of those goals. Understanding the relationship between test case design and different types of testing goals could provide benefits to both researchers and practitioners. For example, such understanding enables characterization of test design practices and the ability to offer clear guidance to developers creating tests for specific types of goals—potentially leading to improved effectiveness or efficiency of the testing process. In addition, characterization of design practices can benefit automated test generation, potentially leading to the development of more human-like generation tools [8,11].

In particular, we are interested in the exploring the types of goals pursued, the relative importance of different goal types, quantitative relations between goal types and test cases—tests-per-goal and goals-per-test—and personal, organizational, methodological, and technological factors that may influence the relationship between goal types and the test design process. To address these topics, we have conducted a series of interviews with software developers in various domains and of varying experience. Thematic analysis of the interviews was then used to develop a survey for wider distribution.

Based on analyses of the interview and survey responses, we have identified nine goal types, including correctness, reliability, performance, quality, security, customer satisfaction, risk management, improving maintenance cost, and process improvement. Correctness was ranked most important, followed by reliability and security. Customer satisfaction and maintenance cost were seen as least important, but were still valued.

We focused on correctness, reliability, and quality for analysis. Test design for correctness forms a "default" design process, which is followed in a modified form for other goals. For all three goal types, several tests are needed to assess goal attainment, and tests focus on 1–2 goals at a time. Testers often start the design process following pre-existing patterns (e.g., using past tests as templates). We also make observations regarding differences in testing practices and tools employed during test design for these three goal types. We further observe that test design can be influenced by process, organization, and team structure.

This study provides a foundation for future research on test case design and testing goals, and enables deeper modeling of test design as a cognitive problem-solving process. To help enable future research, we also make our thematic interview coding and survey responses available[1].

---

[1] Available at https://doi.org/10.5281/zenodo.8106998.

2   Background

During software testing, input is applied to the SUT and the resulting output and other observations are captured [19]. These observations are compared to embedded expectations, called test oracles, to determine whether the SUT operated within expectations. Oracles often directly reflect the goals of test creation [2].

Testing can take place at multiple levels of granularity [19]. At the lowest level, unit tests examine small code elements in isolation with dependencies substituted for "mock" (static) results [21]. During integration testing, dependent units are combined. Then, during system testing, high-level functionality is invoked through interfaces. Tests can be written at all three levels as executable code, using frameworks such as JUnit, PyTest, or Postman [21].

Testing can also be performed manually. This is common during exploratory testing—where humans perform ad-hoc testing based on "tours" [24]—and acceptance testing—where customers offer feedback [22]. Tests are often written after code has been developed. However, test-driven development advocates for test creation before code development [14].

3   Related Work

Enoiu et al. hypothesized that our understanding of test design practices could be improved by formulating test design as a cognitive problem solving model [9]. Their exploratory work proposes that testers follow a seven stage process, including identification and definition of testing goals, knowledge analysis, strategy planning, information and resource organization, progress monitoring, and evaluation. Their research provides inspiration. In particular, we focus on the goal aspect of this model—filling in gaps in our understanding of the goals that testers focus on and how those goals influence test design. Our findings complement, and could lead to elaborations, in this model—as well as in other research that examines testing as a cognitive process, e.g., Aniche et al.'s framework for how developers approach test design [1] or Hale et al.'s cognitive model of how developers choose, implement, and evaluate debugging rules and strategies [12,13].

There has been limited research on how developers approach test case design in practice [9]. For example, Garousi et al. surveyed software developers to examine techniques, tools, methods, and metrics used in test design [10]. They observed that the usage of JUnit and IBM Rational testing tools have been overtaken by NUnit and web application tools. They also observed that organizations were still slow to adopt test-driven development. Eldh et al. asked experts to review 500 test cases written by novice testers [7]. They examined whether the tests matched the IEEE test case template, and also compared the mistakes made by the novices to those made by expert testers. Some mistakes were made by both groups, but others—such as not cleaning up after test execution—were made far more often by novices. Beer and Ramler also investigate how testers' experience impacts the effectiveness of testing methods and tools [3]. They briefly examine test design, noting that experience plays a large role in determining the

Table 1. Demographic information on interview participants.

ID	Role	Development Experience
P1	Software Developer	7.0 Years
P2	Senior Consultant, DevOps Architect	13.0 Years
P3	Software Developer	0.5 Years
P4	Software Developer	9.0 Years
P5	Software Developer	4.0 Years
P6	Software Developer	3.0 Years
P7	Test Manager, Scrum Master	10.5 Years
P8	Quality Manager	6.0 Years
P9	Software Developer	2.0 Years

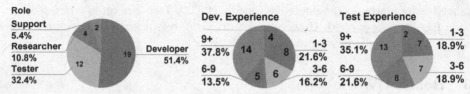

Fig. 1. Demographic information on survey participants.

effectiveness of the designed tests. Although all three studies examine aspects of test design, they—and other past studies—do not closely examine the influence of different goals on test design. Our study contributes to filling this gap.

4   Methodology

We hypothesize that developers follow distinct patterns when designing tests in relation to specific types of testing goals. To examine this hypothesis, we address the following research questions:

– **RQ1:** What types of goals do developers attempt to achieve when designing test cases, and how do they perceive the importance of these goal types?
– **RQ2:** What approaches are taken to design tests for these goal types?
  • **RQ2.1:** How many test cases are generally required to achieve a goal of a specific type?
  • **RQ2.2:** How many goals of each type are generally targeted by a test?
  • **RQ2.3:** Are there patterns that explain the relationship between the selected goal type and the resulting test design process?

To address these questions, we performed semi-structured interviews to gain insight into the test design process. We then performed a thematic analysis of the interview findings, and designed a follow-up survey for wide distribution to provide further evidence for the findings from the interview study, as well as additional quantitative and qualitative data to help answer our research questions.

4.1   Population and Sampling

We performed a series of nine interviews—selected through convenience sampling—with software developers in Gothenburg, Sweden. 37 unique respondents, from around the world, filled out the survey[2]. Table 1 outlines demographic information on the interview participants, including their role and development experience. Figure 1 summarizes the same information for the survey participants, with the addition of testing experience[3]. The interview and survey participants work in many domains—e.g., automotive, data analytics, and telecommunications.

Table 2. Interview questions, linked to research questions

RQ	Interview Question
N/A	1. What is your professional role?
	2. How much experience do you have in software development?
	3. Do you write test cases for code?
	4. How much experience do you have in software testing?
RQ1	5. Can you describe the goals that you target through the creation of test cases?
	6. What are you trying to achieve, avoid, or discover when creating test cases?
RQ2	7. What methods do you use to test your code?
	8. Describe the process you follow to design test cases
	9. What tools do you use to create test cases?
	10. Do you design test cases by yourself or in a group?
	11. How do you perform test design in order to achieve your goals?
	12. How have your testing methods changed over time?
RQ2.1	13. How many test cases do you tend to design for each goal you want to achieve?
RQ2.2	14. Do you design test cases to achieve one or multiple goals at once?
	15. How many goals do you target with each test case?
RQ2.3	16. Do you have any recurring test case design habits?
	17. Do you tend to design test cases in the same way as long as it works, or do you regularly search for new tools and approaches when designing test cases?
	18. How do you assess success or failure at achieving a goal?
	19. In case of failure to achieve a goal, what do you do to address problems?
	20. If you have achieved a goal, how do you proceed?

---

[2] One survey response was discarded, as a respondent answered twice. We retained the first response from this participant.

[3] Job titles have been merged when similar, e.g., "software tester" and "test engineer". The survey asked for both development and testing experience, while the interview only asked about years of development experience.

Table 3. Survey questions, linked to research questions. MC = multiple choice.

RQ	Survey Question	Format
N/A	1. What is your profession?	Free Text
	2. How many years of experience do you have with development?	MC
	3. How many years of experience do you have with software testing?	MC
RQ1	4. Do you have specific goals or types of goals when designing tests?	MC
	5. Please rank the following types of goals by ascending importance	MC (Grid)
(Q6–12 repeated for two goal types indicated as most important)		
RQ2	6. What testing techniques do you use for this goal?	MC, Free Text
	7. Please outline your typical design process when designing a test case to achieve the selected goal type.	Free Text
	8. What tools do you use to design tests for the selected goal type?	MC, Free Text
	9. What type of system do you design tests of this goal type for?	MC, Free Text
RQ2.1	10. How many tests do you typically design for a goal of this type?	MC
RQ2.2	11. How many goals of this type do you try to cover with a single test?	MC
RQ2.3	12. When designing test cases for this goal type, how often do you tend to re-use a particular test case design pattern?	MC, Free Text
	13. Do you design test cases by yourself or in a team?	MC
	14.Are there standards or pre-defined methods used within your organization when designing test cases or goals?	MC, Free Text
	15. How do development and process methodologies (e.g. Scrum/DevOps) influence the way you write tests to achieve different goal types?	Free Text

4.2   Data Collection

Interviews: Interviews were conducted electronically between January–February 2022. At the start of an interview, we gave a brief overview of the research topic. Interview responses were recorded, with permission, for analysis and observer triangulation. The interviews were semi-structured, following the interview guide in Table 2. However, follow-up questions were asked if further discussion was needed. The interviews were transcribed using speech-to-text software, then manually corrected through consultation with the original audio.

Survey: The survey consisted of mostly quantitative questions, with a small number of open-ended questions, and was designed according to the guidelines of Linåker et al. [15]. The questions are listed in Table 3. We focused on quantitative questions to decrease the time burden [16]. To complete the survey, the participants were required to answer all multiple-choice questions, but open-ended questions were optional. The survey was pre-tested with two participants, and the feedback was used to clarify wording and question order. The survey was conducted using Google Forms[4]. Links for the survey were then distributed via email, as well as on social media platforms.

---

[4] https://forms.gle/bhzpUCX9PdXbebiH8.

4.3   Data Analysis

Thematic Analysis: The interview transcripts were analyzed using thematic analysis, following the guidelines of Cruzes et al. [6] and Braun et al. [5]. To conduct this process, we independently examined transcripts, highlighting aspects relevant to the research questions ("codes"). The codes were subsequently organized and aggregated into sub-themes, which were clustered into themes.

After individual coding was completed for the first interview, we compared the codes. After the first iteration, our codes did not achieve an 80% similarity threshold. Therefore, we came to an agreement on sub-theme identification and code classification. After a second iteration, a similarity of over 80% was achieved. This process was conducted iteratively, and was paused for discussion.

An overview of the themes and sub-themes is shown in Table 4. These themes and sub-themes, as well as the underlying codes, were used both to directly assist in addressing the research questions as well as to design the survey instrument.

Survey Analysis: The survey consisted of both quantitative and open-ended qualitative questions. To analyze quantitative data, we used summary statistics (e.g., mean and variance of responses, separated by goal type) [23]. Responses to open-ended questions were assessed using thematic coding. As the survey was designed using the interview codes and themes, no additional themes or sub-themes were identified. Instead, survey responses enriched the existing codes.

Table 4. Themes (bold) and sub-themes from interviews.

Theme	Explanation
Experience	Interviewees' experiences in development and testing
Profession	Interviewees' job titles and responsibilities
Test Case Design	Encompasses sub-themes related to test design planning and execution
Design Process	Steps that interviewees take when designing tests to achieve their goals
Alone/In Group	Whether interviewees work individually or in a group during test design
Design Plan	Specific practices interviewees apply while test design
Design-Goal Relation	Factors that relate goals to test design (e.g., the number of tests to achieve a specific type of goal)
Recurring Habits	Common practices performed while designing test cases, (e.g., basing new tests on earlier tests)
Testing Goals	Specific goal types that interviewees design tests to achieve (e.g., functional correctness or performance)
Measuring Success	How interviewees determine whether goals are achieved (e.g., code coverage, customer satisfaction)
In Case of Failure	Steps taken when goals are not met (e.g., fault analysis)
In Case of Success	Steps taken when tests show goals are achieved (e.g. performing a demo to the client).
Testing Tools	Tools and technologies used to plan, design and execute tests (e.g., JUnit)
Testing Methods	Testing methods or practices (e.g., Test Driven Development) used by the interviewees to achieve their goals
Change Over Time	How interviewees evolved their testing practices following experiences, mistakes, and new technologies or practices.
System Type	The type of system tested (e.g., API end-points, embedded)

5   Results and Discussion

5.1   Goals and Goal Importance

Test design can not take place without *some* reason to design tests in the first place. During the interviews, we identified nine specific types of goals that testers pursue. These types are defined in Table 5. 76% of survey respondents confirmed that they have specified, pre-determined goals when designing test cases.

> **RQ1 (Goals):** The goal types identified include correctness, reliability, performance, quality, security, customer satisfaction, risk management, improving maintenance cost, and process improvement.

Table 5. Goal types identified in interviews.

Goal Type	Definition
Correctness	Tests assess SUT behavioral consistency with specifications
Reliability	Tests assess the ability of the SUT to remain available and failure-free in a specified environment over a period of time
Performance	Tests assess the ability of the SUT to meet performance goals (e.g., response time)
Quality	Tests assess whether the SUT meets specified quality goals (e.g., usability)
Security	Tests assess whether the SUT can protect data and services from unauthorized access
Customer Satisfaction	Tests assess whether the SUT meets the needs of a customer
Risk Management	Tests are used to forecast and evaluate threats and their possible impact on the SUT
Maintenance Cost	Tests are used to make SUT maintenance more efficient
Process Improvement	Tests are created as part of an attempt to improve the testing process (e.g., writing automated test code to replace manual testing)

Survey participants were asked to rank these goal types in importance. The results of this ranking are shown in Fig. 2, along with their average ranking. As might be expected, correctness was ranked as the most important goal (59%).

Interestingly, seven participants indicated correctness as their *least* important goal. At least three of these work with machine learning, where non-determinism often makes assessing correctness difficult. This could be a reason for the low ranking. Among the seven, risk management, performance, customer satisfaction, and maintenance cost reduction ranked highly.

Correctness was followed by reliability. These are followed by assessment of non-functional qualities—security, quality, and performance—and risk management. These goals are important, but are often secondary considerations. In some cases, the participants were highly split in their rankings—e.g., for security, quality, and risk—with a near-even split between high and low importance.

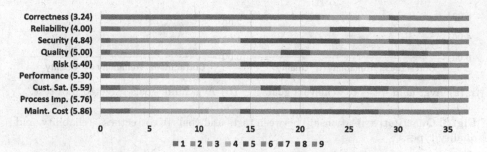

Fig. 2. Ranking of goal importance (1 = most important, 9 = least important). Average ranking indicated in parentheses.

Customer satisfaction and improving process or maintenance are seen, generally, as the least important goals. However, all goal types were highly important among a subset of participants. Some differences could be explained by the nature of the organization that the tester works for. If products are created for clients, then pleasing those clients is—naturally—a high priority. If the organization sells the product widely, then individuals do not have to give approval.

> **RQ1 (Goals):** Correctness was ranked most important, followed by reliability. Customer satisfaction and maintenance cost were seen as the least important. However, all goal types are important for some.

In the survey, we asked participants to answer a set of questions for two chosen goal types. To avoid drawing biased conclusions, we primarily focus in the following subsections on goal types that we received at least five responses for—**correctness** (33 responses), **reliability** (12 responses), and **quality** (8 responses)—or on observations not dependent on specific goal types.

5.2 Quantitative Relationship Between Goal Types and Tests

Test Cases Per Goal: Figure 3(a) shows the average number of tests needed to achieve a goal. Correctness requires the most tests per goal, on average (6.42). Advice on test design often advocates for creating multiple tests for functions that, individually, are simple and focused on a single outcome or facet of the tested function. For example, a common (and highly debated[5]) recommendation is to use a single assertion per test case. Multiple interviewees echoed this advice. Figure 3(a) indicates that this advice is followed, and that multiple tests are needed to demonstrate that a complex function fulfills its specification.

---

[5] E.g., https://softwareengineering.stackexchange.com/questions/394557/should-test s-perform-a-single-assertion-or-are-multiple-related-assertions-acce.

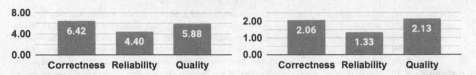

(a) Avg. num. tests to achieve a goal.   (b) Avg. num. goals targeted in a test.

Fig. 3. Quantitative relationship between tests and goals of correctness, reliability, and quality types.

Reliability goals, which typically take different measurements (e.g., failure rate or availability) and compare them to thresholds, require fewer test cases to assess. However, multiple tests are still required to assess a single goal.

> **RQ2.1 (Tests Per Goal):** Several tests are needed to assess whether a single correctness, reliability, or quality goal is met. Correctness requires the most, an average of 6.42 tests per goal.

Goals Per Test Case: Figure 3(b) shows the average number of goals targeted in a single test—on average, approximately two correctness or quality goals, or one reliability goal. This offers further indication that testers tend to focus on creating focused tests over large tests that target many goals at once.

> **RQ2.2 (Goals Per Test):** A single test case tends to focus on 1–2 correctness, reliability, or quality goals.

5.3   Influence of Goals on Test Design

In this subsection, we will explore multiple factors that affect and illustrate the relationship between testing goals and test design practices.

"Typical" Design Process: Survey participants were asked to outline their typical test design process for their selected goal types. Test design for correctness often starts with examination of documentation and discussion with stakeholders. The gathered knowledge is then processed during brainstorming:

> "Identify basic tests to use as foundation..., discussions with others ..., questioning, setting up environments with test data, reviewing tests" - SP10
>
> "I design a simulation of that components usage, and compare with the hand-written solution (done in my head)." - SP3
>
> "I clarify requirements, do mindmaps and discuss with different oracles..." - SP12

Many respondents start by designing basic "happy path" tests for a function showing that the standard outcomes of the function are met. Then—often iteratively—tests are designed to cover additional scenarios:

"Write tests, write minimal code to make tests pass, examine if there are features or corner cases that don't have tests yet, go to step one." - SP13

Respondents stressed the importance of simplicity:

"I try to isolate requirements and design as simple a test case as possible ... I focus on making the test easy to understand; partly by making it small and independent ... I may write multiple test cases for one requirement because there may be multiple modes of failure." - SP4

There was emphasis on considering perspectives, tools, and environments:

"... cover all aspects of the test, such as—bare minimum—up to maximum range of values, different user types if they exist, positive/negative aspects, etc." - SP30

"1. try to understand the functionality specification 2. try to understand the test environment needed 3. trying to understand what tools are needed 4. trying to understand acceptance criteria 5. create test steps" - SP19

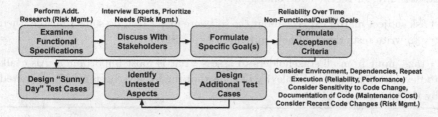

Fig. 4. Typical design process for correctness, with modifications for other goals.

We asked interviewees to describe their typical test design process. Although specific goal types were not considered at that time, their comments largely echo the process outlined above for correctness and illustrated in Fig. 4. Testers collect information, brainstorm, then iteratively create test cases until all functional outcomes are covered—focusing on individually simple and understandable tests.

Enoiu et al. proposed that testers follow a seven stage process—identification and definition of testing goals, knowledge analysis, strategy planning, information and resource organization, progress monitoring, and evaluation [9]. Our observations suggest that this model is largely followed when testers pursue correctness goals. Some aspects of this process may be given more or less weight at times—or even skipped entirely—depending on the form of testing or due to personal experience and preferences. For example, during unit testing, there may not be active discussions with stakeholders. However, this basic process offers a basic outline for discussions on test design.

The responses written about other goal types suggest that the process in Fig. 4 is followed—in a modified form—when pursuing the other goals. For example, the core differences for reliability-demonstrating tests are that (a) reliability must be measured over a period of time, and (b), the SUT should be tested in a realistic environment—which may contain unreliable dependencies. For both reliability and performance, it was also suggested that tests must execute operations multiple times:

> "... stress test both that failing dependencies are correctly handled and that failures don't happen too often over a longer time of nominal operation." - SP4

For quality goals, tests examine both functional correctness and attainment of non-functional properties:

> "... to improve the quality, there could be some overlap of functional and non functional requirements testing here." - SP7

To reduce maintenance costs, testers should design tests that are sensitive to inadvertent code change and use tests to document the code:

> "... ensure that the changes to the interface are documented through tests, with the goal of making tests that would be sensitive to inadvertent changes ..." - SP21

Risk management often requires interviews and research, prioritization, and understanding of recent code changes:

> "I ask subject matter experts about the software under test, do some research, then try to write tests that will help mitigate risk." - SP33

> "I take input from all stakeholders to assess what is most important ... Also talk to developers to assess complexity of code that might have been mostly impacted by the change ..." - SP12

RQ2.3 (Relationship Factors): Test design for correctness goals starts with knowledge gathering and brainstorming, then design of "happy path" tests, then design of tests covering alternative outcomes. When assessing reliability or performance, tests should utilize a realistic environment, assess behavior over time, and be executed multiple times. Tests for quality blend functional and non-functional aspects. Tests can reduce maintenance costs by documenting and detecting changes. Risk management requires research, discussion, and awareness of change.

Use of Recurring Design Patterns: Survey participants were asked if they follow recurring patterns when designing tests for different types of goals. This could include, for example, using past test cases as templates or following specific structures for writing test cases for that goal. Figure 5 indicates that the majority of respondents use such patterns as a starting point:

> "... I overwhelmingly look for similar tests that I can adapt ... initially, then use it to get to the happy path. Following that I'll typically duplicate the test and ensure that some critical conditionals are covered. If it feels like there isn't a test case I can steal, or that setup is too onerous, then I will manually repeat the happy path process until it works before considering adding a test case or two." - SP21

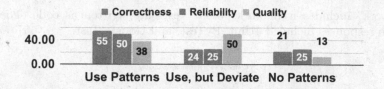

Fig. 5. % of participants re-using patterns when designing tests for correctness, reliability, and quality goals.

> **RQ2.3 (Relationship Factors):** Testers often start test design following patterns. For quality goals, testers often deviate from these patterns.

System Type: The type of system may influence the goal types pursued and their importance. In Fig. 6, we indicate the percentage of respondents who target various system types. We observe a potential relationship between reliability's importance and the level of required trust in a SUT.

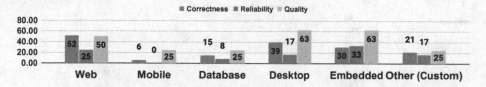

Fig. 6. % of respondents designing tests for correctness, reliability, and quality goals for different system types.

Embedded systems make up the largest proportion of reliability responses. Such systems have high safety demands, and testers may need to show evidence of correctness, reliability, and quality. No respondents indicated that they develop reliability tests for mobile applications. This may be due to the *lack* of criticality in such programs. This observation should be further explored in future work.

> **RQ2.3 (Relationship Factors):** Demonstrating reliability is a focus for embedded systems. Reliability may not be important for mobile apps.

Practices and Tools: The testing practices employed—as well as the tools—may differ between goal types. Figure 7 indicates the percentage of respondents who employed different approaches, including levels of granularity (e.g., unit testing), focuses (e.g., functional versus non-functional testing), and other practices (e.g., mocking, test-driven development). Figure 8 does the same for different types of tools. For both, the initial set of options were derived from interviews. However, some respondents suggested additional options. "Automated Testing

Framework" includes frameworks where tests are written as code. The most common responses included JUnit, PyTest, and Google Test.

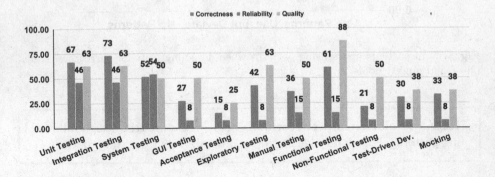

Fig. 7. % of respondents performing testing practices when designing tests for correctness, reliability, and quality goals.

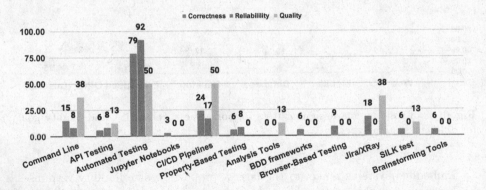

Fig. 8. % of respondents using different tools when designing tests for correctness, reliability, and quality goals.

All three goal types are pursued at all major levels of granularity. However, reliability is relatively uncommon when using human-driven practices—i.e., acceptance, exploratory, and manual testing. Reliability is often demonstrated by executing tests repeatedly or over a period of time [19]. This typically requires automation. In addition, reliability is often attained before presenting the SUT to a client, reducing the importance of acceptance testing. Test design for reliability also typically does not seem to use mocking or test-driven development, perhaps because reliability is most meaningful for a near-final product.

In contrast, quality is often a focus of GUI and human-driven practices. Some typical quality types, such as usability, rely on replicating the typical user experience. This may lead to prominent use of human-driven practices. Correctness, as the "default" goal of testing, necessitates use of almost all practices, with the exception of acceptance testing. Acceptance testing is generally conducted at a late stage of development—when developers have a product to demonstrate [22]. At this stage, correctness testing may have largely concluded.

Automated testing frameworks, CI/CD pipelines, API frameworks, and command-line scripting are used for all three goal types. Property-based testing tools, which generate random input to violate properties, are used to assess correctness or reliability, but not quality goals. Test management tools, such as Jira and its Xray plug-in, are used for correctness and quality. However, they are less useful for reliability, which depends primarily on executing tests on demand.

> **RQ2.3 (Relationship Factors):** Reliability is often pursued using code-focused, automated practices on a near-final product. Quality is often pursued using human and GUI-focused practices. Acceptance testing is rare for correctness and reliability, but more common for quality. Automated and API testing frameworks, CI/CD pipelines, and command-line scripting are common for all goal types.

Organizational Factors: Organizational policies, process, and team composition could also influence test design, regardless of the goal type. We asked survey participants whether there are test design constraints enforced by their organization or legal regulations. Figure 9(a) indicates that constraints affect the majority (48.60%) percent of respondents.

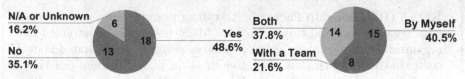

(a) Whether participants must follow company or legal policies during test design.

(b) Whether participants design tests alone or in teams.

Fig. 9. Organizational factors that may affect test design.

We also asked respondents whether they design tests alone, in a team, or both, as collaborative design may lead to different tests than design by a single tester. Figure 9(b) indicates that a slight plurality (40.50%) work along, but that many work in team settings at all (21.60%) or some (37.80%) times. Interviewees suggested that the need for teamwork increases with project complexity:

"If design strategies are needed, teamwork is mandatory." - P4

In a group setting, test design is also often led by test leads with assistance from others working under them:

> "Test leads can do a pretty good job there. So, trust your test leads." - P2

Survey participants were also asked about the influence of development processes on test design. Many felt that there was no influence—other than the positive increase in the use of CI tools and DevOps—or even that testers are the ones that influence development practices:

> "Most often we influence them... We are also the gateway that demands documentation." - SP19

Others discussed positive and negative aspects of short development cycles:

> "Short cycle times encouraged by an agile-like methodology do make it difficult sometimes to add test cases, but some of our PRs tend to be quite self contained (i.e. the change is proposed with several test cases)." - SP21

Multiple respondents indicated that agile processes can be beneficial for getting feedback and offering structure:

> "It helps me to be structured. Keep track of things, like if all the functionalities are covered by the test suits are not." - SP7

Respondents also warned that rigid enforcement of practices can waste testing resources that could otherwise be devoted to more productive goals:

> "large suite that must pass ... makes the teams 'waste' time when making sure that as many as possible checks will pass when pushing to master." - SP23

RQ2.3 (Relationship Factors): Test design can be influenced by process, organization, and team structure. Many testers are constrained by organization or regulatory policies. Testers perform design individually somewhat more often, but also often work in teams. Testers feel they can influence development methodologies, and that agile processes offer feedback and structure. However, there are positive and negative aspects of short release cycles, and rigid practice enforcement can waste time.

---

6   Threats to Validity

Conclusion Validity: The number of responses may affect conclusion reliability. However, our thematic findings reached saturation within nine interviews, and the qualitative survey results fell within the same themes and sub-themes. Further interviews or survey results could enrich our findings, but may not produce significant additions.

Construct Validity: The interviews or survey could have missing or confusing questions, and there was opportunity for misinterpretation. There is also a risk that participants may not be familiar with particular terminology. However, as all participants had prior experience in testing, this risk is minimized. We also provided a brief introduction before the interviews and the survey to further reduce this risk. The use of semi-structured interviews allowed us to ask follow-up questions. We also conducted pre-testing of the survey.

External Validity: The generalizability of our findings is influenced by the number and background of participants. Our participants represent a variety of development roles, experience levels, and product domains. Therefore, we believe that our results are relatively applicable to the software development industry.

Internal Validity: We applied thematic coding, a qualitative practice that suffers from known bias threats. We mitigated these threats by performing independent coding and comparing results, finding sufficient agreement. We make our results available for further analysis, increasing transparency.

7 Conclusion

Our interviews with testers suggest nine common types of goals pursued when designing test cases, as well as an indication of the relative importance of each goal type. Our findings also shed light on the process of test design for different goals, as well as the factors that can influence this design process.

This research provides a basis for understanding how test design is influenced by particular types of testing goals. Our observations should be confirmed and expanded in future work with further, focused data collection. In particular, we plan to further explore the collective impact of organization factors, team-versus-individual design, and testing goals on the design process. We would also like to explore situations where multiple types of goals are targeted simultaneously during test design. We additionally plan to expand our model of the test design process, with a focus on how knowledge of tester practices can enhance automated test generation.

References

1. Aniche, M., Treude, C., Zaidman, A.: How developers engineer test cases: an observational study. IEEE Trans. Softw. Eng. **48**(12), 4925–4946 (2022)
2. Barr, E., Harman, M., McMinn, P., Shahbaz, M., Yoo, S.: The oracle problem in software testing: a survey. IEEE Trans. Softw. Eng. **41**(5), 507–525 (2015)
3. Beer, A., Ramler, R.: The role of experience in software testing practice. In: 2008 34th Euromicro Conference Software Engineering and Advanced Applications, pp. 258–265 (2008)
4. Bentley, J.E., Bank, W., Charlotte, N.: Software testing fundamentals-concepts, roles, and terminology. In: Proceedings of SAS Conference, pp. 1–12 (2005)
5. Braun, V., Clarke, V.: Using thematic analysis in psychology. Qual. Res. Psychol. **3**(2), 77–101 (2006)
6. Cruzes, D.S., Dyba, T.: Recommended steps for thematic synthesis in software engineering. In: 2011 International Symposium on Empirical Software Engineering and Measurement, pp. 275–284 (2011)

7. Eldh, S., Hansson, H., Punnekkat, S.: Analysis of mistakes as a method to improve test case design. In: 2011 Fourth IEEE International Conference on Software Testing, Verification and Validation, pp. 70–79 (2011)
8. Enoiu, E., Feldt, R.: Towards human-like automated test generation: perspectives from cognition and problem solving. In: 2021 IEEE/ACM 13th International Workshop on Cooperative and Human Aspects of Software Engineering (CHASE), pp. 123–124 (2021)
9. Enoiu, E., Tukseferi, G., Feldt, R.: Towards a model of testers' cognitive processes: software testing as a problem solving approach. In: 2020 IEEE 20th International Conference on Software Quality, Reliability and Security Companion (QRS-C), pp. 272–279 (2020)
10. Garousi, V., Zhi, J.: A survey of software testing practices in Canada. J. Syst. Softw. 86(5), 1354–1376 (2013)
11. Gay, G.: One-size-fits-none? Improving test generation using context-optimized fitness functions. In: 2019 IEEE/ACM 12th International Workshop on Search-Based Software Testing (SBST), pp. 3–4 (2019)
12. Hale, D.P., Haworth, D.A.: Towards a model of programmers' cognitive processes in software maintenance: a structural learning theory approach for debugging. J. Softw. Maint. Res. Pract. 3(2), 85–106 (1991)
13. Hale, J.E., Sharpe, S., Hale, D.P.: An evaluation of the cognitive processes of programmers engaged in software debugging. J. Softw. Maint. Res. Pract. 11(2), 73–91 (1999)
14. Karac, I., Turhan, B.: What do we (really) know about test-driven development? IEEE Softw. 35(4), 81–85 (2018)
15. Linaker, J., Sulaman, S.M., Höst, M., de Mello, R.M.: Guidelines for conducting surveys in software engineering v. 1.1. Lund University (2015)
16. Litwin, M.S., Fink, A.: How to Measure Survey Reliability and Validity, vol. 7. Sage (1995)
17. McLeod, R., Jr., Everett, G.D.: Software Testing: Testing Across the Entire Software Development Life Cycle. Wiley, Hoboken (2007)
18. Newell, A., Simon, H.A., et al.: Human Problem Solving, vol. 104. Prentice-Hall, Englewood Cliffs (1972)
19. Pezze, M., Young, M.: Software Test and Analysis: Process, Principles, and Techniques. Wiley, Hoboken (2006)
20. Quadri, S., Farooq, S.U.: Software testing-goals, principles, and limitations. Int. J. Comput. Appl. 6(9), 1 (2010)
21. Runeson, P.: A survey of unit testing practices. IEEE Softw. 23(4), 22–29 (2006)
22. Sommerville, I.: Software Engineering, 9th edn. Addison-Wesley Publishing Company, USA (2010)
23. Upton, G., Cook, I.: A Dictionary of Statistics 3E. Oxford University Press (2014)
24. Whittaker, J.A.: Exploratory Software Testing: Tips, Tricks, Tours, and Techniques to Guide Test Design. Pearson Education (2009)

Multi-device, Robust, and Integrated Android GUI Testing: A Conceptual Framework

Riccardo Coppola$^{(\boxtimes)}$ ⓘD, Luca Ardito ⓘD, and Marco Torchiano ⓘD

Department of Control and Computer Engineering, Polytechnic University of Turin,
Corso Castelfidardo, 34/d, 10138 Torino, Italy
{riccardo.coppola,luca.ardito,marco.torchiano}@polito.it

Abstract. Android GUI (Graphical User Interface) testing is often over-looked by developers, even if it holds the potential to guarantee sufficient quality for the apps. It is typically regarded as a burdensome activity. High maintenance costs, fragmentation, fragility, and flakiness of the test artifacts are the main hurdles for wider adoption in practice. This article identifies the main modules that could enable efficient and robust mobile testing in continuous development environments. On top of them, we sketch the infrastructure of a conceptual framework for the generation, execution, and maintenance of mobile test suites. We also present a call to action for software testers, developers, and researchers towards the framework realization in practice.

Keywords: GUI testing · Mobile Testing · Android development · Testing Framework

1 Introduction

According to recent analyses, Android has achieved the highest overall market share among all - not just mobile - operating systems[1]. Nowadays, Android apps have reached a very high complexity in terms of both graphical appearance and provided features. The above characteristics, and the fact that most interactions with Android apps take place through their GUI (Graphical User Interface) widgets, justify the need for thorough employment of GUI testing techniques.

Many tools for automating Android GUI testing are available in the market [15]. However, research has shown that manual testing through the GUI is still preferred to test automation because many challenges about the latter are still lingering [18]. In recent years, academic literature and tools from the industry have tackled many mobile-specific GUI testing challenges. However, to the best of our knowledge, no comprehensive approach or framework is available, which considers all the principal issues of the three phases of the test cases lifecycle: generation, execution, and maintenance.

---

[1] https://gs.statcounter.com/os-market-share#monthly-202111--202303.

© IFIP International Federation for Information Processing 2023
Published by Springer Nature Switzerland AG 2023
S. Bonfanti et al. (Eds.): ICTSS 2023, LNCS 14131, pp. 115–125, 2023.
https://doi.org/10.1007/978-3-031-43240-8_8

Here we put forward a comprehensive conceptual framework for mobile GUI testing: to do so, we summarize the most critical challenges of the practice, survey the existing techniques and tools tackling them, and propose an agenda for practitioners aiming at incorporating mobile GUI testing in continuous development pipelines.

2 Mobile GUI Testing: State of the Art and Practice

Both industry and academia have proposed many different tools and techniques to perform GUI testing on mobile applications and identified several challenges for the practice. We adopt two orthogonal classification schemes to categorize mobile GUI testing techniques. The process of GUI testing revolves around the identification of elements on the GUI. The properties and means to identify the elements are called *locators*. Test cases also require *oracles*, i.e., properties that have to be verified with assertions to verify that the test executed correctly. GUI testing techniques can be classified according to how the elements on the GUI are identified (i.e., based on the type of locator that is used) [1]:

- *Coordinate-based* GUI testing techniques identify widgets through exact on-screen candidates. Due to major volatility of such properties, these techniques have been largely abandoned in practice.
- *Layout-based* GUI testing techniques identify widgets through properties that are declared in the Android layout descriptor of the current screen (e.g., ids, text content, content description, widget type).
- *Visual*, or *Image recognition-based* GUI testing is based on computer vision techniques, utilizing screen captures as locators. State-of-the-art image-based approaches leverage techniques ranging from pixel-per-pixel comparison to more elaborate matching algorithms (e.g., SIFT, SURF or Akaze feature vectors [3]).

GUI testing techniques can also be classified according to how the test sequences are generated. Adopting a taxonomy proposed by Linares-Vazquez et al. [19]:

- *Automation APIs* or *Scripted* testing tools allow manual writing of test scripts, using platform-specific scripting languages; test scripts can then be executed using dedicated or universal test runners.
- *Capture & Replay* (C&R) testing tools automatically generate test scripts from sequences of user interactions with the AUT (Application Under Test), thus 'capturing' (recording) real usage scenarios [10].
- *Automated Test Input Generation* techniques automate the definition of the test sequences; the generation can be based on heuristics (e.g., a random selection of locators and verification of the occurrence of exceptions or bugs) or on the coverage of a GUI model, which can be itself automatically generated [5].

Despite the availability of tools for Android GUI testing, research has highlighted that the practice is often conducted manually by developers [7]. The reasons behind the limited adoption of automated tools are manifold and specific to the mobile domain:

Fragmentation: One of the main issues for Android GUI testing is the intrinsic *Fragmentation* of the domain: developers must verify and validate the compatibility of the AUT with multiple target configurations where it may be deployed [16]. Such configurations include screen sizes, screen densities and aspect ratios (*hardware fragmentation*) or different versions of the operating system where the AUT has to be installed (*software fragmentation*). The fragmentation issue particularly plagues the Android domain because of the multitude of devices running the operating system and the coexistence of many releases of the o.s. (Operating System) that receive parallel support. Therefore, the tester must run identical test sequences on multiple devices, either real or emulated. This repetition represents an obstacle to the adoption of continuous integration/development practices.

Fragility and Flakiness: Test scripts (either manually written or automatically generated) for mobile applications need critical maintenance to cope with even small changes in the application GUI during its life cycle. This issue is typically referred to as *Fragility* and is considered among the main hindrances to a wide adoption of GUI testing tools [9]. Fragility can be caused by changes in the GUI layout properties that invalidate layout-based locators and oracles or by aesthetic changes of the widgets that invalidate visual locators and oracles. The Fragility in GUI tests requires the tester to analyze the outcome of each test execution carefully. This action is needed because functionally valid test sequences may lead to false positives due to the inability to find the locators, and proper refactoring is therefore needed for fragile locators. Test cases are hampered also by a high level of *flakiness*, i.e., they may have a non-deterministic outcome over repeated runs. Flaky executions can be related to unpredictable execution times, network availability, concurrency in the test devices, and interaction with the execution environment [12].

Limited generalizability: The high complexity of the GUI and the many different ways of composing the individual screens (with orchestrations of *Activities*, *Fragments* and other components) pose relevant generalizability issues to GUI testing techniques. It is not trivial to identify universal models able to represent the GUI states of any application at the desired granularity. Several efforts have been provided for mutation testing [11]. As well, to the best of our knowledge, no coverage models have been defined yet in the academic literature [6]. Therefore, evaluating the quality of generated test sequences or comparing multiple testing tools' results over multiple AUTs is still a complex task.

Hybrid application testing: Finally, even though *Native* mobile applications still represent the vast majority in the Android marketplace, many different frameworks are available to construct *hybrid* or *progressive* web applications that are rendered on a mobile browser to guarantee a similar – if not equivalent

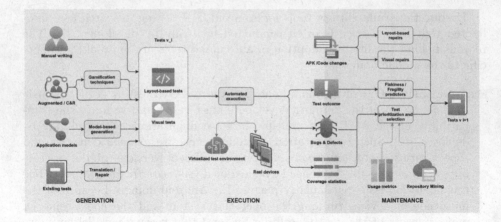

Fig. 1. Modules of the GEM framework: high-level view

– user experience to that of apps specifically designed for the mobile system. Such frameworks typically define components using properties that differ from those specified in the layout files of native apps, therefore making scripted *layout-based* testing tools harder to generalize to all Android apps.

3   Conceptualization of the GEM Framework

The proposed framework, summarized in Fig. 1, is structured according to the three main life cycle phases: Generation, Execution, and Maintenance (GEM).

3.1   Test Generation and Translation

The test generation module of the framework provides new test sequences to add to the test suite for the AUT. The tools should expose multiple and coexisting ways of defining test cases to generate test sequences sharing a common syntax. As the first basic way of developing test cases, the tools shall allow traditional *manual writing* of test sequences in the specific syntax adopted by the tool.

The framework should also offer ways of directly capture the interaction of testers with the GUI of the AUT through the implementation of *Capture & Replay* test sequence generation mechanisms. The literature about C&R testing has recently witnessed some evolution for the concept, in the form of *augmented* layers providing live information and suggestions to the tester to generate input sequences and assertions. C&R test case generation can also be enriched by incorporating concepts that can increase testers' user experience and engagement during the test capture sessions. Recent Software Engineering literature has explored the benefits offered by the implementation of gamification mechanics in software testing. Gamification consists in applying concepts that are proper of game design to other practices, e.g. scoring mechanisms and leaderboards, or graphical live feedback [14]. Gamification has been applied to the phase of test case generation in Capture & Replay tools, where the testers can be incentivized in performing more thorough exploration by the usage of scoring schemes, leaderboards, progression indicators and live feedback [13].

Test generation should be guided by knowledge of the structure of the GUI and the nature of the AUT. Traditional model-based approaches, which mainly apply coverage-based heuristics on automatically built graph-based models, can be paired with AI-based test generation techniques. The latter apply learning mechanisms to automatically adapt general test sequences written in natural language to the specific AUT after classifying it and its activities (i.e., individual screens shown to the user). AI-based test case generation can significantly lower the effort in writing test case sequences and allow stakeholders without software development skills, to easily write test cases without having access to the application code or knowing the internal GUI structure of the AUT [4].

In our conceptualization, testing tools should allow the coexistence of variants of the same test sequences, based on *layout-based* and *visual* locators and oracles. The benefits of having both variants of test cases are manifold. Firstly, it enhances the expressive power of the test suite since the type of bugs found by the two approaches are different: layout-based oracles can only verify the GUI structure and properties of the AUT, while the application of image-recognition based assertions can only spot defects in the visual rendering of the widgets. Similarly, the two types of locators and oracles are fragile to a complementary type of changes in the GUI of the AUT: pictorial changes invalidate visual test cases, whilst changes in the layout properties invalidate the Layout-based test cases. In our conceptualized framework, we envision applying a translation-based mechanism, allowing the automated creation (or regeneration) of layout-based locators and oracles from visual ones and vice versa. Such an approach has already been proven effective for both the web and mobile domains [8,17] in enhancing the test suites' effectiveness and mitigating graphic fragilities.

In the generation phase of the framework, we identify a primary research gap in the generation of visual test cases and the application of gamified mechanics. Both methodologies have been explored for general-purpose or web-based tools, but not specifically for the Android domain.

3.2   Test Execution

Once the test cases are generated, the Execution phase must take place for each test sequence. The most important issue to tackle in this phase is the software and hardware fragmentation of the Android OS and devices. Therefore, it is fundamental to pair real devices with virtualized environments emulating most of the available hardware, software and graphical configurations the AUT must provide compatibility.

Several infrastructures have been conceptualized to provide virtual testbeds to deploy mobile applications. Infrastructure-as-a-Service solutions have been provided to perform layout-based GUI testing or performance testing [2]. Existing commercial tools (e.g., test.io) allow crowd-sourced execution of test cases on real hardware devices; however, they mainly allow pure manual and exploratory test sequences. In general, the current state of the art and practice lacks ways to automatically and extensively execute image-recognition based test suites on multiple configurations. At the end of the test execution, we envision the generation of complete test reporting, including the test cases outcome, found defects, statistics and analyses of the execution issues that can lead to refinement and enhancements of the test suites.

We envision that each testing environment should track the quantity of fragile or *flaky* test cases. A possible solution to identify flaky test cases is to execute each test case multiple times in order to flag the test cases as passing (all executions are passing), flaky (some executions are passing) or failing (all executions fail). Failing tests can furtherly be divided into true positives (i.e., test cases failing due to real defects in the AUT) and fragile tests (i.e., test cases failing due to unrelated changes in the AUT). Sets of change-based metrics have been defined in the empirical software engineering literature to measure the number of fragile tests and their impact on the maintenance effort for the test suite [9]. The objective of fragility tracking is to mark the test cases as fragile if they require too much intervention during the evolution of the AUT. Other modules of the framework can use this flagging activity to aid test prioritization.

Regarding the *Execution* phase of our framework, we identify a primary research gap about the coverage measurement when mobile test cases are executed since no coverage model for mobile applications has been widely accepted by research in the field. Albeit several precise coverage models exist (e.g., multi-device coverage proposed by Vilkomir et al. to measure the reduction of the fragmentation issue [22]), a universally generalizable coverage model is still missing.

3.3 Test Maintenance and Repair

The literature highlights that test scripts maintained manually (either layout-based or visual) can be tedious and costly when they become obsolete. Since mobile applications typically have a quick evolution, the cost of test case maintenance can be required frequently and become unsustainable for developers.

In our framework, we envision a module in charge of automatically adapting the test cases to the changes in the APK, in the GUI pictorial appearance and the application code. Since two equivalent sets of locators and oracles are maintained for the test suite, both layout properties and visual locators have to be updated automatically. Several approaches have been proposed for the automated repair of test cases. Some tools are based on event-sequence models describing the behaviour of the application and abstracting the changes made to the GUI between different releases of the same application. These tools, however, are mainly aimed at preserving the connection between different screens of the AUT traversed during the execution of test sequences and still require the manual intervention of the testers for the preparation of the original models that guide the testing process. Alternative model-less approaches rely on the definition of similarity indexes for the widgets to be interacted during test cases to identify locators that should be treated as the same one even in the presence of changes in their properties or visual appearance [23].

Even incorporating a sophisticated mechanism for test case repair, some test sequences may still need manual maintenance during the evolution of the application. The execution of test cases on multiple devices and configurations, especially when the GUI has to be rendered and verified through computer vision algorithms, can also become unsustainable if the test suite grows significantly. Therefore, a module for the maintenance of test cases should include mechanisms to prioritize and select them to reduce the execution and maintenance time for the subset of test sequences to execute in continuous integration and development settings. Test prioritization should be guided from metrics resulting from the test case execution module, e.g., generated bugs and coverage reports. At the same time, the test prioritization and selection module should incorporate diverse information gathered from repository mining. Usage metrics gathered through mobile APIs on pilot users can help identify the activities and user interaction sequences on which test cases should focus. Suppose the AUT is available as an open-source repository (e.g., on GitHub). In that case, mechanisms can be developed to mine and interpret the issues left by contributors to the project to identify the most critical sections of the code. As well, if the AUT is released on a marketplace, techniques of marketplace analysis can be deployed to mine the user reviews and identify typical usage patterns leading to crashes.

We identify important research gaps regarding the Maintenance phase of our framework. To the best of our knowledge, no automated mobile test suite repair tools have been validated with real-world test suites. Similarly, no prioritization model has been specifically described for mobile GUI test cases used for regression testing, and existing ones are mostly applied to non-functional properties (e.g., for security testing [21]).

4   Discussion

The proposed framework constitutes a vision for the modules that may enable a mobile testing pipeline incorporating multiple means to generate test cases, execute tests on both real and virtual devices, and ease test suite maintenance along the evolution of a mobile app. In our vision, a platform implementing all the modules described in the framework would guarantee:

– Seamless Continuous Integration execution with tracking of test metrics on multiple device and screen configurations. This could enable writing the tests once and run them on all devices (solving the *hardware fragmentation* issue);
– Incremented robustness of tests to changes in structural layout and visual appearance, reduced maintenance effort, and reduced time to find bugs when tests are used with regression purposes. This would allow writing the test once and run it for the whole mobile app lifecycle (solving the *test fragility* issue).

Currently, no testing tool, either available on the market or described in the literature, implements all the features described in our framework. The generation, execution and maintenance pipeline could be partly obtained by combining multiple available instruments. Without claims of exhaustiveness, Table 1 reports, for each module of the framework, existing examples from academia and industry. As reported in the table, there is a high availability of tools for manual test case generation and acquisition of test sequences through the Capture & Replay technique. Several of these tools come embedded in the Android development environment (namely, UIAutomator, Espresso and the related Recorder). Many tools, mostly academic, have been developed for model-based generation of mobile test sequences. Several commercial platforms for crowdsourced testing on multiple devices are also available. Definition and execution of visual test cases can still be performed by utilizing multi-domain visual testing tools (e.g., Sikuli or EyeAutomate) that can be applied to emulated devices on a desktop environment. Conversely, most of the modules in the frameworks related to the maintenance of test cases are not fully implemented by available tools. Some of them are still in early-stage academic investigation (e.g., fragility prediction mechanisms and translation-based tools). However, academic literature in the field proposed heuristics and metrics that can be adapted as add-ons to existing open-source testing frameworks. Finally, research on gamified mechanisms is still in an early stage, and mainly tied to the practice of software engineering in general, with very few verticalizations on the practice of desktop and web application testing.

Table 1. Available tools implementing modules of the framework

Module	Tool	Origin	Open-Source	URL/Notes
Manual test case writing	UIAutomator	Industry	Yes	https://developer.android.com/training/testing/ui-automator
	Espresso	Industry	Yes	https://developer.android.com/training/testing/espresso
	Appium	Industry	Yes	https://appium.io
	Ranorex	Industry	No	https://lp.ranorex.com
	Calabash	Industry	Yes	https://github.com/calabash/calabash-android
Gamified test case generation	–	–	–	Described in academic research for web application testing
Model-based generation	MobiGUITAR	Academia	Yes	https://github.com/AndrewZcc/mobiGUITAR/actions
	Tricentis Tosca	Industry	No	https://www.tricentis.com/products/automate-continuous-testing-tosca/
	Quantum	Industry	No	https://www.perfecto.io/integrations/quantum
	STOAT	Academia	Yes	https://github.com/tingsu/Stoat
	Droidbot	Academia	Yes	https://github.com/honeynet/droidbot
Translation-based tools	TOGGLE	Academia	No	[8]
Capture & Replay	TestProject	Industry	No	https://testproject.io/mobile-test-recorder/
	Repeato	Industry	No	https://www.repeato.app
	RERAN	Industry	No	https://www.androidreran.com
	Espresso Test Recorder	Industry	Yes	https://developer.android.com/studio/test/espresso-test-recorder
	Barista	Academia	Yes	https://github.com/AdevintaSpain/Barista
Automated Execution Environments	Test.io	Industry	No	http://test.io
	CrowdSprint	Industry	No	http://crowdsprint.com
	Firebase TestLab	Industry	No	https://firebase.google.com/products/test-lab
Visual Test Case Execution	Sikuli	Academia	Yes	http://sikulix.com
	EyeAutomate	Industry	No	http://eyeautomate.com
Test Repair Mechanisms	GUIDER	Academia	No	[23]
Fragility Prediction	Coppola et al	Academia	No	[9]
Test Prioritization and Selection	Michaels et al	Academia	No	[20]

5   Call to Action

Based on the proposed framework and the relative mapping to existing and missing tools, we can issue a call to action for three distinct stakeholders:

- *Software Testers* can leverage the framework to identify the tools needed to generate test cases efficiently and adopt instruments for each of the categories for which tools are already available (♦);
- *Tool developers* can leverage the framework to assess the existing tools against the most crucial needs of the practice of GUI testing in industrial settings. Practitioners can find opportunities for new implementations in the categories of tools that have been – to the best of our knowledge – explored exclusively by academic research, e.g. gamified testing tools, test repair and fragility prediction mechanisms (■);
- *Researchers* can leverage the framework to guide future research efforts, discriminating between categories of tools that are widely implemented by the industry and others that have not yet been explored for the mobile testing domain. Systematic research efforts can be conducted in Software Engineering literature to categorize and classify all available tools for mobile testing and provide a comprehensive state of the art mapping according to the framework's modules. Empirical research and industrial case studies are needed to assess the benefits produced by each module of the framework in reducing fragility, fragmentation, and maintenance effort required by test suites (●).

6   Conclusions

In this paper, we envisioned future trends in the automated GUI testing landscape and provided action points for different stakeholders in the field. Our framework can serve as an instrument for researchers and developers of testing tools to assess which among envisioned modules are available in the literature and the market and which need further research and development.

A tentative evaluation of the proposed framework would involve assessing its potential to address the challenges and goals it sets out to achieve. In particular, the framework aims to tackle issues related to hardware fragmentation, test fragility, and test maintenance costs. It is important to note that a full evaluation would require empirical research and industrial case studies, to fully validate the benefits produced by each module of the framework in addressing the challenges it aims to tackle.

It is still worth stressing that some of the modules in the framework, such as fragility prediction mechanisms and translation-based tools, are still in early-stage academic investigation or have not been fully implemented by available tools. The success of the proposed framework in reducing test maintenance costs would rely on the development and integration of these modules and their effectiveness in practical scenarios.

References

1. Alégroth, E., Gao, Z., Oliveira, R., Memon, A.: Conceptualization and evaluation of component-based testing unified with visual GUI testing: an empirical study. In: 2015 IEEE 8th International Conference on Software Testing, Verification and Validation (ICST), pp. 1–10. IEEE (2015)
2. Ali, A., Maghawry, H.A., Badr, N.: Automated parallel GUI testing as a service for mobile applications. J. Softw. Evol. Process **30**(10), e1963 (2018)
3. Ardito, L., Bottino, A., Coppola, R., Lamberti, F., Manigrasso, F., Morra, L., Torchiano, M.: Feature matching-based approaches to improve the robustness of Android visual GUI testing. ACM Trans. Softw. Eng. Methodol. (TOSEM) **31**(2), 1–32 (2021)
4. Ardito, L., Coppola, R., Leonardi, S., Morisio, M., Buy, U.: Automated test selection for Android apps based on APK and activity classification. IEEE Access **8**, 187648–187670 (2020)
5. Choudhary, S.R., Gorla, A., Orso, A.: Automated test input generation for Android: are we there yet?(e). In: 2015 30th IEEE/ACM International Conference on Automated Software Engineering (ASE), pp. 429–440. IEEE (2015)
6. Coppola, R., Alégroth, E.: A taxonomy of metrics for GUI-based testing research: a systematic literature review. Inf. Softw. Technol. **152**, 107062 (2022)
7. Coppola, R., Ardito, L., Morisio, M., Torchiano, M.: Mobile testing: new challenges and perceived difficulties from developers of the Italian industry. IT Professional **22**(5), 32–39 (2020)
8. Coppola, R., Ardito, L., Torchiano, M., Alégroth, E.: Translation from layout-based to visual Android test scripts: an empirical evaluation. J. Syst. Softw. **171**, 110845 (2021)
9. Coppola, R., Morisio, M., Torchiano, M.: Mobile GUI testing fragility: a study on open-source android applications. IEEE Trans. Reliab. **68**(1), 67–90 (2018)
10. Di Martino, S., Fasolino, A.R., Starace, L.L.L., Tramontana, P.: Comparing the effectiveness of capture and replay against automatic input generation for Android graphical user interface testing. Softw. Testing Verification Reliab. **31**(3), e1754 (2021)
11. Escobar-Velásquez, C., et al.: Enabling mutant generation for open-and closed-source Android apps. IEEE Trans. Softw. Eng. **48**(1), 186–208 (2020)
12. Fazzini, M., Gorla, A., Orso, A.: A framework for automated test mocking of mobile apps. In: 2020 35th IEEE/ACM International Conference on Automated Software Engineering (ASE), pp. 1204–1208. IEEE, Washington, DC, USA (2020)
13. Fulcini, T., Ardito, L.: Gamified exploratory GUI testing of web applications: a preliminary evaluation. In: 2022 IEEE International Conference on Software Testing, Verification and Validation Workshops (ICSTW), pp. 215–222. IEEE (2022)
14. Fulcini, T., Coppola, R., Ardito, L., Torchiano, M.: A review on tools, mechanics, benefits, and challenges of gamified software testing. ACM Comput. Surv. (2023)
15. Kong, P., Li, L., Gao, J., Liu, K., Bissyandé, T.F., Klein, J.: Automated testing of Android apps: a systematic literature review. IEEE Trans. Reliab. **68**(1), 45–66 (2018)
16. Lanui, A., Chiew, T.K.: A cloud-based solution for testing applications' compatibility and portability on fragmented Android platform. In: 2019 26th Asia-Pacific Software Engineering Conference (APSEC), pp. 158–164. IEEE (2019)
17. Leotta, M., Stocco, A., Ricca, F., Tonella, P.: Pesto: automated migration of DOM-based web tests towards the visual approach. Softw. Testing Verification Reliab. **28**(4), e1665 (2018)

18. Linares-Vásquez, M., Bernal-Cárdenas, C., Moran, K., Poshyvanyk, D.: How do developers test Android applications? In: 2017 IEEE International Conference on Software Maintenance and Evolution (ICSME), pp. 613–622. IEEE, Washington, DC, USA (2017)

19. Linares-Vásquez, M., Moran, K., Poshyvanyk, D.: Continuous, evolutionary and large-scale: a new perspective for automated mobile app testing. In: 2017 IEEE International Conference on Software Maintenance and Evolution (ICSME), pp. 399–410. IEEE, Washington, DC, USA (2017)

20. Michaels, R., Khan, M.K., Bryce, R.: Test suite prioritization with element and event sequences for Android applications. In: 2021 IEEE 11th Annual Computing and Communication Workshop and Conference (CCWC), pp. 1326–1332. IEEE, Washington, DC, USA (2021)

21. Sadeghi, A., Esfahani, N., Malek, S.: Mining mobile app markets for prioritization of security assessment effort. In: Proceedings of the 2nd ACM SIGSOFT International Workshop on App Market Analytics, pp. 1–7. Association for Computing Machinery, New York, NY, USA (2017)

22. Vilkomir, S.: Multi-device coverage testing of mobile applications. Softw. Qual. J. **26**(2), 197–215 (2018)

23. Xu, T., et al.: Guider: GUI structure and vision co-guided test script repair for Android apps. In: Proceedings of the 30th ACM SIGSOFT International Symposium on Software Testing and Analysis, pp. 191–203. Association for Computing Machinery, New York, NY, USA (2021)

RQCODE: Security Requirements Formalization with Testing

Ildar Nigmatullin[1]([✉]), Andrey Sadovykh[2], Sophie Ebersold[1], and Nan Messe[1]

[1] University of Toulouse - IRIT - CNRS, Toulouse, France
i.nigmatullin@yahoo.com
[2] Softeam, Paris, France

Abstract. Secure software systems are crucial in today's digital world, where there is an ever-increasing amount of IT systems, leading to more risks of exposing sensitive data and service outages. One of the key aspects of secure software development is ensuring that security requirements are met through the various stages of software development. The process of testing security requirements is often complex and time-consuming, notably because of the gap between the verification process of security requirements and the testing process. To address this issue and simplify the testing of security requirements, this paper proposes to use the Requirements as Code approach (RQCODE). RQCODE combines security requirements with code in a way to support automated testing and continuous verification of security requirements throughout the software development life cycle. This paper contributes to the field of software security by providing a practical and effective approach to bridge the gap between verification of security requirements and testing, ultimately leading to more secure software systems. Additionally, it discusses the benefits of this approach, such as its ability to improve the accuracy and consistency of testing, enabling the early detection of security issues, and reducing the time and effort required for security testing. It also discusses the challenges and limitations of the approach.

Keywords: Security Requirements · Security Testing · Seamless Object-Oriented Requirements · Requirements As Code

1 Introduction

1.1 Importance of Security by Design

In today's digital world, cyber-attacks are becoming increasingly common, which leads to high risks of exposing sensitive data and service outages. It is thus essential to build secure software systems and thus be able to withstand attacks from malicious actors. One of the most important aspects of secure software development is ensuring that security requirements are met throughout the various stages of software development. Security requirements are an important part of software requirements and are intended to ensure that the software system is

S. Bonfanti et al. (Eds.): ICTSS 2023, LNCS 14131, pp. 126–142, 2023.
https://doi.org/10.1007/978-3-031-43240-8_9

secure and can withstand attacks such as unauthorized access attempts. According to [10], security requirements are defined as "statements of the desired properties or attributes of a system that are necessary for it to be secure." Security requirements are identified and specified early in the software development process. This ensures that the system is secure from the start. It can be achieved through various activities, such as threat modeling, risk assessment, and misuse case analysis, as described in [17]. By identifying and specifying security requirements early, potential security risks can be mitigated or eliminated, reducing the risk of vulnerabilities and attacks.

According to NIST SP 800-53 [?], security requirements should be verifiable, and a verification plan should be developed to ensure that security requirements are met. The verification plan should include testing and evaluation procedures that verify the software's compliance with the security requirements.

The Security-by-Design principle [20] is a key approach to achieving security in software development. It is a proactive approach towards designing and building secure software systems from the ground, rather than trying to retrofit security features at the final steps or even in the production or operation environments. Secure software development emphasizes the importance of building security in each stage of the software development lifecycle.

Secure-by-Design ensures that IT systems are constructed to protect against cyber threats aiming at accessing devices, data, and connected infrastructure. Integrating Secure-by-Design practices in the development of new technology products can significantly and efficiently enhance its security level, minimizing risks of cyberattacks. Security-by-Design helps organizations to comply with various security regulations and standards, such as the General Data Protection Regulation (GDPR) [2] and the Payment Card Industry Data Security Standard (PCI DSS) [3], by ensuring that security considerations are integrated into the design of their systems and applications.

According to ISO 27034-1 [6], the Security-by-Design approach can help achieve security requirements by ensuring that security is integrated early into the software development process. By incorporating security into the design phase, software developers can identify and address security issues early in the development cycle. Incorporating secure design practices early on can minimize the impact of potential security vulnerabilities and reduce the need for costly and time-consuming security fixes later in the development process. By addressing security requirements from the outset, Security-by-Design principles minimize the impact of potential security threats and ensure that the system is able to perform its intended function while remaining secure.

In the scope of the Security-by-Design paradigm, addressing security requirements is fundamental for building secure software. Verifiability ensures that the security requirements are objective, clear, and measurable. It also helps in identifying potential weaknesses in the software and mitigating them before they can be exploited by attackers. Additionally, verifiable security requirements provide a means for stakeholders to evaluate the security of software and assess whether it meets their needs and expectations.

1.2 Importance of Security Testing

Testing is a critical aspect of software verification and validation, and several testing techniques are available to verify and validate software requirements, including functional testing, performance testing, and security testing [16]. Security testing is a crucial part of ensuring that these security requirements are met. By checking whether these requirements are satisfied under various conditions, security testing aims to uncover vulnerabilities that could be exploited by attackers. Due to the openness of modern service-oriented systems, security testing has gained much interest in recent years and has become a vast field of research [5].

Security testing involves the evaluation of security requirements that pertain to key security properties such as confidentiality, integrity, availability, authentication, authorization, and nonrepudiation. The goal of security testing is to determine whether the specified or intended security properties are correctly implemented for a given set of assets of interest. This can be achieved through conformance testing, where the system's conformance to the security properties is assessed based on well-defined, expected inputs. Alternatively, known vulnerabilities can be addressed through destructive testing, which involves the use of malicious, non-expected input data that is likely to exploit the identified vulnerabilities [?].

According to Tiang-yang and et al. [21], there are two primary approaches in security testing: security functional testing and security vulnerability testing. Security functional testing aims to validate the correct implementation of specified security requirements, including security properties and mechanisms. On the other hand, security vulnerability testing focuses on identifying unintended vulnerabilities in a system. This type of testing involves simulating attacks and penetration testing to assess the system's resilience against potential threats. However, security vulnerability testing requires specific expertise and can be challenging to automate.

The security testing method the following techniques [21]: Model-based security testing, Code-based testing and static analysis, Penetration testing, and dynamic analysis, and Security regression testing.

Model-based security testing relies on requirements and design models created during the analysis and design phase. This includes testing based on architectural and functional models, threat, fault, and risk models, as well as weakness and vulnerability models. Code-based testing and static analysis involve manual code reviews and static application security testing using source and byte code developed during the development phase. Penetration testing and dynamic analysis focus on running systems in test or production environments. This includes techniques such as penetration testing, vulnerability scanning, dynamic taint analysis, and fuzzing. Security regression testing is performed during the maintenance phase and includes approaches like test suite minimization, test case prioritization, and test case selection.

Even though security testing techniques are crucial for identifying vulnerabilities and ensuring the security of software systems, have certain limitations that can impact their effectiveness for customers. Some of the limitations include:

Incomplete Coverage: Security testing techniques may not provide complete coverage of all possible security vulnerabilities. It is challenging to anticipate and test for every potential security weakness, and new threats can emerge over time. Therefore, there is always a possibility of undiscovered vulnerabilities remaining in the system. False Sense of Security: Customers may develop a false sense of security if they rely solely on security testing techniques without considering other security measures. Security testing alone cannot guarantee a completely secure system. It is important to implement other security measures such as secure coding practices, regular security updates, and user awareness training. Resource Intensiveness [13]: Comprehensive security testing requires significant resources, including time, expertise, and tools. Small businesses or individual customers with limited resources may find it challenging to implement and afford rigorous security testing practices. Limited Human Expertise [13]: Security testing techniques rely on human expertise and judgment, which can introduce limitations. Testers may overlook certain vulnerabilities, misinterpret results, or lack the necessary skills to uncover complex security issues. Evolving Threat Landscape: Security threats are constantly evolving, and new vulnerabilities can emerge rapidly. Security testing techniques may struggle to keep pace with the evolving threat landscape, leading to potential gaps in security coverage.

To overcome these limitations, it is important for customers to adopt an approach to cover security requirements. However, there are certain lacks in security requirements specifications. They are often very high-level or vague - mainly specifying the need to comply with a specific cyber-security standard. There is definitely a need to make security clear and verifiable or at least as verifiable as security tests.

This work introduces an approach to formalize the security requirements by means of associated security tests. We present our approach and provide examples from the cyber-security domain. Section 2 discusses the related work. Section 3 presents our approach and provides illustrative examples. Section 4 discusses differences between RQCODE in comparison with security testing in general. Section 5 gives the final conclusions.

2   Related Work

The SQUARE methodology [11] is designed to guide the development of security requirements, with a focus on the quality attributes of software systems. The methodology emphasizes the importance of identifying and prioritizing security requirements early in the software development lifecycle.

SQUARE includes nine steps [11] that cover the entire software development process. These steps are: identifying stakeholders, defining security objectives, identifying security requirements, analyzing security risks, specifying security requirements, validating security requirements, tracing security requirements, managing security requirements, and ensuring ongoing security.

Through these steps, SQUARE ensures that security requirements are clearly defined, traceable, and measurable. It helps to identify potential security risks and provides a framework for identifying security controls to mitigate those risks. It also ensures that security requirements are integrated into the software development process and that security considerations are taken into account throughout the development lifecycle.

Some potential SQUARE's limitations include [11]:

- Time-Consuming Process: SQUARE can be a time-consuming process, which may not be suitable for projects with tight schedules.
- Requires Skilled Practitioners: SQUARE requires a team that has a good understanding of security concepts, as they have to identify, categorize, and prioritize security requirements.
- Lack of Automation: The SQUARE process is largely manual, which can lead to human errors. Also, the lack of automated tool support may make the process slower and more expensive.
- Lack of Formalization: SQUARE does not provide a notation that enforces formalization and verifiability of security requirements.

For the automated verifiability of requirements, one may consider Behaviour-Driven Design (BDD) [19]. BDD promotes starting development by specifying a scenario for a feature to be developed. In BDD, a scenario in natural language is automatically translated into an acceptance test. This is achieved through the use of a structured, natural language format such as Gherkin, which is easy to read and understand even for non-technical stakeholders.

Gherkin can be useful for several reasons in the context of security requirements. Firstly, Gherkin supports the creation of scenarios that clearly describe the expected behavior of a secure system. This aids in ensuring that security requirements are properly defined and understood. Secondly, Gherkin scenarios can be used to create automated security tests that verify that the system is functioning as expected. This helps to identify security vulnerabilities early in the development process when they generally are easier and less expensive to fix. For example, a security requirement for a banking application is that "only authorized users are able to access account information". A Gherkin scenario for this requirement may look as follows:

```
1   Only authorized users can access account information
2     Given I am logged in as an unauthorized user
3     When I try to access my account information
4     Then I should see an error message
5     And I should not be able to access the information
```

Listing 1.1. Gherkin example

This scenario describes the behavior that should occur when an unauthorized user attempts to access account information. By creating automated tests based on this scenario, developers can verify that the system is secure and functioning as expected.

In the meantime, Gherkin has the limitations:

- Limited expressiveness: While Gherkin is designed to be easily understandable by non-technical stakeholders, its simplicity also means it can lack the expressiveness necessary to define more complex behaviors [22].
- Requires good communication: Since Gherkin relies on collaboration between technical and non-technical stakeholders, any communication breakdowns can lead to poorly defined behaviors [18].
- Lack of automation support: Gherkin scenarios need to be manually translated into automated tests by developers. If the scenario is not well defined, this can be a time-consuming and error-prone process [22].
- Maintenance overhead: If the software changes frequently, maintaining Gherkin scenarios and corresponding tests can become a significant overhead [1].

3   The ReQuirements as CODE Approach (RQCODE)

3.1   RQCODE Definition and Concepts

ReQuirements as CODE (RQCODE) is an approach to software development that involves writing requirements in a code-like format, rather than as traditional text-based documentation. This approach enables developers to use code to test requirements, automates the process of verifying requirements, and improves collaboration between developers and other stakeholders. RQCODE aims to bridge the gap between requirements and tests, enabling more efficient and effective testing and earlier identification and resolution of issues [15]. This approach supports modern software development practices, such as continuous integration and automated testing, thereby improving the quality and accuracy of requirements [1].

RQCODE, as described in [9], introduces a new way of utilizing the Seamless Object-Oriented Requirements (SOOR) paradigm in Java programming. RQCODE involves representing requirements as classes that encompass multiple forms of representation, including a natural language description of the requirement, along with methods for testing and verifying the requirement, such as acceptance tests. This creates a direct traceability link between a requirement and its implementation, which can be verified at any time through the execution of the associated test.

Furthermore, the object-oriented approach facilitates the reusability of requirements and tests via standard mechanisms, such as inheritance in Java. A requirement can be either an extension or a specialization of another requirement and can serve as a template for similar requirements by initializing a requirement class with different parameters.

Seamless Object-Oriented Requirements (SOOR) [14] focuses on the seamless integration of requirements and object-oriented modeling, with the goal of establishing a close relationship between requirements and design elements. SOOR uses a domain ontology to specify the concepts and relationships relevant to the application domain, and it emphasizes modeling requirements in a way that is consistent with the object-oriented paradigm [14].

The SOOR methodology documents requirements as software classes to improve their verifiability and reusability. The key concepts of the approach are specification drivers and semantic assertions expressed by pre- and post-conditions. Specification drivers are contracted routines that serve specification purposes, taking objects to be specified as arguments and expressing the effect of operations on those objects with pre- and post-conditions. SOOR utilizes concrete classes as Seamless Object-Oriented Requirements, capturing requirements as specification drivers. Each specification driver includes a comment that describes a natural language version of the requirement.

The usage of SOOR in RQCODE for security requirements intends to provide several benefits. Firstly, RQCODE can enhance the traceability and transparency of security requirements, making it easier to identify and track changes to the requirements. This can lead to better collaboration and communication among stakeholders involved in the development process, as well as easier compliance with industry standards and regulations [12].

Secondly, RQCODE supports the use of formal methods and techniques for security requirements modeling and verification, such as model checking and theorem proving. These methods can help identify potential security vulnerabilities and ensure that the security requirements are consistent and complete.

3.2   RQCODE Example

The section demonstrates the following example of how RQCODE can be used to meet security requirements, specifically in ATM Withdrawal:

```
1  Case:
2    As a bank customer
3    In order to withdraw cash
4    I want to use an ATM
5
6    Scenario: Successful withdrawal
7      Given the ATM has sufficient cash
8      And my account balance is greater than the withdrawal amount
9      When I insert my card
10     And enter my PIN
11     And select the withdrawal option
12     And enter the withdrawal amount
13     Then the ATM should dispense the cash
14     And update my account balance
15
16   Scenario: Insufficient funds
17     Given the ATM has sufficient cash
```

```
18     And my account balance is less than the withdrawal amount
19     When I insert my card
20     And enter my PIN
21     And select the withdrawal option
22     And enter the withdrawal amount
23     Then the ATM should display an error message
24     And not dispense any cash
25     And not update my account balance
26
27   Scenario: Incorrect PIN
28     Given the ATM has sufficient cash
29     And my account balance is greater than the withdrawal amount
30     When I insert my card
31     And enter an incorrect PIN
32     Then the ATM should display an error message
33     And not allow me to proceed with the transaction
```

The above security requirement can be transformed into code with RQCODE:

```
1  public class SuccessfulWithdrawal implements RQCODE {
2      private final int MIN_WITHDRAWAL_AMOUNT = 20;
3      private final int MAX_WITHDRAWAL_AMOUNT = 500;
4
5      private final ScriptRequirement requirement = new STIGScript("
           ↪{WITHDRAWAL_AMOUNT}",
6              "Withdrawal amount must be between " +
                   ↪MIN_WITHDRAWAL_AMOUNT + " and " +
                   ↪MAX_WITHDRAWAL_AMOUNT);
7
8      @Override
9      public ScriptRequirement requirement() {
10         return requirement;
11     }
12
13     @Override
14     public CheckStatus check() {
15         int withdrawalAmount = Integer.parseInt(requirement.
               ↪getSettingValue());
16         if (withdrawalAmount < MIN_WITHDRAWAL_AMOUNT ||
               ↪withdrawalAmount > MAX_WITHDRAWAL_AMOUNT) {
17             return CheckStatus.FAIL;
18         }
19         return CheckStatus.PASS;
20     }
21
22  public class InsufficientFunds implements RQCODE {
23      private final int MIN_BALANCE = 0;
```

```
24
25      private final ScriptRequirement requirement = new STIGScript("
            ↪{ACCOUNT_BALANCE}",
26          "Account balance must be greater than or equal to " +
                ↪MIN_BALANCE);
27
28      @Override
29      public ScriptRequirement requirement() {
30          return requirement;
31      }
32
33      @Override
34      public CheckStatus check() {
35          int accountBalance = Integer.parseInt(requirement.
                ↪getSettingValue());
36          if (accountBalance < MIN_BALANCE) {
37              return CheckStatus.FAIL;
38          }
39          return CheckStatus.PASS;
40      }
41
42  public class IncorrectPIN implements RQCODE {
43      private final String VALID_PIN = "1234";
44
45      private final ScriptRequirement requirement = new STIGScript("
            ↪{PIN}",
46          "PIN must match the valid PIN");
47
48      @Override
49      public ScriptRequirement requirement() {
50          return requirement;
51      }
52
53      @Override
54      public CheckStatus check() {
55          String pin = requirement.getSettingValue();
56          if (!pin.equals(VALID_PIN)) {
57              return CheckStatus.FAIL;
58          }
59          return CheckStatus.PASS;
60      }
```

Listing 1.2. Example of RQCODE for ATM Withdrawal

In this example, the **PasswordLength** class implements the Pattern interface and defines a pattern that checks whether a password's length is within the minimum and maximum bounds. The **RQCODEScript** object defines the setting name **PASSWORD** and a message to display if the check fails.

RQCODE provides a formalized verification of security requirements through its built-in verification mechanism, which can output results of **PASS**, **FAIL**, or **INCOMPLETE**. This feature ensures that the security requirements are met and verified according to their intended specifications.

The **check()** method extracts the password from the pattern, checks its length, and returns a **CheckStatus** value of **PASS** or **FAIL** depending on whether the length is within the required bounds.

The **enforce()** method is not applicable for this pattern, as enforcing a password length requirement would require modifying the application code or configuration.

RQCODE provides a class-based approach that enables to define the security requirements along with verification means. The Object-Oriented nature of the definition makes it possible to reuse security requirements and tests, simplifying maintenance and enhancing traceability. RQCODE includes specific packages for baseline concepts and temporal patterns, as well as STIG (Security Technical Implementation Guide) [4] related classes that can be adapted to specific platforms, such as Windows and Ubuntu.

Next, we discuss the RQCODE application to the Security Technical Implementation Guide in the following section.

3.3   Use Case of Security Technology Implementation Guide

In this study, we have taken into account four STIG requirements that are designed to ensure the security of Windows 10 [7]. We have applied both security testing and the RQCODE approach to evaluate their effectiveness. Our comparison focuses on the efforts required to satisfy these requirements using the two approaches.

STIG stands for Security Technical Implementation Guide, which are a set of guidelines produced by the Defense Information Systems Agency (DISA) [4] to help secure computer systems and networks. STIG provides detailed information on how to configure and secure various operating systems, applications, and network devices in accordance with security best practices and compliance regulations.

The group of Security Policies in OS Windows 10 comprises four STIG security requirements. These requirements have a common description related to maintaining an audit trail of system activity logs. STIGs v-63447 and v-63449 relate to *User Account Management records events such as creating, changing, deleting, renaming, disabling, or enabling user accounts.* The description of STIGs v-63463 and v-63467 is *Logon records user logons. If this is an interactive logon, it is recorded on the local system. If it is to a network share, it is recorded on the system accessed* [7].

The following are the differences observed in these STIGs (Table 1):

- STIG v-63447 is responsible of User Account Management in case of failure. It is described by "the system must be configured to audit Account Management". It is named "Account Management **failure**".

- STIG v-63449 is described by "the system must be configured to audit Account Management". It is named "User Account Management **successes**".
- STIG v-63463: "The system must be configured to audit Logon/Logoff ". It is named "Logon - **failures**".
- STIG v-63467: "The system must be configured to audit Logon/Logoff". It is named "Logon - **successes**".

The Table 1 below describes some test cases for the above-mentioned STIGs. The test cases include the **Steps to Reproduce** that are common for all four STIGs. They can be used for further creation of a common Java class using RQCODE approach (see the listing 1.4). The differences are in **Expected Results** that will be represented as final Java classes (see the listing 1.5).

Table 1. Test Cases for 4 STIGs

STIG Requirement	Steps to Reproduce	Expected Result
STIG v-63447	1. Set "Enabled" Security Option "Audit: Force audit policy subcategory settings (Windows Vista or later) to override audit policy category settings" for the detailed auditing subcategories to be effective	If the system does not audit "Account Management > > User Account Management - Failure", this is a finding.
	2. Use the AuditPol tool to review the current Audit Policy configuration	
	3. Open a Command Prompt with elevated privileges ("Run as Administrator")	
	4. Enter "AuditPol /get /category:*"	
	5. Compare the AuditPol settings with the following. If the system does not audit the following, this is a finding:	
STIG v-63449		If the system does not audit "Account Management > User Account Management - Success", this is a finding
STIG v-63463		If the system does not audit "Logon/Logoff > > Logon - Failure", this is a finding
STIG v-63467		If the system does not audit "Logon/Logoff > > Logon - Success", this is a finding

In the example below, we will demonstrate how the creation of RQCODE patterns can streamline the execution of test cases for repetitive requirements. The RQCODE approach involves the Requirement abstract class, which includes a mandatory statement attribute for the requirement's textual representation. The **Checkable** interface's **check()** method is redefined to facilitate built-in requirement verification, providing three possible outcomes: **PASS**, **FAIL**, or **INCOMPLETE**. **PASS** signifies successful verification, while **FAIL** indicates incorrect outputs and **INCOMPLETE** applies when verification cannot be completed.

When a requirement can guide environment modifications to meet its specifications, the **Enforceable** interface is utilized. The **enforce()** method also returns the status of **SUCCESS**, **FAILURE**, or **INCOMPLETE**, making it useful for initiating countermeasures in security requirement scenarios.

In the RQCODE structure, dedicated packages are designated for baseline concepts, temporal patterns, and STIG-related classes. Specific packages are included for Windows 10 OS, and each platform package contains sub-packages with platform-specific patterns, such as **AuditPolicy**. This modular organization facilitates easy reuse of STIG requirements and guidelines.

With RQCODE, the *STIGPattern* is illustrated by the following example of code (listing 1.3):

```
1  public interface STIGPattern extends Checkable, Enforceable {
2      public STIGScriptPattern pattern();
3
4      public boolean checkProcess(String script, String settingName,
           ↪ String settingValue) throws Exception;
5  }
```

Listing 1.3. Example of STIGPattern

The *AuditPolicy* pattern, which inherits from *STIGPattern*, is represented on the listing 1.4 as follows:

```
1  public abstract class AuditPolicyPattern implements STIGPattern {
2
3      @Override
4      public CheckStatus check() {
5          String settingName = pattern().getSettingName();
6          String settingValue = pattern().getSettingValue();
7
8          String script = pattern().prepareCheckScript();
9
10         boolean auditPolicyCheck;
11         try {
12             auditPolicyCheck = checkProcess(script, settingName,
                   ↪settingValue);
13         } catch (Exception e) {
14             e.printStackTrace();
15             return CheckStatus.INCOMPLETE;
16         }
17
18         if (auditPolicyCheck)
```

```
19                return CheckStatus.PASS;
20            else
21                return CheckStatus.FAIL;
22        }
23
24        @Override
25        public EnforcementStatus enforce() {
26            String script = pattern().prepareEnforceScript();
27
28            try {
29                Process process = Runtime.getRuntime().exec(script);
30                process.waitFor();
31            } catch (Exception e) {
32                e.printStackTrace();
33                return EnforcementStatus.FAILURE;
34            }
35            return EnforcementStatus.SUCCESS;
36        }
```

Listing 1.4. Example of AuditPolicy pattern

The STIG requirement *V-63447* is expressed in the listing 1.5 below.

```
1    public class V-63447 extends AuditPolicyPattern {
2        private final AuditPolicyScriptPattern pattern =
3                new AuditPolicyScriptPattern(
                    ↪AUDIT_POLICY_SCRIPT_PATTERN_ENFORCE,
4                    AUDIT_POLICY_SCRIPT_PATTERN_CHECK,
5                    "{0CCE9235-69AE-11D9-BED3-505054503030}",
6                    "failure",
7                    "enable");
8        @Override
9        public STIGScriptPattern pattern() {
10            return pattern;
11        }
```

Listing 1.5. Example of STIG V-63447

The provided code is an abstract class called **AuditPolicyPattern** which implements the **STIGPattern** interface. It includes two methods, **check()** and **enforce()**, which are used to verify and enforce the STIG requirement, respectively.

0CCE9235-69AE-11D9-BED3-505054503030 is a Microsoft SubcategoryGUID[1]. It identifies the User Account Management audit subcategory. Overall, this code is used to implement the STIG pattern for Audit policy verification and enforcement using the RQCODE framework.

---

[1] https://learn.microsoft.com/en-us/openspecs/windows_protocols/ms-gpac/77878370-0712-47cd-997d-b07053429f6d.

AuditPolicy pattern remains unchanged and is created only once. The only parameters that need to be updated are within the public class *V-63447*, such as **AUDIT_POLICY_SCRIPT_PATTERN_CHECK**, 0CCE9235-69AE-11D9-BED3-505054503030. This means that the **AuditPolicy** pattern can cover a large number of final Java classes related to specific STIG requirements, thereby saving considerable effort given the huge number of STIGs.

4 Discussion

4.1 Background Needed

Individuals involved in implementing the RQCODE approach should possess an understanding of OOP concepts such as inheritance. This knowledge enables them to design and develop code that accurately represents the security requirements.

Additionally, a strong grasp of requirements engineering is essential for the successful implementation of the RQCODE approach. It is necessary to effectively communicate with stakeholders understanding their security concerns and translating them into clear and concise requirements. By leveraging this knowledge in object-oriented programming, quality assurance and requirements engineering, practitioners can effectively apply the RQCODE approach to bridge the gap between security requirements specification and implementation.

4.2 Security Testing

RQCODE and security testing are two distinct approaches that serve different purposes in addressing security requirements. While both approaches contribute to ensuring the security of a system, they cannot be directly compared in terms of their objectives and focus.

Security testing primarily aims to identify errors, vulnerabilities, and gaps in the system and its code. It involves various techniques such as penetration testing, vulnerability scanning, and dynamic analysis to uncover potential security weaknesses. The main goal of security testing is to assess the security posture of the system and identify areas that require improvement or remediation. It is more focused on detecting and mitigating security risks rather than directly verifying the implementation of security requirements.

On the other hand, RQCODE is an approach that focuses on formalization and verification of security requirements. It involves encoding security requirements into the software development process, allowing for automated verification and analysis of the implemented security measures. RQCODE enables the integration of security requirements into the development workflow and ensures that the implemented security measures align with the specified requirements.

The key distinction between RQCODE and security testing lies in their primary objectives. Security testing aims to identify and address security vulnerabilities, while RQCODE focuses on verifying the compliance and implementation of security requirements. Security testing is more concerned with uncovering potential issues and gaps in the system, while RQCODE ensures that the security requirements are met through automated verification.

5   Conclusion and Future Work

In conclusion, our research has shown that adopting the RQCODE approach can contribute to formalizing the security requirements by specifying corresponding security tests along with the requirements description expressed in natural language. For that, RQCODE leverages programming languages, such as Java, to express requirements as classes that incorporate verification means, we have demonstrated the potential for enhanced reusability and traceability in requirements specifications.

The code-like representation of security requirements in Java programming language can provide a more developer-friendly approach compared to other formalization methods that often require expert knowledge and lack tool support for developers. The investigation we carried out in the security domain, specifically with the STIG requirements, has provided concrete examples of how RQCODE can be applied. These examples highlight the potential of security tests for clarifying and formalizing security requirements. This can be considered as the starting point for the analysis and verification of security requirements, thereby achieving the development of secure software systems. This shift towards expressing requirements as code not only facilitates the integration of verification mechanisms, such as tests but also enables seamless collaboration between stakeholders involved in the software development process.

In the context of security requirements and RQCODE, BDD, and SQUARE can also be considered.

BDD [19] focuses on collaboration and communication among stakeholders to define and verify system behaviors. It uses a structured language called Gherkin to describe system behavior in a human-readable format. BDD can be used to capture security requirements by expressing them as behavior scenarios, facilitating clear documentation and alignment of stakeholders.

SQUARE is a methodology specifically designed for security requirements engineering. It provides a systematic approach to elicit, analyze, specify, and validate security requirements [8].

RQCODE [9], or Requirements as Code, involves expressing requirements in a coded form. It treats requirements as executable code and focuses on automating their verification. RQCODE translates security requirements into executable code, allowing for automated testing and analysis to ensure compliance with the specified security requirements.

Each approach has its strengths and can be beneficial for addressing security requirements. BDD promotes collaboration and clear documentation of security expectations. SQUARE provides a systematic methodology for thorough security requirements engineering. RQCODE enables automated verification and testing of security requirements.

In future work, we plan to gather feedback from industry partners through a dedicated tutorial to evaluate the perceived benefits of the RQCODE approach.

By comparing this approach with Test-Driven Development and exploring its integration within Continuous Integration and Delivery practices, we aim to further validate the effectiveness and applicability of RQCODE.

References

1. Adzic, G.: Specification by Example: How Successful Teams Deliver the Right Software. Manning Publications (2011)
2. Regulation, General Data Protection: General data protection regulation (GDPR) - official legal text (2023). https://gdpr-info.eu. Accessed 11 July 2023
3. PCI Security Standards Council: Official PCI security standards (2023). https://www.pcisecuritystandards.org/. Accessed 15 May 2023
4. DoD Cyber Exchange: Security technical implementation guides (STIGs) - DoD cyber exchange (2023). https://public.cyber.mil/stigs/. Accessed 5 July 2023
5. Franke, U., Brynielsson, J.: Cyber situational awareness - a systematic review of the literature. Comput. Secur. **46**, 18–31 (2014). https://doi.org/10.1016/j.cose.2014.06.008. https://www.sciencedirect.com/science/article/pii/S0167404814001011
6. Frontiers: ISO/IEC 27034-1:2011 (2023). https://www.iso.org/standard/44378.html. Accessed 20 Apr 2023
7. Frontiers: Windows 10 Security Technical Implementation Guide - DoD cyber exchange (2023). https://www.stigviewer.com. Accessed 23 MAy 2023
8. Gross, D., Yu, E.: From non-functional requirements to design through patterns. Requirements Eng. **6**(1), 18–36 (2001)
9. Ismaeel, K., Naumchev, A., Sadovykh, A., Truscan, D., Enoiu, E.P., Seceleanu, C.: Security requirements as code: Example from VeriDevOps project. In: 2021 IEEE 29th International Requirements Engineering Conference Workshops (REW), pp. 357–363. IEEE (2021)
10. Jürjens, J.: Secure Systems Development with UML. Springer, Berlin (2005). https://doi.org/10.1007/b137706
11. Mead, N.R., Stehney, T.: Security quality requirements engineering (SQUARE) methodology. ACM SIGSOFT Softw. Eng. Not. **30**, 1–7 (2005)
12. Mellado, D., Blanco, C., Sánchez, L.E., Fernández-Medina, E.: A systematic review of security requirements engineering. Comput. Stand. Interfaces **32**(4), 286–295 (2010)
13. Mukherjee, S., Roy, S., Bose, R.: Defining an appropriate trade-off to overcome the challenges and limitations in software security testing. J. Xidian Univ. **14**(2), 1471–1479 (2020)
14. Naumchev, A.: Seamless object-oriented requirements. In: 2019 International Multi-Conference on Engineering, Computer and Information Sciences (SIBIRCON), pp. 0743–0748. IEEE (2019)
15. Nigmatullin, I., Sadovykh, A., Messe, N., Ebersold, S., Bruel, J.M.: RQCODE-towards object-oriented requirements in the software security domain. In: 2022 IEEE International Conference on Software Testing, Verification and Validation Workshops (ICSTW), pp. 2–6. IEEE (2022)
16. Pressman, R.S.: Software Engineering: A Practitioner's Approach, European edn. McGraw-Hill (1994). Adapted by Darrel Ince
17. Sindre, G., Opdahl, A.L.: Eliciting security requirements with misuse cases. Requirements Eng. **10**(1) (2005). https://doi.org/10.1007/s00766-004-0194-4

18. Smart, J.: BDD in Action: behavior-driven development for the whole software lifecycle. Manning (2014)
19. Software: Behaviour-driven development - Cucumber documentation (2023). https://cucumber.io/docs/bdd/. Accessed 1 May 2023
20. Team: Secure product design - OWASP cheat sheet series (2023). https://cheatsheetseries.owasp.org/. Accessed 2 July 2023
21. Tian-yang, G., Yin-Sheng, S., You-yuan, F.: Research on software security testing. In. J. Comput. Inf. Eng. 4(9), 1446–1450 (2010)
22. Tooke, S.: The Cucumber Book: Behaviour-Driven Development for Testers and Developers. The Pragmatic Bookshelf (2017)

Understanding Problem Solving in Software Testing: An Exploration of Tester Routines and Behavior

Eduard Paul Enoiu[1]([⊠])[iD], Gregory Gay[2,3][iD], Jameel Esber[1],
and Robert Feldt[2,3][iD]

[1] Division of Networked and Embedded Systems,
Mälardalen University, Västerås, Sweden
{eduard.enoiu,jameel.esber}@mdu.se
[2] Department of Computer Science and Engineering,
Chalmers University of Gothenburg, Gothenburg, Sweden
greg@greggay.com
[3] Department of Computer Science and Engineering, University of Gothenburg,
Gothenburg, Sweden
robert.feldt@chalmers.se

Abstract. Software testing is a difficult, intellectual activity performed in a social environment. Naturally, testers use and allocate multiple cognitive resources towards this task. The goal of this study is to understand better the routine and behaviour of human testers and their mental models when performing testing. We investigate this topic by surveying 38 software testers and developers in Sweden. The survey explores testers' cognitive processes when performing testing by investigating the knowledge they bring, the activities they select and perform, and the challenges they face in their routine. By analyzing the survey results, we provide a characterization of tester practices and identify insights regarding the problem-solving process. We use these descriptions to further enhance a cognitive model of software testing.

Keywords: Test Design · Problem Solving · Software Testing

1 Introduction

During software testing, test cases—sequences of input and expectations on the resulting behavior of the system-under-test (SUT)—are designed and executed as a method of determining whether the SUT is functioning correctly [15]. Testing is the most common verification technique [15], and consequently, one of the most researched topics in the software engineering field [14]. However, a significant portion of past research has focused on improving the tools that testers use—there is a lack of investigation of and, consequently, evidence regarding *human aspects of software testing.*

Support provided by Software Center Project 30: "Aspects of Automated Testing", H2020 under grant agreement No. 957212 and Vinnova through SmartDelta project.

S. Bonfanti et al. (Eds.): ICTSS 2023, LNCS 14131, pp. 143–159, 2023.
https://doi.org/10.1007/978-3-031-43240-8_10

To that end, in previous research, we proposed a cognitive model of software testing based on how problem solving is conceptualized in cognitive psychology [5]. This model mapped software testing to a cyclical problem solving model, consisting of activities related to four major phases of the testing process—understanding testing goals, planning testing strategy, executing tests, and checking test results.

The purpose of this study is to gain a deeper understanding of the personal routines of testers, including both their external behaviors and internal processes. While our general knowledge of software testing is vast, there is a lack of clear understanding of the personal decision-making processes of testers and developers—e.g., how they reason, which test design techniques they apply, what kind of difficulties they face, how they decide which test cases to create, and how they decide to stop testing in different testing situations.

As a step towards narrowing this knowledge gap, in this study, we utilize our earlier cognitive model as a foundation for collecting data on the testing process [5]. We have surveyed 38 developers and testers working in the Swedish software development industry, focusing on the *activities performed, knowledge utilized, and challenges encountered* during each major phase of the testing process, as defined in the cognitive model. We utilize thematic analysis of the survey results to characterize how testers approach each of these phases. In turn, we use this characterization to deepen the cognitive model.

Closing this knowledge gap has implications for both researchers and practitioners. The development of a realistic cognitive model enables the formulation of clear guidance on performing effective and efficient testing. In addition, a cognitive model can benefit future approaches to automated test generation, potentially leading to the development of more human-like generation tools [4]. This study provides a foundation for this future research on both human testing practices and human-like test generation.

2   Background and Related Work

The field of *Behavioral Software Engineering* (BSE) focuses on understanding the mental, social, and behavioral aspects of software engineering performed by individuals, teams, and organizations [11]. As an example, Hale et al. [7] created a model of the mental abilities required by programmers during software maintenance. This cognitive process model of debugging combines declarative models, such as a program understanding model, with problem-solving models, based on the idea of structural learning. The proposed model was later tested by Hale et al. [8] through a controlled experiment where participants debugged a program with an unknown fault, and their verbal protocols were analyzed.

Robillard et al. [18] studied the thought processes of developers in mixed teams comprised of engineers and psychologists to develop best practices. Thematic analysis was utilized to define cognitive behaviors. This research showed that software review involves three mental activities—review, alternative solution development, and synchronization.

Fig. 1. Overview of the method used for collecting data and developing the problem-solving model of test design.

Letovsky [12] delved into the cognitive processes behind program comprehension, with a focus on specific moments that occur within seconds or minutes, such as understanding the purpose behind a line of code. This investigation led to the creation of a categorization system for questions and hypotheses, along with a theory of the mental images and processes that produced them. The questions were defined as procedures that evaluate the coherence and accuracy of a person's developing mental model, while the hypotheses were identified as a planning process that draws on various forms of knowledge.

Recently, Aniche et al. [1] investigated the thought processes and decision-making developers experience when manually engineering test cases. Using observations from developers and survey data, it provides a broad framework for understanding developers' approach to test case development.

Despite the diverse range of approaches, it is essential to examine software testing as part of a problem-solving process to identify commonalities and gain insights into the processes involved in problem-solving. These processes seem to vary [1,5,10] depending on the specific testing problem/activity and how the goal is mentally represented. As a first step towards investigating the problem-solving perspectives, we previously hypothesized [5] that *a cognitive test design model could be represented as a cyclical problem-solving process* and conducted a pilot study with five students. As an initial approach, the software testing cycle, considered as a traditional problem-solving process, contains the following phases where a human tester needs to: (i) understand the test goal, (ii) formulate the test strategy, (iii) execute the tests, and (iv) check the test results.

3   Method

In this research, we are interested in addressing the following questions: (1) *How do testers utilize cognitive resources, knowledge sources, and problem-solving processes during testing?* (2) *What are the main challenges testers face in their testing routine?*

To address these questions, we followed a mixed-methods research approach outlined in Fig. 1. This approach combines both qualitative and quantitative data analysis using a survey, allowing us to develop a more comprehensive understanding of the problem-solving processes involved in software testing. We utilized survey research to explore the opinions and decisions of individuals during

Table 1. Survey questions.

Survey Question	Format
1. How many years of experience do you have with development?	Choice
2. How long have you been working with testing?	Choice
3. What is the size of the company you work in?	Choice
4. What role are you presently working in?	Choice
5. Can you summarize what you typically do in your current role?	Text
6. What programming languages do you use in your company?	Choice
7. What activities do you perform when understanding the testing purpose/goal?	Text
8. What knowledge do you bring when trying to understand the purpose/goal?	Text
9. What kinds of purposes/goals do you use during testing?	Choice
10. What are the difficulties you face when you try to understand the purpose/goal?	Text
11. What activities do you perform when planning test strategy and/or creating tests?	Text
12. What knowledge do you bring when you plan test strategy and/or create tests?	Text
13. What difficulties do you face when planning test strategy and/or creating tests?	Text
14. What test design techniques do you use to create tests?	Text
15. What activities do you perform when executing test cases?	Text
16. What knowledge do you bring when executing test cases?	Text
17. What automated tools/frameworks do you use during testing?	Text
18. What activities do you perform when checking test results?	Text
19. What knowledge do you bring when checking test results?	Text
20. What software testing tools do you use to check results?	Text
21. Provide your top three challenges when checking test results	Text
22. What criteria are used in your projects to decide to stop testing?	Text
23. Do you agree with the purpose of this survey?	Likert
24. Were there questions that were not clear?	Text
25. Do you have any feedback on the survey topic?	Text

testing. We developed an exploratory cross-sectional survey, utilizing both qualitative and quantitative descriptive methodology, and distributed it. We then performed a thematic analysis of the qualitative data to obtain an extended problem-solving model of software testing.

3.1   Survey Development

We started by identifying the related work on problem-solving models that have been developed based on Polya's phases in solving mathematical problems to represent problem-solving processes [16] on which our earlier model of test creation and execution [5] was based. Psychologists have also described problem-solving as a cyclical process, as noted by Bransford et al. [2], Hayes [9], and Pretz et al. [17]. We used the overall phases previously outlined by Enoiu et al. [5] to understand how this model of test creation happens in practice, and we focused on the overall activities, knowledge, and other human aspects of different steps. Based on these steps, we developed the questionnaire questions by concentrat-

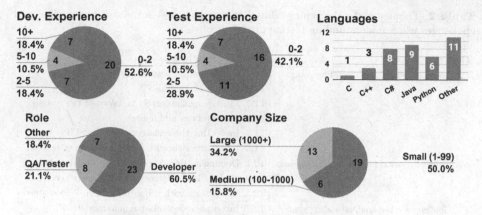

Fig. 2. Demographic information on survey participants.

ing on the activities that participants perform when performing software testing according to the initial problem-solving model of Enoiu et al. [5]. To start the questionnaire, a brief explanation was provided about the survey's objective. In addition, participants were informed of ethical and social considerations and were assured that all collected data would be anonymized.

The survey questions are listed in Table 1. The questions were split into several sections, starting with demographic information. It then asked about the activities that participants undertake when understanding the testing goal, when planning a testing strategy, when executing testing activities, and when checking their results. We then allowed participants to provide feedback.

3.2 Survey Population and Sampling

We targeted professionals in the software development industry. Our primary distribution method was convenience sampling. Connections with organizations were utilized to reach a large number of testers, developers, and practitioners in Sweden to gather diverse opinions and perspectives. A total of 38 responses were submitted. To ensure anonymity, we do not report the identities of respondents.

Demographic information is provided in Fig. 2. The participants had a strong knowledge of software development, with all reporting at least one year of experience. The participants work for companies of all sizes, with half working for small companies and in various roles—with the majority identifying as developers. The most common programming language reported was Java, but many different languages were reported as being in use[1].

3.3 Thematic Analysis

The open-ended questions in the questionnaire were subjected to thematic analysis, a qualitative technique for analyzing data [3]. This approach involves

---

[1] The "other" languages include PHP, MATLAB, Flutter, JavaScript, and Simulink.

Table 2. Themes and sub-themes related to participants' activities, knowledge, and challenges when understanding testing goals/purpose.

Theme	Important Sub-themes
T1. Activities when understanding goals.	T1.1. Understanding software requirements
	T1.2. Document analysis
	T1.3. Identifying the correct behavior of the system
	T1.4. Finding bugs and faults
	T1.5. Inspecting the architecture of the SUT
	T1.6. Using experience from previous testing sessions.
T2. Knowledge used in understanding goals.	T2.1. Documentation, Specifications, Requirements
	T2.2. Code. , T2.3. Memory., T2.4. Experience
	T2.5. Discussions with colleagues., T2.6. Web resources
T3. Challenges when understanding goals.	T3.1. Incomplete or unclear requirements
	T3.2. Complex and highly configurable scenarios

analyzing a collection of text—in this case, participants' responses to open-ended questions—to identify common themes, patterns, and topics that arise frequently. We carried out our thematic analysis using a six-step process: becoming familiar with the data, coding the responses, identifying themes, checking the themes, naming the themes, and reporting our findings.

To begin with, we familiarized ourselves with the data by gathering and reading the responses and making preliminary notes to obtain a comprehensive understanding of the obtained data. The next step involved coding, which entailed identifying specific words or sentences in the responses and assigning them short labels or "codes" to describe their content.

After coding the responses, we reviewed and identified connections between the codes and grouped them into broader themes. This involved combining multiple words and sentences to form cohesive themes. We then verified that the themes accurately reflected the data by comparing them to the responses and making modifications if necessary. Finally, we gave each theme a descriptive and concise name. These themes were then used to extend our problem-solving model of software testing.

4   Results and Discussions

This section presents the findings of the thematic analysis and introduces the extension of the problem-solving model of software testing.

4.1   Survey Results

This section summarizes the results of analyzing the survey data. The results are organized based on the sections of the survey, as explained in Sect. 3.1.

Understanding Testing Goals/Purpose: We asked participants to describe their activities when understanding the purpose or goals of testing. As shown in

Table 3. Themes and sub-themes related to participants' activities, knowledge, and challenges when planning a test strategy.

Theme	Important Sub-themes
T4. Activities while planning test strategy.	T4.1. Identify the SUT., T4.2. Identify the test level
	T4.3. Gather information from sessions in "previous" test levels
	T4.4. Identify the requirements
	T4.5. Identify the interfaces and create test cases
	T4.6. Define the test environments., T4.7. Prepare documentation.
T5. Knowledge used in planning test strategy	T5.1. Documents (Documentation, Specifications)
	T5.2. Code., T5.3. Knowledge and Memory
	T5.4. Experience., T5.5. Web resources.
T6. Challenges when planning test strategy	T6.1. Difficulty in coming up with edge cases/out-of-bound bugs
	T6.2. Correctly selecting the test steps
	T6.3. Handing ambiguous/not clear requirements
	T6.4. Lack of time., T6.5. Communication
	T6.6. The use of testing documents created by others
	T6.7. Unstable environment
	T6.8. Test automation tooling understanding

Table 2, their answers revolved around understanding software requirements and identifying the precise correct behavior of the SUT. This information was needed to understand the recognition, definition and representation of goals before creating test cases.

Our thematic analysis revealed that, during the process of understanding testing goals, participants follow a set of steps, including examining the architecture of the SUT, followed by identifying the interfaces (e.g., hardware, software, and user interfaces) and determining which levels to test them on. Finally, testers identify the responsibilities for the different test levels, if applicable. One participant emphasized the value of conversations with colleagues:

> "Firstly, I turn to the other team members since they ... have developed the new functionality. Then if needed, I turn to code and/or documentation."

Our thematic analysis yielded several sub-themes related to the knowledge utilized during this step (Table 2). 61% of participants selected documents as a source of knowledge. However, multiple sources are often required. The majority of the same participants also chose code as another source of knowledge:

> "I use multiple resources such as documents, code, and my memory, and consult experts whenever necessary."

A small number of participants indicated that they utilize knowledge from previous testing experience, familiarity with the software and hardware, comprehension of the implementation and testing guidelines, web resources, their memory, or conversations with colleagues. For example:

> "I rely on my previous experience, as well as discussions with architects and developers, and an inspection of the architecture and requirement specifications."

We inquired about whether test goals were discovered, created, or presented. Most participants reported a blend of options. 66% (25) discovered goals, 47%

Table 4. Themes and sub-themes related to participants' activities, knowledge, and tool use when executing test cases.

Theme	Important Sub-themes
T7. Activities when executing a test case.	T7.1. Test environment setup
	T7.2. Selecting and running test cases
	T7.3. Validate the test coverage
	T7.4. Continuously observe and analyze outcomes.
T8. Knowledge used when executing tests.	T8.1. Documents (Documentation, Specifications)
	T8.2. Code., T8.3. Knowledge and Memory
	T8.4. Experience
	T8.5. Knowledge of administering the tests
T9. Automated tools/frameworks used.	T9.1. Selenium., T9.2. Pytest., T9.3. Azure pipelines
	T9.4. Xunit., T9.5. IntelliJ., T9.6. Apache JMeter
	T9.7. MATLAB., T9.8. Eclipse., T9.9. Ranorex
	T9.10. Laravel

(18) created their own goals, and 61% (23) utilized test goals that were defined by someone else. One participant noted:

> "The testing goals are already pre-defined as part of the company's test strategy. When creating test cases, we apply different test design techniques such as BVA and equivalence partitioning."

When examining the challenges faced when comprehending the purpose/goals of testing, most participants identified incomplete or unclear requirements as one of the most common difficulties encountered during this phase. One participant noted that vague requirements "*cannot be developed and cannot be tested.*" Additionally, some participants reported facing challenges related to complex or highly configurable scenarios, often exacerbated by communication gaps between developers, testers, and clients.

Planning a Testing Strategy: Table 3 presents the activities involved in test strategy planning and test case creation. For example, analyzing the application before creating test cases based on experience or test specifications. Before commencing testing activities, testers strive to gain an understanding of the SUT by learning everything they can about it, obtaining detailed requirements, and comprehending the developed solution.

Regarding knowledge that participants use when planning a test strategy, we observed that most rely on documentation and the code. Additionally, testers draw on previous testing experience, knowledge of testing guidelines, and specifications from earlier versions of the SUT. Participants who had been testing for more than ten years mentioned that they preferred to use test strategy templates, knowledge of the SUT's architecture, their own experience, and regulatory requirements during the planning phase. One participant provided the following:

Table 5. Themes and sub-themes related to participants' activities, challenges, and criteria when planning to check test results.

Theme	Important Sub-themes
T10. Result checking activities.	T10.1. Compare test specifications with results obtained
	T10.2. Discuss results with the development team
	T10.3. Modify requirements, test cases, or code-under-test.
T11. Challenges in checking results.	T11.1. Communication and interaction with other roles
	T11.2. Lack of skilled testers skilled in test result analysis
	T11.3. Lack of easy-to-use test analysis tools
	T11.4. Lack of automation in test result checking
	T11.5. Lack of historical test trends
	T11.6. Difficulty understanding if the result is correct
	T11.7. Challenging debugging process
	T11.8. Misunderstanding of test specifications and requirements
	T11.9. Incomplete historical record of test reports
	T11.10. Unstable environment
	T11.11. Challenging test selection based on result analysis
	T11.12. Missing links between sources of documentation and logs.
T12. Completion criteria.	T12.1. When testing done on all items in the testing plan
	T12.2. Coverage of edge case scenarios and "normal" scenarios
	T12.3. UI functionality is covered
	T12.4. All specified tests and exploratory test sessions executed
	T12.5. All found discrepancies are analyzed
	T12.6. Human judgment., T12.7. Experience., T12.8. Budget

> "Knowledge of the software and hardware, previous testing knowledge, knowledge of the testing guidelines, and review of relevant documentation."

Regarding challenges while planning test strategy or creating test cases, many struggled with understanding complex or ambiguous requirements:

> "Lack of clear requirements is the most common difficulty."

Participants also identified limitations of testing tools, such as forced tool use leading to an unstable environment. Additionally, participants mentioned that lack of time for planning or tight deadlines were significant difficulties.

We also examined the test design techniques that participants employ. 26% of participants (10) design test cases based on specifications, 29% (11) use code as a basis for test design, and 24% (9) rely on their prior experience. 45% (17) employed a combination of experience, specification, and code. One participant provided a brief description of their creation techniques:

> "We ensure that each public interface has at least some tests, and we also consider code coverage. If a module has insufficient coverage, we add tests there. We also consider different levels of testing and aim to conduct both unit tests, module-integration tests, and system-level tests."

Executing Test Cases: Participants were asked to describe their activities during test case execution (Table 4). Responses indicated that activities include reviewing test specifications, writing test scripts, executing test scripts, and reviewing results.

Multiple tasks were performed by participants during test case execution, such as test environment setup, test case execution (including fulfilling pre-conditions), log-file gathering, archiving of execution and log files, documentation, and analysis of any found discrepancies. Automation of the test environment was also discussed, with one participant stating that they try to automate everything, including the setup of the test environment, running test cases, and observing the output. Some participants focused on debugging and defect identification when software bugs appeared during test execution, while others emphasized the importance of regression testing.

When executing test cases, participants often rely on documents and code to review specifications, report bugs, and document test results. However, one participant claimed that documentation is unnecessary once the tests are ready to be executed, except for instructions on how to report the results. Another participant mentioned that they only require knowledge of administering tests for automated test runs.

The most popular tools used by testers and developers during test execution were Selenium and Pytest, as they provide frameworks for automating web application testing and scalable and straightforward tests, respectively. Some participants perform tests manually, while others use custom-made tools.

Checking Test Results: Participants were asked to describe their routine for checking test results (Table 5). Their answers largely centered around comparing test specifications with the results they obtained. Testers undertake several activities while checking test results, e.g., comparing the requirements with the test results. One participant emphasized that, during this process, it is important to keep an eye on any events not specified in the test case. Some participants also discussed the results with the development team or other testers, examined test scripts, or provided feedback to the designers.

In the event of a test failure, testers and developers iteratively modify either the tests or code until achieving the desired outcome. One participant shared:

> "We rerun the test multiple times to confirm if it's a fluke. We then proceed to fix the test, the code being tested, or even the testing environment. This may involve checking for errors in parameters when setting up dockers or regenerating test data."

In terms of the knowledge utilized when checking test results, documents and code remain the most common sources. One participant emphasized the significance of documentation testing:

> "When tests fail, we almost always refer to the test case documentation. Though sometimes insufficient, we write at least one sentence about the test's purpose. Since the test cases are usually small, this is usually adequate."

However, one participant stated that the tests alone are adequate:

"The tests created contain all the necessary information to check the results."

Participants identified the three primary challenges encountered while checking results that they would like to see addressed in software testing research. One participant highlighted some challenges that arise when tests fail:

"1: It can be difficult to recognize that a failed test already has an open bug report. 2: Multiple failed tests may be caused by the same underlying error. 3: It can be challenging to differentiate between failing test cases due to actual software errors versus test environment issues."

Another also mentioned lack of observability into the causes of SUT behavior:

"The primary challenge is understanding whether the obtained result is correct by chance or if the application is performing as intended."

Other challenges identified include the need for test selection (due to having too many tests to execute) and challenges that emerge from having to make this selection—e.g., the time between executions and lack of certainty in SUT correctness—visualization of test results over time, establishing traceability between documentation sources, and the difficulty of knowing who is responsible for dealing with test results (e.g., the test case creator, the feature developer, or the test environment developers).

We also asked about the criteria participants utilized to determine whether testing activities had been completed. One of the criteria that participants used was ensuring that all the tests were executed successfully and met the desired coverage levels of code and functionality requirements. Another participant stated that all planned tests must be executed without any stopping errors. Other participants mentioned budget and deadline constraints. Another participant indicated that the stopping criterion is when all test steps in the test specification have been executed and assigned a pass/fail grade.

4.2   The Extended Problem Solving Model

Analyzing the survey results, we augmented our test design model [5] using a detailed human problem-solving process model [13]. It operationalises the steps testers take, clarifies the multiple sources of knowledge used and the internal representations the activities are based on and updates. The extended model is depicted in Fig. 3, with the new, process model in the inner circle of the original problem solving model (outer two circles). The extension can be applied throughout the problem-solving phases (mid circle) of the original model [5]. Below we provide further details, overall and per phase.

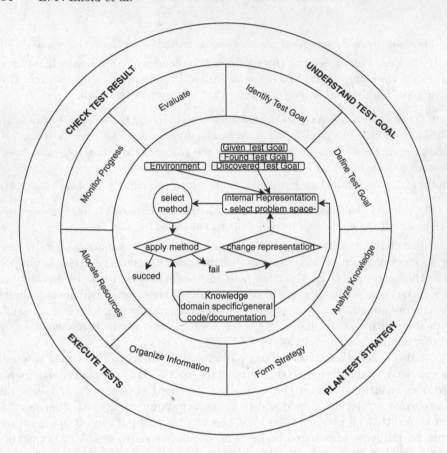

Fig. 3. The extended problem-solving model of software testing.

The Overall Problem-Solving Process: To initiate the testing process, the tester first analyzes the test goal and divides the goal into manageable components, then creates a generic solution for each component—known as a test case. These individual solutions are then combined to form a full test scenario that covers the initial test goal. In Table 6 we consider a specific test goal of security testing and go through the steps outlined in the process, providing practical examples. It is important to note that the testing cycle is not always a linear process, and skilled testers are able to remain flexible. Often, the completion of the cycle leads to the identification of a new test goal, which requires the repetition of the process itself as well as its phases.

In Fig. 3, we depict the interaction between the problem solver and a testing environment. Initially, the tester inspects the environment and generates an internal representation based on the context of the test goal (e.g., a flowchart that illustrates potential SQL injection attacks and vulnerabilities). This representation involves selecting a problem space to define the test goal's representation, the context of problem-solving, and the inferences that can be drawn

Table 6. An example of the steps outlined in the problem-solving process for a specific test goal in security testing.

Overall Steps	Practical Examples
Understand the Test Goal	Identify the Test Goal: Recognize potential security vulnerabilities in the login mechanism of a web application
	Define the Test Goal: Design a test case that bypasses the login mechanism using SQL injection and brute-force attacks.
Plan Test Strategy	Analyze Knowledge: Analyze the login mechanism's code and infrastructure, review security guidelines and understand common attack vectors used to exploit login vulnerabilities
	Form Strategy: Craft a test case that attempts to inject malicious SQL statements into the login form fields to check if the application has implemented proper input validation to prevent SQL injection attacks.
Execute Tests	Organize Information and Allocate Resources: Document the different attack scenarios, list the expected outcomes, and prepare the necessary tools, such as automated security testing tools or proxy servers, to capture and analyze network traffic during the test.
Check Test Results	Monitor Progress: Execute the test case, observe if the application properly rejects the malicious input, and monitor if any unauthorized database queries or errors occur
	Evaluate: Analyze the test results, identify any successful security breaches or vulnerabilities

from it based on general knowledge and past experience (e.g., understanding where the system might be vulnerable and what signs might suggest a failing test case). Equipped with this representation, the tester selects a problem solving method associated with each phase of software testing. For instance, in the solution-searching phase, the tester may revisit the mental representation (e.g., fault trees, checklists), apply different methods for test design (e.g., boundary value analysis), and employ heuristic strategies to facilitate the creation of test cases. The results of these steps are then monitored, and feedback is provided, which may lead to modifications in the representation of the test goal. The survey results suggest that testers rely on multiple and varied sources of knowledge when creating and executing test cases. Among these, documentation is the most commonly used across all testing activities. Testers refer to documents such as specifications, project requirements, and testing guidelines to ensure that needs are met, defects are identified, quality and risk are assessed, confidence is established, and defects are prevented. In practice, code is the most crucial knowledge that testers and developers use during the testing process. It is used to inspect and verify the SUT and detect faults throughout the testing process. Finally, experience and skills are also fundamental sources of knowledge that testers and developers leverage in their routines.

During the testing process, testers engage in different activities at each phase specified by the mid-circle. *The process model of the inner circle thus applies throughout the phases of the mid-circle.* For example, when understanding the test goal, testers mainly focus on comprehending the software requirements and outlining the acceptable behavior of the system. Some of the primary activities they perform include inspecting the system's architecture, identifying the various interfaces (hardware, software, and user), determining the appropriate testing level, and clarifying the responsibilities for the different test levels.

Identify the Test Goal: This is the phase when a tester understands and defines the test objective as a problem that requires a solution. Getzels [6] identifies three types of problems—those that are given, those that are discovered, and those that are created or generated. A given test goal is presented to the tester (e.g., a pre-defined criteria-based test goal, such as applying particular input partitions). A discovered test goal, however, must be identified. Such a test goal exists but has not been clearly stated to the tester, which has to seek out the knowledge gap to discover what the test goal is. In contrast to given and discovered test goals, a created test goal must first be recognized and formulated. In these cases, testers may use exploratory test methods and develop new test objectives based on their knowledge, skills, and interactions with the SUT.

Define the Test Goal: This relates to how one can mentally define the test goals and what the linked tests must accomplish. The test goal definition phase of testing is when the scope and objectives of each test are established and defined precisely. A test goal presents a collection of "givens". When dealing with these constraints, a tester performs certain procedures to achieve the desired state (i.e., creating a test fulfilling a test goal). A test goal can be expressed in many ways, including graphically or audibly. For example, to achieve pairwise coverage, one must describe the objective as the task of generating all available pairs of parameter values that may be applied by at least one test case.

Analyze Knowledge: This phase structures the tester's knowledge concerning testing scenarios. Every tester addresses a particular scenario with a different set of knowledge. For example, someone familiar with test design techniques will assess their past knowledge and use various methods and representations of the test goal to clearly state the needed strategies. To develop test cases, we might have to use broad abilities such as inference, case-based logic, and generalization to organize the data gathered throughout the various processes. On a broader level, higher cognitive abilities such as inspiration and allocating mental resources such as awareness and effort must be used. Additionally, domain expertise, such as electrical, mathematics, computer science principles, programming concepts, and regulations, would be required. We discovered that testers' primary activities involve acquiring a deep understanding of the SUT, obtaining the exact requirements that led to its development, and comprehending the generated test solution. They also develop tests that cover a distinct portion of the system or algorithms.

Form Strategy: In this step, one needs to create a solution approach for generating the required test cases using certain operators. These operators are cognitive frameworks of the operations that a tester may conduct on the "givens." For instance, some computations require the use of mental operators. The activities required to reach the target state are the set of actions required to construct test cases that satisfy a particular test goal. While the operators are often not listed in the test goal, we may infer them based on our past knowledge (e.g., mathematical operators, cognitive operators).

Organize Information and Allocate Resources: After defining the test goals, the next step for the tester is to manage their cognitive and physical resources to develop and execute test cases. Testers can use automation tools to develop test cases as executable scripts and allocate computer resources to run test cases. Alternatively, when tests are performed manually, testers allocate physical resources and document the test outcomes. We found that testers' primary activities include reviewing test specifications, documenting test scripts, and running these tests. Testers also archive test cases and log files and monitor test execution to constantly document and analyze the SUT.

Monitor Progress and Evaluate: In the end, it is crucial for testers to monitor the advancement towards the test objective(s). This phase involves tracking the results of the test generation and execution procedures. In cases where the correct output cannot be easily defined, test oracles are incorporated into scripts or results are manually monitored. This allows for the evaluation of test case quality. If testers determine that a test goal is not being met, they investigate the issue and make adjustments. Testers analyze the sequence of procedures to determine if the test cases fail to validate the test objective. Our results suggest that the testers' main activity in this step involves comparing the software requirements and specifications with the obtained test results. Testers also discuss the results with the development team or other testers to obtain feedback about the outcomes. If the test fails, testers modify the test cases multiple times to achieve the desired result. The primary activities testers and developers perform include comparing test specifications with test results, discussing the results with the team, and modifying the test cases.

5   Discussion

Based on our previously proposed problem solving model of testing we surveyed 38 professionals in the software development industry. The 25 questions of the survey focused on the activities and knowledge they use and the challenges they face in their daily test design, creation, and execution. The thematic analysis then allowed us to extend the problem solving model with a process model that can be instantiated in the phases of the overall process. While the specific method changes between the phases, the extension clarifies that an internal representation, formed based on knowledge about the environment and specific test goals, first helps select and apply a phase-specific activity which in turn leads to the internal representation being updated. Our results also clarify the information that is used in this external-action-internal-refinement loop. Specific challenges that testers face during the process were also identified.

In practice, companies can use the extended model as a basis for discussions among testers and thus create a higher awareness of both the importance of internal representations, the information and knowledge needed during the process, and how to overcome or mitigate specific challenges. Researchers can use the extended model as a basis for further data collection but also as a basis for further theoretical refinement. They can also consider how their proposed new testing technologies and methods fit with the problem-solving methods of testers and how it addresses existing challenges.

In comparison to most related works (e.g., [1,10]), our research proposes a broader perspective on software testing as a problem-solving activity, emphasizing the cognitive processes involved. The study of Aniche et al. [1] aligns with our model as it also acknowledges the presence of a mental model in test case development. They also found that this mental model is updated when failures and unexpected behavior surface during testing. However, our results also highlight that the internal representations affect not only the test case that is developed but help select the specific activity the tester uses during test creation and execution. Our extended model also places the detailed inner updating process in the context of an outer, general problem-solving process which guides which activities are appropriate.

5.1   Threats to Validity

A survey method was chosen because it allowed us to contact potential participants directly, and they could respond anonymously at their convenience. However, as the survey was conducted digitally and anonymously, we were unable to follow up with participants for clarifications or further questions regarding their responses. Consequently, it is possible that our survey participants misunderstood the questions or that we did not have a clear understanding of the testers' perspectives when formulating the questions. To mitigate this risk, an expert in software engineering reviewed the material provided and guided the respondents. To prevent confusion during the survey, we provided brief explanations for each attribute included in the questionnaire.

The survey garnered 38 responses which limit generalizability. To enable comparisons and statistical evaluation, such as based on company size and years of experience, a larger sample would be necessary. We thus focused only on general trends across the entire dataset.

6   Conclusions

This study aimed to understand the routine and behavior of software testers when performing testing, to improve software testing tools and environments to better serve their needs. We surveyed software testers with an average of five years of experience in the field and used thematic analysis to identify main themes, including knowledge, activities, and challenges related to software testing. Through this analysis, we gained insights into how testers use different sources of information and perform various activities, such as understanding software requirements, learning about the software, and discussing results with other team members to get feedback. We refined an existing test design model to show how knowledge and internal representations help select activities that develop test cases that in turn, after execution, then lead to refined internal representations. Overall, our study provides insights into the routine and behavior of software testers during testing, which can inform the development of better software testing advice, tools, and environments.

References

1. Aniche, M., Treude, C., Zaidman, A.: How developers engineer test cases: an observational study. IEEE Trans. Software Eng. **48**(12), 4925–4946 (2021)
2. Bransford, J.D., Stein, B.S.: The ideal problem solver. New York: W. H (1984)
3. Braun, V., Clarke, V.: Using thematic analysis in psychology. Qual. Res. Psychol. **3**(2), 77,101 (2006)
4. Enoiu, E., Feldt, R.: Towards human-like automated test generation: perspectives from cognition and problem solving. In: International Workshop on Cooperative and Human Aspects of Software Engineering, pp. 123–124 (2021)
5. Enoiu, E., Tukseferi, G., Feldt, R.: Towards a model of testers' cognitive processes: software testing as a problem solving approach. In: International Conference on Software Quality, Reliability and Security Companion, pp. 272–279. IEEE (2020)
6. Getzels, J.W.: The problem of the problem. In: New Directions for Methodology of Social and Behavioral Science: Question Framing and Response Consistency, vol. 11, pp. 37–49 (1982)
7. Hale, D.P., Haworth, D.A.: Towards a model of programmers' cognitive processes in software maintenance: a structural learning theory approach for debugging. J. Softw. Maintenance Res. Pract. **3**(2), 85–106 (1991)
8. Hale, J.E., Sharpe, S., Hale, D.P.: An evaluation of the cognitive processes of programmers engaged in software debugging. J. Softw. Maintenance Res. Practi. **11**(2), 73–91 (1999)
9. Hayes, J.R.: Cognitive processes in creativity. In: Glover, J.A., Ronning, R.R., Reynolds, C.R. (eds.) Handbook of Creativity, pp. 135–145. Springer, Boston (1989). https://doi.org/10.1007/978-1-4757-5356-1_7
10. Itkonen, J., Mäntylä, M.V., Lassenius, C.: The role of the tester's knowledge in exploratory software testing. IEEE Trans. Softw. Eng. **39**(5), 707–724 (2012)
11. Lenberg, P., Feldt, R., Wallgren, L.G.: Behavioral software engineering: a definition and systematic literature review. J. Syst. Softw. **107**, 15–37 (2015)
12. Letovsky, S.: Cognitive processes in program comprehension. J. Syst. Softw. **7**(4), 325–339 (1987)
13. Newel, A., Simon, H.A.: Human Problem Solving. Englewood Cliffs, NJ (1972)
14. Orso, A., Rothermel, G.: Software testing: a research travelogue (2000–2014). In: Proceedings of the on Future of Software Engineering, FOSE 2014, pp. 117–132. ACM, New York, NY, USA (2014)
15. Pezze, M., Young, M.: Software Test and Analysis: Process, Principles, and Techniques. John Wiley and Sons, October 2006
16. Polya, G.: How to solve it (1957)
17. Pretz, J.E., Naples, A.J., Sternberg, R.J.: Recognizing, defining, and representing problems. Psychol. Problem Solv. **30**(3) (2003)
18. Robillard, P.N., d'Astous, P., Détienne, F., Visser, W.: Measuring cognitive activities in software engineering. In: Proceedings of the 20th International Conference on Software Engineering, pp. 292–300. IEEE (1998)

Who Is Afraid of Test Smells? Assessing Technical Debt from Developer Actions

Zhongyan Chen(✉) [ID], Suzanne M. Embury[ID], and Markel Vigo[ID]

Department of Computer Science, The University of Manchester,
Manchester M13 9PL, UK
zhongyan.chen@manchester.ac.uk

Abstract. Test smells are patterns in test code that may indicate poor code quality. Some recent studies have cast doubt on the accuracy and usefulness of the test smells proposed and studied by the research community. In this study, we aimed to determine whether developers view these test smells as sources of technical debt worth spending effort to remove. We selected 12 substantial open-source software systems and mapped how 19 test smells from the literature were introduced and removed from the code base over time. Out of these 19 smells, our results show that: 1) four test smells were rarely detected in our selected projects; 2) three test smells are removed rapidly from the projects while another three are removed from code bases slowly; 3) the remaining nine test smells did not show a consistent pattern of quick or delayed removal. Our results suggest that the test smells currently being studied by researchers do not capture the true concerns of developers regarding test quality, with current testing tool sets, with only three of the 19 smells studied showing clear evidence of developer concern.

Keywords: Test Smells · Software Testing · Empirical Software Engineering

1 Introduction

Software testing plays a vital role in revealing hidden defects in software and in detecting functional regression. To maintain the quality of software over the long term, a high quality test suite is needed. As with production code, quality problems in test code are captured through the concept of *code smells* [7]: design or other quality problems that may represent a source of technical debt. Code smells that apply specifically to test code are called *test smells*. To help developers to write better test code, researchers have proposed a range of test smells, based on evidence from developers [8,14,18]. These smells have been used as the basis for other studies of test code quality [4,10,13,15,16,19].

However, the empirical evidence regarding whether the proposed test smells actually represent poor practice is limited or even conflicting. One study found that most developers surveyed considered 19 test smells shown to be poor testing practices [14], while another studying 5 overlapping test smells found that

© IFIP International Federation for Information Processing 2023
Published by Springer Nature Switzerland AG 2023
S. Bonfanti et al. (Eds.): ICTSS 2023, LNCS 14131, pp. 160–175, 2023.
https://doi.org/10.1007/978-3-031-43240-8_11

developers did not consider them to be actual design problems [17]. A more recent study concluded that current definitions of test smells do not reflect real test quality concerns [13]. If research is to assist developers in writing good test code, a set of test smells for which there is consensus across the practitioner community is needed.

Technical debt is a metaphor that refers to designs or implementations that trade software quality for speedy delivery [6]. In this study, we use developer actions to assess whether test smells are perceived as carrying technical debt. We hypothesise that if developers are putting effort into removing test smell instances, that supports the claim that the smell describes genuine technical debt, whereas if developers allow smell instances to exist for long periods in code bases then that calls into question whether the test smell represents a source of genuine technical debt. Our study aims to answer the following research question:

RQ: Which of the test smells proposed by the research community are viewed as sufficient sources of technical debt for developers to put effort into their removal?

To answer the RQ, we investigated the occurrence of 19 test smells consistently studied by the research community in 12 open-source software projects, tracking their introduction and removal al across the commit history of the project. We then conducted a quantitative analysis, looking at the frequency of introduction of each smell type and the length of time the smell types were allowed to remain within the code base. From this, we classified the technical debt potential of each test smell based on the developers' actions in response to them.

Our results found that only 3 of the 19 test smells studied were rapidly removed from code bases by developers, indicating a consensus that they represent genuine technical debt. A further 3 test smells were found to be long-lived in the code bases, indicating a consensus that they do not represent serious forms of technical debt. Four of the test smells were only rarely introduced into the code bases, making interpretation of their technical debt difficult. Either these smells describe patterns of code that do not occur in practice, or they represent such serious technical debt that developers work hard to make sure they are never committed. The remaining 9 smells were observed throughout our code bases but were removed neither quickly nor slowly by developers. Of these, 5 smell types showed a lack of consensus across the projects, being removed quickly in some projects and slowly in others. Our results suggest that the current set of test smells does not map well to developer views on technical debt in test code and that further research is required to address this.

2   Related Work

In this section, we present the foundations for our study in the existing literature on test smells. We summarise the origins of the test smells we study, work on tools to automatically detect them and other efforts to evaluate test smells, which should be considered alongside the results from our study.

One of the earliest proposals, by Van Deursen et al., introduced 11 smell types covering various aspects of test quality and proposed refactorings to remove them [18], demonstrating the value of studying quality of test code independently from production code. Later researchers expanded the set of test smells [8, 14]. They provided unified names, and definitions for each test smell, setting the foundation for future work on test code quality.

Techniques for detecting test smell instances have also been investigated. In a systematic mapping study, Aljedaani et al. summarized the test smell detection tools proposed by the research community in the last two decades and found that recent tools are more adopted by further studies for their high scalabilities [1]. Popular tools like tsDetect [15], JNose [19], and the tool by Bavota et al. [5] can detect more test smells than earlier tools and have high correctness [1]. The proposed tools provide the means to study test smells at scale in real software systems.

Other researchers have looked for evidence in support of the test smells proposed so far. Tufano et al. used Bavota's tool [4] to detect 5 of the test smells proposed by van Deursen et al. [18] in 152 systems to study how long test smells survived in the code, reporting that the smells had high survivability [17]. They also interviewed 19 developers and found that they did not recognize these smells as design problems [17]. Spadini et al. used tsDetect [15] to detect test smells in around 1,500 open-source projects and used a benchmark-based threshold derivation methodology [2] to generate severity thresholds for 11 test smells [16]. They asked developers to rate the severity of each test smell and found that they did not recognize some of the smells as design problems [16].

Kim et al. used the same tool to detect 18 test smells in 12 open-source projects to investigate how the number of test smells evolved and was addressed during the project's development. They found that only 17% of the test smells were deliberately addressed by developers [10]. This is supported by other test smell evaluation studies. Panichella et al. used two tools [4, 15] to detect instances of 6 test smells in 10 projects and manually validated the results. They concluded the smells studied do not reflect real maintainability concerns [13]. Bai et al. assessed the impact of the *Assertion Roulette* test smell [18] on tests written by 42 computer science students. They concluded that this test smell should not be considered a genuine test smell as it had minimal impact on students' programming accuracy and effectiveness [3]. While these studies question developers' ability to recognize and address test smells [10, 16, 17], others concluded that the test smells themselves do not reflect genuine quality concerns [3, 13].

Among the above 5 evaluation studies, 3 studies [3, 13, 17] only studied a small number of test smells proposed by van Deursen et al. [18]. Two studies [10, 16] included some smells proposed by both van Deursen et al. [18], and Peruma et al. [14]. In four studies that used open-source projects, two analyzed more than 1,000 commits [16, 17]. If the research community is to provide tools for developers to understand, correct and avoid poor practices in test code, a definitive set of complete test smells backed by developers' actions is needed.

3   Methodology

Our study aims to objectively assess the technical debt that developers associate with test smells by observing the actions developers take when the smells are present in code. In this section, we describe our evaluation context, and explain the quantities we use to assess technical debt concerns, our data collection processes and our analysis process.

3.1   The Evaluation Context

Test Smells Selection. Table 1 shows the 19 test smells that are included in our study, selected from the literature [1,4,13–15,18,19].

To locate commits in which test smells are introduced and removed from a range of large code bases, we need a way to automatically detect test smell instances. Specifically, to allow us to track the existence of specific smells across sequences of commits, from their introduction to their removal, we need a tool that can tell us in which file and on what lines of code each smell is located. Therefore, we focus on detection tools with this capability. Based on the mapping study by Aljedaani et al. [1], most existing tools focus on smells in Java systems. Thus, we selected Java open-source projects and the smell detection tool JNose [19] for our study. JNose can detect all test smells in Table 1. It reuses the detection rules of tsDetect, achieving better precision and recall in a later evaluation study [20].

Selected Target Projects. We selected open-source projects from GitHub based on the following criteria. Each selected system must:

1. Be a non-fork Java project.
2. Be a software development project, rather than a tutorial or example project.
3. Contain at least one file having ".java" and "Test" in its name (to ensure the project contains some test code).
4. Have at least 5 years of history and 500–10,000 commits (to ensure there is sufficient time for even low severity technical debt to become visible to developers and possibly removed; the upper limit is to ensure all commits can be analysed within the time scales of this study).
5. Have either MIT or Apache-2.0 licenses which allow us to conduct derivative work.

We used GitHub's search function to find candidate projects meeting criteria 1., 3., 4. and 5., ordered by star counts (as a rough measure of popularity). Criteria 2. was manually assessed. The top 12 systems meeting these criteria were selected for our study, as shown in Table 2.

Table 1. Test Smells Selected for the Study

Test Smell	Description
Test Smells Proposed by Van Deurse et al. [18]	
Assertion Roulette	A test method contains more than one assertion statement without using the *message* parameter in the assertion method, which makes it hard to locate the failed assertions of the test.
Eager Test	A test method contains multiple calls to multiple production methods. This smell results in difficulties in test comprehension and maintenance.
General Fixture	Not all fields instantiated within the *setUp()* method of a test class are utilized by all test methods in the same test class. This smell may execute unnecessary code and waste resources.
Lazy Test	Multiple test methods calling the same production method. This smell may make the test harder to maintain.
Mystery Guest	A test method containing object instances of files and databases classes, introducing hidden dependencies.
Resource Optimism	A test method making optimistic assumptions about the state/existence of external resources can cause the test result unpredictable.
Sensitive Equality	A test method invokes the *toString()* method of an object. Changes to the implementation of *toString()* might result in failure.
Test Smells Proposed by Peruma et al. [14]	
Conditional Test Logic	A test method that contains one or more control statements, which negatively impacts the ease of comprehension by developers as failing to meet the condition could also be the cause of failure.
Constructor Initialization	A test class that contains a constructor declaration. Ideally, initialization of fields in tests should use *setUp()* method instead of a constructor.
Default Test	A test class is named either *ExampleUnitTest* or *ExampleInstrumentedTest*. Some IDEs give default names for new test classes but giving test classes meaningful names is considered good practice.
Duplicate Assert	A test method that contains more than one assertion statement with the same parameters.
Empty Test	A test method that does not contain a single executable statement.
Exception Catching Throwing	A test method that contains either a throw statement or a catch clause. Developers should utilize JUnit's exception handling to automatically pass/fail the test instead of using exception handling code.
Ignored Test	A test method or class that contains the *@Ignore* annotation.
Magic Number Test	An assertion method that contains a numeric literal as an argument. Magic numbers do not indicate the meaning of the number and will reduce the comprehensibility and maintainability of the test.
Redundant Print	A test method that has print statements. Print statements in unit tests are redundant as unit tests are automatically executed with little to no human intervention.
Redundant Assertion	A test method that contains an assertion statement in which the expected and actual parameters are the same.
Sleepy Test	A test method that invokes the *Thread.sleep()* method, which may introduce additional delays to the test execution [16].
Unknown Test	A test method that does not contain a single assertion statement

Table 2. The Target Projects (at the Point of Cloning)

GitHub Project Name	Date of the Latest Observed Commit	Project Lifetime (Years)	Number of Analyzed Commits
caffeine	2022/12/18	9	664
dubbo	2022/09/22	12	1203
HikariCP	2023/02/01	11	330
javapoet	2021/04/15	10	231
Java-WebSocket	2022/07/04	13	95
jib	2023/01/09	7	959
mockito	2022/11/28	16	1513
mybatis-3	2023/03/13	14	803
redisson	2022/12/06	10	1028
retrofit	2023/03/31	14	412
RxJava	2022/02/10	11	1299
vert.x	2022/12/20	12	1774

3.2 Mean Time to Removal

Technical debt is usually assessed using the presence of code smells, with other measures such as time/cost of removal also being used [11]. Since we aim to assess test smells from technical debt, not the other way around, we cannot use the smell-based approach. Instead, we choose time to removal (TTR) of the smell, i.e., the interval between the timestamps of the commits introducing and removing it, as our main measure, on the assumption that smells are removed due to the actions of developers, reflecting their views on what makes for valuable use of their time for their system. To aggregate the actions of many developers, we use a mean time to removal (MTTR) score, applied to individual code bases and across code bases.

3.3 Data Collection

The evaluation process followed for each target system is shown in Fig. 1[1]. We clone the target system and analyse it to select the commits that will be the target for smell detection. JNose then runs on each selected commit, and the details of the detected smells are stored. The TTR is calculated for each smell instance removed during the project's lifetime, and the results are aggregated to give the MTTR for each smell type. These steps are explained below[2]

Target Commit Selection. To determine how long test smells exist in the target projects, we run the smell detection tool over each major version of the code to determine commits where test smells are introduced and removed from the code base. Typically, many commits will change only production code. Therefore, to make our pipeline more efficient, we run smell detection only on commits

---

[1] The study design was approved by Computer Science Department Panel, The University of Manchester Ref: 2023-15405-27595. All authors are available for clarifications.

[2] The pipeline code is available at https://github.com/ZhongyanChen/tsObservatory..

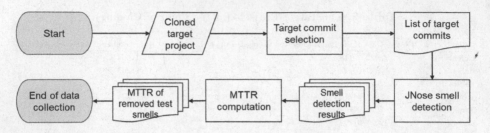

Fig. 1. Data Collection Process (**Rounded rectangle:** state; **Rhomboid:** input; **Rectangle:** process; **Wavy base rectangle:** document)

where some change has been made to test code. To do this, we scan through the commit history and identify the commits that meet the conditions below:

- **Commits on the development mainline:** The development mainline of a repository records the key versions of the code base that contain only completed and integrated feature implementations. We limited our analysis to commits on the development mainline and ignored work-in-progress commits on feature branches. To do this, we manually identify the mainline branch for each target project and configure the pipeline to seek out the first parent commits on that branch.
- **Commits changing at least one file having ".java" and "Test" in its name:** we use the approach of Peruma et al. [15] to identify test files, which is based on best practice recommended by JUnit[3]. A commit is selected for analysis if it adds, deletes or modifies a file meeting these criteria.

The number of commits in each project meeting both conditions is shown in the rightmost column of Table 2.

Test Smell Detection. In this step, we check out each target commit and run JNose to detect test smells for every detected smell instance, JNose records the path of the file containing the instance, the path of the corresponding production file (if applicable), the detected smell type, the test or production method names involved in the smell, and the line number(s) on which the smell instance is located. At the end of this step, we have a set of CSV files detailing the smells detected in every target commit.

MTTR Computation. To compute the time to removal for each smell instance, we need to know the commit when it was introduced into the code base and the commit when it was removed. To do this, we must track a smell instance across a sequence of commits. This is complicated by the fact that other changes to the file may cause the smell to change its position, even if the smell itself is unaffected by the commit. Therefore, when checking whether a smell has

---

[3] https://junit.org/junit4/faq.html#running_15, accessed on 2023/03/30.

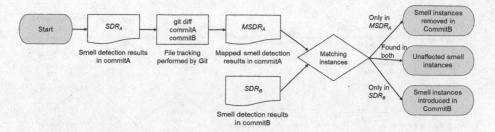

Fig. 2. The Mapping Process from CommitA to CommitB (**Rounded rectangle**: state; **Wavy base rectangle**: document; **Rectangle**: process; **Rhombus**: Decision)

survived into the following commit, we worked out its expected new position in the file based on the changes that have been made during the commit.

Given two consecutive commits, A and B, where A is an ancestor of B, we use the following concepts to map a smell instance from A to B:

- SDR_A: The smell detection results for commit A.
- SDR_B: The smell detection results for commit B.
- $MSDR_A$: The mapped smell detection results for commit A.

Git provides information on what file paths and which lines of code were changed from commit A to B. We use this to produce $MSDR_A$ by updating the file paths and line number(s) of every smell instance in SDR_A. Every smell instance in $MSDR_A$ that does not exist in SDR_B is considered to have been removed by commit B. Every instance in SDR_B that is not in $MSDR_A$ is considered to have been introduced in commit B. This process is illustrated in Fig. 2.

We run this process for all consecutive pairs of target commits and find, for each smell instance, the commit in which it is introduced and removed. From the commit timestamps, we calculate the time to removal for that particular instance. Various MTTR can be calculated from the times to removal for all instances, by aggregating against different sets.

Unfortunately, this process of mapping smell instances across commits is not 100% accurate, since it is impossible to distinguish between the modification of a line and the insertion and deletion of lines. We ran a short study of how this impacted our results and found that the effect on the overall accuracy of our approach was low. We discuss these impacts in Sect. 5.

3.4   Data Analysis

We use the data described above to classify the 19 test smells according to the support given to them by the developers' actions. We use a two-step process (Fig. 3) to classify each test smell into one of four categories: **Underrepresented test smells**, **Rapidly removed test smells**, **Slowly removed test smells**, and **Mid-range removal test smells**. To perform this classification for n target projects, we compute:

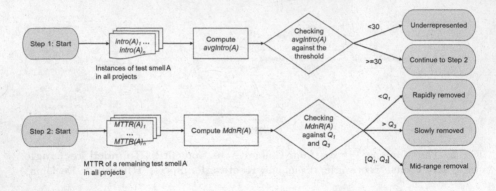

Fig. 3. Data Analysis Process (**Rounded rectangle**: state; **Wavy base rectangles**: documents; **Rectangle**: process; **Rhombus:** Decision)

- $intro(A)_x$: the number of instances of test smell A introduced across all commits in project x.
- $avgIntro(A)$: the average of $intro(A)_x$ across n target projects.
- $MTTR(A)_x$: the mean time to removal across all instances of test smell A in project x.
- $R(A)_x$: the ratio $\frac{MTTR(A)_x}{Lifetime_x}$ for test smell A in project x.
  To allow MTTRs to be compared across projects, we normalize by dividing by the project's lifetime. Since no tests may have been written in the early stages of a project, we use the interval between the first commit in our target set for project x and the latest observed commit as the project lifetime.
- $MdnR(A)$: the median of $R(A)_x$ across all n projects.
- $\sigma_{R(A)}$: the standard deviation of $R(A)_x$ across all n projects.
  Smells classed in the mid-range removal are neither removed rapidly from the code bases we studied nor left to languish for long periods of time. To distinguish them, we can look at the level of agreement on their positioning on our scale from the different projects using the standard deviation of $R(A)$ across all n projects.

The first step of our analysis separates out those test smells for which we found insufficient examples to allow us to draw any firm conclusions. For each project x, we calculate $Intro(A)_x$ and $avgIntro(A)$ for each test smell A. Based on central limit theorem [9], we set 30 as the threshold and classify all smells for which $avgIntro(A)$ is below that as under-represented, and therefore providing insufficient samples from which to make a significant statistical inference.

The next step is to use the $MdnR(A)$ and $\sigma_{R(A)}$ to classify each remaining test smell. We use the first and third quartiles (denoted Q_1 and Q_3 respectively) as thresholds for this classification. A test smell A will be classified as rapidly removed if $MdnR(A)$ is below Q_3. If $MdnR(A)$ is within the interquartile range, it will be a mid-range test smell. Finally, if $MdnR(A)$ is in the range above Q_3, it will be classified as a slowly removed test smell.

Table 3. Results and Classifications of Test Smells

Test Smell	avgIntro	MdnR	σ_R	Classification
Constructor Initialization	2.333	-	-	Under-represented
Default Test	0	-	-	
Empty Test	6.167	-	-	
Redundant Assertion	19.917	-	-	
Mystery Guest	34.583	0.700%	0.075	Rapidly removed
Redundant Print	69.083	1.483%	0.078	
Resource Optimism	40.083	5.454%	0.068	
Lazy Test	1269.083	9.743%	0.038	Mid-range removal with consensus
Eager Test	1443.583	12.786%	0.048	
Unknown Test	1660.167	9.930%	0.049	
Ignored Test	384.833	7.912%	0.051	
Exception Catching Throwing	614.417	11.931%	0.064	
General Fixture	76.167	8.200%	0.157	Mid-range removal with mixed opinions
Conditional Test Logic	569.917	8.656%	0.068	
Sensitive Equality	230.833	10364%	0.121	
Sleepy Test	129.500	12.385%	0.090	
Duplicate Assert	353.417	14.427%	0.074	Slowly removed
Assertion Roulette	5344.000	15.250%	0.087	
Magic Number Test	2155.667	15.550%	0.096	

4   Results and Discussion

The results from our study are shown in Table 3[4] The average introduction count is given for each smell type. Four test smells are classified as underrepresented due to their low average introduction rate across all the projects. These smells do not participate further in the analysis. For the remaining 15 test smells, the $MdnR$ and σ_R are shown in Table 3.

Among the remaining 15 test smells, the $MdnR$ of *Ignored Test* is Q_1, and the $MdnR$ of *Eager Test* is Q_3. This gives the classification to the other test smells, as shown in the table. We divide the test smells in the interquartile range based upon the standard deviation in their median removal rates, separating those for which there is agreement across the projects in the study from those where developer actions in the different projects give very different mean times to removal.

---

[4] The full data set of this study are provided as supplementary information accompanying this paper at https://figshare.manchester.ac.uk/projects/Evaluating_Test_Smells_in_Open-Source_Projects/164461.

4.1   Under-Represented Test Smells

We found 4 test smells that were rarely or never introduced in any of our selected projects. We hypothesise two reasons for this:

- The smell is a source of serious technical debt, so most of its instances were removed before the code was committed or through code review before integration into the development mainline.
- The detection rule for this smell is too strict and is under-reporting the instances that are introduced.

We discuss each test smell placed in this category below.

Default Test: we observed no introductions of this smell in any of our selected projects. It was originally proposed in a study of Android systems, so the detection rule is designed around the default test method names used by the Android Studio IDE [14]. Other IDEs for other languages and frameworks would use different default names. The lack of observed instances of this smell type could therefore be put down to the overly strict detection rule, rather than questioning the rationale for the smell itself. We recommend broadening the detection rule for this smell if it is to be used in future research.

Constructor Initialization: in the 12 studied projects, 5 yielded no examples of this smell while the others introduced fewer than 10 examples each. Following best practice, fixture set up should be done in a *setUp()* method instead of using a constructor. The rationale for proposing this smell [14] is therefore sound, and the detection rule aligns with best practice. A possible explanation for the lack of examples is that developers are accustomed to using the *setUp()* methods for fixture initialisation and do this without considering alternatives.

Empty Test and Redundant Assertion these two smells cause a test to always pass or always fail, regardless of the behaviour of the production code it pertains to test. Most of the participants in the survey conducted by Peruma et al. agreed that these two smells should be removed from code. Peruma et al. also noted that these smells are likely for debugging purposes only [14], which could be the reason why they are rarely seen in mainline commits.

4.2   Rapidly Removed Test Smells

Three test smells fell into this category, with average times to removal of between 24 and 200 days. Instances of these smell types were removed promptly across all our selected projects, suggesting that developers view them as significant sources of technical debt worth putting time and effort into removing.

Redundant Print: print statements in test cases are redundant because test suites are expected to execute with little or no human supervision. Peruma et al. found that one cause of this smell is when print statements introduced for temporary debugging purposes are not removed [14]. Although print statements are poor practice, they don't waste much time or computational resources unless they occur in high numbers. The removal of this smell would likely be for code cleanup than paying back technical debt. Although the average introduction rate for *Redundant Print* is clearly above our threshold, 5 of our 12 projects contained no examples of this smell while 4 projects introduced fewer than 10 instances. RxJava has the most, with 602 instances, which skews the overall result. Thus, the average may overstate the presence of this test smell in our data set.

Mystery Guest and Resource Optimism: significant loss of time and testing power can be experienced when the Mystery Guest smell is present. The use of external resources turns unit tests into integration tests and exposes them to instability and performance costs. Resource Optimism reports situations where important checks of test preconditions are omitted from the test definition. If a test precondition is not satisfied then the test results cannot be properly interpreted and the time spent running this test is wasted. Therefore, these two test smells seem serious, compared to the smells discussed so far. However, the detection rules for both these smells have some limitations. The rule for Resource Optimism looks for specific tests on the File objects, ignoring other resource types. Mystery Guest's detection rule is slightly broader by including a check for instances of a database class, but it also misses other external resources. Therefore, we are likely under-reporting these two test smells.

4.3 Slowly Removed Test Smells

The 3 test smells in this category take, on average, between 527 and 568 days to be removed, suggesting that they may not be perceived by developers as representing sufficient technical debt to be worth the effort of removal.

Duplicate Assert: this smell occurs when a test method has multiple assertions with the same parameters. Peruma et al. suggest that developers grouping multiple test cases within single test methods may be one possible cause, along with accidental copy-paste effects [14]. However, in their survey, they received mixed responses and concluded that the spread of test conditions across test methods is based on individual developer preferences [14]. Since the standard deviation for Duplicate Assert is the median standard deviation of all the test smells, our data is in line with the inconsistent responses to their survey. While differing developer preferences is one explanation, in the projects we studied, we also found that some duplicated assertions test the same variable's value in different states of the process under test. In this case, separating the assertions across test case methods might be prohibitively expensive. Therefore, the smell as currently defined may not be a true source of technical debt.

Assertion Roulette: this smell instance is found when the original JUnit assert methods are used without providing the optional string "message" parameter that is displayed when the assertion fails. The original rationale for this was that without this parameter it is hard to locate which assertion in the test suite failed [18]. However, as Panichella et al. conclude, this rationale was reasonable for JUnit 3 tests but makes less sense for later versions [13]. On this basis, Panichella et al. concluded that this smell is obsolete and should no longer be considered a test smell [13]. Our results support this conclusion. Its average introduction rate is the highest among the 19 test smells, and on average, its instances take the second longest time to be removed.

Magic Number Test: we found that it takes on average 568 days to remove an instance of Magic Number Test, while its average introduction rate is the second highest across all the test smells. This is perhaps surprising, as the presence of numeric and other literals in production code is a well-known and long-respected code smell [7]. A possible explanation for this smell's survival in test code could be found in the differences between production code and test code. In test code, numeric literals are often needed to specify the input values for test cases and the expected output values. Unlike in production code, these literals are intended to represent typical domain values that might be seen in production use, rather than special literals with a specific meaning. They are included in the code in a one-time-use fashion, scoped only within the test method. The results of our study support the conclusion that this smell does not in fact describe a source of significant technical debt for test code. However, if the same numeric literal is used by multiple test methods or classes, it could cost developers more time to refactor the code should a new value be needed. The current detection rule will flag any assertions containing a numeric literal as an argument without checking the numeric literal's scope. Therefore, we recommend an improved detection rule for this smell which can check the scope of the literal and can report on non-numeric literals.

4.4   Mid Range Test Smells

As explained in Sect. 3.4, this remaining group of smells are the ones which are neither removed rapidly nor left in the code bases for long periods of time. To distinguish them, we look at the level of agreement on their ranking from developers on the different projects. We use the standard deviation of the $R(A)$ to class each smell in this group into one of the two sub-groups listed in Table 3.

Test Smells with Mixed Opinions: our data shows that, of the smells in this category, 4 have high standard deviations in their mean time to removal rates. On average, their removal times range from 299 to 452 days. Sleepy Test, where delays are inserted into tests to synchronise with distributed parallel components, may be more prevalent (and harder to avoid) in projects with a significant distributed element. Similarly, Conditional Test Logic and General Fixture are easy to avoid on some projects but may be a significant time saver for projects with complex fixture requirements. These must be treated as true smells, sometimes indicating the presence of technical debt and sometimes indicating a reasonable solution to a difficult testing task.

Sensitive Equality, however, is a different case. It occurs when the writer of a test case uses the *toString()* method to check that the expected instance is returned, rather than implementing and using a true equality check for the class in question. This can cause instability in the tests because the definition of the *toString()* method can be changed without realising the effect on the tests. The detection rule in JNose looks for any use of a *toString()* method in a test case to find instances of the smell. Unfortunately, this will also mark legitimate uses (such as test cases verifying that a desired *toString()* functionality has been implemented correctly) as smells. In our study, we found a reasonably high level of occurrence of this smell but did not find evidence to suggest that developers are rushing to remove it when it is present. We were unable to distinguish legitimate from poor practice uses of *toString()*; it is possible that we would see different patterns of removal in each case if we could.

Test Smells with Consensus: the standard deviations of the 5 test smells in this group (Lazy Test, Eager Test, Unknown Test, Ignored Test, and Exception Catching Throwing) are the lowest among all 19 test smells. There seems to be a general agreement on the handling of these smells among our projects. They are sometimes removed (perhaps when convenient) but are often left in place.

5   Threats to Validity

Strict detection rules: as discussed, the detection rules for Default Test, Mystery Guest, and Resource Optimism in JNose are too strict compared to the test smell definition. This leads to the strong possibility that we may have under-reported instances of these test smells. We mitigated this by filtering out smells with very low introduction rates to avoid drawing conclusions about smells for which we had insufficient data. On the other hand, the detection rules for Magic Number Test and Sensitive Equality are too weak, finding examples of smells that do not really fit their definitions. By using these detection rules, we may be over-reporting the number of instances of the affected smells.

Lacking information about the reasons for smell removal: our study design allowed us to detect and track the existence and removal of test smells across sequences of commits. However, we have not attempted to discover the reasons why each test smell was removed. Was it because a developer identified and intended to remove the smell deliberately? Or was it the result of other changes made to the code base (i.e. removal of features, changes in design) that accidentally caused the smell instance to be removed? Ideally, the accidentally removed test smells should not be included in our data set as they cannot reflect developers' views on technical debt. Since our study design does not distinguish the reason for removal, it is likely we are over-reporting the number of removed test smells and maybe under or over-reporting the time to removal.

Limitations of smell instance mapping algorithm: as mentioned, our algorithm for mapping test smells across sequences of commits has some limitations. For example, suppose a commit refactors a test case where a smell instance is located. The test case contains the smell both before and after refactoring. However, our mapping algorithm cannot distinguish between this refactoring and a smell deletion and insertion of a different smell of the same kind. Both are represented the same way in the Git commit. In this example, our algorithm would report that a smell instance was deleted and a new one was added in this commit. This could cause over-reporting of the numbers of both introduced and removed smell instances and under-reporting of the MTTRs.

6 Conclusions and Future Work

We have presented the results of a study into the introduction and removal of test smells by developers in established open-source software projects, with the aim of determining where there might be consensus on the smells that represent genuine technical debt. Our aim is to supplement earlier studies evaluating test smells and to understand which of the smells are suitable targets on which to build future research. The results, shown in Sect. 4, give our classification for each test smell included in this study into four categories. We only found 3 test smells that tend to be rapidly removed from all the projects in our study, and that would appear to represent sources of significant technical debt. This raises questions as to the suitability of these smells to be included in the "canon" of test smells or as subjects for further research on test code quality.

Several future directions are possible. One is the improvement of the detection rules used to identify smell instances for the test smells so that the scale of occurrence of the smells in code can be more accurately assessed. In addition, it would be useful to be able to distinguish the intentional removal of smells by developers from the accidental removal as a result of other changes. It may also be useful to study smell instances in non-mainline commits, to see if code quality management processes are helping to remove smell instances before integration into the mainline. Information on developer intention may also be present in commit messages and code reviews, or in discussions on pull/merge requests and on issue trackers.

Beyond this, the number of test smells that survived our analysis is small—far smaller and more limited in scope than the well-documented and accepted production code smells. It seems unlikely that these surviving smells are a complete reflection of all the quality issues that can arise when writing test code. Indeed, several important aspects of modern testing practice are not covered, particularly in the writing of fixture code, with the use of test doubles [12], for example, as well as the role of test harness code. Yet more smells may be found in the pragmatic aspects of test run configurations and CI pipeline definitions. Perhaps sufficient time has now elapsed since the first test smells were proposed to justify a revisiting of best practices in automated testing, to derive new smells that reflect the concerns of current developers aiming to manage the quality of their systems through testing.

References

1. Aljedaani, W., et al.: Test smell detection tools: a systematic mapping study. Eval. Assessment Soft. Eng., 170–180 (2021)
2. Alves, T.L., Ypma, C., Visser, J.: Deriving metric thresholds from benchmark data. In: 2010 IEEE International Conference on Software Maintenance, pp. 1–10. IEEE (2010)
3. Bai, G.R., Presler-Marshall, K., Fisk, S.R., Stolee, K.T.: Is assertion roulette still a test smell? An experiment from the perspective of testing education. In: 2022 IEEE Symposium on Visual Languages and Human-Centric Computing (VL/HCC), pp. 1–7. IEEE (2022)

4. Bavota, G., Qusef, A., Oliveto, R., De Lucia, A., Binkley, D.: Are test smells really harmful? An empirical study. Empir. Softw. Eng. **20**, 1052–1094 (2015)
5. Bavota, G., Qusef, A., Oliveto, R., De Lucia, A., Binkley, D.: An empirical analysis of the distribution of unit test smells and their impact on software maintenance. In: 2012 28th IEEE International Conference on Software Maintenance (ICSM), pp. 56–65. IEEE (2012)
6. Cunningham, W.: The WyCash portfolio management system. ACM SIGPLAN OOPS Messenger **4**(2), 29–30 (1992)
7. Fowler, M.: Refactoring. Addison-Wesley Professional (2018)
8. Garousi, V., Küçük, B.: Smells in software test code: a survey of knowledge in industry and academia. J. Syst. Softw. **138**, 52–81 (2018)
9. Hogg, R.V., Tanis, E.A., Zimmerman, D.L.: Probability and Statistical Inference, vol. 993. Macmillan New York (1977)
10. Kim, D.J., Chen, T.H.P., Yang, J.: The secret life of test smells-an empirical study on test smell evolution and maintenance. Empir. Softw. Eng. **26**(5), 1–47 (2021)
11. Lenarduzzi, V., Besker, T., Taibi, D., Martini, A., Fontana, F.A.: A systematic literature review on technical debt prioritization: strategies, processes, factors, and tools. J. Syst. Softw. **171**, 110827 (2021)
12. McDonough, J.E.: Automated unit testing with ABAP. In: Automated Unit Testing with ABAP, pp. 43–98. Apress, Berkeley, CA (2021). https://doi.org/10.1007/978-1-4842-6951-0_5
13. Panichella, A., Panichella, S., Fraser, G., Sawant, A.A., Hellendoorn, V.J.: Test smells 20 years later: detectability, validity, and reliability. Empir. Softw. Eng. **27**(7), 170 (2022)
14. Peruma, A., Almalki, K., Newman, C.D., Mkaouer, M.W., Ouni, A., Palomba, F.: On the distribution of test smells in open source android applications: an exploratory study. In: Proceedings of the 29th Annual International Conference on Computer Science and Software Engineering, pp. 193–202 (2019)
15. Peruma, A., Almalki, K., Newman, C.D., Mkaouer, M.W., Ouni, A., Palomba, F.: tsDetect: an open source test smells detection tool. In: Proceedings of the 28th ACM Joint Meeting on European Software Engineering Conference and Symposium on the Foundations of Software Engineering, pp. 1650–1654 (2020)
16. Spadini, D., Schvarcbacher, M., Oprescu, A.M., Bruntink, M., Bacchelli, A.: Investigating severity thresholds for test smells. In: Proceedings of the 17th International Conference on Mining Software Repositories, pp. 311–321 (2020)
17. Tufano, M., et al.: An empirical investigation into the nature of test smells. In: Proceedings of the 31st IEEE/ACM International Conference on Automated Software Engineering, pp. 4–15 (2016)
18. Van Deursen, A., Moonen, L., Van Den Bergh, A., Kok, G.: Refactoring test code. In: Proceedings of the 2nd International Conference on Extreme Programming and Flexible Processes in Software Engineering (XP2001), pp. 92–95. Citeseer (2001)
19. Virgínio, T., et al.: JNose: Java test smell detector. In: Proceedings of the XXXIV Brazilian Symposium on Software Engineering, pp. 564–569 (2020)
20. Virgínio, T., et al.: On the test smells detection: an empirical study on the JNose test accuracy. J. Softw. Eng. Res. Dev. **9**, 8 (2021)

Model Based Testing

A Systematic Literature Review on Prioritizing Software Test Cases Using Markov Chains

G. Barbosa[1,2], É. Souza[3], L. Rebelo[4,5](✉), M. Silva[4], J. Balera[2], and N. Vijaykumar[2]

[1] Universidade Estadual Paulista - Unesp, Guaratinguetá, Brazil
[2] Instituto Nacional de Pesquisas Espaciais - INPE, São José dos Campos, Brazil
[3] Universidade Tecnológica Federal do Paraná - UTFPR, Cornélio Procópio, Brazil
[4] Instituto Federal de Educação, Ciência e Tecnologia de São Paulo - IFSP, Jacareí-Campos do Jordão, Brazil
[5] Gran Sasso Science Institute - GSSI, L'Aquila, Italy
luciana.rebelo@gssi.it

Abstract. Software Testing is a costly activity since the size of the test case set tends to increase as the construction of the software evolves. Test Case Prioritization (TCP) can reduce the effort and cost of software testing. TCP is an activity where a subset of the existing test cases is selected in order to maximize the possibility of finding defects. On the other hand, Markov chains representing a system, when solved, can present the occupation time of each of their states. The idea is to use such information and associate priority to those test cases that consist of states with the highest probabilities. This journal-first paper provides an overview of a systematic survey of the state-of-the-art to identify and understand key initiatives for using Markov chains in TCP.

1 Extended Abstract

This journal-first paper summarises our recently published survey on the topic of test case prioritization and Markov chain, published in 2022 on the Information and Software Technology Journal [1]. Prioritizing test cases refers to choosing those cases that are more important based on some metric, but without decreasing the number of faults to be detected [4]. Test Case Prioritization (TCP) presents techniques that propose to order test cases based on a defined criterion, which can be fault detection rate, coverage rate, or probability of execution history, among others. Markov chain may represent the software system, considering its available states, while the arcs indicate transitions among states and are assigned probabilities that refer to the probability of a state to move to another. With these probabilities, Markov chains can be solved to obtain steady-state probabilities. Steady-state probabilities represent the percentage of time occupied by each state. This characteristic can be applied for TCP, using the probabilities to define priorities of what states are more active than others. So, test cases going through states which have high probabilities, tend to

Published by Springer Nature Switzerland AG 2023
S. Bonfanti et al. (Eds.): ICTSS 2023, LNCS 14131, pp. 179–182, 2023.
https://doi.org/10.1007/978-3-031-43240-8_20

higher usage of those specific paths. Therefore, if one must choose test cases, it is interesting to exercise the paths that contain states with a high percentage of occupation. These features applied in TCP can generate some benefits.

The objective of our work was to conduct a Systematic Literature Review (SLR) in order to understand how Markov chains have been applied on TCP. Aspects such as approaches, developed techniques, programming languages, analytical and simulation results, and validation tests were investigated. The major contribution is to gather and explore the main test case prioritization techniques using Markov chains that were and are being used now. In addition, we believe that these SLR results can help to identify a body of knowledge to support future research in Markov chains and TCP, providing a basis for other researchers as well as students who consider learning about and contributing to this area.

Three research questions were identified and investigated: **RQ1:** When and where the studies have been published? **RQ2:** How Markov chains have been applied to prioritize test cases? and **RQ3:** What are the algorithms and/or tools to support TCP using Markov chains in each study? In order to answer these questions, the search string [("Software Testing" OR "Software Test" OR "Test Case" OR "Test Sequence") AND ("Markov chains" OR "Markovian")] was applied on five different scientific bases (IEEE Xplore, ACM Digital Library, Scopus, ScienceDirect, and SpringerLink), using inclusion and exclusion criteria. After searching the selected sources, a total of 480 publications were returned considering the studies published until July 2021 (no start date has been set). As a result after applying the criteria a set of 10 studies remained. Over these 10 studies that remained, we performed backward snowballing process, looking at all the references from the 10 studies selected (306 references), resulting in 2 studies. At the end, we got to 12 studies to be analyzed. We briefly summarise how the results of our survey address the research questions listed above.

In answer to **RQ1**, 10 different publication sources were identified. It is worth pointing out that four studies were published in the Journal *Information and Software Technology*, showing that it can be a well-established forum for discussing the topic. Regarding the year of publication of the studies, it has spread over the last two decades (from 2000 to 2017). This indicates that prioritization of test cases, regardless of the applications and techniques used, has only been recently employed. Among them, two papers are most recent, both published in 2017. And four papers are the oldest, published in 2000. Although the search was carried out until July 2021, the last prioritization study using Markov chain returned is from 2017, which shows an exploration gap in the last four years. Also, to better understand the possible relationship between the 12 selected studies, we created a citation relationship. Analyzing the citations, we realized that there is no significant relationship between the studies, as there are only four citations between them. It is believed that this happens because the nature of the test case prioritization applications in each study is quite different. Another important aspect to better understand a research segment is where this type of work has been carried out. From the 12 studies remained, institutions of these authors belongs to six different countries. Among them, the largest concentration is in China, containing five studies, followed by the USA with three.

To understand key initiatives of using Markov chains in the priority test cases context, **RQ2** investigates which approaches have been proposed or applied in the selected studies, that is, the main contexts in which test case prioritization using Markov chains are inserted. Six forms of approaches were found, which are – (i) *Usage model*: this approach explores test sequences according to the use of software instead of testing a specific code [7]; (ii) *Controlled Markov chains (CMC)*: explores the interplay between software and control in order to introduce some concepts of test case prioritization [2]; (iii) *Model-based testing (MBT)*: when probability-based heuristic is created to increase the search for paths in graphs [6]; (iv) *Regression testing*: the test suite prioritization method is based on fault activation analysis, and error propagation analysis – important key to occur prioritization of test cases using Markov chains [5]; (v) *Statistical testing*: allows cases to find the most probable and the rarest tests in a specification [3]; and (vi) *Random testing*: it is an alternative random-coverage-based algorithm, applied specially to cover large problems [8]. Most of the studies have generated new techniques in which Markov chains are used in the TCP process so that the application of Markov chains plays a significant role within each technique.

Table 1 compiles the main information for **RQ3**, which refers to developed techniques, programming languages, analytical and simulation results, and validation tests. An important piece of information that could be present in the table would be an open-source application that was developed. However, none of the studies produced one. Except for A_5, A_7, A_{10}, and A_{12}, all others have generated some new techniques in which Markov chains are used in the test case prioritization process. As a major highlight, the study A_6 has the most directly applied technique, where automation of test cases prioritization is developed. Most of the studies do not indicate the programming language used in their development. In A_3 and A_9, MATLAB is used and A_6 uses MATLAB Simulink. With this information, we can better identify how the generated techniques were developed, in terms of paradigms, for example. The last three columns of the table bring us how the results were generated. Only studies A_7, A_8, and A_{11} did not generate results analytically. On the other hand, studies A_5 and A_{12} were the only ones that did not use some numerical form to demonstrate their results. This combination of analytical and numerical results and in most cases demonstrates how complete the results are. And finally, which brings even more assurance and confidence in the techniques developed and, in the results presented, only study A_5 does not present a validation test.

To conclude, our motivation for this work was the fact that TCP is a profitable field from the point of view of the entire software development cycle, as its application can be useful in many ways, such as saving time and budget since the goal is to optimize the process of software testing, which often consumes a good deal of effort on the part of the development team. Overall, the major contribution of this study was to elucidate the context of the application of this subject. Based on the analysis of all 12 studies, we realized the benefits of applying Markov chains for TCP. Thus, as a proposal for future work, we will develop a test case generation and prioritization technique using Markov chains.

Table 1. Information on the methodology used in the development of works on the use of Markov chains for prioritizing test cases

ID	Context	Developed technique	Programming language	Analytical results	Simulation results	Validation tests
A_1	Usage model	measure of the complexity of a software specification	-	✓	✓	✓
A_2	Usage model	optimal test transition probabilities in a Markov software usage model	-	✓	✓	✓
A_3	Controlled MC	adaptive software testing	MATLAB	✓	✓	✓
A_4	Controlled MC	adaptive software testing (extended)		✓	✓	✓
A_5	Controlled MC	-	-	✓	-	-
A_6	Model-based testing, Regression testing	automatic prioritization of test cases	MATLAB Simulink	✓	✓	✓
A_7	Statistical testing	-	-	-	✓	✓
A_8	Model-based testing	ant colony optimization algorithm and model-based testing	-	-	✓	✓
A_9	Model-based testing	model driven approach for system validation	MATLAB	✓	✓	✓
A_{10}	Usage model, Statistical testing	-	-	✓	✓	✓
A_{11}	Regression testing, Random testing	Markov chain Monte Carlo Random Testing	-	-	✓	✓
A_{12}	Controlled MC	-	-	✓	-	✓

Our technique in the initial testing phase will use the probabilities of each test sequence to perform the ranking. We also intend to make this tool available.

Acknowledgements. The authors acknowledge the support of the MUR (Italy) Department of Excellence 2023 - 2027 for GSSI.

References

1. Barbosa, G., de Souza, É.F., dos Santos, L.B.R., dà Silva, M., Balera, J.M., Vijayku-mar, N.L.: A systematic literature review on prioritizing software test cases using Markov chains. Inf. Softw. Technol. **147**, 106902 (2022). https://doi.org/10.1016/j.infsof.2022.106902
2. Cai, K.Y.: Optimal software testing and adaptive software testing in the context of software cybernetics. Inf. Softw. Technol. **44**(14), 841–855 (2002)
3. Devroey, X., et al.: Statistical prioritization for software product line testing: an experience report. Softw. Syst. Model. **16**(1), 153–171 (2015)
4. Elbaum, S., Malishevsky, A.G., Rothermel, G.: Test case prioritization: a family of empirical studies. IEEE Trans. Software Eng. **28**(2), 159–182 (2002)
5. Morozov, A., Ding, K., Chen, T., Janschek, K.: Test suite prioritization for effi-cient regression testing of model-based automotive software. In: 2017 International Conference on Software Analysis, Testing and Evolution (SATE), pp. 20–29 (2017)
6. Sayyari, F., Emadi, S.: Automated generation of software testing path based on ant colony. In: 2015 International Congress on Technology, Communication and Knowledge (ICTCK), pp. 435–440. IEEE (2015)
7. Walton, G., Poore, J.: Measuring complexity and coverage of software specifications. Inf. Softw. Technol. **42**(12), 859–872 (2000)
8. Zhou, B., Okamura, H., Dohi, T.: Application of Markov chain Monte Carlo ran-dom testing to test case prioritization in regression testing. IEICE Trans. Inf. Syst. **E95.D**(9), 2219–2226 (2012)

Complete Property-Oriented Module Testing

Felix Brüning[ID], Mario Gleirscher[ID], Wen-ling Huang[ID], Niklas Krafczyk[ID],
Jan Peleska[✉][ID], and Robert Sachtleben[ID]

Department of Mathematics and Computer Science, University of Bremen,
Bibliothekstrasse 1, 28359 Bremen, Germany
{fbrning,mario.gleirscher,huang,niklas,peleska,rob_sac}@uni-bremen.de

Abstract. We present a novel approach to complete property-oriented
white box module testing: a finite test suite, created and extended online
(that is, during test execution), in combination with model learning and
model checking allows to prove or disprove that a software module fulfils
an arbitrary LTL property. The approach is applicable for modules with
possibly infinite input and output domains. The testing strategy is based
on the concept of black box checking proposed by other authors and on
a complete model-based equivalence testing strategy developed previously by the authors of this paper. Since the white box approach allows
for static analyses, basic information about internal states, guards and
assignment expressions can be extracted from the module code. With this
information at hand, the approach effectively performs a proof whether
the implementation satisfies the specified property. The "classical" black
box checking method is accelerated by means of coverage-guided fuzzing,
in combination with effective methods for learning, failure monitoring,
and conformance testing. This combination allows to reduce the overall effort for proving that the software fulfils the desired property in a
considerable way.

Keywords: Property-oriented testing · Module testing · Linear
Temporal Logic · Model learning · Formal verification

1 Introduction

Objectives. In this paper, we apply the concept of *black box checking*, as originally presented by Peled et al. [21,22], in the context of white box module testing.
Given an LTL property φ, tests are executed for learning the true behaviour of
an implementation under test (IuT) which is a software module I; this behaviour
is expressed by means of an initially unknown symbolic finite state machine B.

Niklas Krafczyk is funded by the Deutsche Forschungsgemeinschaft (DFG, German
Research Foundation) – project number 407708394. Felix Brüning, Wen-ling Huang,
and Jan Peleska are funded by the German Ministry of Economics, Grant Agreement 20X1908E.

© IFIP International Federation for Information Processing 2023
Published by Springer Nature Switzerland AG 2023
S. Bonfanti et al. (Eds.): ICTSS 2023, LNCS 14131, pp. 183–201, 2023.
https://doi.org/10.1007/978-3-031-43240-8_12

While trying to learn the true representation of B from the test cases executed so far, violations of φ are detected either by means of a monitor checking the reactions of I to the test case inputs, or during model checking the model increments $B = M_1, M_2, \ldots$ learnt so far. If a complete test of I against $B = M_k$ proves the language equivalence between I and B, the verification campaign terminates: I fulfils φ if and only if B fulfils this property. This "proof by testing and property checking" holds under certain hypotheses about the maximal number n of distinguishable states in I, and the guard expressions and output assignments used by I. This information can be extracted from the IuT by means of static analyses. Since these analyses are fairly simple and do not require the full understanding of the programming language semantics, this approach to property verification is a suitable method for testing modules programmed using complex programming languages like C++, Java, C#, where software model checkers accepting the complete syntax do not exist.

Background: Black Box Checking. In the original work by Peled et al. [21, 22], model learning was performed using Angluin's L^* algorithm [1]: under the assumption that I has at most n distinguishable states, the black box B can be reconstructed incrementally by executing finitely many tests against I.

Some tests serve to elaborate a new hypothesis about B (say, $B = M_i$), other tests serve to verify or falsify that I is language-equivalent to the current version of B. For the latter task, the W-Method [9,26] was used in [21,22]. This is a *complete* testing method in the sense that, under the hypothesis that I has at most n states, I passes the tests generated by the W-Method if and only if it is language-equivalent to M_i. Failed test cases can be used by the L^*-algorithm to modify and extend M_i, in order to create a refined model version M_{i+1}.

Using model checking, each new version of B is verified against φ. To this end, the product of B and a Büchi-automaton P accepting $\neg\varphi$ is constructed. If the language of product automaton $B \times P$ is non-empty, this indicates the existence of a *counterexample*, that is, an infinite input/output sequence π violating φ [2]. For safety properties, the violation of φ can already be demonstrated on a finite prefix π' of π [24]. For liveness properties, omega regularity implies that the infinite counterexample π can be written as $\pi_1\pi_2^\omega$ (infinitely many copies of π_2 are appended to π_1), with finite input/output sequences π_1, π_2 [2]. Since I is assumed to have at most n states, it accepts $\pi = \pi_1\pi_2^\omega$ if and only if it accepts $\pi_1\pi_2^n$, since the latter already implies the existence of a "lasso" [4] starting with π_1 and ending in a loop endlessly repeating π_2. Therefore, either π' or $\pi_1\pi_2^n$ are run against I. If the counterexample is accepted by I, an error has been found, and the combined learning and testing process can be aborted. If I does not accept the counterexample, this information can again be used to update B via continued learning. If the latest increment $B = M_k$ passes the check against φ, and the complete test suite proves that I and B are language-equivalent, the black box testing campaign has *proven* that I satisfies φ, under the hypothesis that I has at most n distinguishable states.

Contributions. In this paper, we refine and optimise the black box checking approach in several ways and specialise it for the purpose of white box software module testing, including tool support. For B, we admit (nondeterministic) *symbolic finite state machines (SFSM)* with finite state space, input and output variables over arbitrary primitive data types (including infinite types like $\mathbb{Z}$ and $\mathbb{R}$) and transitions labelled by guard conditions over input variables and output expressions over output and input variables. We advocate a white-box approach which is quite realistic for software in safety-critical systems, where source code needs to be verified by independent verification teams [28]. This allows us to determine upper state bounds n and identify the guard and assignment expressions used in the code by means of static analyses. These static analyses ensure that a passed black box checking suite corresponds to an actual *proof* that I satisfies property φ.

Regarding methodological contributions, the application of black box checking to software with conceptually infinite input and output types is enabled by an equivalence class partitioning method previously developed by the authors [14]. Otherwise black box checking would be infeasible, due to the large size of the alphabets involved, when using interface variables of type `double`, `float`, `int` directly.

Furthermore, we reduce the number of situations where tentative models $B = M_i$ need to be checked by means of a complete testing method. In particular, our strategy allows to check tentative models *later*, after many distinguishable states (say, ℓ) of the IuT have already been discovered. This significantly reduces the exponential term $p^{n-\ell+1}$ influencing the size of the complete test suite, where $n \geq \ell$ is the upper bound of potential distinguishable states in I, and p is the number of input/output equivalence classes derived from guard conditions and output expressions extracted from the code, as described below. Instead of the "classical" L^*-algorithm, we use a novel, highly effective state machine learning algorithm proposed by Vaandrager et al. [25]. For generating complete test suites, a variant of the complete H-Method [12] is used, which needs significantly fewer test cases than the W-Method in the average case [13]. We have modified the H-Method for *online testing*: this means that the test case generation is incremental and interleaved with the test execution, so that it is unnecessary to create a complete suite, when tests of I against the current version of B fail early. We apply the monitor concept proposed by Bauer et al. [3] for detecting safety violations on the fly, during tests intended for model learning. This reduces the need to perform complete model checking runs of $B \times P$ against φ. To speed up the learning process and to avoid having to create complete suites for too many intermediate increments of B, we apply coverage-guided fuzz testing [5,17] for finding many distinguishable states of the implementation at an early stage. Again, this leads to small exponents $n - \ell + 1$ in the term $p^{n-\ell+1}$ dominating the number of test cases to perform for a complete language equivalence test.

While these techniques for effort reduction cannot improve the worst case complexity that was already calculated by Peled et al. [21,22], their combination significantly improves black box checking performance in the average case.

We confirm this by several experiments verifying control software from the automotive domain. These experiments also show that the property testing approach described in this paper is effectively applicable for testing modules performing control tasks of realistic size and complexity. Therefore, the approach advocated here is an interesting alternative to proving code correctness by means of code-based model checkers or proof assistants. From the perspective of standards for software development in safety-critical systems [8,16,28], our approach even has a significant advantage in comparison to "pure" code verification, since tests are actually *executed* against the IuT. The standards emphasise that verification may never be based on static analyses (model checking, formal proof) alone: it is always necessary to perform dynamic tests of the integrated HW/SW system as well.

To the best of our knowledge, the approach presented here is the first to use equivalence class abstractions for enabling complete property testing of source code with large interfaces, using black box checking in combination with fuzzing.

Regarding the implementation of the approach, we present the open source library `libsfsmtest` for complete model-based or property-oriented module testing[1], whose latest version supports the module testing strategy described in this paper. For users only interested in the application of the library for practical testing, a cloud interface[2] is provided, supporting both test suite generation and module test execution.

Related Work. Meng et al. [18] confirm that fuzz testing can be effective for testing software against properties specified in LTL. However, their approach does not provide any completeness guarantees: the tool LTL-FUZZER created by the authors is to be used as an effective bug finder.

Pferscher et al. [23] also combine model learning and fuzzing, but with the objective to check whether an implementation conforms to a reference model, while our focus here is on property-oriented testing. The fuzzer is not guided by the code coverage achieved, as in our approach, but by the coverage of a reference model. Since the latter has not been validated with respect to completeness and consistency, the testing process can only reveal discrepancies between reference model and implementation, but not a correctness proof.

The model learning aspect of black box checking has received much attention since Angluin's seminal paper [1], and a comprehensive overview about improvements and alternative approaches to automata learning is given by Vaandrager et al. [25]. We could have made use of the LearnLib library [15] for the model learning part in our Algorithm 2 (see Sect. 3). However, we would not have used the W-Method or Wp-Method implemented there for equivalence testing and finding counter examples, since our own library `libfsmtest` provides methods like the H-Method that requires far less test effort in the average case. Moreover, the new data structure and associated algorithms for learning that has been pro-

---

posed by Vaandrager et al. [25] is not yet available in LearnLib, and it seemed particularly attractive with respect to maintainability and performance to us.

An alternative to LearnLib is AALPY by Aichernig et al. [19]. While its Python implementation seems less attractive to us, due to the better performance of C++, AALPY uses a strategy for disproving conformance between preliminary model versions and an implementation that is an interesting alternative to our current implementation: AALPY tries to avoid the generation of unnecessary complete conformance test suites by combining random testing with the W-Method, expecting to find early discrepancies between a preliminary version of the model and the implementation by means of random testing. In our approach, we prefer to focus the application of random testing in an initial phase using coverage guided fuzzing with the objective to find an initial candidate for machine B with as many states as possible. After that, we relay on conformance tests without randomisation, but create the cases of the H-Method incrementally, which also avoids the creation of a full conformance test suite as long as B and I do not conform.

Waga [27] presents a black box checking approach that is complementary to ours in several ways. (1) The main objective is bug finding for cyber-physical systems, while we focus on *complete* property checks for software modules. (2) Waga applies signal temporal logic, while we apply LTL. (3) Waga does not use any means of abstractions comparable to the equivalence class abstractions we consider to be crucial for complete property checking. Summarising, Waga's approach performs well for the purpose of bug finding on system level, while the method advocated here provides complete checks on module level.

Overview. In Sect. 2, we summarise the foundations required for the combined testing and black box checking approach described in this paper. In Sect. 3, the methodological main result is presented. In Sect. 4, a short summary of the available tool support is given. In Sect. 5, the application of our approach with this tool platform is described, and performance data is presented. Section 6 contains a conclusion.

2   Theoretical Foundations

2.1   Black Box Checking

The strategy for combined learning, model checking, and testing proposed by Peled et al. [22] is shown in Algorithm 1, with some adaptations for the notation used in this paper. The strategy uses two sub-functions for learning and testing: (1) As the first sub-function, Angluin's L^*-algorithm [1] is invoked (lines 6, 25) for learning the internal structure of the black box B representing the true behaviour of implementation I. The L^*-algorithm is called in Algorithm 1 with three parameters (I, M_i, π): I is the implementation, and the L^*-Algorithm may execute additional tests against I, in order to produce a new model. Parameter M_i specifies the latest assumption for the representation of B, and π is a word representing a counterexample that is either accepted by M_i, but not by B, or vice versa. Based on this information, L^* returns a more refined model M_{i+1}.

(2) As the second sub-function, the W-Method [9, 26] $VC(I, M_i, \ell, k)$ is used as a conformance test that is able to prove or disprove the language equivalence between M_i and I, under the hypothesis that I has no more than k distinguishable states. The algorithm is called with the implementation I to be used in the test, the currently learnt, minimised model M_i that may or may not be equivalent to I, the number ℓ of distinguishable states in M_i, and the currently assumed upper bound $k \leq n$ of distinguishable states in I. Note that the worst case estimate for the number of test steps to be executed for such a conformance test is $O(\ell^3 p^{n-\ell+1})$ [9].

Initially, the L^*-algorithm is set up with the empty machine (line 6). Then the implementation is tested until (a) either the learnt model B satisfies φ and has been shown to be language-equivalent to I by means of complete tests, under the hypothesis that I has at most n states (line 18), or (b) an approximation M_i of B has been learnt that *violates* φ on an infinite word $\pi_1\pi_2^\omega$, and this word is accepted by the implementation (line 22).

Algorithm 1. Black box checking strategy, as proposed by Peled et al. [22].

```
1  function BlackBoxChecker(in I : Implementation;
2                          in φ : LTL formula to be fulfilled by I;
3                          in n : maximal number of states of I) : {pass, fail}
4  begin
5    P := Büchi-Automaton accepting ¬φ;
6    M₁ := L*(I,empty,−); -- initialise learning algorithm with empty machine
7    i := 1;
8    while ( true )
9    begin
10     X := Mᵢ × P; -- Product of machine learnt so far and BA checking ¬φ
11     if L(X) = ∅ then -- Mᵢ does not violate φ
12     begin
13       ℓ := number of states of Mᵢ; k := ℓ;
14       do
15         (conforms, π) := VC(I, Mᵢ, ℓ, k); -- apply the W-Method
16         k := k + 1;
17       while (k ≤ n ∧ conforms);
18       if ( conforms ) then return pass; -- Implementation conforms to Mᵢ, and Mᵢ
                            fulfils φ
19     end
20     else begin -- current model Mᵢ violates φ
21       let π₁, π₂ such that π₁π₂^ω ∈ L(X); -- this word violates φ
22       if I passes test π₁π₂ⁿ then return fail;
23       else  π := shortest prefix of π₁π₂^ω not accepted by I;
24     end
25     Mᵢ₊₁ := L*(I, Mᵢ, π); -- extend model, using counterexample~π
26     i := i + 1;
27   end
28 end
```

Once a hypothetical model M_i has been proposed by the L^*-algorithm, its product with the Büchi-automaton P accepting $\neg\varphi$ is constructed (line 10). If the language of this product is empty, this implies that M_i does *not* accept a word violating φ. Therefore, it is checked whether M_i is language equivalent to I, under the hypothesis that I does not have more than n states (lines 11— 19). This is done incrementally over $k = \ell, \ldots, n$, in order to avoid superfluous tests if the non-equivalence can already be detected with a smaller value $k < n$. Therefore, the full number of $O(\ell^3 p^{n-\ell+1})$ test steps only needs to be executed if I conforms to M_i. If language equivalence between M_i and I can be established by the conformance tests, the strategy terminates with verdict 'pass', since I conforms to a mealy machine $B = M_i$ that fulfils φ.

If the language of the product $X := M_i \times P$ is non-empty, this means that M_i accepts a word satisfying $\neg\varphi$. Omega regularity implies that such a word can be written as $\pi_1 \pi_2^\omega$, with finite prefix π_1, followed by an infinite repetition of finite word segment π_2. To test whether the implementation accepts $\pi_1 \pi_2^\omega$, it suffices to check whether it accepts $\pi_1 \pi_2^n$, since I is assumed to have at most n distinguishable states. If I accepts the finite test $\pi_1 \pi_2^n$, we know that it accepts a word violating φ and can stop the procedure by returning 'fail' (line 22). There is no further need to look for a more refined model $B = M_{i+j}$ representing the true behaviour of I, since the implementation must be fixed anyway.

If, however, I rejects $\pi_1 \pi_2^n$, this implies that the implementation cannot be language-equivalent to the currently assumed representation M_i of B. Now we look for the shortest prefix π of $\pi_1 \pi_2^\omega$ that is rejected by I. This prefix is suitable as a "teacher's response" for the L^*-algorithm, to be used to construct a more refined version M_{i+1} of the true implementation behaviour (line 25).

Peled et al. prove ([22, Theorem 3]) that if the implementation satisfies φ, the worst-case time complexity of the strategy described above is $O(\ell^3 p^\ell + l^3 p^{n-\ell+1} + l^2 mn)$, otherwise (error case), it is $O(\ell^3 p^\ell + l^2 mn)$. The higher complexity in the no-error case given by term $l^3 p^{n-\ell+1}$ in the complexity sum is derived from the fact that the equivalence tests of the implementation against the learnt model B need to execute all test steps required for the conjecture that I has at most n states. In the error case, these tests can be aborted earlier.

2.2 Equivalence Class Construction for SFSM

We summarise here previously obtained results [14] that are relevant for the present paper. A symbolic finite state machine (SFSM) M is a state machine operating on a finite set of control states and input variables and output variables from a symbol set $V = I \cup O$. Variables are typed by some (possibly infinite) set D. A variable valuation is a function $\sigma \in D^V$, associating a value $\sigma(v)$ with each variable symbol $v \in V$. Given a quantifier-free first order expression e with free variables in V, we say that σ is a model for e (written $\sigma \models e$), if and only if the formula $e[v/\sigma(v) \mid v \in V]$, that is created from e by exchanging every occurrence of a variable symbol $v \in V$ by its valuation $\sigma(v)$, evaluates to true.

A transition relation $s_1 \xrightarrow{g/a} s_2$ connects certain control states s_1, s_2. The transition label g/a consists of a guard expression g, that is, a quantifier-free first order expression over variables from I, and update expressions a that are

---

Table 1. Construction method for I/O equivalence classes (from [14]).

1. Let $\Sigma = \Sigma_I \cup \Sigma_O \cup AP$ be the set of all first-order formulae occurring in guard conditions or output expressions of the IuT, or in the property specification φ.
2. For a set of formulae $P \subseteq \Sigma$, define a new first-order formula which is a conjunction of formulae from P and negated formulae from $\Sigma \setminus P$:

$$\phi_P \equiv \bigwedge_{e \in P} e \wedge \bigwedge_{e \in \Sigma \setminus P} \neg e. \tag{1}$$

3. Let $\mathbf{P}$ denote the set of all formulae ϕ that have been constructed according to Eq. (1) and that possess at least one valuation $\sigma \in D^V$ as model, so that $\sigma \models \phi$.
4. For each $\phi \in \mathbf{P}$, define an *input/output equivalence class* io(ϕ) by

$$\mathrm{io}(\phi) = \{\sigma \in D^V \mid \sigma \models \phi\}.$$

5. Let $\mathcal{A} = \{\mathrm{io}(\phi) \mid \phi \in \mathbf{P}\}$ denote the set of all input/output equivalence classes.

---

first order expressions over at least one output variable and optional variables from I. The language of M is the set $L(M) \subseteq (D^V)^\omega$ of all infinite traces of valuations $\sigma_1, \sigma_2, \cdots \in D^V$, such that there exists a sequence of states $s_0, s_1, \ldots$ starting in the initial state and guard and output expressions $(g_1/a_1)(g_2/a_2)\ldots$, such that

$$\forall i > 0 \,\textbf{.}\, s_{i-1} \xrightarrow{g_i/a_i} s_i \quad \sigma_i \models g_i \wedge a_i.$$

The property testing approach described in this paper applies to all software modules whose input/output behaviour can be described by means of an SFSM. The class of real-world applications that can be modelled by SFSM is quite large, examples are airbag control modules, anti-lock braking systems (see Sect. 5) or train control systems.

An input/output equivalence class io is a set of valuations $\sigma \in D^V$ constructed according to the specification in Table 1. The intuition behind this specification is that the input/output equivalence classes partition the set D^V of valuations: two members of the same class are models for exactly the same conjunction over all guard conditions, output expressions, and atomic propositions occurring in the LTL property φ to be verified, each conjunct occurring either in positive or negated form. No valuation can be in more than one class, since two classes differ in the sign (positive/negated) of at least one conjunct.

Two sequences $\pi_1, \pi_2 \in (D^V)^\omega$ of valuations are equivalent if each pair of corresponding sequence elements $(\pi_1(i), \pi_2(i))$, $i = 1, 2, \ldots$ is contained in the same input/output equivalence class. The following properties of equivalent

traces $\pi_1, \pi_2 \in (D^V)^\omega$ are crucial in the context of this paper [14, Theorem 2][3]:
(1) $\pi_1 \in L(M)$ if and only if $\pi_2 \in L(M)$. (2) π_1 and π_2, when contained in $L(M)$, cover the same sequences of states in M (there is only one uniquely determined state sequence if M is deterministic). (3) $\pi_1 \models \varphi$ if and only if $\pi_2 \models \varphi$.[4]

3 Optimisation of the Test Method

Based on black box checking (Algorithm 1), we propose the new white box module testing strategy specified in Algorithm 2 and incorporating several optimisations. This strategy is divided into three phases: (1) setup, (2) fuzzer-guided exploration, and (3) learning as explained below.

Algorithm 2. White box module testing strategy.

```
 1  function FuzzingBlackBoxLearner(in I : Implementation;
 2                              in ΣI : guard conditions;
 3                              in ΣO : output expressions;
 4                              in φ : LTL property to be verified;
 5                              in n : maximal number of states of I;
 6                              in rmax : maximum number of rounds of fuzzing;
 7                              ) : {pass, fail}
 8  begin
 9      -- Phase 1: Setup
10      AP := atomic propositions of φ;
11      A := input/output equivalence classes based on ΣI ∪ ΣO ∪ AP;
12      H := set of input valuations σ1, σ2, ..., such that for each ψ ∈ A, there exists
              some σ ∈ H extendable to a valuation satisfying ψ;
13      T := {ε}; -- initialise a prefix-closed set of traces observed in I
14      P := construct a property monitor accepting ¬φ;
15
16      -- Phase 2: Fuzzer guided exploration
17      r := 0; -- number of performed fuzzing iterations
18      ℓT := 1; -- lower bound on the number of distinct states already observed
19      while ( r < rmax and ℓT < n )
20      begin
21          b̄ := non−empty sequence of integers obtained from fuzzer;
22          x̄ := map each element b̄ to an element of H;
23              -- e.g. by selecting the (b mod |H| + 1)th element of H
24          outputQuery(I, T, P, x̄); -- apply x̄ to I and update T with the observed
                      output; return fail if P observes a violation of φ
25          r := r + 1;
26          ℓT := |maximalPairwiseDistinguishableSubsetOf(T)|
27      end
28
29      -- Phase 3: Learning using L#
```

---

[3] Note that this theorem has only been formulated for finite traces π_i in [14]. The proof, however, holds for infinite traces $\pi_i \in (D^V)^\omega$ as well, because $\pi_1, \pi_2 \in (D^V)^\omega$ are equivalent if and only if all finite prefixes of π_1, π_2 with identical length are equivalent.

[4] Recall that LTL formulae over free variables from V have infinite sequences of valuations in D^V as models [10].

```
30   M₁ := L#(I, H, A, T, P, −) -- start learning using input alphabet H, output
                alphabet A, and the observations T observed during fuzzing
31   i := 1;
32   while ( true )
33   begin
34     X := Mᵢ × P; -- Product of machine learnt so far and BA checking ¬φ
35     if L(X) = ∅ then -- Mᵢ does not violate φ
36     begin
37       ℓ := number of states of Mᵢ;
38       (conforms, π) := H(I, Mᵢ, T, P, ℓ, n); -- apply an online H-Method
39       if ( conforms ) then return pass;
40           -- Implementation conforms to Mᵢ, and Mᵢ fulfils φ
41     end
42     else begin -- current model Mᵢ violates φ
43       let π₁, π₂ such that π₁π₂^ω ∈ L(X); -- this word violates φ
44       if I passes test π₁π₂ⁿ then return fail;
45       else  π := shortest prefix of π₁π₂^ω not accepted by I;
46     end
47     Mᵢ₊₁ := L#(I, H, A, T, P, π); -- learn more elaborate model,
48                                  -- based on counterexample π
49     i := i + 1;
50   end
51 end
```

Phase 1: Setup. In the first phase, we exploit white box knowledge on the IuT in order to abstract from its possibly infinite input and output domains to finitely many equivalence classes. To this end, the algorithm uses the two input parameters Σ_I and Σ_O, denoting the guard conditions and output expressions occurring in the IuT, respectively. Together with the atomic propositions AP occurring in the LTL property φ to check, these are employed in computing input/output classes A (lines 10 and 11) using the techniques described in Sect. 2. These classes could then already serve as symbolic inputs. However, since multiple input/output classes may share the same input valuations, this could introduce superfluous inputs. Thus, line 12 of the algorithm attempts to minimise the number of inputs by only selecting sufficiently many input valuations $\sigma \in H$ to provide input representatives of all input/output classes. In the following, we use elements of H both as symbols and as concrete input valuations.

The first phase concludes by initialising a tree T representing a prefix-closed set of symbolic traces observed in the IuT (line 13), as well as a property monitor P constructed as proposed by Bauer et al. [3] (line 14) to accept $\neg\varphi$. This monitor detects violations of safety properties φ observed during the subsequent execution of Algorithm 2. Since violations of liveness properties can only be determined on infinite traces, these are accepted, but do not lead to failure indications by the monitor.

Phase 2: Fuzzer-Guided Exploration. In the second phase, coverage-guided fuzzing is employed to quickly reach a large number of distinct states in the IuT and record observations on the behaviour of the IuT, with the aim of speeding up the subsequent learning phase. Experiments confirming the efficacy of this approach are discussed in Sect. 5.

Fuzzing is used for several iterations (lines 19—27). In each iteration, a non-empty sequence of integers $\bar{b}$ is obtained from the fuzzer and translated into a sequence of input symbols $\bar{x}$ by mapping each integer to an element of $\mathcal{H}$ (lines 21 and 22). Thereafter, $\bar{x}$ is applied to the IuT (line 24). All such invocations of the IuT in Algorithm 2 occur via calls to procedure outputQuery$(I, T, P, \bar{x})$. These reset the IuT and P to their initial states and initialise a symbolic trace $\gamma = \epsilon$. The following steps are then performed for each input symbol x in $\bar{x}$ in turn: First, x is translated into the concrete input valuation σ_I it symbolises, which is then applied as input to the IuT. Next, the outputs σ_O observed in response are used to create a valuation $\sigma_I \cup \sigma_O$ ranging over all input and output variables. This valuation belongs to exactly one input/output class $y \in \mathcal{A}$, which is considered as the output symbol observed for input symbol x. Thereafter, x/y is appended to observation γ, which is then added to T. Finally, P is used to check whether γ violates φ, in which case Algorithm 2 returns fail.

The fuzzer-guided exploration terminates as soon as one of the following conditions is satisfied: (1) Fuzzing has been performed for r_{max} iterations, where r_{max} is another input parameter of the algorithm, and the number of iterations is tracked in variable r (lines 17 and 25), or (2) fuzzing has identified n distinct states in the IuT. A lower bound on the number of identified distinct states in the IuT is tracked in variable l_T (lines 18 and 26), which is updated after each iteration. This is realised via function maximalPairwiseDistinguishableSubsetOf(T) as follows: First, pairs of traces are identified that are distinguishable in T.[5] From these, a maximal set $S \subseteq T$ is selected such that any pair of distinct traces in S is distinguishable.[6] Variable l is then set to $|S|$, as distinct traces in S must reach distinct states in IuT I and hence $|I| \geq |S|$.

Phase 3: Learning. The third phase (lines 30—50) finally implements learning in analogy to Algorithm 1. It differs from the latter in two aspects: First, instead of Angluin's L^* algorithm [1], learning is performed using an adaptation of the efficient $L^\#$ algorithm proposed by Vaandrager et al. [25] (lines 30 and 47). $L^\#$ follows the same *minimally adequate teacher* framework as L^* in generating hypothesis state machines and providing these to the teacher to check for equivalence with the IuT; hence it can directly replace the original calls to L^* in Algorithm 1. In contrast to line 6 of Algorithm 1 and also differing from the original description of $L^\#$, which starts without prior knowledge, line 30 of

---

[5] Traces α, β are distinguishable in T if there exists $\alpha.(\bar{x}/\bar{y}), \beta.(\bar{x}/\bar{y}') \in T$ with $\bar{y} \neq \bar{y}'$.

[6] Note that finding the largest such set is equivalent to finding the largest clique [6] in an undirected graph with vertexes T where traces are adjacent if and only if they are distinguishable. This constitutes a computationally expensive problem, so that we currently apply a greedy heuristic.

Algorithm 2 provides initial knowledge to the learning algorithm in the form of T, the previously observed traces.

The second difference consists in the conformance testing strategy employed to check whether the current hypothesis M_i is language-equivalent to the IuT (line 38). Instead of the W-Method [9,26], we employ the H-Method [12]. While both strategies exhibit the same worst case behaviour in terms of test steps, the H-Method has been observed in practice to require on average significantly fewer test steps [13]. We adapted the H-Method for online testing. That is, instead of computing the entire test suite and only thereafter applying it to the IuT, we interleave test case generation and application in an attempt to find failures early. This is particularly effective if the current hypothesis contains fewer than n states, as the term $|\mathcal{H}|^{n-\ell+1}$ dominates the number of test cases to consider.

Finally, recall that all interactions with the IuT within Algorithm 2 are performed via function outputQuery first called in the second phase. Thus, for every query to the IuT performed by the H-Method or by $L^\#$ (lines 30, 38, 47), property monitor P continues to check for violations of φ.

4   Tool Support: libfsmtest and libsfsmtest

We have implemented the described approach as a C++ framework based on libFuzzer[7], the coverage-guided fuzzing engine distributed as a part of the LLVM project and on ltl3tools[8] supporting the generation of runtime monitors for LTL properties [3].

The implementation I is integrated into a *test harness*, which contains an implementation of Algorithm 2. Alphabets Σ_I and Σ_O and the LTL property φ are read from files using the libsfsmtest[9] library, which also extracts the atomic propositions AP occurring in φ. From these, the equivalence classes over $\Sigma_I \cup \Sigma_O \cup AP$ and a propositional abstraction of φ are constructed, from which ltl3tools can construct a runtime monitor in a specific pseudo code representation. Using libsfsmtest again, this monitor is transformed into an executable version reading and checking input/output valuations observed on I. We have implemented the $L^\#$ algorithm in libfsmtest[10]. The fuzzer invokes the test harness, which orchestrates the translation from fuzzer inputs to input equivalence classes, the application of inputs to I and the feedback of the observations on I to the runtime monitor for φ and the learning algorithm.

Libraries libfsmtest and libsfsmtest are available as open source under MIT license. If users are not interested in obtaining the source code, they can perform the whole testing approach described here by using a cloud service.[11]

---

[7] https://llvm.org/docs/LibFuzzer.html.
[8] https://ltl3tools.sourceforge.net/.
[9] https://gitlab.informatik.uni-bremen.de/projects/29053.
[10] https://bitbucket.org/JanPeleska/libfsmtest/.
[11] https://fsmtestcloud.informatik.uni-bremen.de.

5   Experiments

For evaluation of the property testing approach described in this paper, we re-implemented an *anti-lock braking system (ABS)* for cars with lane stability control, as designed and published by Bosch GmbH [11]. The full functionality described there has been reduced to ABS for the front-left wheel only, and we do not consider gravel road conditions.

The ABS system implements two fundamental tasks: (1) locking a wheel should be avoided if the driver brakes too hard or brakes on slippery roads. The ABS controller prevents wheel locking by alternately holding, reducing and increasing the brake pressure for each wheel individually so that each wheel rotates recurringly while braking, in order to keep the car steerable. (2) The ABS controller implements a lane stability control to prevent the car from swerving on asymmetric road conditions during braking with straight steering angle. The ABS controller then adjusts the braking force in a car for all wheels, to facilitate the steering intervention by the driver, while still applying the maximal possible braking force. The ABS controller measures constantly the wheel velocity v_U and calculates the brake slip λ_B for each wheel, relative to the vehicle target speed v_R, which in this example is measured at the car powertrain. The equation to calculate the slip is [11]

$$\lambda_B = \frac{v_U - v_R}{v_R}.$$

The ABS controller evaluates the momentary acceleration α of each wheel to detect each wheel's tendency to lock. If α falls below the threshold $-a < 0$, a possible wheel lock is detected and the input valve VI (in front of the brake fluid inlet of the wheel brake cylinder) is closed, as well as the output valve VO (after the brake fluid outlet of the wheel brake cylinder) to hold the current brake pressure. The additional brake pump P to artificially increase the brake pressure is set to mode OFF. Consequently, the negative wheel acceleration α is not reduced any further. Then, if the brake slip falls below the maximum slip threshold, the output valve is opened again. Thus, the brake pressure decreases again, and α and the slip increase.

When $\alpha = -a$, the valves are switched to hold pressure (both valves closed, pump off). Now, the acceleration increases and can exceed two thresholds $+a, +A$ satisfying $+a < +A$. In the first iteration, the brake pressure will be increased when $\alpha > +A$, by setting VI := OPEN, VO := CLOSED, and P := ON. After a certain time, α decreases and reaches $+A$, so that the ABS controller switches again to hold pressure. The braking pressure is held until the $+a$ threshold is reached. At this point, the second iteration begins (henceforth repeating) and the brake pressure is slowly increased until $-a$ is reached. In the following cycles, α is kept between the two thresholds $-a$ and $+a$ by the ABS controller. If the ABS controller receives a signal from the yaw sensor that the car rotates around the z axle during braking, an asymmetric road condition is detected. If the car rotates to the direction of the current wheel, the driver is braking and the steering angle is in direction straight ahead, the controller then tries to facilitate the steering intervention by the driver by alternately reducing and increasing the brake pressure of the current wheel but applying maximum possible braking force in threshold $-a_{\text{GMA}}$ (slightly higher than $-a$) and $+a$ until the rotation is within the yaw threshold again.

The C++ implementation consists of one model with approx. 700 lines of code. It processes 6 input variables of type `double` and writes to three output variables with small enumeration types. The module behaviour depends on 11 (not necessarily pairwise distinguishable) internal control states. Table 2 shows the LTL properties we tested on the example implementation.

The atomic propositions in the LTL formulae, together with the guards and update expressions contained in the code, result in up to 784 input/output equivalence classes $\text{io}_i \in \mathcal{A}$ that were calculated in about 203 s.

For each LTL property, we created one mutant that violates that property. For properties 1, 2 and 4 we did so by manually applying one of the five mutation operators[12] described in [20] at random locations in the program, until we found a mutant that violated that property. For each mutant we determined how fast it could be found with our approach for different numbers of fuzzing rounds. The time it took for a mutant to be killed for each run is shown in Table 3.

From this small set of data we can already conclude that the fuzzing can enable a learning-based approach to be used on problems where it would otherwise be not a sensible choice for economic reasons: While a purely learning-based approach was able to find the property violations for properties 2 and 3, it ran out of memory space in the other cases. This happens when equivalence queries are done with too large of a difference between the number of discovered states and the specified upper bound on the number of states. In all cases, we noticed that some amount of fuzzing usually drastically reduced the runtime of the approach. However, we also see that there is a trade-off to be made between making sure that learning does not start too early, as can be seen for the case where we used 100 fuzzing rounds for property 1, and taking too much time fuzzing, as can be seen for the other approaches where 100 fuzzing rounds found the violation faster than most other settings. Obviously, a violation for property 2 was rather easy to find on the corresponding mutant, and we attribute the runtime differences in the different fuzzing round configurations to runtime noise in the execution setup.

To investigate the runtime of the approach when there is no property violation found, we also ran it for the unmutated implementation which satisfies all four properties. In this case, the full model for the implementation, which has 11 states, has to be learnt. Due to the differing amounts of input/output equivalence classes for the properties, the runtimes can differ significantly for runs with different properties. We ran the approach with 5000 fuzzing cycles once for each property and logged the runtimes, number of applied input sequences and number of applied inputs of the fuzzing and learning portions of the approach, separately. For the number of applied inputs and input sequences we also separately noted how many were applied during equivalence queries. Table 4 shows the average, minimum and maximum numbers determined this way over all

---

[12] ABS, AOR, LCR, ROR, UOI.

Table 2. The set of LTL properties checked on the example implementation.

LTL formula	Description
$\mathbf{G}((\text{driverBrakes} \wedge v_R \geq v_{\min} \wedge$ $\lambda_B \leq \phi \wedge \alpha \leq -a \wedge$ $\|\text{yaw}\| \leq \theta \wedge \|\beta\| \leq \xi)$ $\implies (\neg \text{VI} \wedge \text{VO} \wedge \neg \text{P}))$	Whenever the driver brakes while the velocity is above the minimum activation velocity $v_{\min}$ and when there is negative slip that is less than threshold ϕ, the wheel circumference is decelerating and the car is not yawing to either side more than θ radians per second while the driver is not steering more than ξ radians to either side, then valve VI shall be closed, VO opened, and the brake pump P shall be off to release brake pressure.
$\mathbf{G}((\text{driverBrakes} \wedge v_R \geq v_{\min} \wedge$ $\text{yaw} < -\theta \wedge \|\beta\| < \xi)$ $\implies (\neg \text{VI} \wedge \text{VO} \wedge \neg \text{P}))$	Whenever the driver brakes while the velocity is above the minimum activation velocity $v_{\min}$, the car is yawing to the left more than θ radians per second while the driver is relatively straight (not more than ξ radians to either side), then valve VI shall be closed, VO opened, and the brake pump P shall be off to release brake pressure.
$\mathbf{G}(\text{P} = \text{SLOW} \wedge$ $\mathbf{X}(\text{driverBrakes} \wedge v_R \geq v_{\min} \wedge$ $\alpha > -a \wedge \|\beta\| < \xi \wedge \text{yaw} \geq -\theta)$ $\implies$ $\mathbf{X}(\text{P} = \text{SLOW}))$	Whenever the brake pump is increasing the pressure slowly, it will continue to do so if the pressure is still too low for the acceleration α of the wheel's circumference to be below $-a$ and if the driver continues braking and steering straight ahead, the road conditions stay symmetric and the vehicle is moving fast enough for the system to be active.
$\mathbf{G}((\alpha < -a \wedge \text{driverBrakes} \wedge$ $v_R \geq v_{\min} \wedge$ $\|\beta\| < \xi \wedge \text{yaw} \geq -\theta)$ $\implies$ $((\neg \text{VI})$ $\mathbf{U}$ $\neg(\alpha < -a \wedge \text{driverBrakes} \wedge$ $v_R \geq v_{\min} \wedge$ $\|\beta\| < \xi \wedge \text{yaw} \geq -\theta)))$	Whenever the acceleration of the wheel's circum- ference is less than $-a$ while the driver is braking, the vehicle velocity is above the minimum activation velocity, the driver is steering relatively straight ahead (no more than ξ radians to either side), and the vehicle is not turning to the left more than θ radians per second, the brake pressure will not be increased until any of these conditions change.

Table 3. Program runtimes for the example described above. These were recorded on a kubernetes cluster with 1 CPU core and 16 GiB of RAM allocated to the task. *OOM* denotes that the property violation was not found during fuzzing, and the learning approach ran out of memory. r_{max} denotes the maximal number of fuzzing rounds performed.

r_{max}	Execution time			
	Property 1	Property 2	Property 3	Property 4
0	OOM	310 ms	12.3 s	OOM
100	OOM	5 ms	4.1 s	7.5 s
5000	21.4 s	10 ms	8.0 s	11.7 s
10000	39.1 s	4 ms	23.5 s	28.4 s

properties. We performed these experiments with the same fixed seed initializing the random choices for the fuzzer, starting with seed = 1. This was incremented by one only when the fuzzer would not discover enough states for the learning to be able to learn the rest of the states without posing equivalence queries with too few discovered state. For the four properties tested on the conforming IuT, we succeeded with seed 1 twice, and with seeds 2 and 3 once. While this could seem inconvenient, we found that simply launching several fuzzing runs with different seeds was inexpensive and fast enough to still be practical.

Table 4. Runtime, number of applied input sequences and number of inputs applied during testing all properties against the implementation satisfying all properties.

	Prop. 1	Prop. 2	Prop. 3	Prop. 4
I/O Eq. Classes	600	600	784	714
Input Eq. Classes	120	117	138	124
Input Seq. Fuzzing	5000	5000	5000	5000
Input Seq. Learning	3311	3022	3764	5377
Input Seq. Equivalence Queries	38956	27862	32654	29522
Inputs Fuzzing	15245	19229	15595	17889
Inputs Learning	12409	10642	14217	19954
Inputs Equivalence Queries	47856	39325	45259	33577
Runtime Fuzzing	22.7 s	37.2 s	25.8 s	36.6 s
Runtime Learning	29.6 s	36.7 s	42.4 s	41.3 s

Compared to testing the mutants, testing the conforming implementation takes significantly longer, which matches the complexity results. In our set of problems, the equivalence queries are consistently the most expensive part of the whole approach which is also supported by the complexity results reported in Sect. 2.1. Furthermore, some of the runtime variations can be explained by the variations in input/output equivalence classes caused by the atomic propositions of the respective properties.[13]

6   Conclusion

In this paper, a novel white box module testing strategy based on learning has been presented. This strategy is complete: given an LTL property φ and an implementation under test I, it decides whether I satisfies φ under the assumption that a representation of I as a symbolic finite state machine contains at most n states and employs only guard and assignment expressions contained in a set of expressions Σ. As n and Σ can be determined from static analysis of I, the strategy effectively performs a proof whether I satisfies φ.

The strategy improves previous checking strategies based on learning [22] in several aspects. First, it performs input/output abstraction and hence allows

---

[13] To reproduce these results, our implementations of Algorithm 2 and of the ABS experiment can be accessed at https://doi.org/10.5281/zenodo.8143283.

checking of implementations with possibly infinite input and output domains. Next, it employs fuzzing in order to quickly reach distinct states in I, speeding up subsequent learning. Thereafter, it applies the efficient $L^\#$ learning algorithm [25] and reduces the number of required test cases for equivalence checks by using the H-Method [12]. Finally, throughout the algorithm, violations of φ observed in interactions with I are efficiently detected using a monitor [3]. The efficacy of these optimisations has been demonstrated in experiments with modules performing control tasks of significant size and complexity

For future work, we plan to fully implement the LTL model checking performed in Algorithm 2 in our tool and to pursue several further optimisations. These include the use of parallelisation within computationally extensive tasks such as the construction of input/output equivalence classes or applications of the H-Method. Furthermore, we plan to evaluate various heuristics for tasks such as the selection of input valuations (line 12 of Algorithm 2). Additionally, we plan to lift the restriction that our current implementation of Algorithm 2 supports only deterministic IuT (the underlying theory already covers nondeterministic IuT behaviour). Finally, we plan to develop an argument for the tool qualification [7] of our implementation based on the idea that if the strategy claims that I satisfies φ, then the final hypothesis $B = M_i$ of I's model representation can be used as reference model for and independent model-based testing algorithm to be executed against I.

References

1. Angluin, D.: Learning regular sets from queries and counterexamples. Inf. Comput. **75**(2), 87–106 (1987)
2. Baier, C., Katoen, J.: Principles of model checking. MIT Press (2008)
3. Bauer, A., Leucker, M., Schallhart, C.: Runtime verification for LTL and TLTL. ACM Trans. Softw. Eng. Methodol. **20**(4), 14:1–14:64 (2011). https://doi.org/10.1145/2000799.2000800
4. Biere, A., Heljanko, K., Junttila, T., Latvala, T., Schuppan, V.: Linear encodings of bounded LTL model checking. Logical Methods Comput. Sci. **2**(5), November 2006. https://doi.org/10.2168/LMCS-2(5:5)2006, http://arxiv.org/abs/cs/0611029, arXiv: cs/0611029
5. Böhme, M., Pham, V., Roychoudhury, A.: Coverage-based greybox fuzzing as markov chain. In: Weippl, E.R., Katzenbeisser, S., Kruegel, C., Myers, A.C., Halevi, S. (eds.) Proceedings of the 2016 ACM SIGSAC Conference on Computer and Communications Security, Vienna, Austria, October 24–28, 2016, pp. 1032–1043. ACM (2016). https://doi.org/10.1145/2976749.2978428
6. Bomze, I.M., Budinich, M., Pardalos, P.M., Pelillo, M.: The maximum clique problem. In: Du, D., Pardalos, P.M. (eds.) Handbook of Combinatorial Optimization, pp. 1–74. Springer (1999). https://doi.org/10.1007/978-1-4757-3023-4_1
7. Brauer, J., Peleska, J., Schulze, U.: Efficient and Trustworthy Tool Qualification for Model-Based Testing Tools. In: Nielsen, B., Weise, C. (eds.) ICTSS 2012. LNCS, vol. 7641, pp. 8–23. Springer, Heidelberg (2012). https://doi.org/10.1007/978-3-642-34691-0_3
8. CENELEC: EN 50128:2011 Railway applications - Communication, signalling and processing systems - Software for railway control and protection systems (2011)

9. Chow, T.S.: Testing software design modeled by finite-state machines. IEEE Trans. Softw. Eng. **SE-4**(3), 178–186 (1978)

10. Clarke, E.M., Grumberg, O., Peled, D.A.: Model Checking. The MIT Press, Cambridge (1999)

11. Dietsche, K.H., Reif, K.: Kraftfahrtechnisches Taschenbuch, 2nd edn. Springer Vieweg (2018)

12. Dorofeeva, R., El-Fakih, K., Yevtushenko, N.: An improved conformance testing method. In: Wang, F. (ed.) FORTE 2005. LNCS, vol. 3731, pp. 204–218. Springer, Heidelberg (2005). https://doi.org/10.1007/11562436_16

13. Endo, A.T., da Silva Simão, A.: Evaluating test suite characteristics, cost, and effectiveness of FSM-based testing methods. Inf. Softw. Technol. **55**(6), 1045–1062 (2013). https://doi.org/10.1016/j.infsof.2013.01.001

14. Huang, W.l., Krafczyk, N., Peleska, J.: Model-Based Conformance Testing and Property Testing With Symbolic Finite State Machines - Technical Report. Zenodo, October 2022. https://doi.org/10.5281/zenodo.7267975. https://zenodo.org/record/7267975, to appear in Science of Computer Programming SCP (Part I) and Proceedings of the 10th IPM International Conference on Fundamentals of Software Engineering FSEN 2023 (Part II)

15. Isberner, M., Howar, F., Steffen, B.: The Open-Source LearnLib. In: Kroening, D., Păsăreanu, C.S. (eds.) CAV 2015. LNCS, vol. 9206, pp. 487–495. Springer, Cham (2015). https://doi.org/10.1007/978-3-319-21690-4_32

16. ISO/DIS 26262-6: Road vehicles - functional safety - Part 6: Product development: software level (2009)

17. Manès, V.J.M., Han, H., Han, C., Cha, S.K., Egele, M., Schwartz, E.J., Woo, M.: The art, science, and engineering of fuzzing: a survey. IEEE Trans. Software Eng. (2019). https://doi.org/10.1109/TSE.2019.2946563

18. Meng, R., Dong, Z., Li, J., Beschastnikh, I., Roychoudhury, A.: Linear-time temporal logic guided greybox fuzzing. In: Proceedings of the 44th International Conference on Software Engineering, ICSE 2022, pp. 1343–1355. Association for Computing Machinery, New York (2022). https://doi.org/10.1145/3510003.3510082

19. Muskardin, E., Aichernig, B.K., Pill, I., Pferscher, A., Tappler, M.: Aalpy: an active automata learning library. Innov. Syst. Softw. Eng. **18**(3), 417–426 (2022). https://doi.org/10.1007/s11334-022-00449-3

20. Offutt, A.J., Lee, A., Rothermel, G., Untch, R.H., Zapf, C.: An experimental determination of sufficient mutant operators. ACM Trans. Softw. Eng. Methodol. (TOSEM) **5**(2), 99–118 (1996)

21. Peled, D., Vardi, M.Y., Yannakakis, M.: Black box checking. In: Wu, J., Chanson, S.T., Gao, Q. (eds.) Formal Methods for Protocol Engineering and Distributed Systems. IAICT, vol. 28, pp. 225–240. Springer, Boston (1999). https://doi.org/10.1007/978-0-387-35578-8_13

22. Peled, D., Vardi, M.Y., Yannakakis, M.: Black box checking. J. Automata Lang. Combinatorics **7**(2), 225–246 (2002). https://doi.org/10.25596/jalc-2002-225

23. Pferscher, A., Aichernig, B.K.: Stateful black-box fuzzing of bluetooth devices using automata learning. In: Deshmukh, J.V., Havelund, K., Perez, I. (eds.) NFM 2022. LNCS, vol. 13260, pp. 373–392. Springer, Cham (2022). https://doi.org/10.1007/978-3-031-06773-0_20

24. Sistla, A.P.: Safety, liveness and fairness in temporal logic. Formal Aspects Comput. **6**(5), 495–511 (1994). https://doi.org/10.1007/BF01211865. http://link.springer.com/article/10.1007/BF01211865

25. Vaandrager, F., Garhewal, B., Rot, J., Wißmann, T.: A new approach for active automata learning based on apartness. In: TACAS 2022. LNCS, vol. 13243, pp. 223–243. Springer, Cham (2022). https://doi.org/10.1007/978-3-030-99524-9_12

26. Vasilevskii, M.P.: Failure diagnosis of automata. Kibernetika (Transl.) 4, 98–108 (July-August 1973)

27. Waga, M.: Falsification of cyber-physical systems with robustness-guided black-box checking. In: Proceedings of the 23rd International Conference on Hybrid Systems: Computation and Contro, HSCC 2020. Association for Computing Machinery, New York (2020). https://doi.org/10.1145/3365365.3382193, https://doi.org/10.1145/3365365.3382193

28. WG-71, R.S.E.: RTCA DO-178C - Software Considerations in Airborne Systems and Equipment Certification. 1140 Connecticut Avenue, N.W., Suite 1020, Washington, D.C. 20036, December 2011

Compositionality in Model-Based Testing

Gijs van Cuyck[1]([⊠]), Lars van Arragon[1], and Jan Tretmans[1,2]

[1] Institute iCIS, Radboud University, Nijmegen, The Netherlands
{gijs.vancuyck,lars.vanarragon,jan.tretmans}@ru.nl
[2] TNO-ESI, Eindhoven, The Netherlands

Abstract. Model-based testing (MBT) promises a scalable solution to testing large systems, if a model is available. Creating these models for large systems, however, has proven to be difficult. Composing larger models from smaller ones could solve this, but our current MBT conformance relation **uioco** is not compositional, i.e. correctly tested components, when composed into a system, can still lead to a faulty system. To catch these integration problems, we introduce a new relation over component models called *mutual acceptance*. Mutually accepting components are guaranteed to communicate correctly, which makes MBT compositional. In addition to providing compositionality, mutual acceptance has benefits when retesting systems with updated components, and when diagnosing systems consisting of components.

Keywords: model-based testing · component-based testing · compositional testing · labelled transition systems · uioco

1 Introduction

Modern software systems are becoming increasingly large and complex. Traditional testing scales poorly for systems of these sizes. This causes the development and maintenance of test suites to become costly and time consuming, which slows down the development of new functionality. Model-Based Testing (MBT) is a technique that has been developed to increase the efficiency and effectiveness of testing. With MBT, testers create a model of the system under test from which an MBT tool can then automatically generate and execute test cases. This reduces the problem of creating and maintaining a test suite to creating and maintaining a model of the system under test.

Creating models for complex systems, however, is still difficult and laborious, since often no single person understands the whole system well enough. A solution is to divide and conquer: the system is decomposed into its components which are modelled and tested separately. This requires that the applied MBT methodology is *compositional*: if each component implementation is correct with

This work is part of the project *TiCToC - Testing in Times of Continuous Change*, project nr 17936, part of the research program *MasCot - Mastering Complexity*, which is supported by the Dutch Research Council NWO.

© IFIP International Federation for Information Processing 2023
Published by Springer Nature Switzerland AG 2023
S. Bonfanti et al. (Eds.): ICTSS 2023, LNCS 14131, pp. 202–218, 2023.
https://doi.org/10.1007/978-3-031-43240-8_13

respect to its component model, then it can be inferred that the composition of component implementations, i.e. the system under test, is correct with respect to the composition of component models, i.e. the system model.

In this paper, we investigate compositionality for MBT with labelled transition systems as models, **uioco** as the conformance relation, and parallelism modelling component composition [4]. We define a relation over component specification models, called *mutual acceptance*, which guarantees that components communicate neatly, and that **uioco** is preserved under composition. We generalise existing results on compositionality [4,8,11] by making less restrictive assumptions and using a composition operator that is associative so that also compositions of more than two components can be easily considered. Moreover, we use the more recent **uioco** conformance relation instead of **ioco** [19]. A more detailed comparison with related work can be found in Sect. 8.

In addition to compositionality, mutual acceptance also benefits testing evolving systems and software product lines. It enables more effective testing when a component is replaced by an updated version, as will be elaborated in Sect. 7. Diagnosis is the converse of compositionality: if the whole system has a failure, then diagnosis tries to localise the failure in one of its components; Sect. 7 will also discuss the use of mutual acceptance in diagnosis.

Overview. Section 2 contains preliminaries. Section 3 shows why the current approach to compositional model-based testing is not desirable by means of an example. Section 4 formalises what it means for two models to be compatible with each other for use in model-based testing, and defines the mutual acceptance relation $\leftrightharpoons$. Then Sect. 5 goes on to prove that this leads to desirable properties, after which Sect. 6 revisits the example. Section 7 discusses how these properties also lead to a reduced testing effort when substituting components, and how $\leftrightharpoons$ can be used in diagnosis. Section 8 describes some of the large body of related work previously done in the area of compositional model-based testing. Finally, Sects. 9 and 10 discuss possible future work and summarise the main results of this paper, respectively. All proofs for lemmas and theorems can be found in the extended version of this paper [6].

2 Preliminaries

We give the formal definitions for the MBT theory that we consider. We base our work on the theory developed in [4,18]. The main formalism used is that of labelled transition systems (LTS) (Definition 1). An LTS has states and transitions between states that model events. An event can be an input, an output or τ; τ represents an internal transition which is not observable from the outside and can therefore not be tested. I_s, U_s, etc., indicate inputs and outputs, respectively, coming from LTS s. The shorthand L_s means $I_s \cup U_s$. The name of an LTS is sometimes used as shorthand for its starting state. $\mathcal{LTS}(I, U)$ denotes the domain of labelled transition systems with inputs I and outputs U, or just $\mathcal{LTS}$ if I and U are known. For technical reasons we restrict this class to strongly converging and image-finite systems. Strong convergence means that infinite sequences of τ-actions are not allowed to occur. Image-finiteness means that the number of non-deterministically reachable states shall be finite. In examples, inputs and outputs are given implicitly by prefixing inputs with ?, and outputs with !. The same label can be in the input set of one LTS and in the output set of another.

Definition 1. *A* Labelled Transition System *is a 5-tuple* $\langle Q, I, U, T, q_0 \rangle$ *where:*

- *Q is a non-empty, countable set of states;*
- *I is a countable set of input labels;*
- *U is a countable set of output labels, which is disjoint from I;*
- *$T \subseteq Q \times (I \cup U \cup \{\tau\}) \times Q$ is a set of triples, the transition relation;*
- *$q_0 \in Q$ is the initial state.*

Reasoning about labelled transition systems uses the concept of traces. A trace is a sequence of labels that can occur when walking trough an LTS. Common notation used when describing traces is repeated in Definition 2.

Definition 2. *Let $s \in \mathcal{LTS}$; $p_1, p_2 \in Q_s$; $\ell \in L_s$; $\sigma \in L_s^*$; $\ell_\tau \in L_s \cup \{\tau\}$; $\sigma_\tau \in (L_s \cup \{\tau\})^*$, where ϵ denotes the empty sequence of labels.*

$$
\begin{aligned}
p_1 \xrightarrow{\epsilon} p_2 &\overset{def}{=} p_1 = p_2 \\
p_1 \xrightarrow{\ell_\tau} p_2 &\overset{def}{=} (p_1, \ell_\tau, p_2) \in T_s \\
p_1 \xrightarrow{\ell_\tau \cdot \sigma_\tau} p_2 &\overset{def}{=} \exists p_3 \in Q_s : p_1 \xrightarrow{\ell_\tau} p_3 \wedge p_3 \xrightarrow{\sigma_\tau} p_2 \\
p_1 \xrightarrow{\sigma} &\overset{def}{=} \exists p_3 \in Q_s : p_1 \xrightarrow{\sigma} p_3 \\
p_1 \xnrightarrow{\sigma} &\overset{def}{=} \nexists p_3 \in Q_s : p_1 \xrightarrow{\sigma} p_3 \\
p_1 \xRightarrow{\epsilon} p_2 &\overset{def}{=} \exists \varphi \in \{\tau\}^* : p_1 \xrightarrow{\varphi} p_2 \\
p_1 \xRightarrow{\sigma \cdot \ell} p_2 &\overset{def}{=} \exists p_3, p_4 \in Q_s : p_1 \xRightarrow{\sigma} p_3 \wedge p_3 \xrightarrow{\ell} p_4 \wedge p_4 \xRightarrow{\epsilon} p_2 \\
p_1 \xRightarrow{\sigma} &\overset{def}{=} \exists p_3 \in Q_s : p_1 \xRightarrow{\sigma} p_3 \\
p_1 \xnRightarrow{\sigma} &\overset{def}{=} \nexists p_3 \in Q_s : p_1 \xRightarrow{\sigma} p_3
\end{aligned}
$$

While specifications are often given as an LTS, $IOTS$ are used to represent implementations. In MBT, we commonly assume that we can always give any input to an implementation. $\mathcal{IOTS}$ denotes the domain of all input-enabled transition systems, and $\mathcal{IOTS}(I, U)$ denotes the domain of all input enabled transition systems with input set I and output set U.

Definition 3. *$i \in \mathcal{LTS}$ is an* Input-Enabled Transition System *(IOTS) if in every state for every input, its transition relation either contains that input, or reaches with just internal transitions another state that does so:*

$$\forall q \in Q_i, \ell \in I_i : q \xRightarrow{\ell}$$

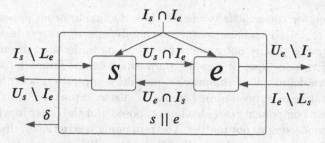

Fig. 1. Parallel composition of system s and its environment e.

Multiple labelled transition systems can be composed to form larger models. For component specifications this is often done using parallel composition (Definition 5). The result of parallel composition represents a system where all the components are being executed at the same time independently of each other. Synchronisation occurs on shared labels. An overview of the label sets of a parallel composition is shown in Fig. 1. Note that we do not require the input sets of the components to be disjoint, which will be explained below. Parallel composition assumes synchronous communication between components. Systems with asynchronous communication can still be modelled, but this requires giving explicit specification for the communication medium.

Definition 4. $s, e \in \mathcal{LTS}$ are composable iff their respective output sets U_s and U_e are disjoint: $U_s \cap U_e = \emptyset$

Definition 5. Parallel composition $\parallel$ on two composable labelled transition systems s and e is defined as: $s \parallel e \stackrel{def}{=} \langle Q, I, U, T, q_0 \rangle$, where

- $Q = \{ p \parallel q \mid p \in Q_s, q \in Q_e \}$
- $I = (I_s \setminus U_e) \cup (I_e \setminus U_s)$
- $U = U_s \cup U_e$
- $q_0 = q_{0_s} \parallel q_{0_e}$
- T is the minimal set satisfying the following inference rules
  (where $p, p_1, p_2 \in Q_s, q, q_1, q_2 \in Q_e$):

$$
\begin{array}{llll}
p_1 \xrightarrow{\ell} p_2 & \ell \in (L_s \cup \{\tau\}) \setminus L_e & \vdash & p_1 \parallel q \xrightarrow{\ell} p_2 \parallel q \\
q_1 \xrightarrow{\ell} q_2 & \ell \in (L_e \cup \{\tau\}) \setminus L_s & \vdash & p \parallel q_1 \xrightarrow{\ell} p \parallel q_2 \\
p_1 \xrightarrow{\ell} p_2,\ q_1 \xrightarrow{\ell} q_2 & \ell \in L_s \cap L_e & \vdash & p_1 \parallel q_1 \xrightarrow{\ell} p_2 \parallel q_2
\end{array}
$$

Lemma 1. Parallel composition is commutative and associative (up to isomorphism $\equiv$), i.e. for $s, e, t \in \mathcal{LTS}$, we have:

$$
\begin{array}{lll}
commutativity: & s \parallel e & \equiv e \parallel s \\
associativity: & (s \parallel e) \parallel t & \equiv s \parallel (e \parallel t)
\end{array}
$$

Our definition for *composable* is weaker than the one in other papers: $I_s \cap I_e = U_s \cap U_e = \emptyset$ [1,4,7]. This is because requiring disjoint input sets leads to a composition operator that is not associative [3]. A more detailed discussion of the properties of various types of parallel composition can be found in [20]. With our less restrictive definition of *composable*, parallel composition is both associative and commutative as expressed in Lemma 1. This is important, as it means that more than two components can also be composed and the order in which components are composed does not matter. The remaining restriction of disjoint output sets does not really restrict the applicability of parallel composition. Output sets can always be made disjoint by renaming one output label and then duplicating the synchronising transitions for the new label.

Another common approach to parallel composition is to replace all synchronised transitions with τ transitions. This is done under the assumption that communication between components is by default not observable by the outside world and therefore should be hidden. A downside is that this removes information, which makes specification-based analysis less useful. Additionally, a large part of the model-based testing theory assumes convergence, i.e. the absence of divergence. This means that there are no infinite paths of just τ-transitions possible in the specification. By automatically hiding the labels of synchronised transitions, divergence is often introduced into the composed specification. For these reasons, we choose not to automatically hide labels during composition.

The main purpose of a labelled transition system when used for model-based testing is to describe when an implementation is considered correct. This is done through a conformance relation.

Two common conformance relations are **ioco** [18] and the more recent **uioco** relation [4]. **uioco** differs from **ioco** in how it deals with *nondeterministic underspecification*, i.e. how non-specified inputs are handled. Among others, **uioco** is better suited for reasoning about composition. A detailed comparison of the two relations can be found in [19].

Definition 6. *For $s \in \mathcal{LTS}$, $\delta \notin L_s$ is a special output denoting the absence of outputs, called* quiescence. *It is defined as follows (with $p_1, p_2 \in Q_s$):*

$$p_1 \xrightarrow{\delta} p_2 \quad \overset{def}{=} \quad p_1 = p_2 \ \wedge \ \forall x \in U_s \cup \{\tau\} : \ p_1 \not\xrightarrow{x}$$

L^δ, U^δ *is used as shorthand for $L \cup \{\delta\}$, $U \cup \{\delta\}$ respectively.*

Definition 7. *Let $s \in \mathcal{LTS}$; $p_1 \in Q_s$; $P \subseteq Q_s$ and $\sigma \in L_s^{\delta*}$.*

$$
\begin{aligned}
p_1 \ \textbf{\textit{after}} \ \sigma \ &\overset{def}{=} \ \{ \, p_2 \in Q_s \mid p_1 \overset{\sigma}{\Rightarrow} p_2 \, \} \\
\textbf{\textit{out}}(p_1) \ &\overset{def}{=} \ \{ \, x \in U_s^\delta \mid p_1 \xrightarrow{x} \, \} \\
\textbf{\textit{out}}(P) \ &\overset{def}{=} \ \bigcup \{ \, \textbf{\textit{out}}(p) \mid p \in P \, \}
\end{aligned}
$$

Definition 8. *Let $i \in \mathcal{IOTS}(I,U)$; $s \in \mathcal{LTS}(I,U)$:*

$$\mathbf{\textit{Utraces}}(s) \overset{def}{=} \{\, \sigma \in L^{\delta^*} \mid s \overset{\sigma}{\Rightarrow} \wedge \,(\, \nexists p \in Q_s,\, \sigma_1 \cdot a \cdot \sigma_2 = \sigma :$$
$$a \in I \wedge s \overset{\sigma_1}{\Rightarrow} p \wedge p \overset{a}{\nRightarrow}\,)\,\}$$
$$i \;\mathbf{\textit{uioco}}\; s \quad \overset{def}{=} \quad \forall \sigma \in \mathbf{\textit{Utraces}}(s):\; \mathbf{\textit{out}}(i \;\mathbf{\textit{after}}\; \sigma) \subseteq \mathbf{\textit{out}}(s \;\mathbf{\textit{after}}\; \sigma)$$

3 Motivating Example: A Parking System

We argue that parallel composition does not work nicely with **uioco**, which we will show with an example in this section. Consider two components that together function as an automatic parking system in a car: a sensor which observes the environment and an actuator that parks the car. An illustration of how these two components communicate with each other and their environment is shown in Fig. 2. Specifications for the behaviour of these components are shown in solid black in Fig. 3. Their behaviour is straightforward: the parking component keeps parking as long as the sensor tells it that it is safe to do so, but stops parking if there is an obstacle, at which point it will stop the car and turn the sensor off. These components are left under-specified on purpose: it does not really matter what the sensor does if it detects an obstacle after it has been turned off, as long as it does not start beeping. This gives an implementer of the actual sensor some freedom, but still specifies the important behaviour.

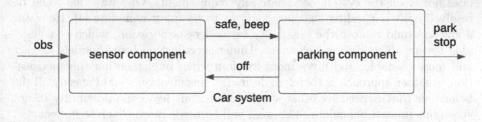

Fig. 2. Two component parking system

Possible implementations that are **uioco** correct are also given in Fig. 3 using the extra dashed blue transitions. On first glance this all seems to make sense, and model-based testing will not find any problems when testing the components. I.E. I_1 **uioco** $S_1 \wedge I_2$ **uioco** S_2. After composing our components using parallel composition, however, which is shown in Fig. 4, the composed implementation is not **uioco** correct to the composed specification.

The problem with the implementation in Fig. 4 is that it contains unspecified output transitions. These can be seen as some of the dashed transitions, which are only present in the implementation and not in the specification. This means that the previously valid implementations are now generating outputs that are not

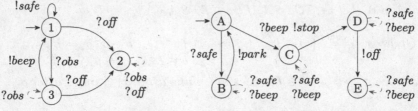

(a) S_1 and I_1: car sensor component   (b) S_2 and I_2: automated parking component

Fig. 3. Car component specifications ($\rightarrow$) and implementations ($\dashrightarrow$)

part of the composed specification. Model-based testing will report an error here, while the components are actually behaving as specified. Additionally, hidden within these false positives, there is also an actual error: if the sensor detects an obstacle after already having communicated that there is no obstacle, the parking system will not respond and will just continue parking. This is represented by the !*beep* transition from B3 to B1, which could for instance happen if a moving obstacle like a person is present. This shows that only looking at the individual components is not enough, as there are real problems that only become visible when looking at combinations of components together.

We argue that the main problem with this example is that the component specifications rely on unspecified behaviour. The sensor specification describes exactly when the sensor is allowed to beep, but the parking specification does not always specify what the result should be. There is no guarantee that the result does not crash the system or violate any requirements. One way this could be resolved is by expanding the specifications to be input complete [4]. However, doing so would remove the possibility for under-specification, which is a desirable feature in modelling behaviour. Under-specification keeps models smaller and more readable, and gives more freedom when implementing the specification. Another approach is therefore desired: a specification should specify all the behaviour that is used by other specifications, but leave the possibility of not specifying unused behaviour. This goal will be made more concrete in Sect. 4.

4   Mutual Acceptance

In order to reason about specified and unspecified behaviour an explicit notion of what it means for behaviour to be specified is required. For **uioco**, the allowance of outputs is always explicitly specified. They are either present in the model and therefore allowed, or absent and disallowed. After a specified input, the model again defines what is allowed. Inputs are always implicitly allowed, but if an input is not part of the model all behaviour after that input is allowed. This means that the behaviour after an absent input is unspecified: the model does not tell us what should or should not happen. Therefore, if all outputs given by one component, are inputs present in the model of the other component, there will be no unspecified behaviour. This requirement is formulated in Definitions 9

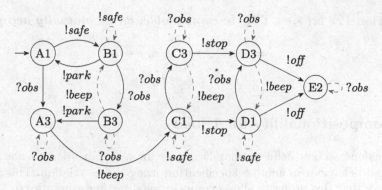

Fig. 4. Car autopark and sensor composed $S_1 \| S_2$ ($\rightarrow$) and $I_1 \| I_2$ ($\dashrightarrow$)

to 11: if after some $\sigma \in \mathbf{Utraces}(s \| e)$ some pair of states s', e' is reached, and s' produces a synchronised output, then e' must have this output as an input. Note that this is trivially holds if e is input enabled which generalises earlier results about component-based testing with **uioco** [4].

Definition 9. *For $s \in LTS$; $p \in Q_s$; $P \subseteq Q_s$, the set of enabled inputs is defined as:*

$$in(p) \overset{def}{=} \{ \ell \in I_s \mid p \overset{\ell}{\Rightarrow} \}$$
$$in(P) \overset{def}{=} \bigcap \{ in(q) \mid q \in P \}$$

Definition 10. *Let $\sigma \in L^{\delta*}$; $\mathcal{L} \subseteq L^{\delta}$; and $\ell \in L^{\delta}$. Projecting a trace to a smaller set of labels is defined as:*

$$\epsilon \restriction \mathcal{L} \overset{def}{=} \epsilon$$
$$(\sigma \cdot \ell) \restriction \mathcal{L} \overset{def}{=} (\sigma \restriction \mathcal{L}) \cdot \ell \quad \text{if } \ell \in \mathcal{L}$$
$$\sigma \restriction \mathcal{L} \qquad \text{otherwise}$$

Definition 11. *Let $s, e \in \mathcal{LTS}$ be **composable**, then s **accepts** e iff:*

$$s \leftharpoonup e \overset{def}{=} \forall \sigma \in \mathbf{Utraces}(s \| e), \; s' \in Q_s, \; e' \in Q_e :$$
$$s \| e \overset{\sigma}{\Rightarrow} s' \| e' \implies out(e') \cap I_s \subseteq in(s') \cap U_e$$

The symmetric version of the $\leftharpoonup$ relation is defined in Definitions 12. Though it might look like an equivalence relation, it is neither reflexive nor transitive. Reflexivity fails because $\rightleftharpoons$ is indirectly defined using parallel composition. This means it is only defined on specifications that are composable, and any specification with outputs is not composable with itself. Transitivity is also not true, because each pair of specifications has its own sets of state pairs and shared labels for which the $\leftharpoonup$ relation must hold. This means each specification pair must be checked independently of any other specifications.

Definition 12. *Let $s, e \in \mathcal{LTS}$ be **composable**, then s **mutually accepts** e:*

$$s \leftrightharpoons e \ \overset{def}{=}\ s \leftharpoonup e \ \wedge \ e \leftharpoonup s$$

5 Compositionalility for Uioco

The previous section defined what it means for a specification to not trigger undefined behaviour in another specification using the $\leftharpoonup$ relation. This section will prove that this property allows compositional testing using **uioco**.

Lemma 2 shows how for composable, input complete systems, traces in the composed system can be transformed into traces in the component systems, and the other way around. This allows for compositional model-based testing in input complete systems. Lemma 3 then goes on to show that for **Utraces**, the same is also possible as long as the two specifications are mutually accepting.

This is also where the **composable** requirement becomes important. It enforces that all labels are either synchronised or only present in one of the two label sets. This means that every trace σ can be split into a unique pair of two projected traces $\sigma \upharpoonright L_s^\delta$ and $\sigma \upharpoonright L_e^\delta$ which can be replayed in s and e, respectively. Without this requirement, it would be unclear what to do with unsynchronised shared labels.

Lemma 2. *let i_s, i_e be **composable** IOTS, $i'_s \in Q_{i_s}, i'_e \in Q_{i_e}, \sigma \in L_{i_s \| i_e}^{\delta}{}^*$.*

$$i_s \| i_e \overset{\sigma}{\Rightarrow} i'_s \| i'_e \iff i_s \xrightarrow{\sigma \upharpoonright L_{i_s}^\delta} i'_s \ \wedge \ i_e \xrightarrow{\sigma \upharpoonright L_{i_e}^\delta} i'_e$$

Lemma 3. *let s, e be **composable** LTS, $s' \in Q_s, e' \in Q_e, \sigma \in \textbf{Utraces}(s \| e)$.*

$$s \leftrightharpoons e \implies (s \| e \overset{\sigma}{\Rightarrow} s' \| e' \iff s \xrightarrow{\sigma \upharpoonright L_s^\delta} s' \ \wedge \ e \xrightarrow{\sigma \upharpoonright L_e^\delta} e')$$

The $\leftrightharpoons$ relation, and by extension Lemma 3, only consider **Utraces** and not arbitrary traces because only states reachable by **Utraces** are important for **uioco**. This does, however, create the extra requirement of checking that after projecting a trace to a specific component, it is still part of the **Utraces** for that component. Lemma 4 shows that the $\leftrightharpoons$ relation ensures that **Utraces** are preserved when projecting from a composed system, in both directions. This is not trivial, as the special label δ is not normally preserved under composition.

Lemma 4. *Let $s, e \in LTS$ be **composable**, $\sigma \in L_{s \| e}^{\delta}{}^*$.*

$$s \leftrightharpoons e \implies$$
$$(\sigma \in \textbf{Utraces}(s \| e) \iff \sigma \upharpoonright L_s^\delta \in \textbf{Utraces}(s) \ \wedge \ \sigma \upharpoonright L_e^\delta \in \textbf{Utraces}(e))$$

We now present Theorem 1, which is the main statement of this paper. It states that for mutually accepting specifications, **uioco** is preserved under parallel composition. The other way around, if there is a problem that causes two

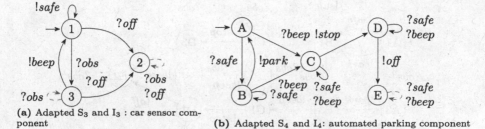

(a) Adapted S_3 and I_3 : car sensor component

(b) Adapted S_4 and I_4: automated parking component

Fig. 5. Mutually accepting versions of Fig. 3. (spec: →, imp: -→)

composed implementations to be **uioco**-incorrect to their composed specifications, then this problem can also be found by testing with at least one of the components. The reverse of this implication, however, does not hold, even if both specifications are mutually accepting.

The reason for this is that the mutual acceptance relation only guarantees that no invalid outputs are communicated. It does not enforce that something is actually communicated. Therefore, it is possible for one of the two implementations to produce quiescence when this is not allowed, which is then masked in the combined system by the outputs generated by the other component. This highlights a property of the **uioco** relation: presence of specific outputs cannot be enforced. One possible way to deal with this might be to extend the **uioco** theory with a more fine grained concept of quiescence, allowing the detection of quiescence in specific components, instead of only over the whole system. This is further explored in [17].

Theorem 1. *Let* $s, e \in LTS$ *be* ***composable****,* $i_s, i_e \in IOTS$*, then*

$$s \rightleftharpoons e \ \wedge \ i_s \ \textbf{\textit{uioco}} \ s \ \wedge \ i_e \ \textbf{\textit{uioco}} \ e \ \implies \ i_s \parallel i_e \ \textbf{\textit{uioco}} \ s \parallel e$$

Another thing to note is that when applying Theorem 1 in practice, this makes the implicit assumption that you can correctly compose components. In order to guarantee the correctness of the composed system, the composition of components i_s and i_e must actually behave as $i_s \parallel i_e$. This means that any communicating channels must be connected as described in s and e, and that there must not be some hidden implicit environment part of the composition setup that further influences the behaviour of either of the components.

6   The Parking System Revisited

Using the results from Sect. 4 and Sect. 5, the problems with the parking system from Sect. 3 can be explained: the two specifications in Fig. 3 are not mutually accepting. A counterexample is the trace $safe \cdot obs$, which is in the **Utraces** of $S_1 \parallel S_2$, and goes to state $B3$. In state 3, however, S_1 can perform output *beep*,

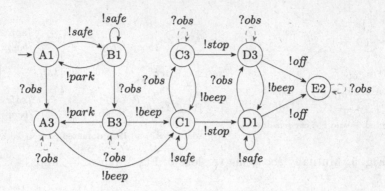

Fig. 6. Adapted car autopark and sensor composed $(S_3||S_4 \rightarrow)$ and $(I_3||I_4 \dashrightarrow)$

while S_2 does not accept input *beep* in state B. A number of other counterexamples can also be given, each one corresponding to one of the dashed output transitions of $S_1||S_2$. These are the states where the composed implementation produces unspecified outputs. Using these counterexamples, the points where the specifications have to be extended can be identified. The result can be seen in Fig. 5. Figure 5b now has several extra transitions for *safe* and *beep* defined in the specification, exactly in those places where the sensor might supply these inputs. The developer is now forced to think about what actually should happen there, while the developer is still free to not specify inputs that should not occur in normal operation. This is especially relevant for the *beep* transition originating from state B, which was previously unspecified. On further inspection, it is revealed that a simple self loop is not desired here, because after a *beep* the car should stop, and not continue to park. This would have resulted in undesired behaviour if the specifications were simply made input enabled in an automatic way, as was done in previous approaches [4]. Using a self-loop here would mean that implementations are possible which pass all tests, but still do not stop when an object is detected.

The result of composing the adapted specifications from Fig. 5 is shown in Fig. 6. This specification now correctly finds that $I_1||I_2$ ~~uioco~~ $S_3||S_4$, which can be seen with the trace *safe · obs · beep* which is present in the **Utraces** of $S_3||S_4$. After this trace, $I_1||I_2$ can produce the output *park*, which is undesirable after detecting an object, and also not allowed by $S_3||S_4$. But if each individual implementation is updated to be **uioco** correct according to its own adapted specification, as is done with I_3 and I_4, then their composition is again correct with respect to the composed specifications, i.e. $I_3||I_4$ **uioco** $S_3||S_4$.

The example shows how the $\leftrightharpoons$ relation can be used to find integration problems between components using their specifications. Possible problems are prevented by expanding the specification, without requiring a full specification of all inputs. This does not yet require any actual implementations, as the reasoning is done over the domain of all possible valid implementations. Finding these integration problems before starting integration testing, allows for fixing them earlier in development.

7   Component Substitution and Diagnosis

In addition to providing compositionality in development and testing, mutual acceptance has benefits when retesting systems with updated components, and when diagnosing systems consisting of components. A common situation is that one component becomes deprecated and needs to be replaced. This traditionally has a high cost, because even if the new component is well tested, there is a chance using it will cause problems with the other components already in use. These issues mainly occur because replacing a component changes the environment for the other components. This means the other components, which are the environment of the replaced component, might be called with new inputs which have not yet been tested. A well known example where reuse of an old, well tested component in a new environment caused the whole system to fail is the crash of the Ariane-5 rocket [15,21]. Here, an important subsystem put implicit requirements on the environment which were not documented or checked to hold. Correctness was inferred from extensive testing, but after changing the environment this testing became invalid, and the component failed anyway.

These problems can be reduced by using a specification-based analysis like $\leftrightharpoons$ in combination with model-based testing. Model-based testing can generate tests for every defined sequence of inputs. If two specifications are mutually accepting, then they only communicate outputs which are defined inputs for the intended communication partner. These two points together mean that all the model-based testing done up to the point of replacing a component is still useful, because it was testing for all possible inputs, and not just the ones that were in current use. This can give a much higher confidence that a component switch will not cause any problems, because testing does not have to start from square one. If the specification of the new component is not mutually accepting with all the rest of the system, then the counterexamples point to all the places where undefined inputs are given. This information can be used to improve the specifications, and focus testing toward these possible problem areas.

The correctness reasoning made possible by the $\leftrightharpoons$ relation can also be used during diagnosis, by taking the converse of Theorem 1. If the whole system contains a problem, and one or more components are found to be **uioco** correct, then the problem must be located within one of the remaining components. Together with Lemmas 3 and 4 this can then be used to narrow down a trace showing **uioco** incorrectness of the whole system to a shorter trace showing **uioco** incorrectness of one specific component. This idea is expressed in Lemma 5. Since **composable** requires each label to be part of at most one output set, the last output of the counterexample uniquely identifies the problem component. This does not work if the last output was δ, which could have been caused by a number of components. In this case we can still find the faulty component by replaying the projected traces in all components until the faulty one is found. This can, for example, more accurately determine the source of bugs from gathered logs containing full system traces.

Lemma 5. *Let* $s, e \in LTS$, $i_s, i_e \in \mathcal{IOTS}$, $s \leftrightharpoons e$, $\sigma \in \textbf{\textit{Utraces}}(s \parallel e)$.

$$\sigma \text{ is a counterexample for } i_s \parallel i_e \textbf{ uioco } s \parallel e \implies$$
$$\sigma \upharpoonright L_s^\delta \text{ is a counterexample for } i_s \textbf{ uioco } s \quad \vee$$
$$\sigma \upharpoonright L_e^\delta \text{ is a counterexample for } i_e \textbf{ uioco } e$$

8   Related Work

The work in this paper is closely related to ideas already discussed in the context of interface automata [8–10]. Interface automata are a type of labelled transition system which can be used to model both the behaviour of a component and the constraints it puts on its environment. These constraints are encoded in the form of missing input transitions, which then signify that the component can only be used in an environment that does not give these inputs. This closely resembles the main idea behind the $\leftrightharpoons$ relation. Apart from a slightly different composability requirement which makes it associative, our definition for parallel composition coincides with the one from [8]. Our definition for $\leftrightharpoons$ also seems to coincide with the absence of reachable (by **Utraces**) error states as defined in [8]. The solution to reachable error states taken for interface automata is to apply a pruning algorithm. This will remove input transitions to further restrict the valid environments until all error states become unreachable. A downside of this approach is that it becomes easy to generate composed models that after pruning no longer give errors, but also no longer express the desired correct behaviour. This is noted in [8] as the observation that the environment that does not give any inputs at all, always avoids all avoidable error states. The interface automata approach consists of removing transitions from the composed specification until problem areas are unreachable. We instead choose to add transitions to the component specifications until the problem areas no longer exist. Another contribution of our work is the inclusion of quiescence, and the direct link to the **uioco** implementation relation. This makes the theory easier to apply in practice in the context of existing MBT tools.

An earlier attempt at formalising the correctness of a component with respect to its environment was developed in [11]. It defines the **eco** (environmental conformance) relation with similar semantics to the accepts relation. The relation **eco**, however, works on a specification for the environment, and a black box implementation of the component. This means that **eco** conformance can only be checked by testing, and this needs to be redone completely whenever a component changes. Additionally, all labels of the component and its environment have to communicate, i.e., there is no external communication, which further restricts applicability. The **eco** approach also has a couple of advantages. Since **eco** is checked using testing, it can be done on the fly. It also does not require how a component calls other components as part of its input specifications. Instead, this information is gathered while testing and compared against the specifications of the components being called. This makes a possible combination of our work with the **eco** theory and algorithms interesting.

In this paper, we describe when a component is a valid environment for another component. Earlier work looking into the set of valid environments for a given component was done in the field of contract-based design. A detailed overview of this field can be found in [2]. A contract is defined as a tuple of a set of valid environments and a set of valid implementations, where every combination of environment and implementation can be composed. The definition of what it means for an environment to be composable with an implementation is very similar to our definitions, and it also describes how a labelled transition system can be seen as a contract. The scope under consideration in [2], however, is limited to receptive environments with the same label set as the components. All components also have to be deterministic, and internal transitions or quiescence are not discussed. A more recent addition to contract theory extends the scope of [2] to hyper-contracts [13]. While this extends the scope of properties that can be expressed as contracts, the current instantiation of the meta-theory for labelled transition systems still has many of the restrictions imposed in [2]. In contrast to the bottom up approach of combining component contracts into a composed contract, a top down approach is also possible and sometimes desired. Decomposing a set of requirements into individual component contracts has been studied in [14].

Another way of describing compatible components is defining a specification for the most permissive communication partner. All concrete communication partners are then in some form of a refinement relation with this "operating guideline". This approach is outlined in [16] for acyclic finite labelled transition systems. It assumes all communications to be asynchronous, while we assume synchronous communication.

9   Future Work

Making specifications mutually accepting involves defining extra behaviour. Some of this extra specification is desirable, for instance the *beep* transition from state B in S_4. This transition represents interesting behaviour that was missed in the specification phase. Most other added transitions, however, are just simple self-loops, which represent that the input has to be ignored. If receiving an input that was not specified is considered undefined behaviour, this is required to ensure correct behaviour. Another possible interpretation would be that unspecified inputs are buffered, until the other component is ready to receive them. In such a setting, it would not be required that every input that can be given is specified immediately. It would then be enough that such inputs are specified always eventually, after some amount of internal actions of the receiving component. In general, it can be investigated how to (automatically) repair non-mutually accepting systems.

In this paper, we have defined mutual acceptance, but no ways for practically checking it have been given. Algorithms to efficiently check mutual acceptance between specifications, or testing procedures to test mutual acceptance, analogous to **eco**, need to be developed.

The theory introduced so far works on two components. Larger systems consist of many components. Mutual acceptance can still be inferred by repeatedly applying the parallel composition operator and Theorem 1. For example, when combining specifications $s1, s2$ and $s3$ into $(s1 \parallel s2) \parallel s3$, we must check that $s1 \parallel s2 \leftrightharpoons s3$. Doing this directly using $s1 \parallel s2$ might be complicated due to the increasing number of parallel components. We postulate that multiway-mutual acceptance can be inferred from pairwise-mutual acceptance. In general, mutual acceptance of many components, with complicated communication structures, should be further investigated.

Requiring $\leftrightharpoons$ for all intermediate steps means that there cannot be any unexpected outputs. For real systems however, these outputs are only a problem if they appear in the final composition of all the components. The fact that two components do not work well in all environments is not a problem if you plan to use them together with other components that will prevent this. Therefore, a different definition of mutual acceptance for more than two components at a time might be investigated.

To apply the theory in this paper to a practical use case, it will need to be extended with the concept of data. Real systems can seldom be modelled with a finite set of labels, but will instead send instances of data types to each other. This has been formalised in the theory of symbolic transition systems (STS) [5,12], which is the underlying formalism of several MBT tools. The concepts in this paper could be extended to STS which would bring them closer to being applied in practice.

10   Conclusion

Model-based testing is a promising technology for increasing the efficiency and effectiveness of testing. The applicability of MBT, however, is limited by the availability of models. Larger system models are hard to create, but can be composed from multiple smaller component models. In this paper, we have defined the mutual acceptance relation $\leftrightharpoons$ between specifications, which guarantees that model-based testing is compositional, i.e. if two components have been tested for **uioco**-correctness with respect to their respective specifications, then the composition of these implementations is also **uioco**-correct with respect to the composition of their specifications, under the assumption that the parallel composition operator itself is faithfully implemented. This is an improvement over previous results which obtained the same conclusion with a stricter requirement, viz. that all specifications must be input-enabled [4]. In addition, we have shown that this result can also help when updating older components with newer ones, and when localising a faulty component during diagnosis of a large, component-based system.

References

1. Beneš, N., et al.: Complete composition operators for IOCO-testing theory. In: Proceedings of the 18th International ACM SIGSOFT Symposium on Component-Based Software Engineering. CBSE 2015. New York, NY, USA, May 2015, pp. 101–110. Association for Computing Machinery (2015). ISBN: 978-1-4503-3471-6. https://doi.org/10.1145/2737166.2737175. Accessed 11 Oct 2021

2. Benveniste, A., et al.: Contracts for system design. Found. Trends ® Electron. Des. Autom. **12**(2-3), 124–400 (2018). ISSN: 1551-3939, 1551-3947. https://doi.org/10.1561/1000000053. http://www.nowpublishers.com/article/Details/EDA-053. Accessed 20 Dec 2022

3. Berendsen, J., Vaandrager, F.: Composition in a Paper by de Alfaro e.a. Is Not Associative. Technical report. Radboud University, May 2008 (2008). https://sws.cs.ru.nl/publications/papers/fvaan/commentdAdSF+.pdf

4. van der Bijl, M., Rensink, A., Tretmans, J.: Compositional testing with IOCO. In: Petrenko, A., Ulrich, A. (eds.) FATES 2003. LNCS, vol. 2931, pp. 86–100. Springer, Heidelberg (2004). https://doi.org/10.1007/978-3-540-24617-6_7 ISBN: 978-3-540-24617-6. Accessed 29 Oct 2021

5. van den Bos, P., Tretmans, J.: Coverage-based testing with symbolic transition systems. In: Beyer, D., Keller, C. (eds.) TAP 2019. LNCS, vol. 11823, pp. 64–82. Springer, Cham (2019). https://doi.org/10.1007/978-3-030-31157-5_5 ISBN: 978-3-030-31156-8. Accessed 23 Fen 2023

6. van Cuyck, G., van Arragon, L., Tretmans, J.: Compositionality in model-based testing. In: CoRR abs/2307.03701 (2023). arXiv: 2307.03701. https://doi.org/10.48550/arXiv.2307.03701

7. Daca, P., et al.: Compositional specifications for IOCO testing. In: Proceedings - IEEE 7th International Conference on Software Testing, Verification and Validation, ICST 2014. March 2014, pp. 373–382 (2014). https://doi.org/10.1109/ICST.2014.50. ISBN: 978-1-4799-2255-0

8. de Alfaro, L., Henzinger, T.A.: Interface automata. In: ACM SIGSOFT Software Engineering Notes 26(5), 109–120 (2001). ISSN: 0163–5948. https://dl.acm.org/doi/10.1145/503271.503226. https://doi.org/10.1145/503271.503226. Accessed 29 Oct 2021

9. de Alfaro, L., Henzinger, T.A.: Interface theories for component-based design. In: Henzinger, T.A., Kirsch, C.M. (eds.) EMSOFT 2001. LNCS, vol. 2211, pp. 148–165. Springer, Heidelberg (2001). https://doi.org/10.1007/3-540-45449-7_11 ISBN: 978-3- 540-42673-8. Accessed 29 Oct 2021

10. de Alfaro, L., Henzinger, T.A.: Interface-based design. In: Broy, M., Grünbauer, J., Harel, D., Hoare, T. (eds.) Engineering Theories of Software Intensive Systems. NSS, vol. 195, pp. 83–104. Springer, Dordrecht (2005). https://doi.org/10.1007/1-4020-3532-2_3 ISBN: 978-1-4020- 3532-6

11. Frantzen, L., Tretmans, J.: Model-based testing of environmental conformance of components. In: de Boer, F.S., Bonsangue, M.M., Graf, S., de Roever, W.-P. (eds.) FMCO 2006. LNCS, vol. 4709, pp. 1–25. Springer, Heidelberg (2007). https://doi.org/10.1007/978-3-540-74792-5_1 ISBN: 978-3-540-74792-5

12. Frantzen, L., Tretmans, J., Willemse, T.A.C.: Test generation based on symbolic specifications. In: Grabowski, J., Nielsen, B. (eds.) FATES 2004. LNCS, vol. 3395, pp. 1–15. Springer, Heidelberg (2005). https://doi.org/10.1007/978-3-540-31848-4_1 ISBN: 978-3-540-25109-5. Accessed 3 Feb 2023

13. Incer, I., et al.: From interface automata to hypercontracts. In: Raskin, J.F., Chatterjee, K., Doyen, L., Majumdar, R. (eds.) Principles of Systems Design. LNCS, vol. 13660, pp. 477–493. Springer, Cham (2022). https://doi.org/10.1007/978-3-031-22337-2_23. ISBN: 978-3-031-22337-2. Accessed 10 Jan 2023
14. Kaiser, B., et al.: Contract-based design of embedded systems integrating nominal behavior and safety. In: Complex Systems Informatics and Modeling, October, pp. 66–91 (2015). https://doi.org/10.7250/csimq.2015-4.05
15. Lions, J.L.: Ariane 5: Flight 501 Failure. Technical Report (1996). https://esamultimedia.esa.int/docs/esa-x-1819eng.pdf
16. Massuthe, P., Schmidt, K.: Operating guidelines - an automata-theoretic foundation for the service-oriented architecture. In: Fifth International Conference on Quality Software (QSIC 2005). September 2005, pp. 452–457. https://doi.org/10.1109/QSIC.2005.47
17. Noroozi, N.: Improving Input-Output Conformance Testing Theories. Ph.D. thesis. Eindhoven: Technische Universiteit Eindhoven, October (2014). https://wiki.hh.se/ceres/images/c/c2/Noroozi_thesis_2014.pdf. Accessed 15 Feb 2023
18. Tretmans, J.: Model Based Testing with Labelled Transition Systems. In: Hierons, R.M., Bowen, J.P., Harman, M. (eds.) Formal Methods and Testing. LNCS, vol. 4949, pp. 1–38. Springer, Heidelberg (2008). https://doi.org/10.1007/978-3-540-78917-8_1 ISBN: 978-3-540-78917-8. Accessed 22 Dec 2022
19. Tretmans, J., Janssen, R.: Goodbye IOCO. In: Jansen, N., Stoelinga, M., van den Bos, P. (eds.) A Journey from Process Algebra via Timed Automata to Model Learning. LNCS, vol. 13560, pp. 491–511 (2022). https://doi.org/10.1007/978-3-031-15629-8_26. ISBN: 978-3-031-15628-1. Accessed 4 Oct 2022
20. Vogler, W., Lüttgen.: A Linear-Time Branching-Time Per-spective on Interface Automata. Acta Informatica **57**(3), pp. 513–550 (2020). https://doi.org/10.1007/s00236-020-00369-4. ISSN: 1432-0525, Accessed 21 Jun 2022
21. Weyuker, E.J.: Testing component-based software: a cautionary tale. IEEE Software **15**(5), 54–59. https://doi.org/10.1109/52.714817. ISSN: 1937–4194

Prioritizing Test Cases with Markov Chains: A Preliminary Investigation

Luciana Rebelo[1,5]($\boxtimes$) (ID), Érica Souza[2] (ID), Gian Berkenbrock[3] (ID),
Gerson Barbosa[4] (ID), Marlon Silva[8] (ID), André Endo[6] (ID),
Nandamudi Vijaykumar[7] (ID), and Catia Trubiani[1] (ID)

[1] Gran Sasso Science Institute - GSSI, L'Aquila, Italy
luciana.rebelo@gssi.it
[2] Universidade Tecnológica Federal do Paraná - UTFPR, Cornélio Procópio, Brazil
[3] Universidade Federal de Santa Catarina - UFSC, Joinville, Brazil
[4] Universidade Estadual Paulista - Unesp, Guaratinguetá, Brazil
[5] Instituto Federal de Educação, Ciência e Tecnologia de São Paulo - IFSP,
Jacareí, Brazil
[6] Universidade Federal de São Carlos - UFSCar, São Carlos, Brazil
[7] Instituto Nacional de Pesquisas Espaciais - INPE, São José dos Campos, Brazil
[8] Instituto Federal de Educação, Ciência e Tecnologia de São Paulo - IFSP, Campos
do Jordão, Brazil

Abstract. Test Case Prioritization reduces the cost of software testing by executing earlier the subset of test cases showing higher priorities. The methodology consists of ranking test cases so that, in case of a limited budget, only the top-ranked tests are exercised. One possible direction for prioritizing test cases relies on considering the usage frequency of a software sub-system. To this end, a promising direction is to identify the likelihood of events occurring in software systems, and this can be achieved by adopting Markov chains. This paper presents a novel approach that analyzes the system scenarios modeled as a Markov chain and ranks the generated test sequences to prioritize test cases. To assess the proposed approach, we developed an algorithm and conducted a preliminary and experimental study that investigates the feasibility of using Markov chains as an appropriate means to prioritize test cases. We demonstrate the strength of the novel strategy by evaluating two heuristics, namely H1 (based on the transition probabilities) and H2 (based on the steady-state probabilities), with established metrics. Results show (i) coverage of 100% for both H1 and H2, and (ii) efficiency equal to 98.4% for H1 and 99.4% for H2, on average.

Keywords: Software Testing · Test Case Prioritization · Markov chain

1 Introduction

One of the primary Verification and Validation (V&V) processes to ensure the correctness of a software product is testing, which basically consists of empir-

Published by Springer Nature Switzerland AG 2023
S. Bonfanti et al. (Eds.): ICTSS 2023, LNCS 14131, pp. 219–236, 2023.
https://doi.org/10.1007/978-3-031-43240-8_14

ically verifying its correctness [12]. The testing process includes several activities, the most challenging being the generation/selection of test cases. This activity consists of deciding the test cases that may present the highest chances of pinpointing problems in the software system under analysis. Several techniques have been developed to deal with this demand, e.g., [9,21]. Test Case Prioritization (TCP) [35], which was first proposed in the context of regression testing, is an approach to deal with the problem of selecting test cases. The technique uses the entire test suite to prioritize test cases to be executed, using some pre-defined criteria, such as fault detection rate, coverage rate, or history-usage profile, among others. In traditional TCP, a set of test cases already exists, the System Under Test (SUT) is modified and there is a need to ensure that new defects are not introduced. Then, based on the knowledge of the change, the existing test cases are ranked, and only the most prioritized run. Although TCP was initially proposed in regression testing, it can also be applied in other general testing scenarios, for example in situations where many (or all) test cases are new [24]. One promising direction relies on the usage frequency of a (sub-) system, since problems are most likely to occur. Kashyap et al. [17] proposes a test plan generation and prioritization technique, through a probabilistic model, where the underlying idea is to capture the critical system functionalities that are most used by the system users. The results showed in [17] suggest that the actual system usage provides a valid contribution when prioritizing test plans since the system most likely improves its reliability by covering more probable bugs during validation. Actual system usage is represented more accurately by the prioritized test plans, if compared to the ad-hoc test plans, and hence, likely to improve the system reliability by uncovering more probable bugs during system validation.

This paper advocates the prioritization of test cases while considering the system usage frequency. One way is to quantify the likelihood of events occurring in software systems, which can be achieved by adopting Markov chain models. As recently outlined by Barbosa et al. [2], although there are some initiatives to prioritize test cases using Markov chains, this is a new subject, still little explored in the literature. This motivates our novel investigation, inspired by the possibility of triggering further studies in this area of research. The software can be modeled by a Finite State Machine (FSM) where the transition arcs are labeled with inputs to be used to generate test cases. The same FSM can be assigned with probabilities on the transition arcs and therefore represent a Discrete Time Markov chain (DTMC). From this formal representation, it is possible to compute the probabilities to obtain the steady-state probabilities. These probabilities represent the percentage of time occupied by each state and, in the long run, they are considered to be steady-state equilibrium. This characteristic can be applied to TCP, using the probabilities to define priorities of what states are more active or visited than others.

In our approach, we first generate the test cases and then reorder them within the suite, leveraging the probabilities of each test sequence to perform the ranking. We define two heuristics to assess the feasibility of Markov chains in the prioritization of test cases: (H1) based on the transition probabilities;

and (H2) based on the steady-state probabilities. We also define some metrics, such as coverage and efficiency, among others, to quantify the feasibility of the proposed approach. About coverage, as proposed in [18,19], we assume that the selected test cases should assure the total coverage, hence our technique must achieve 100% of coverage of all independent paths. About efficiency, as specified in [13,16], we mean the saved computation as an outcome of our prioritization. It is expressed as a percentage value and calculated as the ratio of the number of disregarded test sequences w.r.t. the number of generated test sequences. For instance, with 5k test cases, if our prioritization indicates 200 tests to be run, then efficiency will be 96% (4800/5k).

To validate the proposed approach, we conducted a preliminary study considering different Markov chain models, from distinct domains. Although the evaluated systems are rather small in terms of the number of states and transitions, the obtained results are promising, even more considering this is a preliminary analysis acting as proof of concept. Experimental results demonstrate that our strategy achieves coverage of 100% when using both H1 and H2; the efficiency is estimated to be 98.4% for H1 and 99.4% for H2, on average. We observe that H2 performed slightly better than H1, mainly for those models that generate a large number of test sequences. Yet, further experiments are needed to assess the approach in terms failure detection when compared with other methods. Summarizing, the main contribution of our work is raising attention to considering Markov chain models as a valid support to prioritize test cases, providing means for practitioners and researchers to advance on the prioritization of test cases.

The rest of the paper is organized as follows. Section 2 briefly reviews related work to better position our work. Section 3 introduces the main background concepts. Section 4 presents the details of the approach. Section 5 describes the experimental study and reports the results. Lessons learned are discussed in Sect. 6, along with the conclusion and future research directions. Replication data is publicly available: https://doi.org/10.5281/zenodo.7940360.

2   Related Work

Some initiatives toward employing Markov chains to prioritize test cases can be found in the literature. For instance, Ozawa et al. [25] apply a Markov chain reward model (based on DTMC) to verify how software code metrics affect the test case prioritization. In the context of software testing, Bohme et al. [4] make use of Markov chains to analyze the coverage of test cases on a grey box model. The strategy goal explores more paths fuzzing the path seed, and improving the coverage of the model. Kashyap et al. [17] propose a modeling methodology for generation and prioritization of test cases. This research defines the probability of set of test cases representing actual system usage as a *likelihood* function. The used objective function is represented by the likelihood of a test - which is a measure of how well a test case represents the actual system usage. As outcome of this research, model-based activities are assessed as improving the system reliability. The formalization relies on Markov Modulated Markov Processes (MMMP), whereas the considered system shows two CTMC processes.

Recently, Barbosa et al. [2] conducted a SLR on studies that prioritize test cases using Markov chains. According to this review, 12 initiatives adopting Markov chains in TCP were applied in distinct contexts, which are – (i) *Usage model* [32]; (ii) *Controlled Markov chains (CMC)* [7]; (iii) *Model-based testing (MBT)* [29]; (iv) *Regression testing* [22]; (v) *Statistical testing* [10]; and (vi) *Random testing* [36]. Among the 12 studies presented at SLR, we think that the study of Morozov et al. [22] is the most closely related to our work. In particular, they introduce a method for automatic prioritization of test cases (belonging to an original test suite) to achieve efficient regression testing. The test suite prioritization method considers two principles: (i) the error stimulation in an updated test case block; and (ii) the detection of error propagation, i.e., the stimulated error should propagate to the place where it can be detected. The main difference with our study is that we aim to make use of Markov chains solutions as a solid foundation to generate and rank test cases, according to a test adequacy criterion, as opposed to [22] that instead aims to provide a stochastic error propagation analysis.

Summarizing, to the best of our knowledge, there is no exploratory study on the effort of prioritizing test cases while solving Markov chains as support for identifying the most used system functionalities, as we propose in this paper.

3   Background

3.1   Test Case Prioritization

Test Case Prioritization [35] uses the entire generated test suite and, based on some criteria, prioritizes the suite to exercise those cases (of the suite) that are ordered or ranked first to be exercised. In other words, TCP refers to a set of test cases that are more important based on some metrics, but without decreasing the number of faults to be detected [11]. In traditional TCP when the SUT is modified and there is already a test suite, most of the time it is not possible to exercise the entire test suite, due to resource restriction such as time and budget. So, to achieve efficiency in the regression testing, only a part of this suite might be exercised. In order to classify this test case suite, criteria can be established. Some approaches in this direction make use of data mining [23], Monte Carlo simulation [6], usage frequency techniques [17], and various prioritization techniques [27], among others.

In this paper, although our initial objective is not regression testing of the traditional TCP, we discuss how to make use of system usage frequency. Specifically, we propose to employ both transition probabilities and steady-state probabilities (obtained by solving Markov chains) in order to rank the test cases. We anticipate that our results assess the proposed strategy as a viable criterion to minimize the number of test cases to be exercised on the implementation.

3.2   Markov Chains

Markov chains play a major role in a wide variety of applications. They can be considered probability models in which knowledge about the past is not necessary as long as the present is known, i.e., the memory-less property [14,31]. Markov chains can be represented as state-transition diagrams, whose formalism is based on FSMs [20], consisting of a set of states and transitions linking states. They can be either discrete-time (DTMC) or continuous-time (CTMC). The former uses transition probabilities that represent labels on the transition arcs, while the latter indicates duration of events on the transition arcs. Based on the inputs of probability transitions, methods such as multiplication of matrices, and linear algebra solutions can be employed to generate the steady-state probabilities [28]. These probabilities represent the percentage of time occupied by each state and used to obtain performance metrics.

In this paper, we pursue the idea that these probabilities can play a key role in prioritizing software test cases. Our strategy builds upon systems modeled as ergodic Markov chains [33]. A Markov chain is ergodic when the following criteria are met [5]: (i) transition probabilities linking any two given states must be greater than 0, i.e., any state can be reached starting from a given state; (ii) the chain must not have absorbing (recurrent) states, is irreducible, and aperiodic; and (iii) there is only one steady-state probability vector π as solution for $\pi M = \pi$, and $\sum_i \pi_i = 1$, where M is the transition probabilities matrix.

4 Markov Chains Applied in TCP

This work presents an approach that analyzes scenarios modeled with Markov chains and ranks the generated test sequences to prioritize them. An algorithm is designed to receive different scenarios modeled from an FSM, to generate and rank the test sequences. In this section we present the algorithm and describe its main steps.

Consider the DTMC model shown in Fig. 1, modeled as an FSM, which is ergodic, with states 'S0, S1, S2, S3, S4' and transitions following a stochastic distribution. Nodes represent states, and edges represent transition arcs. The nodes 'S0' and 'S4' are the initial and final states, respectively. The final state has been randomly assigned through the use of the random walk algorithm that requires a final state to complete a path in the FSM (more details are provided later in the sequel of this section). Each edge is labelled with a transition probability. The same chain can be represented by a transition matrix M. The transition matrix is a square matrix of order n, where n is the number of states. Each element corresponds to the probability of transition from one node to another. For example, the matrix $M_{n \times n}$ in (2) represents the Markov chain of Fig. 1, where $n = 5$. The sum of the outgoing transition probabilities from each state is equal to 1, as stated in [31]. In other words,

$$\sum_{i=1}^{n} p_{ij} = 1, \text{for any } j \in [1..n] \tag{1}$$

Using Eq. (1) and the properties of Markov chains, we propose the Algorithm 1 that generates test cases and ranks them based on the probability of

224   L. Rebelo et al.

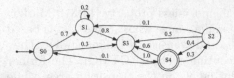

$$M = \begin{bmatrix} 0 & 0.7 & 0 & 0.3 & 0 \\ 0 & 0.2 & 0 & 0.8 & 0 \\ 0 & 0.1 & 0 & 0.5 & 0.4 \\ 0 & 0 & 0 & 0 & 1.0 \\ 0.1 & 0 & 0.3 & 0.6 & 0 \end{bmatrix} \quad (2)$$

Fig. 1. DTMC representing a software model

each sequence. To this end, two heuristics are introduced: (i) **H1**, which performs the calculation using the product of the transition probabilities of a sequence; and **H2**, which performs the calculation using the product of steady-state probabilities of each state in a sequence. The method used to explore the FSM and generate the test sequences is the random walk [34], however with a slight modification, in what it considers the probabilities when choosing the next transition. To complete a path on the FSM exploration, random walk requires an initial and a final state. In the following we explain the main steps of the algorithm considering the example shown in Fig. 1.

Algorithm 1. Markov chain for TCP

---

input: FSM: (list_of_states, transition_matrix (TM), initial_state, end_states); stop_criterion (SC)
output: two lists: i) ordered by arc probabilities, and ii) ordered by state probabilities
1: verify_parameters(FSM)   ▷ check the input parameters
2: SP ← calculate_steady_probability(TM)
3: *stop* ← 0
4: **while** *stop* < SC **do**
5:     seq_arc, seq_state = random_walk(FSM,SP)
6:     **if** seq_arc *not in* list_transitions **then**
7:         *add* seq_arc *to* list_transitions
8:         *add* seq_state *to* list_states
9:         update *stop*
10:     **end if**
11: **end while**
12: decrease_ranking_by_arc_probability(list_transitions)
13: decrease_ranking_by_state_factor_probability(list_states)

---

1. Loading the Input Parameters. The input parameters of the proposed algorithm are the FSM, composed by: Markov process transition matrix, state names, initial and final states; and percentage of inclusion cases (i.e., the percentage of all possible sequences from a Markov chain model). This number will be used as a stopping criterion for the algorithm, and thus, the algorithm will be terminated when this amount of test cases is found. At the beginning of the algorithm, there is a method that checks if the declaration was correctly made (line 1), otherwise, the algorithm stops and outputs an error message. The complete list of the files with the input parameters, as well as the algorithm, can be found in our replication package: https://doi.org/10.5281/zenodo.7940360.

2. Calculating Steady-State Probability. Before starting random walk, the steady-state probability is calculated (line 2). We found the stationary distribution of the Markov chain. To do this, we recall that the FSM must be an ergodic chain (see Sect. 3.2).

3. Initialization of Variables. The first action of the *while* loop (line 4) is the creation of structures that will store the sequences found throughout the algorithm, as well the probability in each iteration. Two lists are created, namely: a list of traversed arcs (*list_transitions*) to calculate H1; and a list of traversed states (*list_states*) to calculate H2.

4. Stop Criterion. At the end of each iteration, the `update stop` (in line) is performed. The calculation is executed as follows: let q_k be the product of all transition probabilities, from state i to state j denoted by p_{ij}, in the newest sequence k added into the list of traversed arcs. Hence, q_k is added to the variable *stop*. This procedure is repeated while $stop < SC$. Otherwise, the random walk stops. In other words,

$$q_k = \prod p_{ij}, \forall (i,j) \in k; i, j \in [1..n] \tag{3}$$

$$stop = \sum_k q_k, \forall k \in \text{list\_transitions} \tag{4}$$

5. Ranking of Test Sequences. When the process of calculating heuristics is completed, the ranking of test cases begins (see lines 12, 13). This ranking is build upon the probabilities of each sequence, for H1 and H2, in descending order, because the higher probability is related to a higher chance to occur.

Using the example in Fig. 1, we can verify the output of our algorithm. Table 1 shows the first test cases prioritized according to their probability, using both H1 and H2. We can observe the travelled states of each sequence, and their probabilities. Note that the same sequences were delivered by H1 and H2, but in different order or priority. Also, the values of the probabilities are quite different relating to the sequences of H1 and H2. This occurs because sequences delivered by H1 use the transition probability, while those sequences delivered by H2 use the steady-state probabilities, and the latter usually leads to much lower values. Let us discuss more thoroughly the sequence 'S0-S1-S3-S4'. Using H1 we have, 'S0-S1' × 'S1-S3' × 'S3-S4' = 0.7 × 0.8 × 1.0 = 0.56 = 56%. Using H2, be π the steady-state probability of a state from a matrix M. So, we have $\pi(S0) \times \pi(S1) \times \pi(S3) \times \pi(S4) = 0.04158 \times 0.051975 \times 0.3659 \times 0.4158 = 0.0003287955 \rightarrow 0.033\%$.

Table 1. List of the first test case sequences generated, revealing the sequences with the highest priorities, for both H1 and H2.

H1		H2	
Travelled states	Probab	Travelled states	Probab.
S0-S1-S3-S4	56%	S0-S3-S4	0.633%
S0-S3-S4	30%	S0-S1-S3-S4	0.033%
S0-S1-S1-S3-S4	11.199%	S0-S1-S1-S3-S4	0.000017%
	$\Sigma = 97.199\%$		$\Sigma = 0.666017\%$

5   Experimental Analysis

The purpose of our experimentation is to assess the feasibility of the proposed approach. We are interested in investigating the ability to prioritize test cases for a bounded number of tests. In particular, we aim to answer the following research question:

RQ: What is the feasibility of using Markov chains in test case generation and prioritization?

In this section we present the application of the approach over three different case studies, from distinct application domains. All examples were adopted from the literature [1,8,30]. Note that some adaptations were made on the FSMs when necessary, but without distorting the examples. For instance, each FSM was assigned a random final state (if it did not have one) due to the use of the random walk algorithm, which needs a final state as a stopping criterion. Besides, when the final state has no transition, it was assigned to it a transition to the initial state, even though we know that this transition will never be exercised, as the algorithm stops when it reaches the final state. This is necessary to fulfill the definition of ergodic chains shown in Sect. 3.2.

It is worth explaining that the stop criterion with the inclusion percentages explained in Sect. 4 was not sufficient to run the experiments. This happens due to a characteristic of the random walk algorithm. The sequence of probabilities usually start quite high, but get smaller and smaller quickly; so it becomes very expensive to reach a high probability inclusion like 90%. As the availability for the laboratory machine was 24 h, we also used this restriction to run the experiments. Therefore, the stop criterion was: reach the probability specified in Sect. 4 (which was 90%) or when running the experiment reaches a timeout set to 24 h. The experiments were run on a Dell computer (Product Name: OptiPlex 5070), Fedora Linux 35 Operating System, Kernel Version: 5.19.7-100.fc35.x86_64 (64-bit), X11 Graphics Platform, Processors: $6 \times$ Intel®Core^{TM} i5-9500, CPU @ 3.00 GHz, and 16 Gb RAM.

5.1   Metrics Definition

To assess the approach and analyze the results, we introduce some metrics, defined as follows:

M_1 – **Number of test cases** (N): this refers to the number of generated test sequences. We also define as set_N the set of all the generated test sequences. This way, N is the cardinality of set_N.

M_2 – **Time** (T): this metric (in seconds) refers to the time for generating the test cases (N), as well as for ordering them using either H1 and H2.

M_3 – **Usefulness - useful number of test cases** (uN): in this metric uN is defined as the number of test sequences, ranked by p, using one of the following two criteria, and the choice is on whichever is greater:

1. all sequences, until all independent paths are covered, see metric M_7;

2. all sequences that have a probability p greater than or equal to $max\_p/1000$, where max_p denotes the highest sequence probability found in set_N.

For instance, observing the example in Fig. 1, sequence 'S0-S1-S3-S4' has the highest probability considering H1, as can be seen in Table 1, which is $max\_p = 56\%$. In this case, we consider all the sequences with probability greater than or equal to 0.056%. Note that the total coverage of independent paths would be enough to define this metric. Since this is a criterion that normally generates very few sequences, we extend our metric to increase the size of the test suite, in order to test more sequences. Hence, we focus on the paths (sequences) that are most likely to be traversed (those that are up to 1k times less likely to happen than the first sequence) while ensuring that all independent paths are covered (i.e., 100% coverage of independent paths).

M_4 – **Efficiency** (ε): it is defined as the ratio of the number of disregarded test cases sequences (N - uN) for the number of generated test cases sequences (N). We consider that the greater ε is, the better the result. This means that with few test cases (uN) we are able to reach the coverage criterion (see metric M_7 - coverage) and point out the sequences of test cases that are more likely to occur. In other terms,

$$\varepsilon = \frac{N - uN}{N} \tag{5}$$

M_5 – **#states:** the number of states in the model.

M_6 – **#transitions:** the number of transitions in the model.

M_7 – **Coverage** (Θ): the sequences generated to be traversed in order to obtain complete coverage of a Control-Flow Graph (CFG), where each of these paths can be interpreted as a test case representing independent paths. Even though we are not working directly with a CFG, this criterion might be applied to Markov chains, as they have a structure very similar to CFGs. To determine the independent paths, the decision graph (or decision-to-decision (DD) path graph), derived from CFGs, can be used [18,19]. DD path graph testing is "the best known code-based testing method, incorporated in numerous commercial tools" [15]. In other words, test cases are generated based on the condition that they cover all independent paths of the FSM to assure the highest coverage.

5.2   Description of Case Studies

In this section, we present the three case studies chosen to assess the approach. We describe the context of each one, showing their DTMC model along with their respective transition matrices. Furthermore, for each case study, the achieved steady-state probabilities as well as the first five test case sequences generated are exhibited, reproducing the states traveled with their respective sequence probability p, i.e., the sequences that have the highest probability to be traversed, for both H1 and H2.

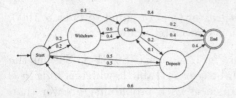

$$CS1 = \begin{bmatrix} 0 & 0.2 & 0.3 & 0.5 & 0 \\ 0.2 & 0 & 0.4 & 0 & 0.4 \\ 0 & 0.6 & 0 & 0.2 & 0.2 \\ 0.5 & 0 & 0.1 & 0 & 0.4 \\ 0.6 & 0 & 0.4 & 0 & 0 \end{bmatrix} \quad (6)$$

Fig. 2. DTMC model for ATM, adapted from [1]

Case Study I (CS I): Automated Teller Machine (ATM). Figure 2 represents the DTMC model of the classical ATM case study, where the ATM interacts with a customer via a specific interface and communicates with the bank over an appropriate communication link. There are several models describing the ATM available in the literature. We constructed a simplified DTMC version for the FSM presented in [1]. Once on the system interface (represented by *start* state), the customer can choose among three options: withdrawal, deposit, and check balance. The model consists of five states: *Start, Withdraw, Check, Deposit,* and *End*. The Markov chain transition matrix CS1 for the model is shown in (6).

After applying the approach to this example, the steady-state probabilities obtained are shown in Table 2 (on the left side). The table exhibits the steady-state probabilities for all the case studies. *Check* is the state with the highest steady-state probability, i.e., the most active state, while state *Deposit* has the smallest one, i.e., the least active state. Table 3 presents the first five 'test sequences generated using H1 and H2. On the left, we see the sequences generated using H1, with the highest transition probability. On the right side, we report the sequences generated using H2, using the steady-state probabilities to rank the sequences. Still, we can observe the probabilities p of each sequence. It is important to note that there is a significant difference in the values of the probabilities, as each heuristic is using a different source to derive the probabilities for the test sequences. The fact that the first sequence produced using H1 '*Start-Deposit-End*' has a probability $p = 20\%$ does not mean that this sequence is more likely to occur or has high priority relating to the first sequence produced using H2 '*Start-Check-End*', which has probability $p = 1\%$. The probability values are

Table 2. The steady-state probabilities for CS I, CS II, and CS III, respectively, sorted in descending order.

CS I		CS II		CS III	
State	Steady-state probab.	State	Steady-state probab.	State	Steady-state probab.
Check	0.2346%	Follower	0.4283%	monitoring	0.3517%
Start	0.2302%	Controller	0.1671%	intrusionDetected	0.2282%
Withdraw	0.1868%	Sensor	0.1671%	initializing	0.1235%
End	0.1864%	GUI	0.1616%	alarm	0.1153%
Deposit	0.1620%	Fail	0.0436%	ready	0.0613%
		End	0.0323%	idle	0.0582%
				policeNotified	0.0565%
				sensorsLost	0.0035%
				assistance	0.0018 %
$\Sigma = 1.0\%$		$\Sigma = 1.0\%$		$\Sigma = 1.0\%$	

only comparable within sequences derived by the same heuristic. Noteworthy to say that there is a strong intersection (80%) among the sequences, even though using different strategies proposed in H1 and H2. The corresponding sequences are labeled in grey in Table 3.

Table 3. List of the first test cases sequences generated for CS I, revealing the sequences with the highest priorities, for both H1 and H2. Notice a strong intersection on the results between the two heuristics.

H1		H2	
Travelled states	p	Travelled states	p
Start-Deposit-End	20%	Start-Check-End	1%
Start-Withdraw-End	8%	Start-Withdraw-End	0.8%
Start-Check-Withdraw-End	7.2%	Start-Deposit-End	0.7%
Start-Check-End	6%	Start-Check-Withdraw-End	0.19%
Start-Deposit-Start-Deposit-End	5%	Start-Withdraw-Check-End	0.19%
	$\Sigma = 46.2\%$		$\Sigma = 2.88\%$

Case Study II (CS II): Robot GUI. This case study illustrates an example of a Robot presented in [30]. The architecture is represented by *Controller*, *Sensor, Follower* and *GUI* components. Transition probabilities are derived from an operational profile [3]. The DTMC model can be seen in Fig. 3. The model consists of six states (*GUI, End, Fail, Follow, Control, Sensor*), one initial state (*GUI*) and two final states (*End, Fail*). We have adapted the model to explicitly set the final states to *End* and *Fail*, and creating for each final state, a transition to the initial state, thus to fulfill the specification of ergodic chains, see Sect. 3.2. The Markov chain transition matrix CS2 for the model is shown in (7).

Applying the approach to this example, the steady-state probabilities obtained for CS II are shown in Table 2 (on the middle). *Follower* is the most active state, while state *End* is the least active. Table 4 presents the first five sequences with the generated highest priority, while using H1 and H2. Similarly

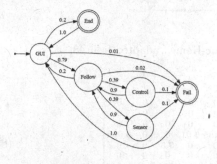

$$CS2 = \begin{bmatrix} 0 & 0.79 & 0 & 0 & 0.01 & 0.2 \\ 0.2 & 0 & 0.39 & 0.39 & 0.02 & 0 \\ 0 & 0.9 & 0 & 0 & 0.1 & 0 \\ 0 & 0.9 & 0 & 0 & 0.1 & 0 \\ 1 & 0 & 0 & 0 & 0 & 0 \\ 1 & 0 & 0 & 0 & 0 & 0 \end{bmatrix} \quad (7)$$

Fig. 3. DTMC model for Robot GUI, adapted from [30]

to the previous case study, we can notice that there is an intersection of 80% among the sequences produced by H1 and H2, labeled in grey.

Table 4. List of the first test cases sequences generated for CS II, revealing the sequences with the highest probabilities, for both H1 and H2. Notice a relevant intersection on the results between the two heuristics.

H1		H2	
Travelled states	p	Travelled states	p
GUI-End	20%	GUI-Fail	0.705%
GUI-Follower-GUI-End	3.16%	GUI-End	0.522%
GUI-Follower-Sensor-Fail	3.081%	GUI-Follower-Fail	0.302%
GUI-Follower-Controller-Fail	3.081%	GUI-Follower-Controller-Fail	0.0504%
GUI-Follower-Fail	1.58%	GUI-Follower-Sensor-Fail	0.0504%
	$\Sigma = 30.9\%$		$\Sigma = 1.63\%$

Case Study III (CS III): Safe-Home System. This case study is a Cyber-Physical System (CPS), namely Safe-Home, i.e., an open-source security software adapted from [8]. It consists of an intrusion detection system to control alarms and sensors that implement some home safety features. Figure 4 illustrates the behavior of the system modeled as a DTMC and the transition matrix is illustrated in (8). We can notice that the model is composed of nine states and seventeen transitions. First, there is a setup (composed of *idle* and *ready* states). Then, there are three main states (*initializing, monitoring,* and *alarm*) which are in charge of sensor initialization, detection, and alarm handling, respectively. If an intrusion is detected, some actions must be done, e.g., calling the police.

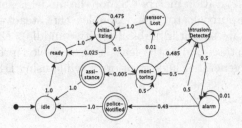

Fig. 4. DTMC model for the Safe-Home, adapted from [8]

$$CS4 = \begin{bmatrix} 0 & 1 & 0 & 0 & 0 & 0 & 0 & 0 & 0 \\ 0 & 0 & 1 & 0 & 0 & 0 & 0 & 0 & 0 \\ 0 & 0.025 & 0.475 & 0.5 & 0 & 0 & 0 & 0 & 0 \\ 0 & 0 & 0 & 0.5 & 0.485 & 0.01 & 0 & 0 & 0.005 \\ 0 & 0 & 0 & 0.5 & 0 & 0 & 0.5 & 0 & 0 \\ 0 & 0 & 1 & 0 & 0 & 0 & 0 & 0 & 0 \\ 0 & 0 & 0 & 0. & 0.5 & 0 & 0.01 & 0.49 & 0 \\ 1 & 0 & 0 & 0 & 0 & 0 & 0 & 0 & 0 \\ 1 & 0 & 0 & 0 & 0 & 0 & 0 & 0 & 0 \end{bmatrix} \tag{8}$$

Some adjustments were necessary also for this model since it was originally represented in [8] as a Markov Decision Process (MDP) [26]. MDPs represent a formalism for modeling systems exhibiting both probabilistic and nondeterministic behavior. In this paper we focus on DTMCs, non determinism is not managed. To handle this, we used the following strategy: whenever the sum of the transition probabilities of each state exceeds 1, a probability is assigned as a proportional value. As an example, the *initializing* state handed over three transitions with the following probabilities: a1=0.05; a2=0.95; a3=1. Considering the normalised probabilities, the values assigned in the corresponding DTMC are: a1=0.025; a2=0.475; a3=0.5. Thus, the system meets the requirements of a DTMC, and we preserve the original transitions among system states. Besides, final states *assistance* and *policeNotified* originally had an auto-transition with probability 1 which we modified by changing the transitions to the initial state, to fulfill the definition of ergodic chains.

Table 2 shows the steady-state probabilities when applying the approach (on the right side). The *monitoring* state is the most active one while the state *assistance* is the least one. Tables 5 and 6 present the first five test sequences generated using H1 and H2, respectively. Notice that the intersection among the sequences generated by H1 and H2 is 40%. Heuristic H2 presents more sequences ending with state *assistance*. However, if we observe the transition probability to achieve state *assistance* is $p = 0.005\%$, which is very low when compared to the other transition probabilities in Fig. 4. As strategy H1 is using the transition probability to derive the sequences, the sequences going through this transition have a lower chance to occur, therefore they are not among the first ones. The overlap in the corresponding sequences is highlighted in grey in Tables 5 and 6.

Table 5. List of the first test cases sequences generated for CS III, revealing the highest probabilities using H1.

Travelled states	p
idle-ready-initializing-monitoring-intrusionDetected-alarm--policeNotified	5.94%
idle-ready-initializing-monitoring-monitoring-intrusionDetected-alarm--policeNotified	2.97%
idle-ready-initializing-initializing-monitoring-intrusionDetected-alarm--policeNotified	2.82%
idle-ready-initializing-monitoring-monitoring-monitoring--intrusionDetected-alarm-policeNotified	1.49%
idle-ready-initializing-monitoring-intrusionDetected-alarm--intrusionDetected-alarm-policeNotified	1.49%
	$\Sigma = 14.73\%$

5.3 Results and Analysis

Table 7 exhibits the metrics (see Sect. 5.1) for all the three case studies which can be identified in the first column (CS). The second column reports the metric

Table 6. List of the first test cases sequences generated for CS III, revealing the highest probabilities using H2.

Travelled states	p
idle-ready-initializing-monitoring-assistance	$2.728 \times 10^{-7}\%$
idle-ready-initializing-monitoring-intrusionDetected-alarm--policeNotified	$2.304 \times 10^{-7}\%$
idle-ready-initializing-monitoring-monitoring-assistance	$9.595 \times 10^{-8}\%$
idle-ready-initializing-monitoring-monitoring-intrusionDetected--alarm-policeNotified	$8.105 \times 10^{-8}\%$
idle-ready-initializing-monitoring-monitoring-monitoring--assistance	$3.375 \times 10^{-8}\%$
	$\Sigma = 7.14 \times 10^{-7}\%$

#states, followed by #transitions, T (in seconds), and stop criterion, defined in Sect. 4 - see Eqs. (3) and (4) - and finally metric N. Then, we report Θ, uN, and ε for H1 and for H2, whereas the last row of the table shows the simple arithmetic mean (AVG) for each metric, considering all case studies. In the following we argue on the results obtained for each case study.

CS I Analysis. The number of generated test sequences is $N = 5008$. CS I requires little time to reach the stopping criterion (27.75 s), with inclusion percentage achieving 95%. For H1, to calculate the usefulness let us first consider the number of sequences to achieve coverage Θ. With the 17 first sequences delivered by H1, all independent paths are covered, i.e., $\Theta = 17$. Considering the criterion of uN, probability $max\_p/1000$, 235 sequences have probability greater than 0.02% (looking at Table 3, probability for sequence 'Start-Deposit-End' is 20%). As the metric states to choose the max of (Θ and $max\_p/1000$), we get the value of $uN = 235$ (please see Sect. 5.1). This leads to an efficiency ε of 95.31% and coverage of 100% of all independent paths. Considering H2, with the 11 first sequences delivered by H2, all independent paths are covered ($\Theta = 11$) and 94 sequences show a probability greater than 0.001%, i.e., $uN = 94$. This originates an efficiency ε of 98.12% and coverage of 100%. For this case study, H2 performed better than H1.

CS II Analysis. We can notice a large number of generated test cases ($N = 836,052$), as well as the time for generating them, which consumed all the available time (24 h or 86400 s) to achieve inclusion of 84.29%. The explanation for this high time is the use of random walk algorithm to travel in the FSM. More details are given at the beginning of Sect. 5. Concerning Θ, with the 12 first sequences delivered by H1 and with the first 9 sequences delivered by H2 all independent paths are covered. Even though N is a large number, for H1 we have usefulness $uN = 316$, i.e., 316 test sequences have probability greater than 0.02%, producing an efficiency $\varepsilon = 99.96\%$. For H2 $uN = 94$, i.e., 94 test sequences show a probability greater than 0.000007%, with an efficiency $\varepsilon = 99.99\%$. The coverage for both H1 and H2 is 100%. We can conclude that for this case study, H2 performed barely better than H1.

Table 7. Summary of the metrics for each case study.

CS	#states	#transitions	$T(s)$	Stop criterion	N	H1 uN	H1 ε	H1 Θ	H2 uN	H2 ε	H2 Θ
I	5	14	27.75	95%	5008	235	95.31%	17	94	98.12%	11
II	6	13	86400	84.29%	836052	316	99.96%	12	94	99.99%	9
III	9	17	86400	83%	1224974	934	99.92%	258	298	99.98%	298
AVG	6.7	14.67	57609.25	87.43%	688678	495	**98.4%**	95.7	162	**99.4%**	106

CS III Analysis. This is the most complex case study, with 9 states and 17 transitions. We also notice a large number of test cases generated ($N = 1{,}224{,}974$). For H1, relating to Θ, with the 258 first sequences delivered all independent paths are covered. Yet, 934 test sequences have a probability greater than 0.006%, producing an efficiency $\varepsilon = 99.92\%$. For H2, the first 114 test sequences show a probability greater than $2.73 \times 10^{-10}\%$. This was the unique result where considering the sequences probabilities ($max\_p/1000$) was not sufficient to achieve full coverage Θ of the FSM. Thus, considering Θ, we have $uN = 298$, and the last sequence of uN is *'idle-ready-initializing-monitoring-sensorsLost-initializing-monitoring-assistance'*, with a probability of occurrence $= 4.17 \times 10^{-11}\%$. Therefore, $uN = 298$ produced an efficiency $\varepsilon = 99.98\%$. The ratio for both H1 and H2 are equivalent to those observed in the other case studies, hence demonstrating evidence that the approach is interesting when applied to more complex models (i.e., including a substantial number of states and transitions). We can conclude that, for this case study, H2 performed better than H1. We remind that the complete list of the models and results can be found in our replication package: https://doi.org/10.5281/zenodo.7940360.

6   Discussion and Conclusion

To answer our research question, we present a preliminary investigation by considering three different Markov chain models, in distinct domains, and producing test sequences through the random walk algorithm. We generate the test cases and we reorder them within the suite using the probabilities of each test sequence to perform the ranking. First, accumulating the transition probabilities of arcs (H1), and then accumulating the steady-state probabilities of the states (H2). Some metrics are defined, such as usefulness, efficiency, and coverage, among others, to study the feasibility of the proposed approach. Considering the examples, efficiency was 98.4% for H1 and 99.4% for H2. On average, H2 performs better than H1, considering all case studies. For instance, case study III (which is the most complex scenario) shows a total of 1,224,974 test sequences, and the useful number of sequences is reduced to 934 and 298, when applying H1 and H2, respectively. Both heuristics lead to 100% of coverage (i.e., all independent paths are wrapped). We think this is valuable, since the criterion of covering all independent paths is robust, as it guarantees that all states and branches will be tested at least once. Our experimental results indicate that Markov chains are indeed suitable modeling abstractions for prioritizing test cases.

The soundness of probabilities reported in DTMC model is an open issue of our approach. This largely depends on the knowledge of the software and its use, and it may require agreement between the customers, the software developers, and test team managers. We used a random walk to generate the test sequences, but this criterion usually generates a large number of sequences and therefore it might be expensive, hence directly impacting the computational time. Besides, random walk requires a final state for the FSMs, which is not always straightforward to find in the case studies. As future work, we intend to complement our research with a comparative analysis by adapting our algorithm with other testing criteria to traverse the FSM, such as Switch Cover, Transition Tour, Breadth First Search, Depth First Search, among others. Such criteria may influence the metrics used in this study, and we are interested to quantify the variations.

To conclude, the achieved results are promising and pave the way for new studies. However, further investigations are essential. Hence, a deeper investigation of Markov chains and TCP is part of our research directions for future work. We are interested to estimate the scalability of the approach while varying the model size (i.e., increasing both the number of states and transitions). We are aware that the requirement of Ergodic chains is quite strong. So, we plan to replicate the study while considering different steady-state distributions, thus to observe if efficiency deteriorates when the system is exposed to variegate distributions. Another limitation concerns the reliability, i.e., the failure detection capability of the present approach has not been evaluated. Although we consider the usage frequency of the software system, and there is evidence that the most used parts tend to present more failures [3,17], this is an assumption that is crucial to be addressed. In the next steps of our experiments, we plan to perform a comparison with state-of-the-art approaches adopting other assumptions, thus learning the pros and cons of our proposal.

Acknowledgements. This work has been partially funded by MUR PRIN 2017TWR-CNB SEDUCE, and the PNRR MUR VITALITY (ECS00000041) Spoke 2 ASTRA - Advanced Space Technologies and Research Alliance. The authors acknowledge the support of the MUR (Italy) Department of Excellence 2023–2027 for GSSI.

References

1. SATM: Simple Automatic Teller Machine. https://slideplayer.com/slide/3835819/. Accessed 4 Oct 2022
2. Barbosa, G., de Souza, É.F., dos Santos, L.B.R., da Silva, M., Balera, J.M., Vijaykumar, N.L.: A systematic literature review on prioritizing software test cases using Markov chains. Inf. Softw. Technol. **147**, 106902 (2022)
3. Bertolino, A., Miranda, B., Pietrantuono, R., Russo, S.: Adaptive coverage and operational profile-based testing for reliability improvement. In: International Conference on Software Engineering (ICSE), pp. 541–551 (2017)
4. Bohme, M., Pham, V.T., Roychoudhury, A.: Coverage-based Greybox fuzzing as Markov chain. IEEE Trans. Software Eng. **45**(5), 489–506 (2019)

5. Bolch, G., Greiner, S., De Meer, H., Trivedi, K.S.: Queueing Networks and Markov Chains: Modeling and Performance Evaluation with Computer Science Applications. John Wiley & Sons (2006)
6. Brémaud, P.: Markov Chains: Gibbs fields, Monte Carlo Simulation, and Queues, vol. 31. Springer, New York (2013). https://doi.org/10.1007/978-3-030-45982-6
7. Cai, K.Y.: Optimal software testing and adaptive software testing in the context of software cybernetics. Inf. Softw. Technol. 44(14), 841–855 (2002)
8. Camilli, M., Gargantini, A., Scandurra, P., Trubiani, C.: Uncertainty-aware exploration in model-based testing. In: IEEE Conference on Software Testing, Verification and Validation (ICST), pp. 71–81 (2021)
9. Cruciani, E., Miranda, B., Verdecchia, R., Bertolino, A.: Scalable approaches for test suite reduction. In: Proceedings of the International Conference on Software Engineering (ICSE), pp. 419–429 (2019)
10. Devroey, X., et al.: Statistical prioritization for software product line testing: an experience report. Softw. Syst. Model. 16(1), 153–171 (2015)
11. Elbaum, S., Malishevsky, A.G., Rothermel, G.: Test case prioritization: a family of empirical studies. IEEE Trans. Software Eng. 28(2), 159–182 (2002)
12. Everett, G.D., McLeod Jr., R.: Software Testing. Testing Across the Entire (2007)
13. Ferreira, A.R.: Análise e Melhoria de Processos, p. 59 (2013)
14. Gagniuc, P.A.: Markov Chains: From Theory to Implementation and Experimentation. Wiley (2017)
15. Jorgensen, P.C.: Software Testing: A Craftsman's Approach. Auerbach Publications (2013)
16. Juntao, W., Mishima, N.: Development of resource efficiency index for electrical and electronic equipment. Procedia CIRP 61, 275–280 (2017)
17. Kashyap, A., Holzer, T., Sarkani, S., Eveleigh, T.: Model based testing for software systems: an application of Markov modulated Markov process. Int. J. Comput. Appl. 46(14), 13–20 (2012)
18. Kaur, A., Goyal, S.: A genetic algorithm for regression test case prioritization using code coverage. Int. J. Comput. Sci. Eng. 3(5), 1839–1847 (2011)
19. Konsaard, P., Ramingwong, L.: Total coverage based regression test case prioritization using genetic algorithm. In: 2015 12th International Conference on Electrical Engineering/Electronics, Computer, Telecommunications and Information Technology (ECTI-CON), pp. 1–6. IEEE (2015)
20. Lee, D., Yannakakis, M.: Principles and methods of testing finite state machines - a survey. Proc. IEEE 84(8), 1090–1123 (1996)
21. Miranda, B., Cruciani, E., Verdecchia, R., Bertolino, A.: FAST approaches to scalable similarity-based test case prioritization. In: Proceedings of the International Conference on Software Engineering (ICSE), pp. 222–232 (2018)
22. Morozov, A., Ding, K., Chen, T., Janschek, K.: Test suite prioritization for efficient regression testing of model-based automotive software. In: 2017 International Conference on Software Analysis, Testing and Evolution (SATE), pp. 20–29 (2017)
23. Muthyala, K., Naidu, R.: A novel approach to test suite reduction using data mining approach. Indian J. Comput. Sci. Eng. 2(3), 500–505 (2011)
24. Ouriques, J.F.S., Cartaxo, E.G., Machado, P.D.: Test case prioritization techniques for model-based testing: a replicated study. Software Qual. J. 26(4), 1451–1482 (2018)
25. Ozawa, M., Dohi, T., Okamura, H.: How do software metrics affect test case prioritization? In: Annual Computer Software and Applications Conference (COMPSAC), vol. 01, pp. 245–250 (2018)

26. Puterman, M.L.: Markov Decision Processes: Discrete Stochastic Dynamic Programming. Wiley (2014)
27. Raiyani, A.G., Pandya, S.S.: Proritization technique for minimizing number of test cases. Int. J. Softw. Eng. Res. Pract. **1**, 3–9 (2011)
28. Saad, Y.: Numerical Methods for Large Eigenvalue Problems. Manchester University Press, Manchester (1992)
29. Sayyari, F., Emadi, S.: Automated generation of software testing path based on ant colony. In: 2015 International Congress on Technology, Communication and Knowledge (ICTCK), pp. 435–440. IEEE, November 2015
30. Singh, L.K., Tripathi, A.K., Vinod, G.: Software reliability early prediction in architectural design phase: overview and limitations. J. Softw. Eng. Appl. **4**, 181–186 (2011)
31. Tijms, H.C., Tijms, H.C.: Stochastic Models: An Algorithmic Approach, vol. 303. Wiley, New York (1994)
32. Walton, G., Poore, J.: Measuring complexity and coverage of software specifications. Inf. Softw. Technol. **42**(12), 859–872 (2000)
33. Whittaker, J.A., Thomason, M.G.: A Markov chain model for statistical software testing. IEEE Trans. Software Eng. **20**(10), 812–824 (1994)
34. Xuan, J., Jiang, H., Ren, Z., Hu, Y., Luo, Z.: A random walk based algorithm for structural test case generation. In: The 2nd International Conference on Software Engineering and Data Mining, pp. 583–588 (2010)
35. Yoo, S., Harman, M.: Regression testing minimization, selection and prioritization: a survey. Softw. Test. Verification Reliab. **22**(2), 67–120 (2012)
36. Zhou, B., Okamura, H., Dohi, T.: Application of Markov chain Monte Carlo random testing to test case prioritization in regression testing. IEICE Trans. Inf. Syst. **E95.D**(9), 2219–2226 (2012)

Probabilistic Approach for Minimizing Checking Sequences for Non-deterministic FSMs

Natalia Kushik[1]($\boxtimes$), Nina Yevtushenko[2], and Jorge López[3]

[1] SAMOVAR, Télécom SudParis, Institut Polytechnique de Paris, Palaiseau, France
`natalia.kushik@telecom-sudparis.eu`
[2] Ivannikov Institute for System Programming of the Russian Academy of Sciences, Moscow, Russia
`evtushenko@ispras.ru`
[3] Airbus, Issy-Les-Moulineaux, France
`jorge.lopez-c@airbus.com`

Abstract. The paper is devoted to model based testing against probabilistic FSMs. Differently from our prior work in 2021, we consider checking sequences and possibilities of test suite minimization through reducing the length of the resulting checking sequence. Given a level of certainty P, we define a P-probably checking sequence under a white box testing assumption and discuss how a suffix of an input sequence can be omitted, such that the resulting sub-sequence is P-probably checking. The specification and possible implementations are non-initialized, i.e., the assumption of 'no reset' is supported.

Keywords: Model Based Testing · Non-deterministic Finite State Machines · Checking sequence · Probabilistic Approach

1 Introduction

Model based test generation strategies, and in particular, Finite State Machine (FSM) test generation strategies are known to have guaranteed fault coverage under certain assumptions. When an implementation under test (IUT) is non-initialized, i.e., each implementation state can be initial, checking sequences are often considered. A checking sequence represents therefore a test suite and often consists of a combination of synchronizing/transfer sequences with the proper distinguishing sequences for a specification and related fault domain.

In this work, we focus on non-deterministic FSMs as related specifications; the specification and implementations are non-initialized, possibly non-deterministic machines, i.e., the 'no strict reset' assumption is supported. A fault domain consists of the FSM implementations that are explicitly enumerated, i.e., similar to [3,7], we consider a test derivation strategy under the white box testing assumption. In our previous publication [4], we studied the possibility of test suite minimization through the introduction of the probabilities to the specification machine. Together with that, we introduced a new P-probably

© IFIP International Federation for Information Processing 2023
Published by Springer Nature Switzerland AG 2023
S. Bonfanti et al. (Eds.): ICTSS 2023, LNCS 14131, pp. 237–243, 2023.
https://doi.org/10.1007/978-3-031-43240-8_15

separability relation to be able to distinguish each faulty implementation from the specification with a given level of certainty, P. We now extend this work by taking away a number of assumptions. First of all, we allow all the machines to be non-initialized and thus, we consider a test suite represented by a single (checking) sequence. Secondly, as no reset can be applied during testing, we do not minimize the test suite cardinality, instead we shorten the overall length of the checking sequence, whenever possible. The latter is based on the introduction of P-probably separating sequences, a P-probably checking sequence and a proper use of related transfer sequences.

The structure of the paper is as follows. Section 2 contains preliminaries. Non-initialized probabilistic machines are introduced in Sect. 3, while the checking sequence minimization strategy is presented in Sect. 4. Section 5 concludes the paper.

2   Preliminaries

An FSM is a 4-tuple $\mathcal{S} = \langle S, I, O, h_S \rangle$ where S is a finite nonempty set of states, I and O are finite input and output alphabets, and $h_S \subseteq S \times I \times O \times S$ is a $transition$ $relation$. The FSM $\mathcal{S}$ is $non\text{-}deterministic$ if for some pair $(s, i) \in S \times I$, there exist several pairs $(o, s') \in O \times S$ such that $(s, i, o, s') \in h_S$; otherwise, the FSM is $deterministic$. The FSM $\mathcal{S}$ is $observable$ if for every two transitions (s, i, o, s_1), $(s, i, o, s_2) \in h_S$ it holds that $s_1 = s_2$; otherwise, the FSM is $non\text{-}observable$. The FSM $\mathcal{S}$ is $complete$ if for every pair $(s, i) \in S \times I$, there exists a transition $(s, i, o, s') \in h_S$; otherwise, the FSM is $partial$ (partially specified). We hereafter consider complete observable FSMs, if not stated otherwise.

A non-deterministic FSM $\mathcal{S} = \langle S, I, O, h_S, pr \rangle$ is $probabilistic$, when for each non-deterministic transition $(s, i, o, s') \in h_S$, the function pr defines the probability for the output o to be produced at state s under input i, $pr : S \times I \times O \longrightarrow [0, 1]$. For a non-deterministic FSM, the function pr is defined in such a way that $\forall s \in S \; \forall i \in I \sum_{o \in O} pr(s, i, o) = 1$, and it is extended over input/output sequences from $(IO)^*$. Given an input/output sequence $\alpha/\beta = (\alpha'/\beta').(i/o)$ and a state s_0, $pr(s_0, \alpha, \beta) = pr(s_0, \alpha', \beta') * pr(s, i, o)$, where s is the α'/β'-successor of the state s_0 of the specification FSM $\mathcal{S}$; if the trace α'/β' is not defined at state s_0 then $pr(s_0, \alpha', \beta') = 0$; $pr(s, \varepsilon, \varepsilon) = 1$.

In this paper, similar to our previous work [4], for test minimization, we consider the following fault model $\langle \mathcal{S}, \cong, FD \rangle$, where $\mathcal{S}$ is complete possibly non-deterministic observable FSM, $\cong$ is the non-separability relation, and all the implementations from FD are explicitly enumerated, $FD = \{\mathcal{I}_1, \mathcal{I}_2, \ldots, \mathcal{I}_k\}$. FSMs $\mathcal{I}_j$ and $\mathcal{S}$ are $separable$, (written $\mathcal{I}_j \not\cong \mathcal{S}$), if there exists a $separating$ sequence $\alpha \in I^*$ such that the sets of output reactions of $\mathcal{I}_j$ and $\mathcal{S}$ to α do not intersect, i.e., $out(\mathcal{I}_j, \alpha) \cap out(\mathcal{S}, \alpha) = \emptyset$. We are interested in $exhaustive$ test suites, such that each $\mathcal{I}_j \in FD$ that is separable with $\mathcal{S}$ can be detected by the test suite. Moreover, we are interested in a test suite containing a single sequence which is referred to as a $checking$ sequence with respect to a corresponding fault model. Therefore such checking sequence α should be able to detect all non-conforming implementations, i.e., all the implementations of the fault domain which are separable with the specification.

The main difference (with our previous work) and the main contribution of this work is that we take away the assumption of having a designated initial state, be that in the specification or in an implementation. Previously a P-*probably separating* sequence was defined as follows: $\alpha \in I^*$ is a P-probably separating sequence for $\mathcal{I}_j$ and $\mathcal{S}$, if $\sum_{\beta \in out(\mathcal{I}_j,\alpha) \cap out(\mathcal{S},\alpha)} pr(s_0, \alpha, \beta) \leq 1 - P$. In the latter, $pr(s_0, \alpha, \beta)$ was the probability to observe β when α is applied at the initial state of the specification machine $\mathcal{S}$. We further adapt this notion to non-initialized FSMs $\mathcal{S}$ and $\mathcal{I}_j$ and explain how a checking sequence α can be shortened for a given level P.

3   Non-initialized Probabilistic FSMs

In this section, we define the probability of an output sequence to appear as a reaction to a given input sequence, when the machine can start at any initial state. We avoid going through the determinization procedure for that matter, i.e., obtaining an initialized equivalent, not to encounter potential state explosion.

Given a non-initialized probabilistic specification FSM $\mathcal{S} = \langle S, I, O, h_S, pr \rangle$, $S = \{s_1, s_2, \ldots, s_n\}$, and an input/output pair i/o, $pr(\mathcal{S}, i, o) = \frac{1}{n} \sum_{s \in S} pr(s, i, o)$. The latter assumes that the probability p for $\mathcal{S}$ to start in state s_i is the same as in any other state $s_j \in S$. In other words, pressing a 'reset' button does not bring any certainty concerning the initial state of the machine. Assume now that for a state s_j, $j \in \{1, \ldots, n\}$, a probability p_j is given, for the machine $\mathcal{S}$ to start in this state (s_j), in this case $pr(\mathcal{S}, i, o) = \sum_{j=1}^{n} p_j * pr(s_j, i, o)$ for an input/output pair i/o. For a given input i, it holds that $\sum_{o \in O} \sum_{j=1}^{n} p_j * pr(s_j, i, o) = 1$.

As an example of a non-initialized probabilistic FSM, consider the machine in Fig. 1 (similar to that one in [4]). Consider an input/output pair i_1/o_1, for $p_1 = 0.8$, and $p_2 = p_3 = 0.1$, it holds that $pr(\mathcal{S}, i_1, o_1) = 0.74$.

As usual, we extend the behavior of the probabilistic machine over input/output sequences from $(IO)^*$. Given an input/output sequence $\alpha/\beta = (\alpha'/\beta').(i/o)$, the probability of the non-initialized $\mathcal{S}$ to produce β on α is $pr(\mathcal{S}, \alpha, \beta) = \sum_{j=1}^{n} p_j * pr(s_j, \alpha, \beta)$. For example, for the FSM in Fig. 1, $pr(\mathcal{S}, i_1 i_1, o_1 o_2) = 0.096$.

We are interested in a checking sequence α that delivers a P-*probably exhaustive* test suite for a given specification $\mathcal{S}$ and a set of its potential implementations $\{\mathcal{I}_1, \mathcal{I}_2, \ldots, \mathcal{I}_k\}$. The P-*probably separability* is therefore adjusted for non-initialized machines. Input sequence $\alpha \in I^*$ is a P-*probably separating* sequence for $\mathcal{I}_j$ and $\mathcal{S}$, if $\sum_{\beta \in out(\mathcal{I}_j,\alpha) \cap out(\mathcal{S},\alpha)} pr(\mathcal{S}, \alpha, \beta) \leq 1 - P$. Note that $out(\mathcal{I}_j, \alpha)$ $(out(\mathcal{S}, \alpha))$ is the union of all output reactions β on the sequence α that can be obtained at any initial state of $\mathcal{I}_j$ $(\mathcal{S})$.

An interesting question arises about the probability distribution for initial states of implementation FSMs. In this paper, we assume that all the states can be initial with the same probability. If this assumption is not supported then the formula for defining a P-probably separating sequence for the specification and such implementation should be modified, accordingly.

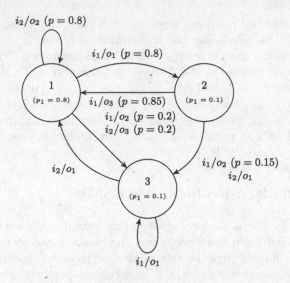

Fig. 1. An example probabilistic FSM $\mathcal{S}$

Coming back to the same example of $\mathcal{S}$, let us consider an implementation $\mathcal{I}_1 \in FD$ in Fig. 2. According to the above definition the sequence $\alpha = i_2 i_2 i_1 i_1 i_1 i_1$ is a 0.9-probably separating sequence for $\mathcal{I}_1$ and $\mathcal{S}$ (Fig. 1).

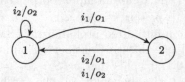

Fig. 2. An implementation FSM $\mathcal{I}_1 \in FD$

A sequence α is *P-probably checking* for the fault model $\langle \mathcal{S}, \cong, FD = \{\mathcal{I}_1, \mathcal{I}_2, \ldots, \mathcal{I}_k\}\rangle$, if this sequence P-probably separates each implementation $\mathcal{I}_j$, $j \in \{1, \ldots, k\}$, from the specification $\mathcal{S}$.

4   Minimizing a Checking Sequence with a Level of *P*-Exhaustiveness

Assume that a sequence α is a checking sequence for the fault model $FM = \langle \mathcal{S}, \cong, FD = \{\mathcal{I}_1, \mathcal{I}_2, \ldots, \mathcal{I}_k\}\rangle$. Given a level P of certainty, the question arises: can we shorten α in such a way that the resulting sequence would be P-probably checking for $\langle \mathcal{S}, \cong, FD = \{\mathcal{I}_1, \mathcal{I}_2, \ldots, \mathcal{I}_k\}\rangle$? We conjecture the following: non-initialized implementations can be hard to test as in the checking sequence a *transfer* to a known state of the implementation, is implicitly used or even explicitly included during its derivation (see some related works on the checking sequence derivation, for example in [1,2,5,6]). We therefore propose the following: before the application of the sequence α or its shorter preamble α', one can apply a synchronizing sequence SS with further verification that the sequence $SS.\alpha'$ is P-probably checking for FM^1. Note however, that the sequence SS should be synchronizing for all the implementations $\mathcal{I}_1, \mathcal{I}_2, \ldots, \mathcal{I}_k$, and this sequence can be derived for a single FSM which is the direct sum of $\mathcal{I}_j, j \in \{1, \ldots, k\}$. The latter contains all the transitions of each implementation $\mathcal{I}_j$ and thus, its synchronizing sequence is also one for each $\mathcal{I}_j, j \in \{1, \ldots, k\}$. Note that if implementations are non-initialized but deterministic then such a sequence can be efficiently computed [8] (in polynomial time, if the number of mutants k is polynomial too w.r.t. n, for the corresponding automaton where the outputs are omitted).

As an example of the proposed strategy, consider again the FSM $\mathcal{S}$ in Fig. 1, and the $FD = \{\mathcal{I}_1, \mathcal{I}_2, \mathcal{I}_3\}$. $\mathcal{I}_1$ is shown in Fig. 2, while $\mathcal{I}_2$ and $\mathcal{I}_3$ in Fig. 3 and Fig. 4, respectively. Note that the sequence $\alpha = i_1 i_1 i_2 i_2 i_1 i_1 i_1 i_2 i_1 i_2 i_2$ is a checking sequence for $\langle \mathcal{S}, \cong, FD = \{\mathcal{I}_1, \mathcal{I}_2, \mathcal{I}_3\}\rangle$. The direct sum for the three implementations possesses a synchronizing sequence $SS = i_2 i_2$; indeed, each of the implementations has the same SS, which can be checked by direct inspection. We append this SS as a prefix to α and start cutting its suffix. For $P = 0.8$, one can cut 8 inputs in the resulting sequence, i.e., $SS.\alpha' = i_2 i_2 i_1 i_1$ is 0.8-probably checking sequence and it is six inputs shorter than the initial α. This approach can be therefore applied iteratively, until the level P of exhaustiveness is respected.

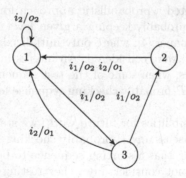

Fig. 3. An implementation FSM $\mathcal{I}_2 \in FD$

The following suggestions for deriving a shorter checking sequence can be made based on the considered example. First of all, the use of proper final state identification sequences such as homing and synchronizing sequences, can help

---

[1] Such checking is needed to assure that $SS.\alpha'$ is P-probably separating for each implementation $\mathcal{I}_j, j \in \{1, \ldots, k\}$, and $\mathcal{S}$.

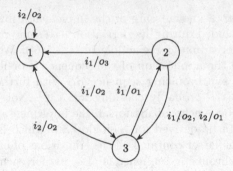

Fig. 4. An implementation FSM $\mathcal{I}_3 \in FD$

to derive a shorter checking sequence with the given level of certainty. Secondly, when deriving a checking sequence it seems to be worth considering a deterministic projection of the specification where transitions and the initial state have the highest probability. In a deterministic projection only one transition is left at each state for every input. Finally, if all the implementations are deterministic it is worth introducing another conformance probabilistic relation such as for example, the P-probably reduction when the behavior of an implementation is P-probably included in that of the specification, for a given level of certainty P. All these challenging issues should be studied in details in the future.

5   Conclusion

In this paper, we presented a probabilistic approach for minimizing the length of a checking sequence, probably keeping a given level of its exhaustiveness. It is a continuation of the paper [4], where only initialized machines (specification and its implementations) were considered. An interesting direction would be to combine both approaches, when some of the test sequences could be regrouped together, i.e., building a P-probably checking sequence for a subset of implementations.

There are many possibilities for future work, we state some of these future directions. We did not discuss any P-probably checking sequence derivation scenarios in detail, assuming that a starting sequence to be shortened is given. At the same time, we did not consider any other testing assumptions nor other conformance relations. Finally, experimental evaluations need to be performed to see how often the approach brings good practical results.

References

1. Hennie, F.C.: Fault detecting experiments for sequential circuits. In: Proceedings of Symposium on Switching Circuit Theory and Logical Design, pp. 95–110 (1964)

2. Jourdan, G., Ural, H., Yenigün, H.: Reduced checking sequences using unreliable reset. Inf. Process. Lett. **115**(5), 532–535 (2015). https://doi.org/10.1016/j.ipl.2015.01.002

3. Kushik, N., Yevtushenko, N., Cavalli, A.R.: On testing against partial non-observable specifications. In: 9th International Conference on the Quality of Information and Communications Technology, QUATIC 2014, Guimaraes, Portugal, 23–26 September 2014, pp. 230–233. IEEE Computer Society (2014). https://doi.org/10.1109/QUATIC.2014.38

4. Kushik, N., Yevtushenko, N., López, J.: Testing against non-deterministic FSMs: a probabilistic approach for test suite minimization. In: Clark, D., Menéndez, H.D., Cavalli, A.R. (eds.) Testing Software and Systems - 33rd IFIP WG 6.1 International Conference, ICTSS 2021, London, UK, 10–12 November 2021, Proceedings. LNCS, vol. 13045, pp. 55–61. Springer, Cham (2021). https://doi.org/10.1007/978-3-031-04673-5_4

5. Nguena Timo, O., Petrenko, A., Ramesh, S.: Checking sequence generation for symbolic input/output FSMs by constraint solving. In: Fischer, B., Uustalu, T. (eds.) ICTAC 2018. LNCS, vol. 11187, pp. 354–375. Springer, Cham (2018). https://doi.org/10.1007/978-3-030-02508-3_19

6. Petrenko, A., Yevtushenko, N.: Conformance tests as checking experiments for partial nondeterministic FSM. In: Formal Approaches to Software Testing, 5th International Workshop, FATES 2005, Edinburgh, UK, 11 July 2005, Revised Selected Papers, pp. 118–133 (2005). https://doi.org/10.1007/11759744_9

7. Poage, J.F., McCluskey, E.J.: Derivation of optimum test sequences for sequential machines. In: 1964 Proceedings of the Fifth Annual Symposium on Switching Circuit Theory and Logical Design, pp. 121–132 (1964). https://doi.org/10.1109/SWCT.1964.7

8. Volkov, M.V.: Synchronizing automata and the Černý conjecture. In: Martín-Vide, C., Otto, F., Fernau, H. (eds.) LATA 2008. LNCS, vol. 5196, pp. 11–27. Springer, Heidelberg (2008). https://doi.org/10.1007/978-3-540-88282-4_4

AI and Smart Contracts Testing

Applying Pairwise Combinatorial Testing to Large Language Model Testing

Bernhard Garn, Ludwig Kampel[✉], Manuel Leithner, Berina Celic,
Ceren Çulha, Irene Hiess, Klaus Kieseberg, Marlene Koelbing,
Dominik-Philip Schreiber, Michael Wagner, Christoph Wech, Jovan Zivanovic,
and Dimitris E. Simos

MATRIS Research Group, SBA Research, 1040 Vienna, Austria
{matris,lkampel}@sba-research.org

Abstract. In this paper, we report on applying combinatorial testing to *large language models* (LLMs) testing. Our aim is to pioneer the usage of combinatorial testing to be used in the realm of LLMs, e.g. for the generation of additional training or test data. We first describe how to create an input parameter model for the input of an LLM. Based on a given original sentence, we derive new sentences by replacing words with synonyms according to a combinatorial test set, leading to a specified level of coverage over synonyms while attaining an efficient diversification. Assuming that the semantics of the original sentence are retained in the derived sentences, we construct a test oracle based on existing annotations. In an experimental evaluation, we apply generated pairwise sentence test sets from the BoolQ benchmark set [4] against two LLMs (T5 [12] and LLaMa [15]). Having automated our approach for test sentence generation, as well as their execution and analysis, our experimental evaluations demonstrate the applicability of pairwise combinatorial testing methods to LLMs.

Keywords: large language models · combinatorial testing

1 Introduction

Recent progresses in research and development of artificial intelligence (AI) systems seem to have yielded a breakthrough in the capabilities of large language models (LLMs) to engage in human-like conversations. Such AI systems currently attain broad attention throughout society, being highly discussed in research, frequently covered by the media and subject to political discussions. The increasing capabilities and improved performance of AI systems often come at the cost of added model complexity, which also requires increased efforts for learning. The resulting financial and environmental costs as approximated in Strubell et al. [14] are significant. For example, training the base version of BERT [14] requires a

B. Garn, L. Kampel, M. Leithner—Equally contributing first authors.

CO_2 emission of 650 kg and expenses of \$3751 to \$12571. *Such numbers emphasize the high costs and large data sets required for training and testing modern AI models.* To address these issues, researchers are working towards generating such data sets automatically, particularly in the domain of natural language processing (NLP) (cf. Bowman et al. [1]). Especially when testing for *semantic consistency* of LLMs, it is extremely challenging to cover all possible variations of formulations of input queries as also mentioned in [8]. Aside from pure training of AI systems, there is a need for the development of appropriate (automated) testing and quality assurance measures [17]. In light of these developments and needs, we investigate the use of combinatorial testing (CT) for the testing of LLMs, with the *aim of establishing this combinatorial coverage based test set generation method for automated test set augmentation and diversification.*

A Brief Overview of Combinatorial Testing. CT is an established black box testing methodology for testing a system under test (SUT) against undesired effects of interactions of its parameters. The essential two pre-requisites for the application of CT are, first, the existence of an *input parameter model* (IPM) [6] of the SUT, which models the SUT's input by means of finitely many parameters that can take on finitely many values. Second, a *testing oracle* is required, which is – conceptually speaking – a method to distinguish *failing tests*, those that trigger faulty behavior of the SUT, from *passing tests*, those that do not. The key idea of CT is to use optimized test sets in which any combination of t parameter-values appears in at least one test. Such test sets are called *combinatorial* or *t-way* test sets. The parameter t is also referred to as the *(interaction) strength*. Pairwise testing, i.e. CT with interaction strength $t = 2$, is likely the most prominent instance of CT. A thorough introduction to CT is provided by Kuhn et al. [10], while a survey on CT is given by Nie and Leung [11].

Fig. 1. Overview of a generic CT process [6].

In this paper, we present how the CT process (see Fig. 1) can be instantiated in order to be applied for the testing of LLMs. Our approach takes as input a sentence, e.g. a question from an existing training data set, and allows us to diversify the input to a chosen degree of *coverage* by deriving additional test sentences according to a combinatorial test set. Thereby our focus is to maintain the semantics of the sentence, such that a potential existing correct or expected answer is also valid for all of the derived sentences.

In particular, the contributions of our work are as follows:

1. An approach to construct an *input parameter model (IPM)* from a sentence which is given as input to an LLM;

2. A method to derive a *combinatorial test set* based on a given sentence and a *covering array* (CA);
3. An initial experimental evaluation, where we use pairwise combinatorial testing against two SUTs.

This Paper is Structured as Follows. In Sect. 2, we review related work on the testing of LLMs. In Sect. 3, we give a general description of our approach for applying CT to the testing of LLMs, and illustrate it by means of a running example. In Sect. 4 we give an outline of our initial experimentation. Finally, in Sect. 5, we briefly discuss potential threats to validity of this work before we summarize the paper and mention some ideas for future work in Sect. 6.

2 Related Work

The approach of mutating input sentences to a LLM while preserving the meaning or sentiment has recently garnered attention. The work by Gardner et al. [5] proposes the generation of *contrast sets* from standard test sets for supervised learning by manually perturbing the test instances, leading to a more accurate and comprehensive assessment of a model's linguistic capabilities. Similarly, Khashabi et al. [9] propose a novel method for generating training datasets by applying *human based natural perturbations* to a small scale *seed dataset*. In contrast to these works, the approach presented in this paper uses an automated way for extending test or training data.

Ruane et al. [13] put forward a framework for using *divergent input examples*, generated by altering a textual user utterance while still maintaining the original intent, for testing the quality of conversational agents. In a continuation, Guichard et al. [7] propose and evaluate an approach with regard to the utilization of paraphrases. They generate divergent input examples by processing the input data through lexical substitutions, i.e. replacing words with their synonyms, using the Oxford Thesaurus for the retrieval of synonyms.

Bozic [2] proposes a metamorphic testing approach for chatbot testing making use of an ontology. The method presented in our work can be used for deriving tests for such a metamorphic testing approach.

3 Instantiating the Combinatorial Testing Process for Testing of LLMs

In this section, we describe the application of the CT process to LLM testing. To briefly outline our approach, we start from a given sentence, e.g. from a training or evaluation set for LLMs. Interpreting each word of the given sentence as a parameter of an IPM, we generate from it several derived sentences by replacing words with synonyms according to a combinatorial test set. The derived sentences can later be submitted to an LLM. Provided *annotations* of the original sentence, such as a `true/false` assignment to a statement or a correct answer to a question, are reused for the derived sentences. Subsequently, they can be used by a test oracle to assess the LLM's responses to the derived sentences. An outline of our approach is given by Fig. 2 and elucidated in this section.

Fig. 2. An overview of the proposed testing approach. CT dependent steps are colored in red, LLM specific steps are colored in gray. (Color figure online)

3.1   A Combinatorial Sentence Model via an IPM

Bridging concepts from LLMs and CT, our key idea is that a given original sentence (a statement or question from a benchmark) gives rise to an IPM, by regarding each word in the sentence as a parameter and its synonyms as the corresponding parameter-values. For each word, we create a list of synonyms with at most v_{max} elements to avoid an uncontrolled size of the IPM, where the original word appears as the first element. It is also possible to consider no synonyms for a specific word, which means to consider the word itself as its only synonym, leading to a parameter in the IPM with only one value. Conceptually, our proposed approach is independent from the way *how* and from *where* these synonyms are selected.

The derivation of the IPM is summarized in the following procedural steps:

***Step 1*:** Select an *original sentence* (e.g., from a given benchmark set).
***Step 2*:** Each word of the sentence gives rise to one *parameter* of the IPM.
***Step 3*:** For each word of the sentence, create a list of synonyms:
  - each synonym serves as one *parameter value* of the corresponding parameter in the IPM;
  - the length of the list of synonyms reflects the parameter domain size and is bounded by v_{max};
  - ensure that the original word appears as first element in the list.

Example 1. *We illustrate the steps of our approach by means of a (running) example, where we consider the following concrete original sentence, which is the 23rd question of the training set in the BoolQ benchmark [4]:*

"can you drink alcohol in public in denmark".

This sentence consists of eight words, and hence the corresponding IPM has eight parameters. We set the maximal number of considered synonyms v_{max} to three, and further for the words 'can', 'you' and 'in' we select themselves as their only synonyms. Table 1 shows the considered synonyms for each word of this sentence. The corresponding parameters $p_1, \ldots, p_8$ can take $1, 1, 3, 3, 1, 3, 1$ and 3 values, respectively. We emphasize again that the first value of each parameter is equal to the corresponding word in the original sentence.

Table 1. The selected synonyms largely maintain the questions' semantics.

p_1	p_2	p_3	p_4	p_5	p_6	p_7	p_8
can	you	drink	alcohol	in	public	in	denmark
		drinking	alcoholic drink		populace		kingdom of denmark
		booze	alcoholic beverage		world		danmark

3.2   Generation of t-Way Sentence Test Sets

We use an IPM as described above to generate a combinatorial test set that achieves coverage of all t-way combinations of synonyms for a specified interaction strength t. For practical applications, there exist dedicated CT tools, such as CAgen [16], which take an IPM as an input and return a combinatorial test set of the desired interaction strength t. Each row of the returned (abstract) combinatorial test set then represents a derived sentence and hence corresponds to one (abstract) test case. The fact that the first element of each synonym list is the original word, together with the properties of the CAgen tool, has the result that the first derived sentence in the combinatorial test set is equivalent to the original sentence. Collectively, all derived sentences in a generated combinatorial test set have the property that every combination of t synonyms for different t words appears within at least one of them.

Example 1. *(continued) The IPM depicted in Table 1 can now be used to generate the pairwise combinatorial test set given in Table 2 derived from the example sentence. The columns headed by $p_1, \ldots p_8$ represent the parameters, respectively the words, and each row $q_1, \ldots, q_9$ represents one test case, i.e. a derived sentence. Altogether, these derived sentences achieve full 2-way coverage, i.e. they have the property that any pair of two synonyms for two different words appears together in at least one of the derived sentences. To illustrate this pairwise coverage property, consider the parameters p_4 and p_8, for which we can verify that each pair in the Cartesian product $\{alcohol, alcoholic\ drink, alcoholic\ beverage\} \times \{denmark, kingdom\ of\ denmark, danmark\}$ appears in at least one of the tests $q_1, \ldots, q_9$. Taking the pair (booze, kingdom of denmark), i.e. the synonym booze for the original word drink and the synonym kingdom of denmark for the original word denmark, we find it in the derived sentence q_7. Similarly, the remaining pairwise coverage requirements can be verified.*

Table 2. A pairwise combinatorial test set for the question *"can you drink alcohol in public in denmark"* and its corresponding IPM with eight parameters. It consists of nine derived sentences. The original sentence appears as q_1.

#	p_1	p_2	p_3	p_4	p_5	p_6	p_7	p_8
q_1	can	you	drink	alcohol	in	public	in	denmark
q_2	can	you	drink	alcoholic drink	in	populace	in	kingdom of denmark
q_3	can	you	drink	alcoholic beverage	in	world	in	danmark
q_4	can	you	drinking	alcohol	in	populace	in	danmark
q_5	can	you	drinking	alcoholic drink	in	world	in	denmark
q_6	can	you	drinking	alcoholic beverage	in	public	in	kingdom of denmark
q_7	can	you	booze	alcohol	in	world	in	kingdom of denmark
q_8	can	you	booze	alcoholic drink	in	public	in	danmark
q_9	can	you	booze	alcoholic beverage	in	populace	in	denmark

3.3 Sentence Test Set Translation and Execution

The generated combinatorial test sets now serve as a basis for test execution against LLMs. Each sentence given as a row of a combinatorial test set is translated to one *test case*, i.e. one query to an LLM. In order to obtain executable test cases from the derived sentences that yield a processable response, adequate prompt design is required; in this step, modifications are applied to the prompt in order to evoke a Boolean answer (cf. Brown et al. [3] for an exploration of this topic). The generated executable test case (i.e., the derived sentence combined with an appropriate prompt) is submitted together with potential further configuration values to an LLM.

Example 1. *(continued) We translate the first derived sentence, i.e. test case q_1 in Table 2, to an executable test case. For the sentence* "can you drink alcohol in public in denmark", *we add a prompt specific to the LLM LLaMa to obtain an executable test case, which yields:*

```
can you drink alcohol in public in denmark. the boolean (1)
answer to this question is
```

3.4 Test Oracle

Under the assumption that synonym replacement preserves the semantics of a sentence, the meaning of the derived sentences in a combinatorial sentence test set should also be equal to the meaning of the original sentence. Making use of this assumption, we can create a *test oracle* for the derived sentences based on an annotation for the original sentence, in case it is available.

For the specific case where the original sentence is a Boolean question with its corresponding annotation given by a `true`/`false` assignment, consider an executable test case obtained from a combinatorial sentence test set derived from this original Boolean question. When submitted against an LLM, we expect the LLM to deal with the truth content of the test sentence, and therefore, it should be possible to categorize its response into one of the three classes `true`, `false` and `undefined`. This categorization can be obtained by textual post-processing using keywords in the returned response. The test oracle then compares the assigned category with the given annotation of the original Boolean question: if the category of the response is equal to the `true`/`false` annotation of the original Boolean question, the test oracle decides this derived sentence to be a `passing test`, otherwise it is a `failing test`.

Example 1. *(continued) The response of LLaMa to the prompt given in (1), is:*

$$\text{\texttt{can you drink alcohol in public in denmark? The boolean}} \quad (2)$$
$$\text{\texttt{answer to this question is Ãĉ}}$$

After removing the prompt (1) from (2), the remaining part "Ãĉ" is transformed to the empty string via the post-processing. Hence, the response is classified as **undefined**. *To give another example, consider the response obtained after executing the test case obtained from the derived sentence q_2 of Table 2:*

$$\text{\texttt{can you drink alcoholic drink in populace in kingdom of}} \quad (3)$$
$$\text{\texttt{denmark? The boolean answer to this question is ◆yes}}$$

After removing the prompt (1) from the response (3), the remaining response "◆yes" is classified as **true**.

4   Outline of Experimental Evaluation

In order to conduct our experimental evaluation, we automated the process of applying CT to LLMs in an extensible testing pipeline that is open to additional LLMs, benchmark sets as well as test oracles. We applied our approach to all $9,427$ questions in the `train.jsonl` file from the BoolQ benchmark set, generating pairwise combinatorial sentence test sets for each of them. Subsequently, we executed all derived questions from all combinatorial sentence test sets ($90,976$ sentences in total) against the two SUTs T5[1] [12] and LLaMa [15], which was sourced via the LLaMa Cpp Port[2]. The results are documented in Table 3.

To outline the results of our experimental evaluation, first, both LLMs are not very accurate, and second, this is independent from the sentence sets. To elaborate, the high percentage of undefined responses by T5 (see column U in the lower part of Table 3) shows that it is difficult to steer T5 towards giving

---

[1] https://huggingface.co/docs/transformers/model_doc/t5v1.1, accessed on 2023-05-03.

[2] https://github.com/ggerganov/llama.cpp, accessed on 2023-05-03.

Boolean answers reliably. Considering that roughly 62% of the original questions of the BoolQ dataset are annotated as true, and the remaining 38% as false, this explains the low accuracy achieved by T5 in our experimental evaluation. Hence, this LLM exhibits a very low accuracy of only 2.02% for our set of derived sentences and 2.76% for the set of original sentences. In contrast, the settings of the LLaMa model together with the applied post-fix mostly yielded responses classifiable as Boolean value. Nevertheless, the accuracy is only 47.45% and 45.75% for original and derived sentence sets, respectively, which is close to a random fair coin flip for a Boolean classification task.

Overall, it seems that the performance of the two LLMs was not meaningfully impacted by our derived sentences, since the accuracy values do not differ by more than 2% in each category. This could suggest that our combinatorial generation approach was successful in generating more sentences from a given set, without reducing its quality. However, the fact that the accuracy of both LLMs for the original sentences was either very low for T5, and close to that of a fair coin flip for LLaMa, relativizes this observation.

5   Lessons Learned and Threats to Validity

Throughout our experimental evaluation, we encountered a variety of issues in connection with the use of synonyms. The most significant one is that replacing a word with a synonym can alter the meaning of the original sentence. Assessing the suitability of synonyms coming from (external) synonym databases is not trivial and goes beyond the scope of this work. We have tried to mitigate this threat by choosing at most three words from a synonym list. Finally, the small number and low accuracy of the considered sample SUTs does not allow for a general evaluation of our approach. However, the primary focus of this work is

Table 3. Confusion (actual/predicted) values (top) and performance results (bottom) of all models by test set, given in percent. Where the acronyms stand respectively for T = true, F = false, U = undefined, AWUP = accuracy without undefined predictions, ACA = average of combinatorial test set accuracies.

SUT	sentences	T/U	T/T	T/F	F/U	F/T	F/F
T5	original	59.44	2.76	0.12	36.20	1.49	0.00
	derived	60.05	1.98	0.10	36.73	1.10	0.04
LLAMA	original	32.88	20.34	9.09	18.37	14.56	4.75
	derived	32.85	19.58	9.71	19.40	12.91	5.56
SUT	sentences	acc	T	F	U	AWUP	ACA
T5	original	2.76	4.24	0.12	95.64	63.26	-
	derived	2.02	3.07	0.14	96.78	62.68	2.15
LLAMA	original	47.45	51.26	34.90	13.84	55.07	-
	derived	45.75	52.25	32.48	15.27	54.00	45.45

to propose a CT method for testing LLMs and we consider a larger evaluation as part of future work.

6 Summary and Future Work

In this work, we proposed an approach for the application of combinatorial testing to LLMs. Based on a set of original questions designed to benchmark an LLM's capabilities and a dictionary of synonyms, we derive an IPM for each original question that allows us to diversify the input to a chosen pairwise degree of coverage. Our experimental evaluation suggest that the accuracy of responses roughly stays on par with those returned for the original test set. However, some test sentences may be impacted by issues related to the use of synonyms.

In order to address such issues, in our future efforts we want to improve the quality of the lists of synonyms, e.g. by querying the SUT itself. Furthermore we want to consider other testing oracles that can handle non-Boolean test sentences, as well as to investigate our method in a larger experimental evaluation featuring more LLMs.

Acknowledgements. SBA Research (SBA-K1) is a COMET Center within the COMET – Competence Centers for Excellent Technologies Programme and funded by BMK, BMAW, and the federal state of Vienna. The COMET Programme is managed by FFG. Moreover, this work was performed partly under the following financial assistance award 70NANB21H124 from U.S. Department of Commerce, National Institute of Standards and Technology.

References

1. Bowman, S.R., Angeli, G., Potts, C., Manning, C.D.: A large annotated corpus for learning natural language inference. In: Proceedings of the 2015 Conference on Empirical Methods in Natural Language Processing, pp. 632–642 (2015)
2. Božić, J.: Ontology-based metamorphic testing for chatbots. Softw. Qual. J. **30**(1), 227–251 (2022)
3. Brown, T., Mann, B., Ryder, N., Subbiah, M., Kaplan, J.D., Dhariwal, P., et al.: Language Models are Few-Shot Learners. In: Advance in Neural Information Proceedings Systems, vol. 33, pp. 1877–1901. Curran Associates, Inc. (2020)
4. Clark, C., Lee, K., Chang, M.W., Kwiatkowski, T., Collins, M., Toutanova, K.: BoolQ: exploring the surprising difficulty of natural yes/no questions. In: Proceedings of the 2019 Conference of the North American Chapter of the Association for Computational Linguistics: Human Language Technologies, vol 1. pp. 2924–2936 (2019)
5. Gardner, M., Artzi, Y., Basmov, V., Berant, J., Bogin, B., Chen, S., et al.: Evaluating models' local decision boundaries via contrast sets. In: Findings of the Association for Computational Linguistics: EMNLP 2020, pp. 1307–1323 (2020)
6. Grindal, M., Offutt, J.: Input parameter modeling for combination strategies. In: Proceedings of the 25th Conference on IASTED International Multi-Conference: Software Engineering, pp. 255–260. SE 2007, ACTA Press, Anaheim, CA, USA (2007)

7. Guichard, J., Ruane, E., Smith, R., Bean, D., Ventresque, A.: Assessing the robustness of conversational agents using paraphrases. In: 2019 IEEE International Conference On Artificial Intelligence Testing (AITest), pp. 55–62 (2019)

8. Jang, M., Lukasiewicz, T.: Consistency analysis of chatgpt. arXiv preprint arXiv:2303.06273 (2023). https://doi.org/10.48550/arXiv.2303.06273

9. Khashabi, D., Khot, T., Sabharwal, A.: More bang for your buck: natural perturbation for robust question answering. In: Proceedings of the 2020 Conference on Empirical Methods in Natural Language Processing (EMNLP), pp. 163–170 (2020)

10. Kuhn, D., Kacker, R., Lei, Y.: Introduction to Combinatorial Testing. Chapman & Hall/CRC Innovations in Software Engineering and Software Development Series, Taylor & Francis Group, CRC Press, Boca Raton, Florida (2013)

11. Nie, C., Leung, H.: A survey of combinatorial testing. ACM Comput. Surv. **43**(2), 1–29 (2011). https://doi.org/10.1145/1883612.1883618

12. Raffel, C., Shazeer, N., Roberts, A., Lee, K., Narang, S., Matena, M., et al.: Exploring the limits of transfer learning with a unified text-to-text transformer. J. Mach. Learn. Res. **21**(1), 5485–5551 (2020)

13. Ruane, E., Faure, T., Smith, R., Bean, D., Carson-Berndsen, J., Ventresque, A.: BoTest: a framework to test the quality of conversational agents using divergent input examples. In: Proceedings of the 23rd International Conference on Intelligent User Interfaces Companion. IUI 20118 Companion, ACM, New York, NY, USA (2018)

14. Strubell, E., Ganesh, A., McCallum, A.: Energy and policy considerations for deep learning in NLP. In: Proceedings of the 57th Annual Meeting of the Association for Computational Linguistics, pp. 3645–3650

15. Touvron, H., Lavril, T., Izacard, G., Martinet, X., Lachaux, M.A., Lacroix, T., et al.: Llama: open and efficient foundation language models. Preprint arXiv:2302.13971 (2023). https://doi.org/10.48550/arXiv.2302.13971

16. Wagner, M., Kleine, K., Simos, D.E., Kuhn, R., Kacker, R.: CAGEN: a fast combinatorial test generation tool with support for constraints and higher-index arrays. In: 2020 IEEE International Conference on Software Testing, Verification and Validation Workshops (ICSTW), pp. 191–200 (2020)

17. Wotawa, F.: On the use of available testing methods for verification & validation of AI-based software and systems. In: CEUR Workshop Proceedings 2808 (2021)

CATANA: Replay Testing
for the Ethereum Blockchain

Morena Barboni[1]([✉])(iD), Guglielmo De Angelis[2](iD), Andrea Morichetta[1](iD),
and Andrea Polini[1](iD)

[1] University of Camerino, Camerino, Italy
morena.barboni@unicam.it
[2] IASI CNR, Rome, Italy

Abstract. Blockchain technology is increasingly being adopted in various domains where the immutability of recorded information can foster trust among stakeholders. However, upgradeability mechanisms such as the proxy pattern permit modifying the terms encoded by a Smart Contract even after its deployment. Ensuring that such changes do not impact previous users is of paramount importance. This paper introduces CATANA, a replay testing approach for proxy-based Ethereum applications. Experiments conducted on real-world projects demonstrate the viability of using the public history of transactions to evaluate new versions of a deployed contract and perform more reliable upgrades.

Keywords: Replay Testing · Smart Contract · Upgrade · Proxy Pattern · Ethereum · Software Testing

1 Introduction

One of the most notable features of blockchain technologies is the capability of storing data so that it cannot be modified in any practical way. Ethereum stands out for its support of smart contracts, tamper-proof programs that can be deployed and executed on the blockchain. This feature allows users to engage with decentralized applications (DApps) more confidently, as they can trust that no one will make arbitrary modifications to the underlying logic. Smart contract immutability, however, is a double-edged sword: it fosters integrity and trust, but it also prevents direct bug fixes and feature updates. To overcome this limitation, developers rely on *smart contract upgradeability* mechanisms, among which the proxy pattern is the most popular [4,17]. The *proxy pattern* permits to upgrade the logic associated with a *proxy smart contract* even after its deployment, bringing about numerous advantages and various concerns. Even a minor change, such as reordering variables, can disrupt compatibility between two different versions of the implementation [15]. Additionally, other smart contracts (or even off-chain software) that rely on upgradeable systems might encounter compatibility issues when the underlying logic is replaced. Thoroughly testing new contract versions before deployment is crucial to prevent such scenarios. *Replay testing* is a technique that leverages recorded interactions between the users and the

© IFIP International Federation for Information Processing 2023
Published by Springer Nature Switzerland AG 2023
S. Bonfanti et al. (Eds.): ICTSS 2023, LNCS 14131, pp. 257–265, 2023.
https://doi.org/10.1007/978-3-031-43240-8_17

system under test to generate replayable test scripts, and is often used to support regression testing activities [3,10,12,13]. In conventional systems, capturing execution traces can be intrusive and introduce performance overhead. Public blockchains offer a significant advantage by permanently and publicly recording all operations (i.e., transactions) executed by their users. Despite this, the public history of transaction was only leveraged for inspection [11], monitoring [5] and test case generation purposes [20]. In this work, we propose the first replay testing approach for proxy-based upgradeable smart contracts. Specifically, we analyze possible complexities and opportunities connected to the Ethereum environment, and we implement the proposed solution in the CATANA (Contract Assessment through TrANsaction replAy) tool. The rest of this paper is structured as follows: in Sect. 2 we provide background about replay testing and smart contracts. Section 3 describes the proposed replay approach, while Sect. 4 presents the experimental evaluation. Related work is reported in Sect. 5, while in Sect. 6 we draw conclusions and identify areas for further research.

2   Background

Ethereum Smart Contracts and Upgradeability. Ethereum is a public blockchain platform that supports the execution of self-enforcing programs called Smart Contracts. These enable the creation of *decentralized applications* (DApps) for various domains, from gaming to finance. Each contract resides at a unique address on the blockchain comprising executable code, storage data, and a balance. Users can interact with the contract functions by issuing *transactions*, with the resulting state changes permanently recorded in the ledger. The source code of a contract is immutable, meaning that its terms cannot be changed after deployment. This property promotes integrity and trust, but it also limits the ability to fix bugs and vulnerabilities. While deploying a new contract is an option, it can be complex and costly as it requires migrating the old contract's state and redirecting users to the new address. In recent years, upgradability mechanisms gained popularity in mainstream projects[1], enabling the release of patches and new features over time. However, upgrading a smart contract is a delicate activity that necessitates caution to avoid breaking previous functionalities or introducing new issues (e.g., the Compound Finance upgrade bug[2]).

The *proxy pattern* has gained significant attention among existing upgradability mechanisms due to its effectiveness and simple design. A comprehensive study on smart contract upgradeability [17] reveals widespread adoption of proxy-based projects on the main chain, with 1.4 million proxy contracts employed in 8,225 upgradeable systems. The proxy pattern aims to *decouple the storage of a smart contract from its logic.* Users interact with the *proxy contract*, which maintains the relevant storage data and balance of the DApp, along with a reference to a specific *logic contract*. The proxy automatically redirects transactions to the referenced logic contract using `delegatecall`, a low-level Ethereum function

---

[1] https://blog.openzeppelin.com/the-state-of-smart-contract-upgrades.

[2] https://protos.com/compound-finance-upgrade-bug-freezes-830m-in-crypto.

that executes the logic of the called contract within the context of its caller. This ensures that any operations performed by the logic contract only impact the state of the proxy. Consequently, the logic contract can be replaced without redeploying the proxy or incurring costly state migrations. Proxy contracts also include an *upgrade function* that allows changing the referenced implementation address. This function is typically integrated into the proxy with appropriate access control mechanisms to prevent unauthorized users from initiating upgrades.

Replay Testing. Replay testing is a technique used to verify system behavior by replaying captured inputs, and it foresees two main phases: The *Capture* phase records interactions between users and the system under test (e.g., the input and output values of each function call). In the *Replay* phase, the collected data is transformed into test scripts and executed to detect unexpected system behaviors. This approach has found widespread use in testing web [14], mobile [3,8], and IoT devices [6]. However, real traffic can also be recorded for regression testing purposes [3,10,12,13], ensuring that software products evolve without negatively impacting users. Using real traffic is a very appealing solution as it enables the automatic generation of tests without in-depth system knowledge. Moreover, tests generated from real-world input can be extremely effective as they reflect *real usage scenarios* observed in production.

3   Methodology

Consider a DApp comprising a Proxy contract P and a logic contract L_1 deployed on the Ethereum Mainnet. At some point, L_1 must be upgraded to version L_2 to improve some functionalities or to fix some bugs. With replay testing we aim to ensure that, when L_1 is upgraded to L_2, the transactions that were executed on L_1 give the same output on L_2. In a Proxy-based project a logic contract executes in the context of its proxy, with the latter holding the state. Therefore, to replay any historical transaction t on the upgraded contract, we must synchronize P's state with the state observed on the main network right before the execution of t. To achieve this we can *fork* the Mainnet right before the execution of t, switch the logic contract used by P with its upgraded version, and replay the transaction without worrying about state set-ups. In the following, we present the methodology implemented in the CATANA tool.

1) Retrieving the transactions To run replay testing we must retrieve the set of transactions T that were run on P while it referenced the logic contract L_1. These can be easily obtained using the Etherscan API. Each returned object includes all the fields required for replaying a transaction (e.g., the invoked method, its input data, and the sender address), except for its historical output. For each transaction $t \in T$ to be replayed, we must then repeat steps 2–5.

2) Forking the main network To replay a transaction $t \in T$, we must retrieve the block b that includes t, and fork the main network at block $b - 1$. This forking capability is provided by the Ganache[3] Ethereum simulator, which allows us to locally copy the Ethereum Mainnet starting from a specified block number, without the need to download the entire blockchain. When a past state, such as a smart contract, is required but not available locally, Ganache dynamically retrieves it from an external source, eliminating the need for mocking contract dependencies. Moreover, this tool allows us to impersonate any account on the main network, enabling the successful replay of transactions sent from different addresses. In our proposed approach, we create a new fork using the following script: `ganache --fork --fork.blockNumber <blockNumber> -u <addressList>`. Here, `blockNumber` is the block $b - 1$ prior to the one including t, while `addressList` specifies all the addresses that must be unlocked for replaying the transaction (i.e., the sender of t, and the addresses used for deployment and upgrade operations).

3) Executing the transaction on the original logic contract Once the main network is forked, we proceed to execute transaction t on Proxy P, which still references logic contract L_1. This step has two purposes: 1) ensuring that the transaction can be successfully replayed on the original logic contract, and 2) building a test oracle. To run the tests we use Truffle[4] a popular testing framework for Ethereum. The defined test script takes t as input and executes two parametric test methods, T_1 and T_2, on the forked network. Listing 1.1 shows an excerpt of T_1, which aims to run t on L_1 and build the test oracle. To replay tests on any project, we require the interface of the proxy P (line 1) and its logic contract L_1 (line 2). After retrieving the transaction to be replayed, we decode its input using the ABI (Application Binary Interface) of L_1 (line 9). To interact with L_1, we create an abstraction of the contract using the Mainnet address of its proxy (line 10). At this point we can replay t (line 12) by calling P from the original sender's address, using the decoded method name, parameters, and value (i.e., the amount of transferred funds). Note that we use `call()` instead of issuing a normal transaction to prevent persisting state changes after the contract execution. In this way we can use the same, unaffected fork for subsequent operations. Most importantly, using `call()` permits us to observe the return value regardless of whether the invoked method is read-only or not (i.e., it is marked as `view` or `pure`). The output of this call serves as a test oracle.

Listing 1.1. Test method T_1

```
1   const Delegator = artifacts.require(config.Delegator);
2   const Delegate = artifacts.require(config.Delegate);
3   ...
4   describe(''Replay'', () => {
5     const tx = JSON.parse(process.env.npm_config_tx);
6     ...
7     it(''should replay tx on L1'', async() => {
8       ...
```

---

[3] Ganache: https://trufflesuite.com/ganache.
[4] Truffle: https://trufflesuite.com/docs/truffle,.

```
9    const decodedInput = decoder.decodeData(tx.input);
10   const proxy = await Delegate.at(config.DelegatorAddr);
11   ...
12   const originalCall = await proxy[decodedInput.method].call(...
        replayValues, {from: tx.from, value: tx.value});
13   });
14   })
```

4) Upgrading the logic contract The fourth step involves deploying the new logic contract L_2 on the fork and upgrading the Proxy P to use L_2 as its implementation. Listing 1.2 shows the test method T_2 responsible for these operations. First, L_2 is deployed on the fork (line 2). Its address is then passed as an argument to the upgrade function of P to change its referenced logic contract. In reality, the upgrade process is often more complex and governed by a voting protocol. However, this process can generally be bypassed during replay testing by impersonating a proxy administrator. Finally, the upgrade method of P is called to update its logic contract to L_2 (line 6). Note that in this case we issue a transaction to persist the state changes on the fork.

Listing 1.2. Upgrading the logic contract

```
1    it(''should successfully replay tx on L2'', async () => {
2      const logicV2 = await Delegate.new({from:config.DelegateDeployer});
3
4      let proxy = await Delegator.at(config.Delegator);
5
6      const txSetImplementation = proxy[config.upgradeFunc](logicV2.
          address, {from: config.DelegatorAdmin});
7      ...
8    });
```

5) Replaying the transaction on the upgraded logic contract At this point, we are ready to replay the transaction on the upgraded implementation of P. This step is very straightforward, as we repeat the same call to the proxy described in Sect. 3, and we check if its outcome is consistent with the oracle.

4   Experimental Evaluation

The objective of this study is understanding whether using historical transaction data is a viable solution to perform regression testing on smart contract upgrades. To this end, we must evaluate: 1) *how many transactions* CATANA *can successfully replay on the original contract* L_1, among the ones stored in the blockchain, and 2) *whether* CATANA *can detect inconsistent behaviors when replaying the same transactions on the upgraded contract* L_2. To find viable subjects we manually searched among Mainnet contracts targeted by recent transactions on the Etherscan explorer, and selected those that respected the following criteria: 1) the project must include a proxy contract P whose logic contract L_1 was upgraded to L_2 at some point; 2) The smart contracts must be verified so that we can access their source code; 3) P must feature a reasonable number of transactions to be replayed on L_2. The resulting projects are: 1) *Compound Protocol*[5] a DApp for supplying and borrowing assets on Ethereum, 2) *USD Coin:*

---

[5] Compound Protocol: https://compound.finance/developers.

an asset that is commonly deployed in decentralized finance (DeFi) protocols, 3) *Land Registry* and 4) *Estate Registry*: two sets of smart contracts for keeping track of the land parcels and estates available in the Decentraland[6] metaverse. For each project, Table 1 reports the address of its proxy P, and the address of the two most recent versions of its logic contract, L_1 and L_2. Generally, Etherscan only keeps track of the current logic address used by a proxy. Therefore, to retrieve L_1, we either queried the proxy from a pre-upgrade network fork, or we analysed the event logs emitted during the upgrade operation. Clearly, such procedure is not needed for the original developers, as they have direct references to the two versions of the contract. We then retrieved all the transactions addressed to P while it was using L_1, to replay them on the next version L_2. Due to the high volume of transactions and associated replay costs, we fed the last 1000 (successful) transactions to CATANA. For each transaction t in the sample, the tool ran the two subsequent tests, $T1$ and $T2$, described in Sect. 3. All the experiments in this work were run on a virtual machine with an Intel Xeon(R) E-2226G CPU @ 3.40 GHz, and 4 GB of RAM, running on Ubuntu 20.04 LTS.

Table 1. Experimental Subjects

Project	Proxy P	Logic L_1	Logic L_2
Compound Protocol	CErc20Delegator	CErc20Delegate	CErc20Delegate
	0x5d3a536E4D6DbD6114c	0xa035b9e130F2B1AedC	0x3363bae2fc44da742df
	c1Ead35777bAB948E3643	733eEFb1C67Ba4c503491F	13cd3ee94b6bb868ea376
USD Coin	FiatTokenProxy	FiatTokenV2	FiatTokenV2_1
	0xA0b86991c6218b36c1d	0xB7277a6e95992041568	0xa2327a938Febf5FEC13
	19D4a2e9Eb0cE3606eB48	D9391D09d0122023778A2	baCFb16Ae10EcBc4cbDCF
Land Registry	LANDProxy	LANDRegistry	LANDRegistry
	0xF87E31492Faf9A91B02	0xA57E126B341B18c262a	0x554BB6488bA95537735
	Ee0dEAAd50d51d56D5d4d	D25B86bb4F65b5e2AdE45	9bED16b84Ed0822679CDC
Estate Registry	AdminUpgrad.Proxy	EstateRegistry	EstateRegistry
	0x959e104E1a4dB6317fA	0x0A820C4e3a9c8D89c9a	0x1784Ef41af86e97f8D2
	58F8295F586e1A978c297	3E78DfE993b3885b229Fa	8aFe95b573a24aEDa966e

For each project, Table 2 shows the percentage of transactions (%Tx) that succeeded on $T1$ and $T2$, failed on $T1$, and failed on $T2$. As it can be observed, $T1$ passed 98,8% of the time, meaning that CATANA can **successfully replay most of the transactions** contained in the blockchain as they are. The remaining 1,2% failed during $T1$ due to an incorrect setup of the fork. Currently, Ganache allows us to copy the state of the main chain at a given block, but not after a specific transaction. To replay a transaction t originally included in block b, we can fork the blockchain at block $b - 1$. Clearly, this fork lacks the state changes caused by the transactions in block b, including those that might indirectly affect the outcome of t. If the test fails on the original smart contract version, we cannot reliably obtain an oracle value. One solution would be executing all the missing transactions to bring the fork in the correct state. However, this can be costly due to the possibly high number of unrelated transactions in each block. In the

---

[6] Decentraland: https://decentraland.org/.

general case, we judge it more reasonable to just discard the failing transactions. From Table 2 we can observe that most transactions **(98,6%) produced the same output before and after the contract upgrade**. This is not surprising, as the experimental subjects are main network releases, which undergo extensive testing prior to deployment. However, 8 transactions that were successfully replayed on Compound Protocol's L_1 **generated a different output** after the implementation was switched to L_2. To determine the cause of failure we analyzed these transactions in relation to the modifications introduced during the upgrade. We found out that the invoked methods always produced an error code on L_1, but caused the same transactions to revert on L_2. Further examination of the two contracts confirmed that the discrepancy is due to a modification in the error-handling mechanisms of the smart contract, and not to a possible issue in the reproduction of the environment made by CATANA. On average, replaying 1000 transactions on each project required ~9,7 h. Replay tests are more time-expensive than regular ones, as CATANA must set up the fork and retrieve past state information for each transaction to be replayed. However, combining test parallelization and appropriate transaction selection strategies can help to significantly reduce costs. Overall, the experimental data confirm the possibility of leveraging historical transactions to perform regression testing on proxy-based smart contracts. Indeed, CATANA was able to successfully replay most transactions without issues, and it also detected inconsistent behaviours resulting from a real upgrade.

5   Related Work

Replay Testing. Replay testing has been extensively studied in various domains, including web [14], IoT [6], and mobile applications [3,8]. This technique was employed for regression testing, ensuring the correctness of evolving programs. Previous research has explored mutable replay approaches [13] to tolerate valid variations caused by security updates and addressed the issue of replay test breakages during regression activities [10,12]. In the blockchain field, the recording capabilities of the ledger were leveraged for monitoring [5], transparency evaluation [11], and test case generation [20] purposes, but never for regression testing of evolving smart contracts.

Blockchain Testing. Releasing reliable smart contract code is a primary concern for industry professionals working with blockchain. To date, developers can rely on a range of static and dynamic analysis tools (e.g., Slither [7], Echidna [9]) for disclosing faults and removing code smells. EVMPatch [16] is a framework that fixes faulty contracts while maintaining functional equivalence, mitigating compatibility issues. Solidity-specific mutation testing approaches were also proposed to improve the fault-detection capabilities of smart contract test suites (e.g., SuMo [1], ReSuMo [2]). Several works do not specifically target smart contracts, but rather build test cases for the whole DApp [18], or detect bugs stemming from the bad synchronization between on-chain and off-chain components [19].

Table 2. Results of replay testing

Project	T1 outcome	T2 outcome	%Tx
Compound Protocol	✓	✓	94,6
	×	–	4,6
	✓	×	0,8
USD Coin	✓	✓	99,9
	×	–	0,1
	✓	×	0
Land Registry	✓	✓	100
	×	–	0
	✓	×	0
Estate Registry	✓	✓	99,8
	×	–	0,2
	✓	×	0

6   Conclusions and Future Work

In this work, we proposed the usage of historical blockchain transactions to enable replay testing of upgradeable Ethereum smart contracts using the *Proxy* pattern. By replaying past transactions, we can verify the consistency of a revised smart contract with its pre-upgrade version deployed on the Ethereum Mainnet. We implemented our approach in the CATANA tool and conducted evaluations on four real-world smart contract projects. The results were promising, with CATANA successfully replaying ~98,6% of the collected transactions on the original smart contract version. Only a few invocations failed due to imprecise state-setting resulting from the block-level fork granularity. Furthermore, we identified eight transactions that produced different outcomes after the contract was upgraded. This highlights the potential of CATANA to detect disruptive upgrades and promote the release of more reliable code. Future work should focus on improving the effectiveness of CATANA by checking the events logged by the smart contract during its execution. Indeed, only observing the output values of a contract invocation might limit the detection of inconsistent behaviors. Additionally, the tool should be enhanced with a mechanism for identifying and replaying relevant missing transactions after a fork, so that any historical transaction could be transformed into a test. Lastly, exploring efficient transaction selection strategies, considering the specific changes introduced by the upgrade, is crucial for accelerating the testing process.

References

1. Barboni, M., Morichetta, A., Polini, A.: Sumo: A mutation testing approach and tool for the Ethereum blockchain. J. Syst. Softw. **193**, 111445 (2022)
2. Barboni, M., Morichetta, A., Polini, A., Casoni, F.: ReSuMo: a regression strategy and tool for mutation testing of solidity smart contracts. Softw. Q. J. (2023). https://doi.org/10.1007/s11219-023-09637-1
3. Bernaschina, C., Fedorov, R., Frajberg, D., Fraternali, P.: A framework for regression testing of outdoor mobile applications. In: Proceedings of MOBILESOFT, pp. 179–181 (2017)
4. Bui, V.C., Wen, S., Yu, J., Xia, X., Haghighi, M.S., Xiang, Y.: Evaluating upgradable smart contract. In: Proceedings of Blockchain, pp. 252–256 (2021)
5. Cook, T., Latham, A., Lee, J.H.: Dappguard : active monitoring and defense for solidity smart contracts. https://courses.csail.mit.edu/6.857/2017/project/23.pdf (2017)
6. Fang, K., Yan, G.: Iotreplay: troubleshooting cots IoT devices with record and replay. In: Proceedings of SEC, pp. 193–205 (2020)
7. Feist, J., Grieco, G., Groce, A.: Slither: a static analysis framework for smart contracts. In: Proceedings of WETSEB, pp. 8–15 (2019)
8. Feng, S., Chen, C.: Gifdroid: automated replay of visual bug reports for android apps. In: Proceedings of ICSE, pp. 1045–1057 (2022)
9. Grieco, G., Song, W., Cygan, A., Feist, J., Groce, A.: Echidna: effective, usable, and fast fuzzing for smart contracts. In: Proceedings of ISSTA, ACM (2020)
10. Hammoudi, M., Rothermel, G., Tonella, P.: Why do record/replay tests of web applications break? In: Proceedings of ICST, pp. 180–190 (2016)
11. Hartel, P., van Staalduinen, M.: Truffle tests for free-replaying Ethereum smart contracts for transparency. arXiv preprint arXiv:1907.09208 (2019)
12. Imtiaz, J., Iqbal, M.Z., khan, M.U.: An automated model-based approach to repair test suites of evolving web applications. J. Syst. Softw. **171**, 110841 (2021)
13. Kravets, I., Tsafrir, D.: Feasibility of mutable replay for automated regression testing of security updates. In: Proceedings of RESoLVE (2012)
14. Long, Z., Wu, G., Chen, X., Chen, W., Wei, J.: Webrr: self-replay enhanced robust record/replay for web application testing. In: Proceedings of ESEC/FSE, pp. 1498–1508 (2020)
15. Meisami, S., Bodell III, W.E.: A comprehensive survey of upgradeable smart contract patterns. arXiv preprint arXiv:2304.03405 (2023)
16. Rodler, M., Li, W., Karame, G.O., Davi, L.: {EVMPatch}: timely and automated patching of ethereum smart contracts. In: Proceedings of USENIX Security, pp. 1289–1306 (2021)
17. Salehi, M., Clark, J., Mannan, M.: Not so immutable: upgradeability of smart contracts on Ethereum. arXiv preprint arXiv:2206.00716 (2022)
18. Wu, Z., et al.: Kaya: a testing framework for blockchain-based decentralized applications. In: Proceedings of ICSME, pp. 826–829 (2020)
19. Zhang, W., Wei, L., Li, S., Liu, Y., Cheung, S.C.: Darcher: detecting on-chain-off-chain synchronization bugs in decentralized applications. In: Proceedings of ESEC/FSE, pp. 553–565 (2021)
20. Zhou, T., Liu, K., Li, L., Liu, Z., Klein, J., Bissyandé, T.F.: Smartgift: learning to generate practical inputs for testing smart contracts. In: Proceedings of ICSME, pp. 23–34 (2021)

GResilience: Trading Off Between the Greenness and the Resilience of Collaborative AI Systems

Diaeddin Rimawi[1]($\boxtimes$) (iD), Antonio Liotta[1] (iD), Marco Todescato[2] (iD),
and Barbara Russo[1] (iD)

[1] Free University of Bozen-Bolzano, Faculty of Engineering, Bolzano 39100, Italy
{drimawi,antonio.liotta,barbara.russo}@unibz.it
[2] Fraunhofer Italia, Bolzano 39100, Italy
marco.todescato@fraunhofer.it

Abstract. A Collaborative Artificial Intelligence System (CAIS) works
with humans in a shared environment to achieve a common goal. To
recover from a disruptive event that degrades its performance and ensures
its resilience, a CAIS may then need to perform a set of actions either
by the system, by the humans, or collaboratively together. As for any
other system, recovery actions may cause energy adverse effects due to
the additional required energy. Therefore, it is of paramount importance
to understand which of the above actions can better trade-off between
resilience and greenness. In this in-progress work, we propose an approach to automatically evaluate CAIS recovery actions for their ability
to trade-off between the resilience and greenness of the system. We have
also designed an experiment protocol and its application to a real CAIS
demonstrator. Our approach aims to attack the problem from two perspectives: as a one-agent decision problem through optimization, which
takes the decision based on the score of resilience and greenness, and
as a two-agent decision problem through game theory, which takes the
decision based on the payoff computed for resilience and greenness as
two players of a cooperative game.

Keywords: Greenness · Resilience · GResilience · Collaborative AI
Systems · Optimization · Game Theory

1 Introduction

A Collaborative Artificial Intelligence System (CAIS) is an example of a Cyber
Physical System that works together with humans in a shared environment to
achieve a common goal, [1]. The collaboration between humans and AI components poses specific challenges for a CAIS to be resilient (i.e., recover from a
disruptive event that causes performance degradation) as disruptive events can
be caused or have effects on humans. Therefore, it is of paramount importance to
define suitable recovery strategies to automatically support the decision-making
process in case of disruptive events affecting CAISs. A recovery strategy typically

© IFIP International Federation for Information Processing 2023
Published by Springer Nature Switzerland AG 2023
S. Bonfanti et al. (Eds.): ICTSS 2023, LNCS 14131, pp. 266–273, 2023.
https://doi.org/10.1007/978-3-031-43240-8_18

detects the performance degradation (detection), then defines mitigation actions (mitigation), and finally, restores the system to an acceptable performance state (recovery), [2]. Recovering from a disruptive event may require additional energy consumption, which, in turn, may increase the CAIS energy adverse effects, such as CO_2 footprint, [6,9]. The efficient usage of energy with minimizing adverse effects is called *greenness*, [6].

In this in-progress work, we are interested in the relation between two properties of a CAIS: resilience and greenness. In particular, we aim to support the decision-making process to trade-off between them. Specifically, we introduce the approach *GResilience*[1] to select automatically recovery action(s) that finds the best trade-off between greenness and resilience while restoring the CAIS services to an acceptable performance state. Our approach formulates the trade-off decision in two ways: i) as a one-agent decision through optimization, and ii) as a multi-agent decision through game theory. In the former case, the decision is taken by selecting actions(s) and optimizing measures of resilience and greenness. While in the latter, actions are selected through a multi-participant game in which the measures of resilience and greenness define the payoff for the actions.

Finally, we plan to apply our approach to a CAIS demonstrator available at our laboratory. The demonstrator is a robotic arm that is equipped with an AI component and performs activities for in-production systems. To this aim, we have devised an experimental protocol that we present in the next sections.

In summary, we aim to *understand the relationship between resilience and greenness and discuss the one-agent and the multi-agent methods in case of CAISs*. To achieve this goal, this study poses the following research questions:

- **RQ1**: Is the optimization model a valuable solution for automatizing the decision-making process that finds a trade-off between the *greenness* and *resilience* in CAISs?
- **RQ2**: Is the game theory model a valuable solution for automatizing the decision-making process that finds a trade-off between the *greenness* and *resilience* in CAISs?
- **RQ3**: What are the major differences between the optimization model and the game theory model solutions?

The rest of this paper discusses the related work (Sect. 2), our approach and experiment protocol to the trade-off between resilience and greenness (GResilience) along with our demonstrator CAIS (Sect. 3), and finally our conclusion and future work (Sect. 4).

2 Related Work

For what concerns our work, we see the following topics as relevant: i) resilience, ii) greenness, iii) multi-objective optimization, and iv) game theory.

---

[1] The name GResilience comes from joining the two words, green and resilience. The name is inspired by the "eco–greslient" technique used in [7] study.

Resilience. Studies are categorized into two classes depending on the model type they use, [5]. The first category addresses quantitative models that discuss structure-based models and define computational metrics, whereas the second category addresses qualitative studies that are more concerned about conceptual frameworks. Henry *et al.* [4] define a generic quantitative approach that uses a function of time to model the resilience process, while Speranza *et al.* [11] propose a social-ecological framework to address policies' effectiveness to build livelihood resilience.

Greenness. Studies have analysed greenness in two ways, technical and non-technical. Pandey *et al.* [8] discuss making Google Tensor Processing Unit resilient against activating sequences error in the systolic array considering a low-voltage operation, which ensures less energy adverse effects, while Rodriguez *et al.* [10] focuses on the business and financial aspect to identify the right location for a green infrastructure component of a sewer system.

Multi-objective Optimization. These techniques help create a simple mathematical representation of problems that have multiple objectives, [3]. Several studies have used scalarization optimization techniques to trade off between different system properties [7]. Mohammed *et al.* [7] create the eco-gresilient model to build an economical, green, resilient supply chain network. It uses a three-objectives-optimization model (economical, green, resilient) to find the right number of facilities to be built in each supply network section. Multi-objective optimization helps find a solution that trades off multiple objectives and it uses one agent that combines the conflicting weighted objectives to find the final solution, [3].

Finally, **Game Theory** searches for strategies (Nash equilibrium) that help the players gain the best payoffs for their interests, [9,12]. Thus, the problem is framed as a multi-agent game for which each agent has a preferred action to achieve a common goal such as the game of "The Battle of Sexes", [12]. The players of the game will try to choose the action that maximizes their payoff. When choosing this action is done independently leads to a mixed strategy Nash equilibrium (MSNE), [9,12].

3   Approach - GResilience

GResilience is our empirical approach to support the decision-making process and trade-off between *greenness* and *resilience* after a disruptive event. The approach provides one or more agents with the measurements required to take the decision and select the recovery action that best balance between the two properties. The approach is applied to CAIS in which the AI component learns from human movements. GResilience monitors and controls the collaboration between the human and the AI component to support the decision-making process after disruptive events. The core common component of the GResilience approach is the measurement framework for resilience and greenness. The framework is then used by two techniques to trade-off between greenness and resilience: optimization and game theory. While the former is typically used for trading off between non-functional properties of a system [7], the latter, to the best of our knowledge, is novel in such context. The use of one or the other depends on the type of problem the decision-maker needs to solve. The goal of each technique is to select a recovery action after the disruptive event to return to an acceptable performance state. Recovery actions are categorized into two classes: i) general actions that are derived from a system or environment policies, and ii) actions defined by the decision maker.

In Fig. 1 we describe the resilience process from two perspectives. Figure 1 (A) describes the performance behavior of the running system over time, while, Fig. 1 (B), illustrates the GResilience approach state diagram based on such resilience process. In Fig. 1 (A), the process starts at a *steady state* and faces a disruptive event at t^e that may *transition* to a *disruptive state* at t^d. During the disruptive state, the system starts the recovery process and selects a recovery action to move to an *acceptable recovery state* at t^r. In Fig. 1 (B), the system starts at a *steady state* and remains in the same state if there is no performance degradation. When a performance degradation occurs, the system moves to a *disruptive state*, where it either recovers by default system actions or policies, or it moves to the *trade-off state*. The trade-off state invokes the GResilience model (optimization or game theory) to select the action that finds the best trade-off between greenness and resilience. As an example in Fig. 1 (B), we illustrate two actions: a1) that targets a *learning state*, and a2) that targets an *operating state* of the AI component. From either state, the performance recovery enters in the *measuring state* looping between one state and the measurement state until the system reaches an acceptable performance (*recovered state*).

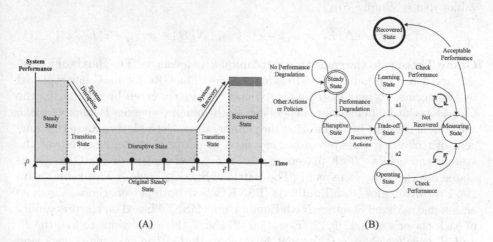

(A)   (B)

Fig. 1. System's Performance States (A) Resilience performance evolution, (B) GResilience State Diagram

The GResilience framework includes three attributes, one attribute to measure the system resilience and the other two to measure the CAIS greenness.

Table 1. The GResilience Game General Payoff Matrix

P_r	P_g		
	$a_1(p)$	$a_2(1-p)$	P_r Expected Payoff
$a_1(q)$	$P_r^2(a_1), P_g^2(a_1)$	$P_r^1(a_1), P_g^1(a_2)$	$pP_r^2(a_1) + (1-p)P_r^1(a_1)$
$a_2(1-q)$	$P_r^1(a_2), P_g^1(a_1)$	$P_r^2(a_2), P_g^2(a_2)$	$pP_r^1(a_2) + (1-p)P_r^2(a_2)$
P_g Expected Payoff	$qP_g^2(a_1) + (1-q)P_g^1(a_1)$	$qP_g^1(a_2) + (1-q)P_g^2(a_2)$	

The first attribute is *the estimated run time* (E_t), which represents the action running time. The other two attributes are *the estimated* CO_2 *footprint* (E_{CO_2}) to emit by the action, and *the human labor cost* (H), which is the number of human's interactions needed by the action. It is worth noticing here that human energy and financial factors are not considered in the framework and will be a matter of future investigation. The measures are then used by each of the two techniques as in the following.

Optimization. The optimization technique uses one agent and the *weighted sum model* (WSM) [7] to trade-off between greenness and resilience by combining the three attributes and define a global score for each action. Equation (1) shows the global score of the action a ($S(a)$), where w_T, w_H, and w_{CO_2} are the weights of the attributes (run time, human labor, and CO_2 footprint). ϵ is the confidence level of the AI component model ($\epsilon \in [0,1]$): the higher the value the more we trust the AI to continue operating. Thus, ϵ multiplies the inverse of the resilience measure, and $1 - \epsilon$ multiplies the inverse of the greenness measures. Each resulting measure is then normalized (N()). Finally, we search the weights' values that maximize $S(a)$.

$$S(a) = w_T \cdot \epsilon \cdot N(E_t^{-1}) + (1 - \epsilon) \cdot \{w_H \cdot N(H) + w_{CO_2} \cdot N(E_{CO_2}^{-1})\} \quad (1)$$

Game Theory. In the game theory technique, we leverage "The Battle of Sexes" [12] and define our game *The GResilience Game*. The GResilience Game is played by two agents: P_g and P_r. P_g aims to make the system green by minimizing the CO_2 footprint by being more dependent on the human whereas P_r aims to make the system resilient by minimizing the running time. Both players share the same goal of recovering the system so they need to adopt a strategy to recover the system and achieve both players' goals. The payoff matrix of the GResilience Game has the same form as in "The Battle of Sexes", Table 1. This table shows two Pure Strategies Nash Equilibria (PSNE) where both players choose the same action and a Mixed Strategy Nash Equilibrium (MSNE) based on the probability of each player's action, [9,12]. Equation (2) shows the expressions to find the P_r and P_g payoffs, where α is the matching factor that is 1 in case the players land on different actions and 2 in case of PSNE.

$$P_r^\alpha(a) = \epsilon \cdot \alpha \cdot E_t^{-1}, \ P_g^\alpha(a) = (1 - \epsilon) \cdot \alpha \cdot H^{-1} \cdot E_{CO_2}^{-1} \quad (2)$$

In the MSNE, P_r chooses a_1 with probability q and a_2 with probability $1 - q$, while P_g chooses a_1 with probability p and a_2 with probability $1 - p$, which results to the *expected payoff* described in Table 1. Thus, to find the probability q (resp. p) with MSNE, we equal the expected payoffs of P_g (resp. P_r) for a_1 and a_2 and solve the resulting equation for q (resp. p).

Experiments Protocol. We plan a series of experiments in three stages, i) setup, ii) iterative execution and data collection, and iii) data analysis. During the setup stage, we need to understand the disruptive events that might occur, and what are the feasible actions to recover from one of these events. As illustrated by Fig. 1 (B), GResilience wraps the system to detect the performance degradation in the second stage, and for each trading off technique, we collect the number of iterations to recover, the performance at the start and the end of each iteration, the selected action per iteration, and the values of the resilience and greenness attributes per iteration. Finally, by analyzing the collected data, we can understand for which disruptive event a technique is a valuable solution to automatize the decision-making process, and what are the major differences between them.

Demonstrator. Our CAIS demonstrator "CORAL"[2] is a collaborative robot arm learning from demonstrations. Figure 2 shows the robotic arm, (where 1, 3, and 4 represent the arm and its controllers) that works with the human (6) to classify objects moving on the conveyor belt (2) based on their colors. In addition to object color learning, CORAL learns background subtraction, object detection, and human movement. CORAL has two vision sensors, one through a Kinect (5) that monitors human movement, and a second above a conveyor belt that moves objects to be classified. Losing the lights that support the vision sensors or having another human in the vision range may disrupt CORAL ability to classify the objects and drop or wrongly classify them. Thus, CORAL requires more time to learn the objects with the faded environmental light and this consumes additional energy. We will apply our approach to CORAL under different disruptive events.

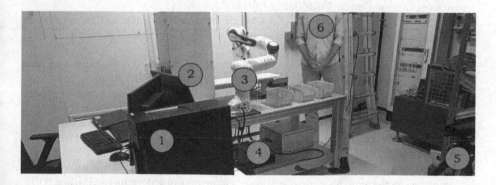

Fig. 2. Collaborative Robot Learning from Demonstrations (CORAL)

---

[2] CORAL is developed by Fraunhofer Italia Research in the context of ARENA Lab.

4   Conclusion and Future Work

This in-progress work proposes an approach to support the decision-making process to recover from a disruptive event that has caused performance degradation and control the energy adverse effects at the same time. To this aim, we have defined a set of measures for resilience and greenness and two techniques leveraging optimization and game theory respectively. The techniques automate the selection process of the recovery actions by measuring the trade-off between the greenness and the resilience capability of CAIS. The first technique evaluates each action separately using an optimization model (WSM), whereas the second technique evaluates greenness and resilience payoffs by selecting an action through a game theory model leveraging "The Battle of Sexes". To verify our approach, we designed experiments to test our techniques on our CAIS demonstrator. In our future work, we plan to run experiments on CORAL. This will help us understand the relationship between resilience and greenness for CAIS and eventually extend our approach to test CAIS for other non-functional properties. In addition, we plan to extend our techniques with reinforcement learning, to incorporate a rewarding mechanism in the optimization and game theory techniques. Moreover, we plan to reconsider further human attributes as for example human energy and financial costs.

References

1. Camilli, M., et al.: Risk-driven compliance assurance for collaborative AI systems: a vision paper. In: Dalpiaz, F., Spoletini, P. (eds.) REFSQ 2021. LNCS, vol. 12685, pp. 123–130. Springer, Cham (2021). https://doi.org/10.1007/978-3-030-73128-1_9
2. Colabianchi, S., Costantino, F., Gravio, G.D., Nonino, F., Patriarca, R.: Discussing resilience in the context of cyber physical systems. Comput. Ind. Eng. **160**, 107534 (2021)
3. Gunantara, N.: A review of multi-objective optimization: methods and its applications. Cogent Eng. **5**(1), 1502242 (2018)
4. Henry, D., Ramirez-Marquez, J.E.: Generic metrics and quantitative approaches for system resilience as a function of time. Reliab. Eng. Syst. Safety **99**, 114–122 (2012)
5. Hosseini, S., Barker, K., Ramirez-Marquez, J.E.: A review of definitions and measures of system resilience. Reliab. Eng. Syst. Saf. **145**, 47–61 (2016)
6. Kharchenko, V., Illiashenko, O.: Concepts of green IT engineering: taxonomy, principles and implementation. In: Kharchenko, V., Kondratenko, Y., Kacprzyk, J. (eds.) Green IT Engineering: Concepts, Models, Complex Systems Architectures. SSDC, vol. 74, pp. 3–19. Springer, Cham (2017). https://doi.org/10.1007/978-3-319-44162-7_1
7. Mohammed, A., Harris, I., Nujoom, R.: Eco-Gresilient: Coalescing ingredient of economic, green and resilience in supply chain network design. In: Parlier, G.H., Liberatore, F., Demange, M. (eds.) Proceedings of the 7th International Conference on Operations Research and Enterprise Systems, ICORES 2018, Funchal, Madeira - Portugal, January 24–26, 2018, pp. 201–208. SciTePress (2018)

8. Pandey, P., Basu, P., Chakraborty, K., Roy, S.: GreenTPU: predictive design paradigm for improving timing error resilience of a near-threshold tensor processing unit. IEEE Trans. Very Large Scale Integr. Syst. **28**(7), 1557–1566 (2020)

9. Rimawi, D.: Green resilience of cyber-physical systems. In: 2022 IEEE International Symposium on Software Reliability Engineering Workshops (ISSREW), pp. 105–109. IEEE (2022)

10. Rodriguez, M., Fu, G., Butler, D.: Green infrastructures and their impact on resilience: spatial interactions in centralized sewer systems. In: Kar, B., Ye, X., Mohebbi, S., Fu, G. (eds.) ARIC@SIGSPATIAL 2020: Proceedings of the 3rd ACM SIGSPATIAL International Workshop on Advances in Resilient and Intelligent Cities, Seattle, WA, 3 November, 2020, pp. 49–57. ACM (2020)

11. Speranza, C.I., Wiesmann, U., Rist, S.: An indicator framework for assessing livelihood resilience in the context of social-ecological dynamics. Global Environ. Change. **28**, 109–119 (2014)

12. Stowe, C.J., Gilpatric, S.M.: Cheating and enforcement in asymmetric rank-order tournaments. Southern Econ. J. **77**(1), 1–14 (2010)

Testing Quality of Training in QoE-Aware SFC Orchestration Based on DRL Approach

Mohamed Escheikh[1], Wiem Taktak[1(✉)], and Kamel Barkaoui[2]

[1] Syscom Laboratory, ENIT, University of Tunis El Manar, Tunis, Tunisia
{mohamed.escheikh,wiem.taktak}@enit.utm.tn
[2] Cedric Laboratory, Paris, France
kamel.barkaoui@cnam.fr

Abstract. In this paper, we propose a Deep Reinforcement Learning (DRL) approach to optimize a learning policy for Service Function Chaining (SFC) orchestration based on maximizing Quality of Experience (QoE) while meeting Quality of Service (QoS) requirements in Software Defined Networking (SDN)/Network Functions Virtualization (NFV) environments. We adopt an incremental orchestration strategy suitable to online setting and enabling to investigate SFC orchestration by processing each incoming SFC request as a multi-step DRL problem. DRL implementation is achieved using Deep Q-Networks (DQNs) variant referred to as Double DQN. We particularly focus on evaluating performance and robustness of the DRL agent during training phase by investigating and testing the quality of training. In this regard, we define a testing metric monitoring the performance of the DRL agent and quantified by a QoE threshold score to reach on average during the last 100 runs of the training phase. We show through numerical results how DRL agent behaves during training phase and how it attempts to reach for different network scales a predefined average QoE threshold score. We highlight also network scalability effect on achieving a suitable performance-convergence trade-off.

Keywords: Learning Quality · DRL · SDN/NFV · SFC Orchestration

1 Introduction

In the last few years, the two disruptive technologies SDN and NFV have revolutionized the way networks are designed, deployed, and managed. SDN enables the separation of the control and data planes, allowing network administrators to centrally manage and program the network [3]. NFV, on the other hand, allows Network Functions (NFs) to be implemented as Virtualized Network Functions (VNFs) that can be deployed on commodity hardware [9]. SFC is a networking concept that delivers customized Network Services (NSs) by directing traffic through a chain organized in a specific sequence of NFs that need to be executed in a specific order to achieve a specific outcome. It can be used to enforce

© IFIP International Federation for Information Processing 2023
Published by Springer Nature Switzerland AG 2023
S. Bonfanti et al. (Eds.): ICTSS 2023, LNCS 14131, pp. 274–288, 2023.
https://doi.org/10.1007/978-3-031-43240-8_19

security policies, implement traffic steering, and provide QoS guarantees [4]. SDN and NFV whenever combined together, bring significant benefits to SFC orchestration, including flexibility, simplified management, resource efficiency, scalability, optimization, and faster service innovation. Modeling SFC orchestration in SDN/NFV environments with DRL is a promising approach that could enable more efficient and effective network management, particularly in complex and dynamic environments where traditional approaches may not be sufficient. However, there are still many challenges that need to be addressed, such as designing appropriate reward functions and ensuring scalability and robustness.

DRL is a type of Machine Learning (ML) that enables an agent to learn how to make decisions by interacting with an environment composed with a Physical Substrate Network (PSN) processing each incoming SFC request according to an incremental strategy [2]. The environment provides feedback in the form of rewards or penalties based on agent's actions. If the agent successfully places and chains the VNFs to achieve a specific performance metric, it receives a reward, otherwise, it receives a penalty. The DRL algorithm then uses this feedback to update the agent's policy, which determines the agent's actions. The policy is updated to maximize the expected future rewards. In this paper, we investigate quality testing of SFC orchestration problem in SDN/NFV environments. The problem is defined as a DRL problem where the agent is responsible for orchestrating VNFs placement and chaining to achieve a specific goal related to maximizing QoE while meeting QoS requirements.

Testing in online DRL is essential to ensure that the agent performs well and to profit from benefits concerning:

- **Performance evaluation**, where the environment is dynamic and unpredictable. This helps also to validate that the agent can learn and adapt to changing conditions and still perform well.
- **Robustness enhancement**, through handling unexpected situations by exposing the agent to a variety of scenarios to identify any weaknesses in the agent's learning process and refine the algorithm accordingly.
- **Scalability evaluation**, as the number of network devices (PSN nodes, PSN links) the complexity of the deployment environment increases as well. Online testing can help ensuring that the agent can handle this increased complexity without compromising performance.

In this paper, we adopt DRL approach to formulate SFC orchestration problem maximizing QoE while meeting QoS requirements in SDN/NFV environment. Along the DRL process we focus on training, testing and evaluation phases and we investigate agent behavior and how it strives to achieve suitable trade-off between performing good learning quality (corresponding to a near-optimal policy) during testing while converging in a reasonable time. The rest of this paper is organized as follows: we address, in Sect. 2, the RL and DRL process including the different phases of training, testing and evaluation. We detail, in this same section, why it is important to find a suitable performance-convergence trade-off. In Sect. 3, we describe next DQN and its variant, Double DQN, used in this paper to implement the DRL approach. In Sect. 4, we investigate the

DRL approach used for SFC orchestration in SDN/NFV environments and we particularly detail the reward design. We devote, Sect. 5, to numerical results and performance evaluation before concluding this paper in Sect. 6.

2   Reinforcement Learning

RL [14] is a ML area where a software agent tries to acquire knowledge and to learn progressively how to behave and to achieve a complex objective (a goal) based on continuous interaction between an Artificial Intelligence (AI) system and its dynamic, unknown and ever changing environment without any human involvement and without explicit instructions. This learning is based on feedback received for its past actions and is acquired by performing a series of decisions or actions through trial and error methods. The goal of learning is to train an agent to fulfill a task and to maximize the cumulative reward based on feedback generated for respective actions.

2.1   RL Agent

The RL agent involves two main components referred to as a policy and a learning algorithm.

- The policy is a (stochastic or deterministic) rule leveraged by an agent to perform decision making actions. It is formalized as a mapping function that selects a feasible action for a problem based on observations from the environment. Typically, DRL [2] trains a Deep Neural Networks (DNNs) with tunable hyper-parameters, to approximate the optimal policy and/or the optimal value functions;
- The learning algorithm belongs usually to a class of learning methods (model-free or model-based) and consists of a loss function and an optimization technique. It aims to find an optimal policy that maximizes cumulative reward (called return) over time by continuously updating policy parameters based on performed actions, made observations, and perceived reward from environment.

2.2   Training (Learning), Testing and Evaluation in RL

In RL, learning refers to the process of training an agent to make optimal decisions in a given environment through trial and error. Testing and evaluation are the processes of evaluating performance of the trained agent and assessing how well it has learned to make optimal decisions.

Training in RL. In RL, training (a.k.a learning) aims to find optimal (or near-optimal) policy or value function that can maximize the expected cumulative reward of an agent over time through using RL algorithms, such as Q-learning.

The goal of training is to improve the agent's performance over time by finding an optimal or near-optimal policy that maximizes the expected cumulative reward. For this purpose, the training process evolves over time by iteratively updating the Q-values using Bellman equation [6], until converging to an optimal Q-function. This update rule is repeated for each state-action pair the agent encounters during training, until the Q-values converge to the optimal values. In DRL, a Neural Network (NN) is used to approximate Q-values or policy function. The NN is trained to change its attributes (such as weights and learning rate) in order to reduce the losses and obtain faster results. The weights of the NN are updated iteratively using back-propagation, which computes the gradient of the loss function with respect to the weights. This gradient is then used to update the weights in the direction that minimizes the loss function, such as the mean squared error between the predicted Q-values and the target Q-values. This update rule is repeated for each batch of training samples, until the NN converges to an optimal policy or value function. The convergence of the training process depends on various factors, such as the complexity of the problem, the quality of the training data, and the choice of DRL algorithm and hyper-parameters.

Testing and Evaluation in RL. Once the agent has learned a policy, it can be tested on a new set of data to evaluate its performance. Testing can be done by running the agent in the environment and measuring its cumulative reward or success rate over a certain number of episodes. The goal of testing is to assess how well the agent has learned to make optimal decisions and to identify areas where it may need further improvements. The testing stage involves evaluating the agent's performance on a separate set of test runs, which are generated by the same environment but are not used for training. The goal of testing is to measure the generalization performance of the agent and to identify potential over-fitting or under-fitting issues. Evaluation is the process of assessing the quality of the agent's learned policy. It evaluates the agent's performance on a specific task or benchmark, which is often used to compare the performance of different RL algorithms or agents. The goal of evaluation is to provide a standardized and objective measure of the agent's performance and to identify potential strengths and weaknesses. One common evaluation method is to use performance metrics such as average reward, success rate, or convergence rate to compare the agent's performance to that of other agents or benchmarks. The goal of evaluation is to ensure that the agent's learned policy is effective and reliable in making optimal decisions in the environment. In practice, the testing and evaluation stages are often combined into a single process and the evaluation phase can actually occur during the training phase. This process can be repeated multiple times using different sets of test runs to obtain a more comprehensive assessment of the agent's performance. During learning (or training), the optimal policy may be unreachable and in such context we attempt to find a near-optimal solution. The evaluation phase is needed to verify whether learned policy to solve actual real-world problem is good enough before deploying RL algorithm. The evaluation phase assesses quality of the learned policy and how much reward the agent obtains if it follows that policy. So, a typical metric that can be used to assess the quality of the policy is to plot the cumulative reward as a function of the number of runs. DRL algorithm is considered dominates another if its plot is consistently above the other. Moreover, assessment may cover the generalization of the learned policy by evaluating it in different (but similar) environments to the training environment. Whereas during training, the goal is to find the optimal policy, the evaluation phase aims to assess the quality of the learned policy (or RL algorithm). Notice that evaluation may be performed in online scenario during training phase. So in online DRL, there is only a learning or training phase and no a separate testing or evaluation phase.

Online Evaluation in DRL. In DRL, online evaluation of the learning phase refers to the process of evaluating the performance of the learning algorithm as it interacts with its environment in real-time. The goal of online evaluation is to monitor the learning process and identify any issues or areas for improvement as they arise. There are several approaches to online evaluation in RL, including:

1. **Monitoring the reward signal:** The reward signal is a critical component of RL, as it guides the learning algorithm towards optimal behavior. By monitoring the reward signal over time, we can get a sense of how well the learning algorithm is performing.
2. **Tracking performance metrics:** Such as the average episode length, the number of episodes required to converge, or the average reward per episode. These metrics can help us identify areas where the learning algorithm is struggling and make adjustments accordingly.
3. **Visualizing the learning process:** In order to understand the learning process in RL, we can use plots, graphs, or animations to visualize the learning algorithm's behavior over time, making it easier to identify patterns and trends.

2.3   Convergence-Performance Trade-Off in Training RL Algorithms

Convergence refers to the process of an RL agent's policy and value function improving over time as it receives more experience or data. Convergence efficiency of RL algorithms refers to how quickly the agent's policy and value function converge to optimal or near-optimal performance. It can be affected by various factors such as the algorithm used, the complexity of the environment, the amount of data available, and the hyper-parameters chosen. In practice, RL algorithm is considered to converge when the learning curve gets flat and no longer increases. A ML model reaches convergence when it achieves a state during training in which loss settles to within an error range around the final value. In other words, a model converges when additional training will not improve the model. The convergence-performance trade-off in training RL algorithms refers to the compromise between how quickly RL agent learns and how well it learns. Typically, a faster learning agent will sacrifice some of its learning performance in exchange for speed, and a slower learning agent will sacrifice speed to achieve better learning performance.

3   DRL Implementation via Double DQN

Double DQN is a variant of DQN. In the rest of this section, we describe first DQN principle and we detail, next, Double DQN concept and related improvements.

3.1   DQN

Unlike Q-learning where a table is used explicitly represent the Q-value function, DQN [11], as a DRL algorithm, extends this representation by approximating Q-value function by a NNs using DNNs [13]. DQN uses a parameterized Q-function $Q(s, a; \theta) \approx Q(s, a)$ where, θ represents the DNN parameters. By training DNN with gradient descent instead of the Q-Learning iterative update process, DQN aims to minimize a loss function at iteration i:

$$L_i(\theta_i) = \mathbb{E}_{s,a,r,s'}[(y_i^{DQN} - Q(s, a; \theta_i))^2] \tag{1}$$

This extension enables more scalability by handling higher dimensional state spaces and allows to solve more complex decision-making problems.

The DQN tackles the instability caused by using function approximation by leveraging two innovative techniques: experience replay and target Q-networks. Experience replay allows to break the correlation between consecutive experience tuples and stabilizes the training process. This is achieved by storing a history of experiences in a buffer and by randomly sampling from the buffer during training [10]. On the other hand, the target Q-network is a copy of the main Q-network that is used to generate the training targets. DQN uses a frozen target network to generate the target Q-values, used to update the main network. By freezing the target network, DQN attempts to improve stability of the training targets by decoupling them from the parameters being updated and prevent over-fitting [11]. Freezing concerns the target network parameters $Q(s', a'; \theta^-)$ for a fixed number of iterations while updating the online network $Q(s, a; \theta_i)$ by gradient descent to minimize the loss function. The specific gradient update is given as follows:

$$\nabla_{\theta_i} L_i(\theta_i) = \mathbb{E}_{s,a,r,s'}[(y_i^{DQN} - Q(s, a; \theta_i))\nabla_{\theta_i} Q(s, a; \theta_i)] \tag{2}$$

Given the state s', reward r, discount factor γ, DQN computes the target Q-value y_i^{DQN} as follows:

$$y_i^{DQN} = r + \gamma max_{a'} Q(s', a'; \theta^-) \tag{3}$$

where θ^- represents the parameters (weights) of a fixed and separate target network.

Despite the advantages of DQN, it is known to be computationally expensive algorithm and may require a large amount of training data. It may also suffer from instability during training due to the network's weights oscillations, which can negatively affect the convergence of the algorithm to an optimal solution. The major challenge is to find suitable performance-convergence compromise while computing NNs.

3.2   Double DQN

In practice, DQN often overestimates Q-values, leading to sub-optimal policies [8]. This actually happens because the algorithm uses the same network to estimate both the target and behavior policies, and this can result in an overestimation bias. To address this issue and in order to provide more accurate Q-value estimates and to improve the stability and performance, a DQN variant referred to as Double DQN [15] is proposed. Its approach consists in decoupling the action selection and action evaluation (Q-value estimation) steps while computing the target Q-value (Eq.(4)).

$$y_i^{DoubleDQN} = r + \gamma Q(s', argmax_{a'} Q(s', a'; \theta_i); \theta^-) \qquad (4)$$

Action selection is fulfilled using the current Q-network with weights θ while action evaluation is accomplished using DQN's target Q-network, with weights θ^-. Decoupling is achieved by using two separate NNs. The first one (i.e., the "online network") selects the action, while the second network (i.e., the "target network") evaluates the Q-value of the selected action. During the learning process, the weights of the target network are periodically updated to match those of the online network. On the other hand Double DQN algorithm uses a loss function that combines the Q-value of the selected action from the online network and the Q-value of the same action from the target networks.

4   DRL Approach for SFC Orchestration in SDN/NFV Environments

4.1   SFC Orchestration

SFC orchestration is an important concept in modern networking and is critical to the successful deployment and management and execution of NFs in SFC. It enables network administrators to create customized NS tailored to their specific requirements. It involves in our case study VNFs placement and chaining to maximize QoE while meeting QoS requirements. SFC orchestration is commonly done through a central controller that communicates with network devices to manage VNFs placement and chaining. The controller uses policy-based decision-making to determine the appropriate VNFs to select and order in which they need to be executed. SFC orchestration process typically involves different steps. The first one concerns the design of Service Function Forwarding Graph (SFFG) to specify the sequence of NFs. The second step involves, based on SFFG, VNF selection and placement in PSN to check the proper execution of SFC. The next step covers traffic steering through SFC to ensure that it follows the prescribed path.

Hence, the last step deals with service function monitoring to ensure that SFC is functioning correctly and to detect any potential issues. On the other hand, automating SFC deployment in SDN/NFV environments involves using tools and techniques to automate the process of creating, configuring, and deploying NFs to create SFC. Among these tools SDN network controllers are essential and are commonly used to achieve Controller-based automation of SFC deployment. The controller can automatically configure NFs and route traffic through SFC based on policy and service requirements. This approach can simplify the deployment process and reduce the risk of human error. Also SFC orchestration technique may be leveraged to automate the management of SFCs, such as scaling, upgrading, and monitoring. Lastly virtualization enables creating VNFs that can be deployed on Virtual Machines (VMs) or containers and greatly facilitates deployment automation of NFs, as virtual resources. By automating SFC deployment, network operators can reduce time and effort required to deploy and manage NFs, and ensure efficient delivery of NS. Also, optimizing SFC in SDN/NFV environments involves balancing various factors such as QoE, service requirements, available resources, network topology and QoS parameters.

4.2   SFC Orchestration Based on DRL Approach

The key steps involved SFC orchestration process based on a DRL approach concerns defining the state space. In our case study it includes information about available resources in the PSN, the SFC request, network topology. It involves also specifying action space including selecting which NFs to deploy, where to deploy them, and how to configure them. Another step concerns designing the reward function to provide feedback to the agent on the quality of its actions. In the case of SFC deployment, the reward function can be based on QoE of NS delivered through the SFC, as well as the QoS constraints that need to be met. The goal is to maximize QoE while meeting QoS constraints. Finally the last step concerns training the agent by using a DRL algorithm such as DQN or its variants to enable the agent to learn to optimize its actions to maximize the cumulative reward over time. By using DRL to optimize automation of SFC deployment in SDN/NFV environments, network operators can reduce time and effort required to deploy and manage NFs, while ensuring the efficient delivery of NS.

4.3   Reward Design

In this paper we adopt similar problem formulation given in [1], and we briefly describe in the rest of this subsection reward function used by DRL agent to take actions that maximize user's satisfaction while meeting QoS requirements. Indeed, designing an effective reward function is a challenging task, and the specific form of the function will depend on application or service being optimized. In this regard, the reward function is designed by balancing the trade-off between maximizing QoE while meeting QoS constraints, to ensure that RL agent learns to take actions leading to good user experience.

$$R_{QoE-QoS} = \begin{cases} 0, & \text{if } (c_1) & \text{(5a)} \\ QoE_{sfc}, & \text{if } (c_2) & \text{(5b)} \\ QoE_{sfc} - P_{sfc}^{req}, & \text{if } (c_3) & \text{(5c)} \\ P = 10, & \text{otherwise} & \text{(5d)} \end{cases}$$

where c_1, c_2, c_3 are logical conditions defined as follows:

- c_1: vnf_i ($i \in [1...N-1]$) $\in r_n$ is successfully deployed
- c_2: $vnf_N \in req$ is successfully deployed and $QoS_{sfc}^t = QoS_{req}^t, t \in \{1, 2, .., L\}$
- c_3: $vnf_N \in req$ is successfully deployed and $QoS_{sfc}^t \neq QoS_{req}^t, t \in \{1, 2, .., L\}$

P_{sfc}^{req} (Eq.(6)) [5]: expresses QoS constraints penalty as follows:

$$P_{sfc}^{req} = P \cdot e^{-\sqrt{\sum_{t=1}^{L} \|QoS_{sfc}^t - QoS_{req}^t\|^2}} \tag{6}$$

Relationships between QoE and measurable QoS parameters: Measuring QoE versus QoS is a complex task that requires careful consideration of the specific application or service being evaluated and the user's individual preferences. Different methods may be more appropriate depending on context, and the ultimate goal is to optimize the user's experience while meeting the necessary QoS requirements. From a service provider or network operator perspective there is an imperative need to apprehend the relationships between QoE and measurable QoS parameters. This is mainly achieved in literature through two different generic and quantitative formula laws. The first one proposed by Fiedler et al. [7] and based on an exponential function called IQX hypothesis to express relationship between QoE and QoS degradation. The objective of such formula is to capture correlations between network-level traffic features and user perceived QoE. The second one, proposed by Weber-Fechner Law (WFL) [12] relies on a logarithmic relationships between relative quality changes in network QoS and user QoE. We use a mixture of the above models to define QoE gain used in designing the reward function. QoE (Eq.(7)) [7,12] specifies reward obtained in response to successful SFC deployment.

$$QoE_{sfc} = \sum_{t=1}^{K} w^t \times QoE_{sfc}^t - \sum_{t=K+1}^{L} w^t \times QoE_{sfc}^t \tag{7}$$

where:

$$QoE_{sfc}^t = \gamma_p \times log(\alpha_p \times qos_{sfc}^t + \beta_p) + \theta_p, t \in \{1, 2, .., k\} \tag{8}$$

$$QoE_{sfc}^t = \gamma_n \times e^{(\alpha_n \times qos_{sfc}^t + \beta_n)} + \theta_n, t \in \{k+1, k+2, .., L\} \tag{9}$$

5   Simulation Results

We investigate, in this section, the DRL agent learning process and we test quality of learning using QoE Threshold Score (QoE_{Th_Sc}). The training process is observed along one episode of 20000 runs. We explore the DRL agent behavior for different levels of learning to be achieved where each learning level is quantified by a QoE_{Th_Sc} to be reached on average in the last 100 runs of the training phase. We proceed by progressively and incrementally increasing QoE_{Th_Sc} and we intend to see for each experience how this factor impacts agent behavior in terms of performance and convergence speed. In other words, we explore how DRL agent attempts to reach better learning quality as close as possible to the optimal (or near-optimal) solution.

Main Assumptions: For the DRL agent a cycle of state-action-reward corresponds to one step and each incoming SFC request involves 5 steps or actions. The training curve describes the evolution of the agent training process along one episode. It represents the reward's trend for each run of the episode. The training curve is plotted by associating to each run the corresponding average accumulated reward of 100 SFC requests. The training phase may be stopped prematurely (before the end of an episode) whenever DRL agent's performance is considered satisfactory enough. Satisfaction is attained whenever a predefined score quantifying the quality of learning is reached. As soon as the training phase is finished, the environment is reset to its initial state and another episode is initiated by the agent. Such process allows the agent to learn from its experience along every episode and uses data incrementally gathered as a knowledge to improve its performance in the following episodes.

We aim through different experiences to get closer to the best reachable learning quality in a reasonable period of time. In other terms we intend to find for the DRL agent through such approach a suitable performance-convergence trade-off. We investigate three scenarios. For each scenario, we fix QoE_{Th_Sc} and we increase progressively the PSN scale (we consider different PSN scales (5, 10, 15)). This is achieved by increasing the number of nodes (M) in the PSN. Notice that the PSN is assumed composed of M nodes with limited capacities fully interconnected. We intentionally choose an episode with a large duration (20000 runs) to allow the agent to reach during the testing phase the desired performance (QoE_{Th_Sc} level).

In Fig. 1 (resp. Figure 2) QoE_{Th_Sc} is fixed to 2500 (resp. 2550) whereas in Fig. 3 QoE_{Th_Sc} is fixed to 2600. Notice that for a fixed QoE_{Th_Sc}, increasing the PSN scale may during exploration, both enhance opportunities for the agent to obtain better rewards but also may increase the risk to be penalized. This justifies the mixed results obtained in the three figures where increasing the PSN scale (for fixed QoE_{Th_Sc}) does not necessarily lead to longer training. We choose QoE_{Th_Sc} values (2500 (Fig. 1), 2550 (Fig. 2), 2600 (Fig. 3)) to reach relatively good performance but also allowing to converge before an episode ends. Such choice justifies the need to find suitable performance-convergence trade-off along the training phase. From another perspective, we attempt to apprehend another facet of the agent behavior and its capacity to achieve a good performance-convergence trade-off by considering PSN scale with fixed size (for example $M = 5$) and by progressively increasing QoE_{Th_Sc} from 2500 to 2600. Indeed, on one hand, for example, rising QoE_{Th_Sc} from 2500 (Fig. 1a) to 2550 (Fig. 2a) yields a decrease of the required number of runs, to attain the desired

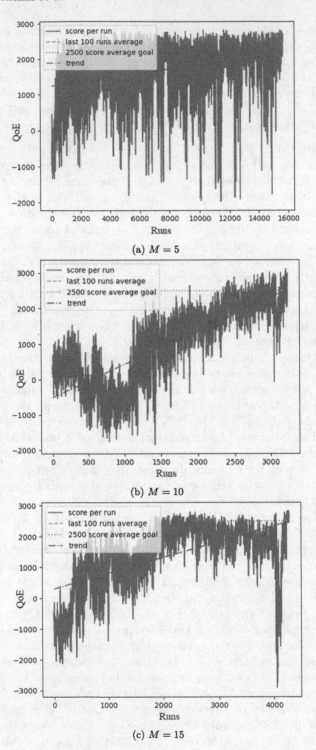

(a) $M = 5$

(b) $M = 10$

(c) $M = 15$

Fig. 1. QoE score vs number of runs ($QoE_{Th\_Sc} = 2500$)

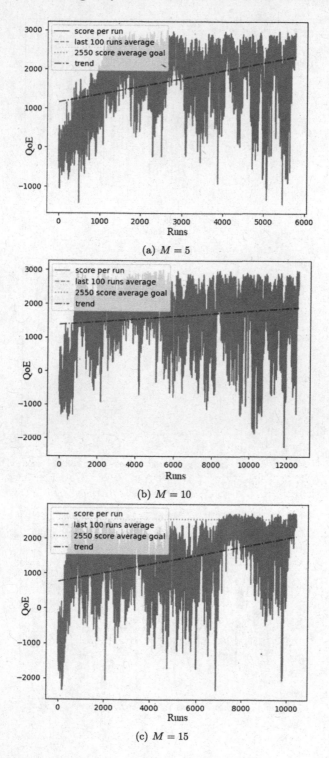

(a) $M = 5$

(b) $M = 10$

(c) $M = 15$

Fig. 2. QoE score vs number of runs ($QoE_{Th\_Sc} = 2550$)

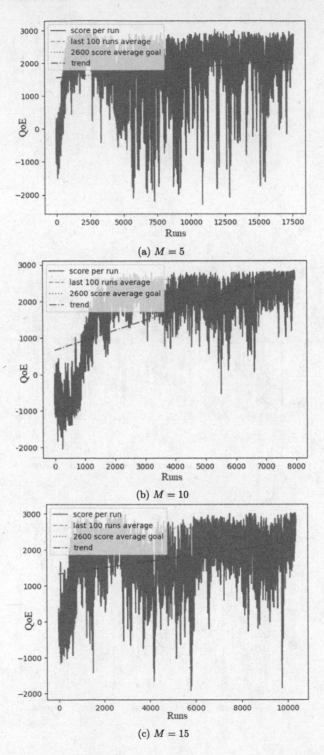

(a) $M = 5$

(b) $M = 10$

(c) $M = 15$

Fig. 3. QoE score vs number of runs ($QoE_{Th\_Sc} = 2600$)

QoE_{Th_Sc}, from 16000 to 6000. Conversely, rising QoE_{Th_Sc} value from 2550 (Fig. 2a) to 2600 (Fig. 3a) increases the required number of runs, to improve the desired QoE_{Th_Sc}, from 6000 to 17500. Such behavior may be explained by the following arguments. Along a training phase, the agent learns through trial and error and tries alternates in a probabilistic manner according to ϵ-greedy algorithm between exploration and exploitation. In a nutshell, due to the stochastic nature of the training process, the required time to train the agent for the same scenario may be longer or shorter depending on experience. We believe that the above explanation fully justifies the agent trend for different QoE_{Th_Sc}.

Notice also that in DRL, the learning phase is of stochastic nature given that agent's actions are often based on probability distributions, rather than deterministic rules. The stochasticity arises from the fact that the agent's policy is often based on a probability distribution over actions, rather than a deterministic mapping from states to actions. This means that the agent may take different actions in the same state, depending on probabilities assigned to each action. Additionally, rewards received by the agent may also be stochastic, as they may depend on random events in the environment. This stochasticity allows agent to explore different actions and learn from experience. However, it also introduces additional complexity, as the agent must learn to balance exploration and exploitation in order to maximize its long-term rewards. This complexity leads to uncertainty about agent's capacity to attain the desired quality within one episode.

6   Conclusion

Testing and evaluation of the quality of learning in DRL is critical for ensuring the generalization of learned policies and to assess their robustness. In this paper, we proposed an investigation of testing and evaluation of learning phase of the Double DQN agent through testing its capacity to learn a near-optimal policy to achieve SFC orchestration maximizing QoE while meeting QoS requirements of PSN in SDN/NFV environments. By evaluating the performance of DRL agent, we attempt to identify areas where the agent under-performs in specific scenarios and how modifying the related parameters to achieve the best quality of training enabling suitable performance-convergence trade-off. Trough numerical investigations, we particularly explore the impact of modifying progressively quality of learning (quantified by a QoE score) and the scale of the network (PSN) on achieving a good compromise between performance and convergence. We show that increasing these parameters often leads to mitigated results and we provide detailed explanations of this behavior based on the stochastic nature of the DRL process. In future works, we intend to make further explorations about other parameters, hyper-parameters and DRL algorithms (DQN variants) that may impact DRL agent behavior and the achieved performance-convergence trade-off during testing in learning phase.

References

1. Escheikh, M., Taktak, W.: Online QoS/QoE-driven SFC Orchestration Leveraging a DRL Approach in SDN/NFV Enabled Networks, April 2023. (submitted to Soft Computing)
2. Arulkumaran, K., et al.: Deep reinforcement learning: a brief survey. IEEE Signal Process. Mag. **34**(6), 26–38 (2017)
3. Benzekki, K., El Fergougui, A., Elalaoui, A.E.: Software-defined networking (SDN): a survey. Secur. Commun. Netw. **9**(18), 5803–5833 (2016)
4. Bhamare, D., et al.: A survey on service function chaining. J. Netw. Comput. Appl. **75**, 138–155 (2016)
5. Chen, X., et al.: Reinforcement learning-based QoS/QoE-aware service function chaining in software-driven 5G slices. Trans. Emerg. Telecommun. Technol. **29**(11), e3477 (2018)
6. Chen, J., Chen, J., Zhang, H.: DRL-QOR: deep reinforcement learning-based QoS/QoE-aware adaptive online orchestration in NFV-enabled networks. IEEE Trans. Netw. Serv. Manage. **18**(2), 1758–1774 (2021)
7. Fiedler, M., Hossfeld, T., Tran-Gia, P.: A generic quantitative relationship between quality of experience and quality of service. IEEE Netw. **24**(2), 36–41 (2010)
8. Hasselt, H.: Double q-learning. In: Advances in Neural Information Processing Systems, vol. 23 (2010)
9. Herrera, J.G., Botero, J.F.: Resource allocation in NFV: a comprehensive survey. IEEE Trans. Netw. Serv. Manage. **13**(3), 518–532 (2016)
10. Lin, L.-J.: RL for Robots Using Neural Networks. Carnegie Mellon University, Pittsburgh (1992)
11. Mnih, V., et al.: Human-level control through deep reinforcement learning. Nature **518**(7540), 529–533 (2015)
12. Reichl, P., et al.: The logarithmic nature of QoE and the role of the Weber-Fechner law in QoE assessment. In: 2010 IEEE International Conference on Communications. IEEE (2010)
13. Sarker, I.H.: Deep learning: a comprehensive overview on techniques, taxonomy, applications and research directions. SN Comput. Sci. 2(6), 420 (2021)
14. Sutton, R.S., Barto, A.G.: Introduction to Reinforcement Learning, vol. 135. MIT Press, Cambridge (1998)
15. Van Hasselt, H., Guez, A., Silver, D.: Deep reinforcement learning with double Q-learning. In: Proceedings of the AAAI Conference on Artificial Intelligence, vol. 30. No. 1 (2016)

Author Index

© IFIP International Federation for Information Processing 2023
Published by Springer Nature Switzerland AG 2023
S. Bonfanti et al. (Eds.): ICTSS 2023, LNCS 14131, pp. 289–290, 2023.
https://doi.org/10.1007/978-3-031-43240-8

Printed in the United States
by Baker & Taylor Publisher Services